D1616028

STATE OF WAR

MODERN WAR STUDIES

Theodore A. Wilson
General Editor

Raymond A. Callahan
J. Garry Clifford
Jacob W. Kipp
Allan R. Millett
Carol Reardon
Dennis Showalter
David R. Stone
Series Editors

STATE OF WAR
THE POLITICAL ECONOMY OF AMERICAN WARFARE, 1945–2011

PAUL A. C. KOISTINEN

UNIVERSITY PRESS OF KANSAS

Published by the University Press of Kansas (Lawrence, Kansas 66045), which
was organized by the Kansas Board of Regents and is operated and funded by
Emporia State University, Fort Hays State University, Kansas State University,
Pittsburg State University, the University of Kansas, and Wichita State University

Library of Congress Cataloging-in-Publication Data

Koistinen, Paul A. C.
State of war : the political economy of American warfare, 1945–2011 /
Paul A.C. Koistinen.
p. cm. — (Modern war studies)
Includes bibliographical references and index.
ISBN 978-0-7006-1874-3 (cloth : alk. paper)
1. War—Economic aspects—United States—History—20th century. 2. United
States—Defenses—History—20th century. 3. Industrial mobilization—United
States—History—20th century. I. Title.
HC110.D4K647 2012
338.4'73550097309045—dc23

                                       2012016382

British Library Cataloguing in Publication Data is available.

Printed in the United States of America

10 9 8 7 6 5 4 3 2 1

The paper used in this publication is recycled and contains 30 percent
postconsumer waste. It is acid free and meets the minimum requirements of the
American National Standard for Permanence of Paper for Printed Library
Materials Z39.48-1992.

For Richard Drinnon,
Daniel Koistinen Harris,
and
Michael Briggs:
The beginning and the end

CONTENTS

ACKNOWLEDGMENTS

I benefited greatly from the assistance of others in putting this volume into its final form. At California State University–Northridge (CSUN), John J. Broesamle read the entire manuscript and Ronald L. F. Davis went over portions of it, as did my son, David J. Koistinen, at William Paterson University. Andrew J. Bacevich reviewed the manuscript for the press and provided an extended and detailed critique. All of them supplied me with excellent insights and advice. Additionally, a host of student research assistants over the years served me in an always diligent and often selfless way. I could not ask for more from a publisher than the services provided by the University Press of Kansas. Michael Briggs, editor in chief, oversaw the project with a sure but gentle hand, and his capable and dedicated staff—including marketing manager Susan Schott and production editor Larisa Martin—went about the wonders of converting manuscripts into published volumes with a high level of professionalism. My debt to all these people is matched only by my gratitude for their labors and contributions. Needless to say, I alone am responsible for all that is said and not said in this book.

Much precedes the review and publication of a manuscript. Archivists and staffs of numerous record collections and papers provided me with invaluable and unfailing guidance and assistance over many years. Without the Oviatt Library at CSUN, especially its Interlibrary Loan Services, I would have been hard-pressed to complete this work. Charlotte Oyer, Donald L. Read, Michael Barrett, Felicia Cousin, and Berhan Arega worked endlessly on my behalf. Both the late Joseph J. Dabbour and Ramon J. Alvarado, heading Circulation Services, went out of their way to make the library's excellent collection conveniently available to me. Finally, the continued support, encouragement, and love of my wife, Carolyn Epstein Koistinen, are crucial to what I do.

For financial support, I had many benefactors, including research fellowships from Harvard's Charles Warren Center for Studies in American History, the American Council of Learned Societies, and the National Endowment for the Humanities. Furthermore, CSUN's History Department, College of Social and Behavioral Sciences, and the university as a whole have assisted me in numerous ways for many years.

The volume is dedicated to three individuals who are actually or symbolically important to this volume and those that preceded it. Richard Drinnon, my mentor at the University of California–Berkeley, suggested the topic for my dissertation, which led to the publication of my volume on labor-military relations during World War II and my subsequent work in the field. Of vital significance, Dick also provided a snug harbor for an intriguing and gifted collection of students who approached graduate studies with a measure of skepticism and a sense of distance.

Daniel Koistinen Harris, our second grandchild, was born in 2004, about the same time my research for this volume was getting under way. Over the years, my wife and I have had the great satisfaction of watching our grandson grow and mature as this volume progressed.

Without Michael Briggs, the quinary, of which this volume is the final part, would never have been published in its current form. Mike not only saw the value of the study; he also acted on the conviction that, economics aside, some scholarship should and needs to be published because of the contribution it makes.

ABBREVIATIONS

ABM	antiballistic missile
ACDA	Arms Control and Disarmament Agency
AEC	Atomic Energy Commission
AID	Agency for International Development
ANMB	Army-Navy Munitions Board
ANSER	Analytical Services Inc.
ARPA	Advanced Research Projects Agency
AT&T	American Telephone and Telegraph
AWACS	airborne warning and control system
BCG	Boston Consulting Group
BRAC	base realignment and closure
CDI	Center for Defense Information
CENIS	Center for International Studies
CEO	chief executive officer
CIA	Central Intelligence Agency
CNS&E	College of Nanoscale Science and Engineering
CRESS	Center for Research in Social Sciences
DARPA	Defense Advanced Research Projects Agency
DOD	Department of Defense
DOE	Department of Energy
FBI	Federal Bureau of Investigation
FEMA	Federal Emergency Management Agency
GAO	General Accountability Office
GDP	gross domestic product

GNP	gross national product
GPS	Global Positioning System
HUMRRO	Human Resources Research Office
IBM	International Business Machines
ICAF	Industrial College of the Armed Forces
ICBM	intercontinental ballistic missile
ICT	information and communications technology
IDA	Institute for Defense Analyses
IMF	International Monetary Fund
IRBM	intermediate-range ballistic missile
JCS	Joint Chiefs of Staff
MB	Munitions Board
MBA	master of business administration
MIC	military-industrial complex
MIRV	multiple independently targeted reentry vehicle
MIT	Massachusetts Institute of Technology
MPRI	Military Professional Resources Inc.
MSUG	Michigan State University Group
NACA	National Advisory Committee for Aeronautics
NASA	National Aeronautics and Space Administration
NASDAQ	National Association of Securities Dealers Automated Quotations
NATO	North Atlantic Treaty Organization
NDRC	National Defense Research Committee
NEBM	new economic business model
NIH	National Institutes of Health
NSC	National Security Council
NSF	National Science Foundation
NSRB	National Security Resources Board
NSS	National Security Strategy of the United States
NYRB	*New York Review of Books*
OASW	Office of the Assistant Secretary of War
ODM	Office of Defense Mobilization
OEBM	old economic business model

OECD	Organization for Economic Cooperation and Development
ONR	Office of Naval Research
OPEC	Organization of Petroleum Exporting Countries
OSRD	Office of Scientific Research and Development
OSS	Office of Strategic Services
OST	Office of the Special Assistant to the President for Science and Technology

PD	Presidential Directive
POW	prisoner of war
PSAC	President's Science Advisory Committee

RAC	Research Analysis Corporation
RAM	random-access memory
R&D	research and development
RCA	Radio Corporation of America

SAC	Strategic Air Command
SAIS	School of Advanced International Studies
SALT	Strategic Arms Limitation Treaty
SDC	System Development Corporation
SDI	Strategic Defense Initiative
SEATO	Southeast Asia Treaty Organization
SIOP	single integrated operational plan
SLBM	sea-launched ballistic missile
SORO	Special Operations Research Organization
START	Strategic Arms Reduction Treaty

TRW	Thompson-Ramo-Wooldridge Inc.

UAW	United Automobile Workers
UMT	universal military training
UN	United Nations

WIB	War Industries Board
WMD	weapons of mass destruction
WPB	War Production Board
WPR	War Powers Resolution

INTRODUCTION

This volume is the last in a five-volume study of the political economy of American warfare—the means the nation has employed to mobilize its economic resources for defense and hostilities. It begins in 1945 and extends virtually to the present day—the Cold War and post–Cold War years. The preceding volumes (all published by the University Press of Kansas), are as follows: volume 1, *Beating Plowshares into Swords: The Political Economy of American Warfare, 1606–1865* (1996), covers the colonial period through the Civil War; volume 2, *Mobilizing for Modern War: The Political Economy of American Warfare, 1865–1919* (1997), focuses on the Gilded Age, the Progressive Era, and World War I; volume 3, *Planning War, Pursuing Peace: The Political Economy of American Warfare, 1920–1939* (1998), deals with the interwar years; and volume 4, *Arsenal of World War II: The Political Economy of American Warfare, 1940–1945* (2004), examines economic mobilization for World War II. The goal of my multivolume project is to provide scholars and other readers with what was previously unavailable: a comprehensive, analytical, and interdisciplinary study of the economics of America's wars from the colonial period to today. In doing so, I demonstrate how the political economy of warfare impacts domestic life and foreign policy and what economic mobilization for defense and war reveals about the nature and operations of power within society. I also seek to expand on the study of military history by examining in depth and in breadth an aspect of warfare that is often ignored or treated in a perfunctory manner. This different perspective leads to different insights and conclusions about civilians, soldiers and sailors, and warfare. If I raise as many questions as I answer, I will have accomplished my purpose.

Analyzing how America has mobilized its economic resources for war and defense is important for a number of reasons. Logistics are basic to warfare and depend on the nation's ability to marshal effectively its economic might. Over the centuries, economic mobilization has followed a discernible evolutionary pattern that illuminates the study of warfare and the military. Furthermore, how the United States has mobilized its economy reveals a great deal about institutional and power structures. Indeed, the stress and demands of warfare make manifest social patterns that are less evident or are obscured during years of peace.

The political economy of warfare involves the interrelationships of political, economic, and military institutions in devising the means to mobilize resources for defense and to conduct war. In each war, the magnitude and duration of the fighting have dictated *what* the nation had to do to harness its economic power, but prewar trends have largely determined *how* this mobilization took place. Four types of factors are essential in determining the method of mobilization: (1) economic, or the level of maturity of the economy; (2) political, or the size, strength, and scope of the federal government; (3) military, or the character and structure of the military services and the relationship between them and civilian society and authority; and (4) the state of military technology.

Patterns of economic mobilization for war have passed through three major stages over the course of American history. The Revolutionary War, the Civil War, and twentieth-century warfare best characterize these stages, which I have labeled preindustrial, transitional, and industrial. Altering the four factors—economic, political, military, and technological—modifies each stage of mobilization. The factors have seldom changed at the same time or pace, but over time, each has had to adjust to the others so that viable patterns of economic mobilization could be maintained.

The preindustrial stage of economic mobilization for war extended from the colonial period to approximately 1815 and included the Revolutionary War and the War of 1812. During the American Revolution, economic, governmental, and military institutions were in an embryonic state and were not clearly distinguished from one another. Military technology was rather primitive and varied little from production in the peacetime economy. Hence, economic mobilization involved increasing civilian output and diverting products from civilian to military use in order to supply the armed forces without converting the economy. Nonetheless, to maximize output, comprehensive regulation of the emerging nation's economic life became essential. Yet the undeveloped nature of economic, political, and military institutions not only prevented such regulation from working well but also resulted in the inextricable intertwining of private and public functions and civil and military activities. Merchants served simultaneously as public officials and military officers while they continued to conduct their private affairs.

The effects of harnessing the economy for war carried over into the years of peace. By highlighting the weaknesses of the Articles of Confederation, economic mobilization helped create the momentum for the ideas underlying the

Constitution. And, during the early national period, intense conflict grew between the factions that became the Federalist and Republican parties over the strength and policies of the national government under the new charter. This strife weakened the federal government and stunted the growth of the armed services, which was a major source of dispute. Consequently, although the economy was much stronger in 1812 than in 1776 and military technology had changed little during that period, economic mobilization for the War of 1812 did not improve measurably over that for the Revolutionary War.

The second, or transitional, economic mobilization stage extended from 1816 to 1865. During this period, the economy developed enormous productive capacity; it became diversified and quite industrialized, and specialized functions emerged in manufacturing, marketing, banking, and the like, although the size of firms remained comparatively small. The federal government was limited in size, scope, and activity, but it was capable of expanding to handle economic mobilization effectively and efficiently. Both the army and the navy had professionalized to the point where they had definable structures and missions. But military technology still had experienced no dramatic change. Since weaponry remained basic, economic mobilization required only expanding and diverting civilian production, not economic conversion.

Harnessing the economy for war was more readily accomplished in the transitional stage than in those stages that preceded and followed it. The pattern was evident in the Mexican War but was best demonstrated by the Union during the Civil War. Operating under the direction of the president, the War, Navy, and Treasury departments acted as the principal mobilization agencies. They relied on market forces in a strong competitive economy, not on the elaborate regulation of the preindustrial and industrial stages, to maintain economic stability while meeting the enormous demands of war. Moreover, institutional barriers were not breached. In the economic realm, little mixing of activities or personnel occurred among private and public, civilian and military affairs. The major exception involved the railroads, which had begun to organize as modern corporations before the hostilities started. The telegraph system followed a similar trend.

Union success contrasted sharply with the Confederacy's failure. The South was closer to the preindustrial than to the transitional stage. Like the colonies and states during the revolutionary years, the Confederacy experimented with comprehensive economic regulation, without much success. Weak economic and political systems consistently undermined the Confederacy's economic mobilization effort and played an important role in the South's defeat.

Modern warfare in the twentieth century represents the third, or industrial, economic mobilization stage. By 1900 the United States had become a mature industrialized nation with a modified capitalist system. Although market forces remained significant in the production and distribution of goods, the administered decisions of several hundred modern corporations exercised a strong, at times dominant, influence over the economy's direction. To make concentrated and consolidated economic power more responsible to the public and to stabilize an enormously complex economy, the federal government started to act as economic regulator. The growth of huge bureaucracies in the corporate and governmental spheres began to blur the institutional lines between them. Businessmen often staffed the government's regulatory agencies, and, as they had during the preindustrial stage, the affairs of government and business touched or merged at many points. A government-business regulatory alliance began to emerge during the Progressive Era.

For a time during the late nineteenth century, the military services entered a period of relative isolation as the nation became absorbed in industrialization, the threat of war receded, and the army and navy became intensely involved in professionalizing their functions. A technological revolution in weaponry in the later years of the nineteenth century, however, drew the civilian and military worlds back together. The consequences of this revolution were first manifest with the navy. In order to build a new fleet of steel, armor, steam, and modern ordnance, a production team consisting of political leaders, naval officers, and businessmen was formed. Although this team's composition, responsibilities, and operation have varied over the years, it has continued to exist. The army was slower to feel the impact of technology, but it eventually experienced the same needs and developed a relationship with industry and civil authorities similar to the navy's.

By the eve of World War I, therefore, the federal government, the industrial community, and the military services had developed complex, modern, and professionalized structures, each dependent on the others in terms of national defense. Economic mobilization for World War I (unlike the brief and limited Spanish-American War) forcefully demonstrated this institutional interdependence. The quantity and sophistication of military demand meant that increasing and diverting civilian production were no longer adequate; market forces could not be relied on. Production had to be maximized, and industries had to be converted to manufacture the often specialized military hardware that war required. Priority, allocation, price, and other controls had to be introduced. Existing governmental departments and agencies were unequal to the task. New mobilization bodies had to be created, the most important being the War Industries Board (WIB). Through the board, centralized control over a planned economy was established and carried out by representatives of the government, the business community, and the military. The process obscured institutional lines. Civilian and military, private and public activities combined. For very different reasons and with quite different results, the first and the third mobilization stages are strikingly similar.

World War I mobilization left an indelible imprint on national life. During the interwar years, direct and indirect economic planning patterned after the WIB was tried. Congress and other governmental bodies repeatedly investigated the methods and consequences of harnessing the World War I economy in order to understand better what had taken place, to prevent future mobilization abuses, and to head off the perceived threats of modern warfare. Moreover, close ties among the civil and military sectors of the government, the industrial community, and other new and old interest groups were maintained to design, produce, and procure specialized munitions and to plan for industrial mobilization. During World War II, a modified form of the World War I model was used to mobilize the economy to meet the astronomical and often highly specialized demands of the armed forces and America's allies. With the Cold War following World War II, the nation—for the first time in years of peace—supported a massive military establishment, one that became inordinately expensive because of its size and because of the continuing transformation of weaponry through scientific and technological advancement. As a result, a defense and war "complex" included and affected most private and public institutions in American life.

Economic mobilization has been carried out largely by political, economic, and, ultimately, military elites. Economic and political elites are closely related and constitute the nation's upper classes. In the late eighteenth and early nineteenth centuries they included merchants, planters and large landowners, and professional elements. As the economy matured, those involved with banks, railroads, and manufacturing gained in importance, and twentieth-century economic elites were based primarily in the vast corporate and financial communities. Military elites as a distinct group did not work in close association with economic and political elites until the industrial stage. In the preindustrial period, no clear line separated the military from the civilian world. During the transitional stage, both the army and the navy distanced themselves from civilians as they began to professionalize and acquire separate identities. But in the industrial stage, military leaders had to join their political and economic counterparts out of necessity to mobilize the economy for war.

Elites shaped economic mobilization in a number of ways. The federal executive—or what approximated it during the Revolution—devised and implemented methods to harness the economy for war. Throughout American history, the highest appointed officials in the executive branch have been drawn predominantly from the wealthy or those associated with them. Moreover, the federal government has turned to the nation's business leaders to assist in economic mobilization. They have acted as temporary or permanent advisers to government mobilizers, served in established or newly created federal agencies with or without pay, or engaged in some combination of these activities.

Harnessing the economy for war has generated a great deal of political controversy in America. Much of the conflict grows from the fact that economic mobilization highlights the nation's most basic contradiction: an elitist reality in the context of a democratic ideology. During years of peace, that dynamic contradiction tends to be obscured; during years of war, it is magnified by elitist economic mobilization patterns. Excluded interest groups and classes inevitably challenge the legitimacy of mobilization systems run by the few, claiming that they are unrepresentative and fail to protect larger public interests. This resentment is exaggerated by the widespread aversion to and fear of government at the national level. Moreover, economic mobilization for war elevates the armed services to a position of central importance, which intensifies the strong antimilitary strains in American thought. Opposition to war among nonelites often leads to critiques of economic mobilization policies. There is a close correlation between antiwar and antielite attitudes.

Controversy over the political economy of warfare was greatest in the preindustrial and industrial stages. Because they require a form of planning, both underdeveloped and highly developed economies make elites quite visible. Market economies do not have such an exaggerated effect because mobilization agencies that combine political and economic elites are unnecessary. Consequently, economic mobilization caused less political turmoil in the transitional stage.

Throughout the course of American history, the role of political, economic, and military elites in economic mobilization for defense and war can be fully understood only within the four-factor, three-stage paradigm. If the preindustrial stage is dated from 1765 to 1815 (instead of including the entire colonial era), it lasted only about fifty years, approximately the same duration as the transitional stage. Accelerated physical and economic growth quickly modified institutions and power operations and, in the process, altered the stages of economic mobilization. Rapid industrialization after the Civil War ushered in the last mobilization stage, one with a permanence of sorts. Since the late nineteenth century, political, economic, and military elites have been absorbed in creating and refining planning structures to cope with the ongoing weapons revolution, a revolution that has comprehensively affected how America prepares for and conducts warfare.

This volume, like the first one in the series, is based primarily on secondary sources. From the early post–World War II period to the present day, publications relevant to the political economy of warfare have appeared at a steady rate, constituting a nearly overwhelming collection. They amply met the reference requirements for this book, without further research in primary documents.

My principal goal in this volume is to analyze the political economy of American warfare from 1945 to the present from a broad perspective. To meet the international challenges of the Cold War and post–Cold War world, the United States, for the first time in its history, has maintained large military structures during years of relative peace. Moreover, the army, navy, air force, and related services have been armed and supplied principally by a formidable, privately owned defense industry, including some of the nation's largest corporations as well as a host of other firms. Large-scale private arsenals are also historically unprecedented in America; their significance is multiplied manyfold by exceptionally sophisticated weaponry centered around nuclear armaments and aerospace and electronic advancements that require extensive research and development by scientists, engineers, and technicians. These developments have led to enormous defense budgets that reach as high as 14 percent of the gross domestic product and 70 percent of annual government spending, and they seldom fall below 5 and 20 percent, respectively. During a period of more than six decades, multiple trillions of dollars have been expended on national security.

Together, a massive Cold War military and a powerful private defense industry have accumulated vast influence and power that directly or indirectly affects practically every area of foreign and domestic life. Their growth and operation so alarmed President Dwight D. Eisenhower that, in his 1961 farewell address to the nation, he warned Americans about the dangers of a "military-industrial complex" and a "scientific-technological elite."

The so-called military-industrial complex (MIC) did not create itself. It grew out of clashing goals for reconstructing and restructuring war-shattered Europe and Japan and weakened or collapsing colonial empires in the Middle East, Africa, and Asia. America's drive for an "open-door" world of democratic capitalism faced the real or perceived ambition of communist-led expansion on the part of the Soviet Union. Drawing on past policies and practices, the United States at the outset intended to shape the world in its own image through the use of its unequaled industrial-financial strength, backed by a modest military.

By 1949–1950, with American plans for stabilizing western Europe stalled, Russia detonating an atomic weapon, China falling under communist control, and war breaking out in Korea, the nation felt compelled to militarize its foreign policies. Thereafter, a bipolar world emerged in stages, with the United States and the Union of Soviet Socialist Republics participating in a potentially catastrophic nuclear arms race, Europe becoming an armed camp, and the two major powers competing for power and position throughout the developing world. The virtual collapse of the Soviet Union between 1989 and 1991 ended what had become a dangerous and destructive running confrontation between two imperial systems.

Although it developed as a result of the militarized Cold War, the MIC eventually began to grow beyond the control of responsible authorities. It has attempted to block or resist efforts to reduce defense budgets or reject favored weapon systems, to control or halt the arms race, to improve relations with the Soviet Union and other adversaries, and to adopt more enlightened policies toward the developing world. Nearly twenty years after the Soviet Union fell apart, defense budgets (excluding the costs of the wars in Iraq and Afghanistan) are higher today than at any time during the Cold War.

My four-factor paradigm for analyzing the political economy of warfare is useful for briefly analyzing the principal characteristics of the MIC and the Cold War that created it. The overwhelming industrial and financial might of the American economy—the first factor—stood practically alone among damaged and destroyed economies in the war-ravaged world. Both before and after its militarizing Cold War foreign policies, the United States depended heavily on the nation's economic prowess for pursuing its international goals. Paradoxically, the corporate community in the post–World War II years began to shift its emphasis away from production in a fashion that weakened the nation's economic strength by the 1970s.

The federal government in general, and the executive in particular—the second factor—was at the pinnacle of its historical powers during the Cold War and after. With foreign policy commanding national attention, the president's authority and reach grew at an accelerated rate as the principal architect of international relations. A vastly expanded State Department, a powerful Department of Defense, and an influential National Security Council, along with a host of intelligence agencies, all added to the executive's clout. Military intervention and wars abroad repeatedly took place either without Congress's consent or with only its implied consent. The legislative branch could and did influence foreign and national security policies, but it was never a match for the executive branch.

Civil-military relations—the third factor—changed dramatically during the post–World War II years. The large U.S. military spent billions of dollars annually, operated facilities throughout the nation and abroad, and relied heavily on nuclear weaponry. As a result of these conditions, the armed services accumulated unprecedented power and influence over the formulation and implementation of national security and foreign policy.

The armed forces' power and influence have been further enhanced by the fourth factor—the sophistication of weaponry. Growing out of economic mobilization for World War II, the privately owned defense industry acted as a valuable partner, ally, and advocate of the armed services. Ultimately, the military-industrial team at the center of the MIC became as much a liability as an asset. Pushing weapons to and beyond the point of technological feasibility often results in systems that are badly flawed and prone to failure. Their escalating costs, moreover, drain Defense Department budgets, resulting in fewer weapons and reduced budgets for their maintenance and repair.

All four factors shaping the political economy of warfare during the Cold War and beyond are significant. Consistent with the industrial stage in general, the federal executive—the second factor—remains the most important. The overall length of American engagement, however, has been as consequential as the various factors shaping the post–World War II political economy of warfare. After more than six decades of modified economic mobilization for purposes of dominating and stabilizing a turbulent world community, it has become nearly habitual, a critical characteristic of the American way of life. Eisenhower's military-industrial complex of half a century ago has become part of an even larger warfare or national security state.

Since national security has affected nearly all aspects of American life, this volume takes a broad, rather than a closely focused, approach in analyzing the MIC. The first chapter deals with the presidency and the shaping of post–World War II foreign and defense policies and, to a lesser extent, civil-military relations. Congress's impact on both foreign relations and national security are the subject of chapter 2. Chapters 3 and 4 focus on the armed services and the defense industry, respectively, and the interaction between the two. Scientists and engineers, who were central to the transformation of weaponry that began during World II and continues today, are discussed in chapter 5. Chapter 6 examines think tanks and similar civilian institutions, many of which were university based or affiliated and were intended to facilitate the formulation and execution of Cold War policies. The transformation of weaponry stemming from jet engines, nuclear advances, and solid-state electronics is covered in chapter 7. Chapter 8 analyzes the consequences of large and sustained defense budgets on the operation of the American economy; it does so within the context of the nation's economic decline since the late 1960s to the present day. Chapter 9 constitutes the conclusion, where the salient themes of the previous chapters are summarized and a number of analytical points are made.

1
THE PRESIDENCY

The military-industrial complex grew out of American Cold War foreign policy rather than creating or shaping it. Over time, however, the complex acted to support and sustain the nation's global thrust. Expansionist from its very origins, the United States set its sights on worldwide hegemony after World War II. Based on its open-door, informal imperial ambitions of the late nineteenth century and pre–World War II twentieth century, the nation at first sought to achieve this goal principally through its overwhelming economic power. Multiplying challenges soon convinced American leaders that massive and broad-based military might, including vast nuclear arsenals, would be essential. The ensuing war machine brought into being a full-fledged MIC and significantly modified civil-military relations.

The nation's Cold War international policies were cast in highly ideological terms, such as exceptionalism, superiority, morality, and mission. Such heady notions were consistent with America's earlier drive across the continent and later into the Pacific, Caribbean, and Latin America. During the Cold War, so-called liberal internationalism centered around such ideas as the "free world" versus "communism," open versus closed systems, and the virtues of democratic capitalism over totalitarian planning.

Ironically and tragically, the ongoing crusade for freedom throughout the world led to violations of democratic principles at home and abroad. With few exceptions, foreign and national security policies were not fully open to public debate. Under the banner of a bipartisan foreign policy, Congress was subordinated to an imperial presidency; the public was manipulated through slogans, exaggerated threats, and distorted and hidden truths; and civil rights and liberties were frequently compromised. An elite made up of elected and appointed members of the executive, a select group of legislators, senior military officers, and corporate and think-tank specialists moving in and out of government service formulated foreign and national security policies. In the developing or third world, policy makers placed a low priority on democracy compared with pro-Western and anticommunist commitments. Cold War "realism" often had a ruthless quality that was at odds with America's ideology.

The MIC that the Cold War spawned ultimately took on a self-perpetuating quality. Hence, in 2009, national security budgets in adjusted dollars matched or exceeded those of the early Cold War period, although there was no relevant enemy to justify such a massive military and, in a sense, the armed services' readiness level declined.

TRUMAN ADMINISTRATION, 1945–1953

America's approach to the international community during the last half century has been shaped by the Cold War polices devised by the Harry S. Truman administration. Liberal internationalism stressed the nation's commitment to maintaining an open, democratic, capitalist world in the face of totalitarian threats. That highly ideological, absolutist end would be pursued through both economic and military might. Although polices have varied among administrations, the continuity from 1946 to the present has been remarkable, even after the Cold War ended with the collapse of the Soviet Union in 1989–1991.

At the conclusion of World War II, the United States faced both enormous challenges and opportunities. Among the major nations, it stood almost alone as a strong, vibrant, growing industrial and financial power. Europe was in ruins. The Soviet Union, although victorious, had suffered almost immeasurable human, economic, social, and political damage and loss. Colonialism was in tatters, and the developing world was in distress, facing instability at best, revolution at worst. The mighty wartime military forces of Great Britain and the USSR, along with what remained of the French, were worn and exhausted. Only the United States had deep reserves of men, supplies, arms, and, more importantly, atomic weapons. Seldom before had one nation had such a near monopoly on world power.

Given these momentous circumstances, Franklin D. Roosevelt's death in April 1945 was a national and international calamity. The president had dominated American wartime diplomacy and military strategy. In doing so, he had remained flexible concerning the USSR because he recognized that, at enormous cost and on their own, the Soviets had played a major role in defeating the Germans and their formidable war machine. Fully 80 percent of German combat deaths took place at Russian hands.[1] Consequently, from the Soviets' point of view, any postwar settlement had to protect the USSR's security interests in central and eastern Europe, provide severe restrictions on Germany, and recognize the USSR's interests in and about the Middle East. Although the

United States opposed the creation of spheres, the Yalta and Potsdam Accords were loosely and ambiguously written to accommodate differing goals and to maintain Allied unity.

As Roosevelt's replacement, Truman was uninformed, insecure, and dependent on others for direction.[2] After months of uncertainty and drift, the administration policy for occupied Europe settled into a hard line toward the Soviet Union. By stages, from 1946 through 1949, the United States implemented a policy of "containing" the USSR. Portrayed as seeking worldwide domination, the former ally was accused of constituting a massive threat to Europe, Asia, and the developing world. In all its destruction and horror, World War II had left a bipolar world with the two major powers in a state of basic conflict.

The Truman Doctrine of early 1947, the European Recovery Program of 1947–1948, the step-by-step division of Germany and the rearming and indirect integration of the Western sector into the North Atlantic Treaty Organization (NATO) of 1949, and the initiation of what became the European Economic Community were all intended to protect Europe, integrate it into America's economic sphere, and isolate the Soviet Union. Later, a containment policy of sorts was aimed at Communist China. It was centered around a reconstructed Japan and incorporated South Korea, Taiwan, Vietnam, the Philippines, Australia, and New Zealand.

The United Nations (UN) came into existence in 1945 and, for the most part, acted to legitimize America's international approach. Nonetheless, the institution could never go beyond the willingness and ability of the major powers to cooperate. More immediately important for American purposes were new institutions and practices designed to further world economic stability and cooperation and to head off autarky, closed trading systems, money manipulation, and the like. These included the International Monetary Fund (IMF), the so-called World Bank, and the General Agreement on Tariffs and Trade.

By 1950, practically no part of the world was free from America's direct or indirect involvement or oversight. Nevertheless, as worldwide commitments grew, military demobilization continued. The number of active-duty personnel for all services dropped from more than 12 million in 1945 to less than 1.5 million by 1950. War and defense budgets fell from over $90 billion in 1944 to around $13 billion in 1950.[3] Truman and his economic advisers insisted on balanced budgets and the restraint of inflationary forces, and they achieved this by cutting Department of Defense (DOD) appropriations to the bone. Such frugality eased the way for the administration to gain conservative Republican acquiescence to Cold War policies.

Although the mismatch between diplomacy and armed strength may have appeared alarming, the administration was not proceeding blindly. It was relying on strategic airpower to guard national interests. Beginning as early as 1943, the Joint Chiefs of Staff (JCS) and high State Department officials had begun planning for postwar military bases around the globe. By 1946, the United States had 170 active airfields, in addition to naval bases and other installations, and it was seeking even more. It had the ability to severely cripple, perhaps even destroy, the Soviet Union or other enemies. By 2000, the United States had more than 725 foreign bases in 38 countries. These bases and installations housed over a quarter of a million military personnel (more than half a million inhabitants, when dependents and civilians were included) and had a replacement value of approximately $118 billion. By then, all real or potential enemies, neutrals, and allies were within America's military and intelligence reach.

At the outset of the Cold War, the U.S. military strength under Truman took on even more menacing proportions with the nation's monopoly on nuclear weapons, its growing stockpile of atomic bombs, and the capacity to deliver them. Through the so-called Baruch Plan of 1946, the United States, in effect, blocked the way to international control of nuclear might.

Crucial developments in 1949 and 1950 dramatically altered American military policies. Late in 1949, Russia tested an atomic weapon, the Communist Party took control of China, and proposals for unifying western Europe under American direction bogged down. The unexpected outbreak of the Korean War in mid-1950 turned the Cold War hot in a limited but vital area.

National Security Council (NSC)-68 of April 1950 assessed the consequences of the USSR's acquisition of atomic capabilities. Authored principally by Paul H. Nitze, who headed the State Department Policy Planning Staff, the document insisted that the loss of a nuclear monopoly required the United States to accelerate its atomic program in order to maintain overwhelming superiority over the Soviets at all times.[4] The same was true for airpower. Conventional forces also had to be vastly expanded for purposes of limited warfare. Such a formidable military posture, supplemented by intelligence operations, economic assistance, military aid, and unwavering diplomacy, would ensure American domination of Europe, Asia, and the developing world. Under such policies, the United States could defeat communist challenges wherever they arose, roll the USSR back to "traditional Russian borders," and alter the Soviet system to satisfy the West. Unmatched military might would allow such an ambitious agenda while keeping the Russians on the defensive and maintaining the support of America's allies.

The Nitze document accurately set forth the prevailing views of Secretary of State Dean Acheson and most of those in the State and Defense departments, the armed services, and elite foreign policy circles. It broke ground only by officially calling for vast increases of military might in every category.

With division in the Truman administration, real and potential Republican opposition still strong, and Congress loath to greatly expand national defense spending, NSC-68 faced nearly insurmountable odds. The Korean War saved the day.[5] Using the conflict to document Soviet aggression and the general threat of a worldwide communist conspiracy, the Truman administration took significant steps toward implementing the Nitze proposal before leaving office. Overall national defense budgets jumped from around $13.1 billion in 1950 to $50.4 billion in 1953. The Korean War itself consumed less than one-third of these expenditures; the remainder went to vastly expanding the army, navy, and air force, in addition to providing military and economic assistance to Europe and other threatened areas.[6] NATO and the future European Economic Community were successfully under way, and programs continued and expanded for stabilizing regions of the developing world to the extent possible. Additionally, in January 1950, Truman authorized an effort to develop a hydrogen, or fusion, bomb, the so-called Super.[7]

American Cold War policies had now become fully militarized. Moreover, an expensive and deadly arms race founded on nuclear weapons had begun. What the Truman administration had put in place set the pattern that lasted throughout the Cold War and beyond.

EISENHOWER ADMINISTRATION, 1953–1961

When Dwight D. Eisenhower took office in 1953, he pledged to meet the threat of the Soviet Union and world communism with greater vigor and effect. High on his list of priorities was lowering defense spending to ensure national security without endangering the stability of the economy. That quest led to the "New Look" defense posture, stressing a growing reliance on tactical and strategic nuclear weapons, or what Secretary of State John Foster Dulles labeled "massive retaliation." To respond to threats in the developing world, the Eisenhower administration increasingly turned to covert operations carried out by the Central Intelligence Agency (CIA). Before long, the president concluded that the danger and expense of Cold War armament and conflict could be reduced only through efforts aimed at peace and arms control.

When Eisenhower left office in 1961, few of his declared goals had been realized. Cold War tensions were higher in 1961 than they had been in 1953; the arms race had accelerated, and nuclear stockpiles had increased enormously; DOD budgets had been reduced, but the New Look was under attack both within and outside the administration; the imperial presidency had been strengthened; and the DOD and CIA were both growing in power and independence. Fundamental contradictions help explain the limitations of Eisenhower's leadership. Expanding international commitments undermined the drive to lower defense spending permanently. Furthermore, responding to practically all nationalism in the developing world as if it were communist inspired led to immediate and future instability throughout a good part of the world. And intense anticommunism thwarted the measure of trust essential for significant movement toward peace and arms limitation.

Despite its failures, the Eisenhower administration created strong and systematized agencies for formulating and executing foreign and defense policies. In those areas, Eisenhower led the way, as scholars have established in revising notions of a passive chief executive.[8] He insisted on full and open analysis and debate from all relevant officials through the operations of a carefully structured and directed National Security Council, but the president, not the NSC, made the decisions. In doing so, he turned to a small circle of his White House staff and most trusted advisers for assistance.[9] Dulles was always a key player, but if the two constituted a foreign policy partnership, Dulles was unquestionably the very junior member.[10]

Under Eisenhower, little changed in Europe. After years of maneuvering, the Western powers formally recognized the Federal Republic of Germany in May 1955, ending the occupation. Shortly thereafter, the republic became a member of NATO. More important, Nikita S. Khrushchev's February 1956 speech denouncing Joseph Stalin triggered unrest in Poland and, in the fall, a full-blown revolt in Hungary, which the USSR ultimately crushed. Republican goals of "liberation" and rollback were laid to rest by U.S. inactivity. Any overt American intrusion into central or eastern Europe would have triggered all-out war. The division of Europe resulting from the Cold War had been tacitly accepted. Confrontations among the major powers gave way to the more usual difficulties and periodic flare-ups.[11]

While Europe stabilized, in a sense, the developing world presented increasing challenges for the United States. The stalemated war in Korea was the Eisenhower administration's first order of business. Through determined negotiations and threats to use atomic weaponry, an armistice was signed in July 1953.[12]

The first test of massive retaliation came in Vietnam. After the French made their last futile stand against the Vietminh at Dien Bien Phu in 1954, top military and civilian officials proposed American intervention, including the use of atomic weapons. Lacking confidence in the French and unwilling to proceed over the opposition of Congress and Britain, Eisenhower vetoed the proposal. Instead, the administration used the Geneva Accords of 1954 to elbow the French out of Indochina, install Ngo Dinh Diem as head of a government in South Vietnam, and begin substantial programs of economic and military aid in the hope of creating a viable government in the South. The Southeast Asia Treaty Organization (SEATO) supposedly gave American efforts a broad base of support in both Europe and Asia.[13]

At all times, China remained the principal enemy in Asia. Such an outlook led to ongoing crises from 1953 through 1958. Ultimately committed to Taiwan through a defensive treaty, the administration repeatedly threatened to use nuclear weapons against the mainland as conflicts erupted between China and the Chiang Kai-shek government. By a lopsided vote in January 1955, Congress approved the vaguely worded terms of the Formosa Doctrine, which authorized the president to use force in beating back Chinese aggression. For the first time in history, the nation's legislators granted the chief executive advance authority to conduct war at a time and place of his choosing.[14]

By endorsing the Eisenhower Doctrine in March 1957, Congress again authorized the president's advanced war-making power to thwart communist aggression, this time in the Middle East. The administration had become active in the region a number of years earlier. In 1953 the White House had authorized, and the CIA had led, the toppling of the Mohammed Mossadeq government of Iran in favor of the shah. The intervention was successful in preserving some British oil interests, increasing American oil companies' stakes in the country, and holding off a growing Russian presence and real or claimed domestic communist influence.[15] Working with the UN in 1956, the United States forced Britain, France, and Israel to pull back from their invasion of Egypt to undo Gamal Abdel Nasser's nationalizing of the British-owned Universal Suez Canal Company. With Nasser maneuvering to expand his power in the area, the administration used the Eisenhower Doctrine in mid-1958 to send troops into Lebanon, supposedly to combat communist subversion in that country's civil war.[16]

In Latin America the Eisenhower administration once more turned to covert operations. In Guatemala, the reformist government of the democratically elected Jacobo Arbenz Guzman was considered to be a threat. It was overthrown in 1954 by another president-approved, CIA-executed coup and replaced by an American-selected strongman.[17]

Relations with the Soviet Union remained central to the Cold War. After Stalin's death in March 1953, Nikolai Georgi Malenkov's call for a relaxation of Cold War conflicts was viewed skeptically by the Eisenhower administration. Yet the USSR's persistence led to a peace treaty with Austria in 1955, followed by the first Cold War summit at Geneva. Nothing concrete resulted from the conference, but at least the two sides had begun talking. In his last years as president, Eisenhower concluded that only movements toward peace and arms control could bring any hope of security. Perhaps a good beginning would be to ban or limit nuclear testing. Small steps in that direction were taken, and the possibility of a meaningful breakthrough seemed to be in sight at the Paris summit scheduled for May 1960. Those hopes were dashed by the U-2 episode.[18]

Eisenhower had taken office in 1953 determined to rein in what he considered to be excessive defense budgets. His continued efforts throughout two terms paid some dividends. A Truman-proposed 1954 defense budget of around $46.3 billion was pared down to about $40.6 billion. Thereafter, the figure dropped as low as $35.6 billion in 1955 and 1956 before beginning to increase again.[19]

For eight years, the president fought the armed services, which regularly demanded more. Switching the members of the JCS proved to be futile. Furthermore, the three services combined forces to oppose the New Look through leaks to the media, testimony before Congress, and published volumes. In an attempt to bring the military under better control, Eisenhower pushed through DOD reforms in 1953 and 1958.[20]

Additionally, Eisenhower constantly had to veto the use of atomic weapons, principally but not exclusively in Asia. Such was the case five times in 1954 alone, when he resisted pressure from the NSC, the JCS, and the State Department. In a sense, however, the president had helped create this exceptionally dangerous situation by accepting the doctrine of massive retaliation, threatening to go nuclear in Korea, accelerating the development of tactical atomic weapons, stockpiling nuclear weapons overseas, allowing subordinate commanders to initiate the use of nuclear weapons in the event of a communications breakdown, and the like.[21] With the commander in chief basing strategic doctrine on nuclear weapons, the much more hawkish military and its supporters were bound to advocate their usage.

Similar conditions emerged with the CIA. Relying on covert operations as a major tool for managing the developing world encouraged the agency's flawed operations. Favoring subversion over intelligence gathering from the outset, the CIA failed to keep the president objectively informed of basic international affairs.[22]

Despite the limitations and contradictions of the Eisenhower administration, the president, unlike his predecessor and numerous successors, achieved his primary goal of avoiding war. Additionally, as set forth in his farewell address, Eisenhower is the only chief executive to acknowledge and take responsibility for the grave threat to basic American values resulting from the militarization of Cold War policies.

KENNEDY ADMINISTRATION, 1961–1963

The eloquence of John F. Kennedy's inaugural address in January 1961 initially obscured its belligerent Cold War message. Ardent anticommunism characterized his presidential years. The beginnings of detente with the Soviet Union were preceded by nuclear showdowns over Berlin and Cuba, and nearly all policies relating to the developing world were formulated to blunt or beat back the real or presumed threat of communism. Idealist rhetoric gave way to hard-headed, "realistic" solutions.[23]

Insisting that the nation had to approach a troubled world through strength, the Kennedy administration reversed Eisenhower's determination to lower or restrict defense spending. Along those lines, the administration vastly increased strategic and tactical nuclear weaponry. Simultaneously, it scrapped the New Look in favor of "flexible response," in which conventional forces in all services and their arms and equipment were expanded and improved. Overall, Kennedy's defense budgets increased by around 15 percent; roughly 80 percent of the new money went to traditional elements.

Intent on shaping foreign policy, the president downgraded the influence of the State Department to the advantage of the Defense Department. He also largely ignored the NSC in favor of its staff, led by McGeorge Bundy, who ultimately operated out of the White House; in effect, he elevated the position of special assistant for national security affairs to that of national security adviser. Preferring to formulate policy through individual contacts and small groups, the president relied heavily on his brother, Attorney General Robert F. Kennedy, as well as Bundy, Defense Secretary Robert S. McNamara, and General Maxwell D. Taylor.

Before his death, Kennedy helped usher in detente between the East and the West over the division of Europe. Reduced conflict was preceded by the final confrontation over Berlin, which entered the critical stage during the last half of 1961 and included nuclear saber rattling. Acceptance of the Berlin Wall signaled America's de facto recognition of two Germanys.

Like its predecessor, the Kennedy administration's attention was drawn increasingly toward the change and tumult in the developing world. Indeed, the first crisis the administration faced was the Cuban situation inherited from the Eisenhower administration. The April 1961 Bay of Pigs fiasco was followed by the Soviet-triggered Cuban missile crisis of October 1962, which brought the world to the brink of nuclear war.

In general, Kennedy's policies toward Latin America differed little from the unenlightened record of the Eisenhower administration, notwithstanding the high promises of the Alliance for Progress and the Peace Corps. Similar ironies and contradictions characterized the administration's approach to the strife-torn Middle East and turbulent Africa.

Asia became the main focus of the Kennedy administration's anticommunist, anti-insurgency, and nation-building emphasis. Fully embracing the domino theory, the new president continued his predecessor's policy of containing China, albeit at a less active and intense level. That was the case in part because Southeast Asia continued to be the principal area of concern. Kennedy had inherited a growing crisis in Laos that threatened to engulf its neighbors, most significantly South Vietnam. Kennedy managed to hold off pressure from inside and outside his administration to intervene militarily in Laos. Instead, a Geneva conference between mid-1961 and July 1962 gradually worked out a neutrality accord. At all times, however, the settlement was precarious. The United States added substantially to the instability by a Kennedy-sanctioned CIA counterinsurgency operation in Laos that persisted for years, cost billions, and left a legacy of destruction and death.

The status of Laos was largely determined by the fate of Vietnam. When Kennedy entered office, the Diem government of South Vietnam was failing. The new administration gradually moved from assisting Diem to becoming his partner in a desperate effort to stabilize South Vietnam and ward off the Vietcong insurgency. Between 1961 and 1963 the number of U.S. military personnel in Vietnam grew from around 700 to nearly 17,000. These increases took place in stages, as the president typically sought the middle ground between his often intensely divided advisers. Moreover, Kennedy insisted that the growing American involvement be kept under wraps, so combat troops were still designated "advisers," and covert and clandestine operations conducted by the CIA and others continued apace. With the American-sanctioned coup and the assassination of Diem and his brother, Ngo Dinh Nhu, on November 1, 1963, the level of U.S. involvement became clear, and America's commitment to Vietnam and responsibility for its future were greatly strengthened. What Kennedy's policies for South Vietnam would have been if he had lived remains unclear and is the subject of ongoing debate.

Contradictions aside, the prospects of a nuclear war and the deadly arms race between the two superpowers generated great fear in the president and moved him to try to reduce risks. In 1961 the administration created the Arms Control and Disarmament Agency to pursue more effective arms-control efforts at Geneva. Stalemated talks ultimately yielded positive results. In mid-1963 the United States, USSR, and Great Britain signed a Limited Test Ban Treaty, restricting nuclear testing in the atmosphere, underwater, and in outer space. Although the seeming breakthrough yielded no quick returns, it slowly led to future progress.

Overall, the Kennedy administration's foreign and national security policies were devoid of coherence. Within a context of strengthening and exercising American power, the president swung between hawkish and conciliatory approaches with no clearly discernible patterns. Kennedy had inherited a volatile, dangerous international order. At the time of his assassination, the world was just as perilous as when he took office, and perhaps more so.

JOHNSON ADMINISTRATION, 1963–1969

The issues surrounding Vietnam became so pervasive during the presidency of Lyndon Baines Johnson that his administration's other international policies have been obscured.[24] Increasingly, however, the Southeast Asian war affected responses elsewhere, and usually negatively. Relations with Latin America had turned sour during the Kennedy years, and that trend grew stronger under Johnson, exemplified in April 1965 by the invasion of the Dominican Republic under the pretext of protecting American lives and thwarting subversive elements.

More seriously, the Johnson administration was unable to head off Israel's preemptive attack leading to the Six Days' War in mid-1967. The war's destabilizing consequences for the Middle East still reverberate today. Less dire but still of great significance, the NATO alliance continued to erode because of the multiple problems the Johnson administration faced, exacerbated by the conflict over and consequences of the Vietnam War.

The Soviet Union and China were always in mind as the Johnson administration continued to escalate the war in Vietnam. The president and his civilian advisers feared what would happen if either nation joined the hostilities and took every precaution to avoid the possibility. Hence, when Russia clearly established at a June 1967 summit that it was anxious to avoid military confrontation with the United States, the president was greatly relieved. That brief conference in Glassboro, New Jersey, may have assisted the negotiations that ultimately resulted in the Nuclear Nonproliferation Treaty of July 1968. Before, during, and after Glassboro, the administration continued to explore prospects for the two superpowers to agree to limit systems for delivering and defending against nuclear weapons. The Soviet invasion of Czechoslovakia in August 1968 short-circuited a proposed Moscow conference on the critical issue. All in all, and despite the war in Vietnam, the Johnson administration continued Kennedy's policies leading toward detente.

Nonetheless, the Johnson administration became increasingly absorbed in, even obsessed with, the Southeast Asian conflict. Although Johnson kept most of Kennedy's key officials, those who were moderates regarding the war either declined in influence or left. Hawks such as Secretary of State Dean Rusk, Bundy, Walt W. Rostow, and, for a time, McNamara gained in power. Johnson seldom welcomed conflicting viewpoints, which was only one of many reasons his relations with the military were worse than that of any of his post–World War II predecessors.

After the assassination of Diem, South Vietnam entered a period of extreme instability as one government after another came and went with amazing rapidity. Refusing to even consider withdrawal, Johnson chose to increase the level of American involvement, leading in August 1964 to the Gulf of Tonkin Resolution. American takeover of the war in Vietnam was well under way. With the presidential election behind him, Johnson proceeded to move more aggressively against the enemy. The systematic bombing of North Vietnam began in February 1965; the approximately 50,000 U.S. troops in Vietnam in early 1965 ballooned to 535,000 by early 1968. A strategy of "escalation" was designed to force North Vietnam to the negotiating table once the level of destruction and suffering became intolerable. The approach failed. By late 1966–early 1967, the war had deadlocked. North Vietnam could not overrun South Vietnam, but no amount of force could persuade the North to negotiate except on its own terms. In March 1968 Johnson finally, albeit tentatively, accepted that reality, but he and his administration could not reach an accord with Ho Chi Minh's government before leaving office.

Defense budgets, most of which involved war costs, shot up around 57 percent during Johnson's years in office, rising from approximately $50.7 billion in 1964 to more than $79.1 billion in 1969. Yet, until a tax surcharge was instituted in 1968, the president refused to raise taxes to cover war expenses. Based on the desire to protect Great Society programs and minimize opposition to the war, Johnson's decision had extremely negative consequences for the economy in both the short run and the long run.

As the war proceeded, Johnson's loss of public support was vastly accelerated by his refusal to be candid with the public and explain the nation's goals for and its conduct of the Vietnam War. Instead, duplicity eroded the administration's credibility as stalemate became obvious in Vietnam.

NIXON AND FORD ADMINISTRATIONS, 1969–1977

Secrecy and deception leading to criminality ended Richard M. Nixon's presidency in 1974.[25] Before that occurred, the president and his national security adviser Henry A. Kissinger, who later simultaneously served as secretary of state, set about fundamentally transforming American Cold War foreign policy. While attempting to end the Vietnam War, the two leaders aimed at ushering in a new age of peace and world stability. Their bold and far-reaching goals were based on accepting the reality that the United States no longer had the resources to act as world hegemon; henceforth, commitments had to match capabilities. The nation would now serve as the first among a number of international power centers, including the USSR, European Common Market states, Japan, and China. These "economic superpowers" would maintain order and harmony in their regions.

According to the Nixon Doctrine of 1969, America would still provide its allies with a nuclear umbrella against atomic threats by the superpowers; however, with regard to nonnuclear aggression, nations had to defend themselves, with the United States restricted to providing economic and military aid where so obligated. There would be no more Vietnams. In working to implement these policies, detente would be fostered with the USSR and outreach would be made to China. Through what Kissinger called "linkage," the administration expected reciprocity from these nations, beginning with cooperation in settling the war in Vietnam.

Detente with the USSR reached fruition in 1972 with the Soviet-American Statement of Basic Principles, which committed the two nations to avoiding confrontation, and the Strategic Arms Limitation Treaty (SALT I), which placed limitations on ballistic missiles and antiballistic missile (ABM) sites. Those agreements were followed in 1975 by the Helsinki Accords, under which the United States, the USSR, and European nations pledged to honor detente, accept Europe's post-1945 borders, and further human rights. A bolder and more surprising venture took place with the "opening" to China, worked out through secret diplomacy and culminating in the president's trip to the nation early in 1972. In the Shanghai Communiqué, the two nations agreed on friendship, trade, and UN membership for China. The United States accepted a "one China" approach, severing relations with Taiwan and agreeing, along with China, to a peaceful settlement of that island's future.

Broader international goals notwithstanding, the early Nixon administration by necessity focused on the Vietnam War. In seeking to extricate the nation from the quagmire, the president began pulling out American troops with the explicit understanding that they would not return, escalating the air war in the North, and expanding hostilities to Cambodia and Laos, all without the desired results. With Russia and China neutralized and perhaps lending modest support to the United States, the administration unleashed an even more brutal bombing of North Vietnam. Under those circumstances, a negotiated settlement was finally reached in January 1973. It was a cynical settlement, dishonorably achieved, and no party to the agreement expected it to last. Nixon and Kissinger appeared to be intent on preventing the North from unifying the nations under its control through ruthless air attacks until after the administration left office. Watergate squelched any efforts along those lines. In the spring of 1975, South Vietnam fell to North Vietnam's offensive, and Cambodia and Laos quickly came under communist control as well.

Although generally supporting the policies of detente with Russia and the opening to China, Europe resented the secrecy and lack of consultation in their implementation. The response of Asian allies ranged from perplexity to consternation. Other regions suffered from America's diverted attention. Despite warnings from the Middle East, the administration failed to try to prevent what became the Yom Kippur War in October 1973 between Israel and the Arab states. With hostilities under way and the administration practically paralyzed by Watergate, it initially responded to the crisis in an uncertain and cautious way. Latin America was also largely ignored until Chile elected the radical Salvador Allende to the presidency. With CIA complicity, the Chilean military overthrew Allende in late 1973 in a bloodbath that continued into the post-coup years.

Concerning broader world affairs, and consistent with their quest for world peace and arms control, both Nixon and Kissinger favored a nuclear strategy of "sufficiency" to replace the "assured destruction" doctrine they had inherited. The revised approach was adopted early in 1974. DOD spending in general was also restricted. Between fiscal year 1969 and fiscal year 1975, defense budgets fell almost 30 percent in constant dollars. Additionally, the overall size of the armed forces dropped by around 1.3 million. The declining budgets and force size stemmed largely (but not totally) from the United States' disengagement from Vietnam. But civil-military relations during the Nixon years took on nightmarish qualities because of the secrecy, deception, and duplicity that were characteristic of the administration.

Overall, the accomplishments of Nixon and Kissinger over five years were stunning. Withdrawal from Vietnam under the terms of the Nixon Doctrine, detente with Russia, the opening to China, and turning away from nuclear superiority all reversed Cold War doctrine as it had evolved since 1946. Neither Nixon nor Kissinger appeared to believe in American exceptionalism or the universality of its ideals, mission, and so forth. Instead, they operated on the assumption of limited and declining national power and the realistic need to share global responsibility with others.

For such fundamental change to endure, it must be achieved through open debate, persuasion, and consensus, not the furtive, disingenuous, manipulative, underhanded, and ultimately criminal operations of the Nixon administration. These methods obscured the momentousness of what had been done and left the policies vulnerable to reversal. The strongest opposition and blowback came from hard-right Republican elements. Assuming office upon Nixon's resignation, Gerald Ford stabilized to a degree the presidency that his predecessor had so defiled and diminished.[26] Interested primarily in domestic affairs, the new president not only kept Kissinger on in his dual roles but also relied on him to play a dominant part in foreign affairs. Nonetheless, Ford had to face the nation's humiliating exit from South Vietnam, Cambodia, and Laos. The ill-fated and clumsily handled *Mayaguez* crisis of May 1975 acted, in the eyes of some, to salvage a measure of America's international self-respect.

The most significant development during Ford's two-plus years in office was the assault on detente. Ultraconservative Republicans, who had been growing in strength since 1970, rejected the Nixon-Kissinger accomplishments in behalf of a new world community, a goal accepted in a low-key manner by the Ford administration. Increasingly, critics began rallying around Ronald Reagan and encouraging him to challenge Ford and detente in the drive for the Republican presidential nomination in 1976. Reagan shared conservative assertions that the Soviet Union sought world domination and constituted a growing threat to the United States. They argued that the nation had to engage in a massive buildup of its military strength to deal with the peril and return to an aggressive, crusading foreign policy of shaping the world order according to American ideology and the alleged superiority of democracy and capitalism.

To meet the challenge in part, Ford reshuffled his administration late in 1975. Among other changes, Kissinger lost his national security adviser's role, Donald Rumsfeld became secretary of defense, and George H. W. Bush took over the top CIA post. By downgrading Kissinger and allowing hard-line conservatives to officially challenge CIA national security estimates, Ford attempted to distance himself from detente. Improved relations with the USSR were becoming a political liability in the president's quest for reelection. Nevertheless, he lost the 1976 election by a small margin.

Although the military in general either had reservations about or opposed arms-control agreements, Ford still managed to rectify civil-military relations and generally win both the respect and the cooperation of the armed services.

CARTER ADMINISTRATION, 1977–1981

Almost from the outset, the foreign and national security policies of the James Earl Carter Jr. administration had an inconsistent, even contradictory, quality. As a result, they confused friend and foe abroad and the population at home.[27]

The problems began with the president. Although a quick and eager study, he lacked the experience and leadership skills required to adroitly handle complexities abroad. These drawbacks might have been overcome through the guidance of able advisers. Although both Cyrus R. Vance as secretary of state and Zbigniew Brzezinski as national security adviser were exceptionally talented, they favored very different and competing approaches to world affairs. Vance was an advocate of detente who sought to work for international stability through cooperation with the Soviet Union. Brzezinski pushed a hard line toward the USSR, with the goal of maximizing American international hegemony. Keeping the two working in harmony was far beyond Carter's ability. That reality goes far in explaining the administration's incoherence in terms of foreign affairs.

For the first two years, Carter attempted to break out of old Cold War patterns by focusing on human rights abroad and the welfare of less developed regions, particularly Africa, the Middle East, Central America, and the Caribbean. Results were mixed at best. The Camp David Accords and the Panama Canal treaties were among the administration's outstanding achievements.

In seeking world order, the Carter administration stumbled badly in its relations with the USSR. Rather than attempting to build on the guidelines of SALT I and the Vladivostok agreement of the Ford administration, Carter began anew with a much more ambitious proposal for nuclear arms control that the Russians predictably rejected. At about the same time, the administration began hectoring the Soviets about the violation of human rights in their own country and in the central and eastern European satellites. With tension growing between the two nations, negotiations for SALT II stretched out over more than two years, and the treaty was finally signed in June 1979.

By that time, detente had been gravely weakened and Cold War animosities rekindled. Three areas of dispute increasingly strained relations between the superpowers: China, NATO, and Africa. In outmaneuvering Vance, Brzezinski was central to the discord. By mid-1978, the Soviet Union was modernizing its missiles in the European theater. The national security adviser persuaded Carter to counter Soviet action by normalizing relations with China and including the latter in an entente aimed at Russia. Then, in 1978 and 1979, Brzezinski oversaw planning to strengthen NATO's nuclear striking power against the USSR, including the introduction of Pershing II and ground-launched cruise missiles.

The less developed world, even more than Europe, acted to erode U.S.-USSR relations. With its influence and presence in the Middle East diminishing, the USSR became increasingly active in Africa in 1978. It began supplying

Libya militarily and supporting Marxist governments in Afghanistan, South Yemen, and, in tandem with Cuba, Ethiopia. Claiming that the USSR's action was threatening vital American interests in a "crescent of crisis," Brzezinski fed the president's national security fears.

By 1979–1980, a second round of the Cold War was well under way, despite the presumed national chastening from the Vietnam disaster. The crowning blow for both the United States and the USSR was Muslim-based movements that threatened or toppled favored governments in Iran and Afghanistan. In 1978 the shah and his close ties to the United States engendered increasingly strident internal dissent; as a result, the shah was virtually driven out of Iran in January 1979. Ayatollah Ruhallah Khomeini took the lead in setting up an Islamic republic. With relations between Iran and America deteriorating, the American embassy in Tehran was stormed in November 1979 and its occupants taken hostage. Carter authorized a military rescue operation in April 1980 that failed in its early stages. Opposed to the venture from the outset, and still at odds with Brzezinski, Vance resigned as secretary of state.

For its part, the USSR invaded Afghanistan in December 1979 to try to salvage a grossly inept Marxist government that was facing growing resistance from popular Islamic nationalist forces. Carter responded, among lesser acts, by withdrawing the already stalled SALT II from Senate consideration, launching a massive military buildup based on a modified and arguably menacing nuclear strategy, and, according to the Carter Doctrine, vowing to fight the USSR if it interfered with access to Persian Gulf oil.

At the outset of his administration, Carter significantly cut the armed services' budgets and a number of favored weapon systems; aimed for a drastic reduction of strategic nuclear weapons, in agreement with the USSR; and considered removing troops from South Korea. As matters worked out, the DOD budget, which, in current dollars, stood at around $89.6 billion in 1976, dropped during the first two Carter years and then skyrocketed in the last two years to approximately $134 billion. Most of the spending was for advanced weaponry, since the size of the armed services remained largely the same. Throughout his tumultuous years in office, Carter's relations with the military were difficult at best because of his shifting, unpredictable policies and his reluctance to consult with the JCS.

The troubled Carter presidency was further challenged by chronic national and international economic dislocation. The principal problem stemmed from the Arab oil boycott following the 1973 Arab-Israeli war and the fall of the shah's government in Iran. Those woes simply added to the sense of failed presidential leadership, resulting in Carter's overwhelming defeat in his quest for reelection in 1980.

REAGAN ADMINISTRATION, 1981–1989

The bellicosity of the later Carter years was continued and greatly escalated by the Ronald Reagan administration.[28] Indeed, between 1981 and 1986, defense budgets (in current dollars) burgeoned from around $158 billion to $273 billion, reaching more than $1.3 trillion in total and constituting the biggest peacetime military spending in American history. (During Reagan's eight years in office, the figure totaled nearly $1.9 trillion.) With unquestioned and unbending support, Secretary of Defense Caspar W. Weinberger encouraged the armed services to request whatever weapons they desired. An exasperated Congress finally began reining in the runaway budgets beginning in 1986. Before it did so, extravagance, waste, corruption, and criminality in military procurement had become widespread.

The conduct of foreign policy during the first six years was equally unstructured and chaotic. Under a hands-off president, endless turmoil occurred as conservatives, moderates, right-wing ideologues, and others maneuvered for position. In the process, the NSC was marginalized, and the CIA under William J. Casey virtually carried out its own clandestine foreign policy. Only after the exposé of the Iran-Contra affair in 1986 and the resignation of Weinberger in 1987 did the Reagan administration put together a professional team that stabilized foreign policy under George P. Shultz as secretary of state, Frank C. Carlucci heading the DOD, and General Colin L. Powell in charge of the NSC staff.

Repeated failures and blunders abroad and a revived gunboat diplomacy characterized most of the Reagan years. It began in El Salvador and Nicaragua shortly after Reagan took office and continued in Grenada. By 1982, the administration became involved in the turbulent Middle East. American troops, along with those of France and Italy, were sent into Lebanon in an attempt to end the fierce fighting in that troubled land. By slow stages, the United States ended up taking sides in the vicious civil war that split the country. As a result, in April 1983 the American embassy in Beirut became the target of suicide bombers, and in October a massive attack on military headquarters killed hundreds of marines and navy personnel. The armed services were then pulled out.

As it had in Lebanon, the Reagan administration became entangled in the bitter and bloody war fought between Iran and Iraq. Furthermore, the navy began patrolling the Persian Gulf to ensure the continued flow of oil. Until the Iran-Iraq war concluded in 1988, tensions ran high in the volatile area, with repeated damage to and loss of military and civilian property and lives. Libya was singled out for harsh treatment. Muammar Khaddafi supported and financed various terrorist attacks in Europe and the Middle East. Consequently, the navy and air force patrolled the Gulf of Sidra and, between 1981 and 1986, engaged Libyan forces and launched bombing attacks on the mainland.

Although involvement in less developed areas engaged the Reagan administration, the USSR always remained its principal focus. At the outset, the administration's approach toward the USSR was extremely hostile, and in the early 1980s, particularly in 1983, the two superpowers veered closer to an all-out nuclear war than at any time since the Cuban missile crisis. Despite that harsh reality and the apparent contradiction involved, Reagan supported an end to the potentially catastrophic nuclear arms race. Negotiations with the USSR over arms reduction continued during the tensest years of the president's first term. Meaningful progress took place only when Mikhail S. Gorbachev came to power in 1985. He realized that the Soviet Union's survival depended on ending the Cold War and the deadly and prohibitively expensive arms race it fed. Between November 1985 and the end of Reagan's presidency, the two heads of state held five summit conferences. Growing out of meetings in Reykjavik late in 1986, the United States and USSR worked out the Intermediate-Range Nuclear Forces Treaty, signed in December 1987. Thereafter, in a remarkably short period, the Cold War ended. The Soviet Union not only withdrew from central and eastern Europe and less developed countries but also surrendered its empire to become Russia once again.

Scholars and other authors differ over whether Gorbachev or Reagan contributed more in the negotiations leading to the termination of the extended conflict between East and West. Reagan's unquestioned anticommunist credentials allowed him to pursue nuclear arms control and improved relations with the USSR where more liberal leaders would have been hampered or deterred. Nonetheless, the president resisted intense pressure from within and outside the administration in his determination to halt the arms race. In the often contentious negotiations leading to that end, however, Gorbachev made most of the critical concessions that were essential for continued progress. What the Soviet leader did not receive was the necessary measure of accommodation from the United States that would have eased the way for the ongoing battles he fought at home in a desperate effort to save the USSR.

Measuring levels of contribution is less important than recognizing the enormous historical significance of what Reagan, Gorbachev, and their assistants achieved. Although Gorbachev lost his struggle to save the Soviet Union, he proved to be a daring and resourceful statesman. For Reagan, achieving nuclear arms control and accelerating the Cold War's end stand out as his greatest foreign policy successes.

Reagan's lavish military spending, arguably, was counterproductive. The problem stemmed from several sources. Money flowed to the DOD in an incoherent, unpredictable manner, thereby denying the services the opportunity to plan for its use over a number of years. Additionally, Reagan and Weinberger emphasized procuring new and technologically sophisticated weapon systems that were much more expensive than those they would replace. With weapons taking years to complete, the Pentagon created reserve funds to pay for them over time and to provide for their operation, maintenance, and repair. The constantly rising costs of DOD procurement across the board drew down the reserve accounts excessively. As a result, budgets became seriously unbalanced, with adverse effects on the military in general. By 1985, all the armed services had declined in size and basic weaponry, and levels of training, munitions stock, and combat readiness were considered inadequate. Although the armed forces had acquired some new weapons and equipment, the military as a whole appeared to be in no better shape in 1989 than it had been in 1981.

Budgetary issues aside, Reagan maintained positive relations with the armed forces. His unfailing support of and praise for the military were greatly appreciated by all the services. They found the president to be a welcome change from a number of his predecessors.

BUSH SR. ADMINISTRATION, 1989–1993

The George H. W. Bush administration faced many of the same issues as the Reagan administration, but with a different tone and under the direction of a more professional and harmonious leadership team.[29] Overall, however, it was more cautious and pragmatic than innovative and daring.

These qualities were fully displayed in the administration's response to the Soviet Union and its leader, Gorbachev. The first meeting between Bush and Gorbachev did not occur until December 1989 at Malta. Thereafter, six summit conferences took place in which the two leaders worked productively together. Most of the initiative came from the USSR, but the Bush administration carefully avoided words or deeds that might make Gorbachev's hazardous transition effort more challenging. By 1989, however, the Soviet Union was beginning its rapid phase of disintegration, with the states of eastern Europe and the Baltic gaining their independence. By adroitly maneuvering around intense Soviet resistance and European concern, the United States played a key role in unifying Germany within the NATO structure in October 1990. At the end of 1991, Gorbachev's resignation as president of the now-defunct USSR brought Boris N. Yeltsin to power as president of the Russian Republic. Yeltsin was not welcomed by the Bush administration because of his unpolished emotionalism and erratic behavior.

Before Gorbachev left office, the United States and USSR moved rapidly ahead on arms control. Under the Conventional Forces in Europe Treaty signed in November 1990, massive reductions in ground forces took place on the part of members of the Warsaw Pact and NATO. Once the USSR became more flexible on the Strategic Defense Initiative (SDI), negotiations on strategic arms moved forward, resulting in the Strategic Arms Reduction Treaty I (START I), signed in July 1991, and START II, signed by Yeltsin in January 1993. Together, the agreements proposed cutting strategic nuclear weaponry on both sides by around two-thirds by the end of the century. Overriding his secretary of defense and military elements, Bush ordered in September 1991 a unilateral demobilization of the nation's ground and naval tactical nuclear weaponry, along with other measures. Shortly thereafter, the USSR followed suit. Hence, before the USSR passed from the scene, the Cold War arms race, particularly as it involved nuclear weapons, had largely ended.

Although the USSR had removed itself from the less developed world, the United States had not. Indeed, Washington could now move without considering Moscow's response. Yet the threat of communism no longer existed as a ready excuse for intervention. Consequently, American policies in the less developed areas became mixed, unpredictable, even confused. During the Bush administration, pragmatism prevailed for the most part in Latin America. The major exception was the December 1989 invasion of Panama to capture and extradite General Manuel Noriega, who had been on the CIA payroll for years but later became an increasing irritant to Washington. Earlier, in the late spring of 1989, the Bush administration had responded coolly to China's bloody slaughter of protesting students in Tiananmen Square but, through quiet diplomacy, maintained friendly relations between the two powers.

If the Panamanian imbroglio stemmed in part from blowback, Iraq was an even more extreme example of American policies gone badly awry. In its efforts to isolate Iran, Washington helped Iraq in multiple ways, including economic, military, diplomatic, and intelligence assistance. Misreading American aims and attitudes throughout the world community, Iraqi leader Saddam Hussein invaded Kuwait in August 1990 and then annexed it. Facing the prospect of the vast Middle East oil reserves falling under the domination of a ruthless dictator backed by a massive, lethally armed military, the United States mobilized the UN and a worldwide coalition to thwart Hussein. When his government turned away all efforts aimed at persuading it to back down, the United States attacked in January 1991. By the end of February, it had achieved a remarkably rapid victory. Anticipating a quick overthrow of Hussein, the administration chose not to push on to Baghdad to topple the dictator and face the hazards of a drawn-out occupation. Hussein, however, not only survived but also brutally attacked Kurds in northern Iraq and Shiites in the south and resisted and harassed UN-appointed weapons inspectors.

Civil-military relations under Bush were sound. Nonetheless, the administration faced ongoing and challenging defense budget problems. The unwieldy spending during the Reagan years had created extraordinary expenses. Additionally, with the Cold War over or ending, Congress was clamoring for meaningful cuts in DOD appropriations. Gradually, under the careful guidance of Colin Powell as chair of the JCS, the administration worked out what was labeled the "base force": a military trimmed in size by about one-third between 1990 and 1995. Moreover, after a slow start, the president was determined to cut American nuclear forces severely.

Overall, the Bush administration established a creditable, though unspectacular, foreign policy and national security record. It navigated the great transition that ended the Cold War with appropriate caution and skill. The one place it definitely faltered was the Congress-led effort to help finance the securing of nuclear and chemical weaponry in the Soviet Union and later the various republics. The DOD and the military impeded the effort, and the administration failed to push the program forward. Bush's modestly positive foreign policy record did not lead to reelection. By 1992, popular concern had shifted to domestic policy and economics in particular—not areas of strength for the administration.

CLINTON ADMINISTRATION, 1993–2001

Elected to the presidency in 1992 principally on domestic issues, William Jefferson Clinton took at least two years to gain a reasonably firm footing in foreign affairs.[30] Although a person of broad interests and a quick study, Clinton was inexperienced in international relations. His foreign policy–national security team did not step in to lead effectively. The administration approached the post–Cold War world with positive goals, including globalization, enlargement of democratic and free market systems, multilateralism, and the like. Too often, however, it ended up supporting American hegemonic and militaristic policies that were little different from those of the past.

With a tumultuous Russia, Clinton did as well as possible. His administration cultivated and maintained good relations with the extremely difficult Yeltsin and probably helped him survive numerous political challenges and keep Russia intact. Similar to Reagan and Bush, Clinton continued to use Russian dependence on the United States to extract whatever the United States wanted without providing the former Soviet Union with any meaningful economic assistance, which it desperately needed.

These conditions changed abruptly when Yeltsin resigned at the end of 1999 and Vladimir Putin replaced him. The troubled nation's transition was entering a new period, one that would be much more confrontational toward the United States. Soon after taking office, Putin began reaching out to Europe as a nationalist and distancing himself from America.

Over substantial objections from the nation's foreign policy establishment, the extreme reluctance of Russia, and the uncertainty of Europe, Clinton pushed through the expansion of NATO to include Poland, Hungary, and the Czech Republic. After preliminary procedures and continued debate, the three nations joined NATO in 1999. The president was determined to link the three most advanced former east European communist states with the West. Increasing American investment and trade opportunities also played a part, as did the prospect of a new area for exploitation by American arms makers.

Compared with Europe, Asia was less affected by the USSR's disintegration. Still, American national security could not be ignored. The rise of China led to a strengthening of America's alliance with Japan. North Korea's nuclear threats that began in 1993 became even more disturbing. Former president Jimmy Carter negotiated a settlement in 1994 that headed off a potentially deadly military encounter. The administration also mediated an even greater crisis farther south when India and Pakistan approached nuclear war over Kashmir in 1999. Late in the 1990s, as it had earlier in Mexico, the United States took the lead in resolving a severe economic disruption in Asia.

Clinton's early years were defined and marred not by what was done in Europe and Asia but by problems largely inherited from the Bush administration in peripheral areas: Somalia, Haiti, and eastern Europe. In 1992 the Bush administration had intervened militarily in Somalia with the intent of quelling clan warfare. Under Clinton, the goal was expanded to reestablish Somalia as a stable, functioning state. A humiliating and costly combat setback in October 1993 led to American troops being pulled out. Badly shaken by the experience, the nation held back when genocidal ethnic violence in Rwanda rocked Africa and the world in 1994.

Closer to home, the situation in Haiti once again flared up. The democratically elected government of Jean-Bertrand Aristide was overthrown by a military junta in 1991, less than a year after taking office. After attempts at a negotiated settlement broke down in 1993, the Clinton administration prepared for military intervention in 1994. Before that took place, Carter prevailed on the junta to step down and allow Aristide, protected by American troops, to complete his term of office.

The former Yugoslavia presented the greatest challenge to American humanitarian intervention. In 1991 ethnoreligious warfare broke out in the province of Bosnia. NATO moved to use air strikes to stop the slaughter only after the United States took the lead. A negotiated settlement was worked out at a Dayton, Ohio, peace conference in November 1995 at which a tripartite Bosnian Republic was created. NATO troops, including those of the United States, implemented and enforced the accord. Once Bosnia began to stabilize, the situation in Kosovo flared up. Although Kosovo was under nominal Serbian sovereignty, it was inhabited principally by Albanian Muslims, or Kosovars. As the Kosovars' insistence on independence became more aggressive, Serbia responded with increasingly brutal military suppression in 1998. With the United States once again out front, NATO launched a seven-week air attack in March 1999 that forced Serbia to back off. By mid-1999, a tense peace agreement was achieved, overseen, as in Bosnia, by NATO forces with American participation.

The Middle East engaged the Clinton administration almost from the outset. Extended efforts to restrict Iraq continued to break down. Greater success appeared possible in easing the Israeli-Palestinian conflict with the Oslo Accords of September 1993; however, those hopes died with the assassination of Israel's prime minister, Yitzhak Rabin, in November 1995. Clinton was unable to reverse the deteriorating relations even with intense negotiations in 1999 between Ehud Barak, the Labor Party's prime minister, and the Palestine Liberation Organization's chairman, Yassir Arafat.

Although the record is far from clear, the Clinton administration appears to have taken seriously the various terrorist attacks at home and abroad. During Clinton's last two years in office, his administration focused on counterterrorism and began to appreciate and warn of the great, even catastrophic, threats to national security.

For a number of reasons, Clinton's relations with the military were always rocky. Certainly, the armed services resented the declining budgets and force structures throughout the Clinton years. Nonetheless, the Clinton administration's record in arms control is in no way outstanding. The nation had stopped making and testing nuclear weapons in 1992, and in 1996 it signed the Comprehensive Nuclear Test Ban Treaty. But the administration took no steps in the direction of demobilizing the Cold War military buildup, and it seemed to favor strengthening the nation's industrial base for purposes of national security; it spoke of preemptive military action; and it adopted the Ballistic Missile Defense Organization in place of SDI, which appeared to violate the 1972 ABM Treaty. While advocating the nonproliferation of armaments, the Clinton administration made the United States the world's leading arms dealer. To complete a rather contradictory record, Clinton intervened in more countries than any president since Woodrow Wilson, although he often did so in collaboration with the UN. Unquestionably, there are positive and negative aspects to Clinton's foreign policy and national security record. Yet Clinton, like Bush, made little progress in modifying or lessening the dimensions of America's national security state.

BUSH JR. ADMINISTRATION, 2001–2009

The George W. Bush administration greatly strengthened and extended the reach of the national security state.[31] Other than continued progress in nuclear arms control, the earlier Bush and Clinton administrations had made little substantive headway in adjusting the nation's response to the post–Cold War world. This Bush administration, by contrast, attempted to reassert an exaggerated and distorted version of the Truman administration's early Cold War hard line. It did so when the United States no longer had the economic or military might, or perhaps even the will, for worldwide hegemony.

The administration's aims and ends were clearly set forth in September 2002 by the National Security Strategy of the United States (NSS). This published document stressed four points: (1) the United States intends to move the world's nations toward the "superior" American political and economic model; (2) the model features democracy and market economics that promise prosperity through pro-growth policies; (3) the United States will launch preventive attacks against potential enemies that might threaten it, especially tyrants and terrorists possessing or seeking weapons of mass destruction (WMD); and (4) America will bypass international organizations and alliances to maintain military superiority over all others, assisted, if necessary, by coalitions willing to follow the nation's lead. NSS was based largely on the Defense Planning Guidance document authored by Secretary of Defense Richard Cheney's department in March 1992 and written by Paul Wolfowitz.

Before 9/11, the Bush administration had indicated its intention to break free of practically all international commitments and restraints. It rejected the Kyoto Protocol, abandoned the ABM Treaty, and turned its back on the Comprehensive Test Ban Treaty, the Chemical and Biological Weapons Convention, the International Criminal Court, and similar agreements and institutions. After

9/11, and in line with its declared global war on terrorism, the administration went much further by refuting the Geneva Conventions and refusing to be bound by UN action, alliances such as NATO, or any other source of authority or previously acknowledged agreements. The administration also pursued the development and output of new tactical nuclear weaponry. In a similar vein, it expanded America's already vast collection of military bases, surveillance sites, and espionage centers, especially in Central Asia and the Persian Gulf. Pentagon publications indicate that such entities totaled between 737 and 860, excluding those that were unacknowledged for various reasons.

On the home front, the Bush administration violated the rights and liberties of American citizens as well as those of legal and illegal aliens. Abroad and on American soil, detainees and enemy combatants and noncombatants were denied protection and were subjected to numerous abuses, including "extraordinary rendition" and torture.

With the Second Gulf War, the United States defied a good part of the world community in launching a preventive attack on Iraq. The invasion was based on distorted intelligence claiming that Iraq was involved in the 9/11 attack, possessed WMD, and constituted a great danger to the world community.

The unilateral and often internationally illegal actions of the Bush administration were consistent with the nation's Cold War past. Since the late 1940s, the United States has overthrown or acted to overthrow unwanted governments. Intervening in other nations' affairs for various reasons, including sheltering authoritarian and dictatorial governments under siege from nationalist movements, has also been typical American behavior. Likewise, the use of distorted intelligence and deception was a common Cold War practice.

Where the Bush administration departed dramatically from America's past conduct was in jettisoning the nation's participation in or commitment to international efforts to achieve a safe, stable, and peaceful world. What the Bush administration pursued instead was aggressive, crusading nationalism. It was intent on reclaiming the international dominance exercised by Washington from 1945 to 1965. The Nixon administration's acceptance of the fact that American preeminence was no longer possible generated an intense reaction among hard-line foreign policy conservatives—principally Republicans, but also a number of Democrats—ultimately leading to the Bush administration's policies at home and abroad.

When Bush took office in 2001, the nation was at peace; when he departed in 2009, America was bogged down in wars in Afghanistan and Iraq, situated in the most volatile regions of the globe. National defense spending during those years more than doubled, climbing from around $341.5 billion in 2000 to $700.7 billion in 2008. In the process, the Bush administration further weakened the nation's economy and its military, badly sullied the U.S. image abroad, and complicated enormously America's relations with its allies.

CIVIL-MILITARY RELATIONS

Civil-military relations went through a major transformation during the Cold War and post–Cold War years.[32] Nonetheless, the fundamental shift grew out of the more distant past. Reaching back to the foundations of the nation, civilian officials and military officers have differed and fought over defense policies and have devised various ways to protect their interests. Except during times of hostilities, especially during long and divisive wars such as the American Revolution and the Civil War, the civil-military conflict was not particularly consequential because the peacetime armed services were purposely kept small, sometimes to the point of insignificance.

With the Cold War, these conditions changed dramatically. Although President Roosevelt achieved a remarkable balance in civil-military relations during World War II, all the services had grown mightily and exercised a range of power and influence never before experienced. In a postwar world that was largely destroyed and where there was widespread danger and the potential for conflict, and given the great uncertainty created by nuclear weapons, both civilian and military leaders accepted that the armed services needed to remain relatively large. A sizable "peacetime" military of long duration changed the nature and consequences of civil-military relations.

Andrew J. Bacevich trenchantly points out that post–World War II civil-military relations must be viewed in two different ways. The first is the official version, which insists that civilians are fully in control of national security policy and that the armed services remain subordinate and deferential. These claims are a myth, he explains, intended to assure the public that large and powerful military services constitute no threat to American democracy: there is no reason for concern or anxiety. A pliant public is unlikely to question the power, position, prestige, and place of the "national security elite" made up of high-ranking elected and appointed civilian officials, senior military officers, select legislators, corporate officials, and policy-oriented academics. This elite determines national security policy to the nearly total exclusion of the general public, and it is intent on maintaining that state of affairs. As long as the official version holds, the people will most likely go along.

In Bacevich's words, the official interpretation is "widely misleading, where not simply dead wrong." Instead, he insists, "civilian control of the military during the postwar era was frequently contested, at times highly contingent, and on a few occasions downright precarious."[33] Throughout that period and right up to the present, civilian leaders have had to engage in hard bargaining with the armed services' leaders as if they were equals; both sides engaged in elaborate maneuvering and positioning based on shared suspicion and mistrust and motivated more by parochial self-interest than national security. Included in that struggle were weighty matters such as the amount and division of the defense budget; the armed forces' size, mission, and weaponry; nuclear weapons and their use; foreign policy; and issues of war and peace. A huge, permanent military system absorbing trillions of dollars insisted on having a voice in, and at times a veto power over, vital policies affecting the nation at home and abroad.

Truman encountered the reality, not the mythology, of civil-military relations in the brutal battles over universal military training; armed services unification; service roles, sizes, and budgets; racial integration; control of nuclear weapons; and the conduct of the Korean War, leading to General Douglas MacArthur's removal from command. Eisenhower's long, distinguished army career did not significantly assist him in dealing with an aggressive, energized military. All the services in one way or another opposed and resisted the policy of massive retaliation and persistently fought for larger appropriations and additional nuclear weapons. Repeated changes in the makeup of the JCS and their stated commitment to follow the president's lead were to no avail. Of particular concern was General Curtis LeMay, commander of Strategic Air Command (SAC), who was determined to follow his own agenda concerning the use of nuclear weapons. Deeply troubled by the costs and consequences of militarizing American foreign policy, Eisenhower felt compelled to warn the nation about the grave dangers it faced in his remarkable farewell address.

Variations on what took place with Truman and Eisenhower continued with Presidents Kennedy and Johnson. Kennedy was familiar with the ways of the military from his World War II service and his experience in the House of Representatives. He neither trusted the military nor held it in high regard. The outcome of the Bay of Pigs fiasco and the Cuban missile crisis confirmed the president's judgment. In the first instance, the JCS dodged responsibility and blamed the White House for the failure; in the second, they pushed for an unlimited attack on and invasion of the island. For Southeast Asia, the joint chiefs again advocated military intervention, including the use of nuclear weapons. All but ignoring the service chiefs, Kennedy turned principally to Secretary of Defense Robert S. McNamara, General Maxwell Taylor, and a few others for national security advice. Although their guidance, for the most part, proved to be disastrous, it was no worse, and probably more restrained, than what he received from the individual and collective armed services. Although dismissing the input of the JCS, Kennedy went out of his way to placate them, fully aware that they could cause his administration great woe.

Even though Johnson knew even more about civil-military relations than his predecessor, he treated the JCS with undisguised contempt and bullying, kept them at a distance, and ignored their advice; he and his contingent of civilian advisers made decisions concerning Vietnam on their own. Only by threatening to resign en masse were the joint chiefs able to persuade the president to include them in his principal Vietnam advisory group. But it was already too late for the military to be heard. The public had turned against the war, and neither the White House nor the Pentagon had much credibility on the subject. The Vietnam War had delivered a death blow to the existing mode of civil-military relations, as evidenced by the muddled and chaotic, if not farcical, interactions of the Nixon and Carter administrations with the JCS and the more placid, though uncertain, relations of the Ford administration.

An unpopular, damaged, and demoralized military finally regained its footing with the warm glow of the Reagan administration. By then, the armed forces were insisting that civilian leaders, defense intellectuals, and the media, not the military, had been responsible for the Vietnam defeat. Moreover, the services regained esprit and confidence when they were required to rely on an all-volunteer force by elevating the positions of enlisted members to those of shared military professionals and expanding their recruitment pool to include unlimited numbers of African Americans and women.

Additionally, the officer corps turned away from the hazards and frustrations of irregular warfare characteristic of the developing world—later known as fourth-generation warfare—to concentrate on the potential for traditional warfare—or second-generation warfare—in defending Europe against the massive forces of the Soviet Union. In short, they returned to the familiar pattern of World War II.

The Reagan administration not only opened the national treasury for DOD but also provided cover for the military with the Weinberger Doctrine of 1984. Henceforth, troops would be called to arms only to defend vital and clearly defined national interests; once war was declared, its conduct would be left to the professional military. The secretary of defense's dictum was expanded by JCS chairman Colin Powell's insistence that "overwhelming force" was essential to ensure a successful outcome to hostilities.

With the Gulf War, the armed services' effectiveness and reputation appeared to be fully restored. While Bush Sr. ostensibly allowed the armed forces to control the battlefield, his lieutenants, in fact, carefully managed all major aspects of hostilities without appearing to upstage the sensitive military leadership. The military's rebirth so emboldened the Pentagon that it treated the Clinton administration with barely disguised disdain. However, owing to 9/11, the military's newly won power and favor were short lived.

Initially, the election of Bush Jr. indicated that the once bipartisan or party-balanced officer corps had become a heavily Republican structure under Reagan. More to the point, this more partisan military was biased. Whereas the Democrat Clinton had been endlessly hounded by the armed forces for his avoidance of military service during the Vietnam War, the strongly Republican military gave the new president, vice president, and numerous other high-ranking members of the administration a free pass on the same issue.

In any event, 9/11 drove the Bush administration to preventive warfare under the direction of the heavy-handed, imperious Secretary of Defense Donald Rumsfeld. To complicate matters further, the armed services' preparation for their preferred second-generation warfare was totally inappropriate for the despised fourth-generation warfare they ultimately encountered in Iraq and Afghanistan. Quagmires resulted, generating major crises once more for civil-military relations, with no resolution apparent or even likely.

The use of private contractors to perform military functions has greatly complicated civil-military relations. The practice began in the late 1970s with basic plant operations and maintenance and then expanded to include troop training, security and intelligence operations, and a host of other duties. As a result, managing the fighting forces has become more challenging for civilian and military authorities alike.

To make the all-volunteer force more attractive to potential recruits, civilian contractors took over onerous and resented duties such as mess hall assignments and barracks and latrine cleanup. The use of such contractors took on much greater importance with the Nixon Doctrine, which called on allied or associated nations to defend themselves against nonnuclear aggression.[34] That goal led the United States to undertake widespread programs to train foreign militaries. Authorization for the training took place under the State Department's International Military Education and Training Program, set up in 1976, and the Defense Department's Joint Combined Exchange Training Program, organized in 1992. DOD has another program called Foreign Military Financing, in which the department grants funds to countries that buy American weapons and provides personnel to instruct the recipients in their use.

Some of the training programs are carried out by American military forces; increasingly, however, the job has been turned over to private contractors such as the Vinnell Corporation of Fairfax, Virginia, a subsidiary of Northrop Grumman Corporation. The firm handles all aspects of preparing foreign troops for hostilities, including constructing facilities, setting up auxiliary operations and training, equipping, writing doctrine, and so forth. It does so under very lucrative contracts. Both political parties have supported the approach, which by 1990 had been implemented to varying degrees in 96 countries; after 9/11, this jumped to 133 nations, constituting 70 percent of states represented in the UN. Joining Vinnell are about thirty-four other companies performing similar or related services.

In the eyes of the foreign policy elite, international training operations have a number of advantages: preparing surrogates to fight for or with American forces against identified enemies or terrorists, increasing the sale of American weapons and equipment, and gaining political influence. Secretary of Defense Cheney pushed privatization much further in 1992, arguing that military logistical operations should be placed in private hands. After leaving the DOD in 1993, Cheney headed the Halliburton Corporation. Kellogg Brown & Root, a Halliburton subsidiary, is among the most profitable military contractors; its fortunes almost doubled under Cheney's leadership and skyrocketed during the Iraq and Afghanistan wars. But Kellogg Brown & Root is only one of many. In addition to Vinnell, firms such as Military Professional Resources Incorporated (MPRI), DynCorp, and Science Applications International Corporation are among the top thirty-five military contractors.

A number of these companies were organized by senior generals and admirals. The founder of MPRI, for example, was General Carl E. Vuono, who served as army chief of staff during the first Gulf War. Staffing comes principally from former service personnel seeking similar duties, soldiers of fortune, those devoted to combat, former law enforcement officers, and related types. More often than not, the founders have become very wealthy individuals.

Besides training foreign troops, these companies construct, maintain, and guard military bases that range from small to large. Hence, they clean and monitor barracks and other facilities, cook and serve food, handle transportation, and operate water and sewerage systems. To varying degrees, private contractors are integral to the operation of about 700 bases abroad. Some of these firms also provide security systems for high-placed foreign leaders. At home and abroad, contractors service and repair weapons and equipment, such as Abrams tanks and unmanned aerial vehicles, that are too complex for the armed services to handle. Some have gone even further, taking over aspects of U.S. Army education, training, and doctrine development; Reserve Officers' Training Corps operations; and military recruiting stations.

Many of these firms are massive, employing hundreds or even thousands of individuals with varying skills and specialties. In 1990 private military companies' available revenue totaled $55.6 billion; by 2010, the figure was expected to reach $202 billion. Of the initial $57 billion appropriated for the invasion of Iraq, at least one-third of the amount went to the numerous services provided by military contractors.

Various knowledgeable scholars, journalists, and concerned citizens, along with military officers, are deeply concerned about the operations of these private contractors. The companies could have a deleterious effect on military professionalism. Furthermore, such firms are not subject to military discipline, and their functions are proprietary information, beyond the reach of any form of public oversight. In effect, privatization circumvents Congress and acts to keep the public uninformed. Civilian control over a vital range of military operations is rarely raised or debated in government circles or among the general population. The DOD cannot be fully relied on to monitor its own creation of what has become, in effect, an extension of the armed services. Even fully exposed abuses and misconduct go largely unpunished. In the late 1990s, for example, DynCorp employees in Bosnia kept underaged females as sex slaves and later sold them in other parts of Europe. Once this activity was publicly reported, no disciplinary action took place other than the firing of the individuals involved.

There is no evidence that the operations of these private companies result in greater efficiency or savings. In light of the armed services' widespread cost-plus and no-bid contracting, costs are usually greater. That becomes even more likely if contracts go to a limited number of well-connected firms. Moreover, as with most military contracting, corruption and abuse appear to be common. According to Chalmers Johnson, Cheney was intent on financially rewarding corporations through his aggressive advocacy of privatization and, in the process, strengthening the bonds of the MIC. In addition, the use of private contractors allows hostilities to be carried out with fewer troops and fewer casualties, reducing public concern and opposition. That senior generals and admirals have led in the formation of these companies speaks volumes about what has happened to military professionalism and the consequences for civil-military relations.[35]

The CIA has followed a similar path in terms of hiring security firms to perform a wide variety of intelligence duties. These include providing security guards, interrogating prisoners and operating "black sites" for doing so, running aborted assassination programs, maintaining sites for and servicing Predator aircraft, collecting intelligence, and operating classified computer networks. Outsourcing of particularly sensitive assignments gives the agency greater cover in the event operations go wrong or trouble arises.

The CIA's ties with Blackwater USA, later renamed Xe Services LLC, became especially close, with some senior agency officials moving directly from public to private service with Blackwater, a firm founded by several former navy

SEALs. According to the CIA, costs increase with the use of private firms because it must pay high salaries to attract those with the necessary expertise. Other intelligence agencies have followed the CIA's lead, as has the State Department in hiring security guards. Unlike military contractors, security firms (particularly Blackwater) have come under congressional and other public scrutiny over questionable conduct in Iraq, including torture and other abuses of captured prisoners.

Irony abounds in the use of private firms to perform military and intelligence functions. The supply arms of the army and navy were created and professionalized beginning in the early nineteenth century to rid the armed forces of unreliable, abusive, and profiteering civilian contractors who threatened military functions during both war and peace.[36] The use of private firms today constitutes a much graver problem than in earlier centuries. They have acted to "hollow out" the government's capacity to conduct national security functions in an increasingly turbulent world. Furthermore, privatization has enormously complicated civil-military relations and the ability of the executive and Congress to effectively monitor and control military activities and operations.

2
CONGRESS

In sharp contrast to the interwar period, and more along the lines of the World War II years, Congress played a subordinate role in the formulation and execution of foreign and national defense policies throughout the Cold War era and beyond. From 1945 through 1960, legislators were especially passive, acting more as the executive's advocate than its overseer. Gradually, in the 1950s, members of Congress sought to ease Cold War tensions and began to question presidential directions. Major challenges, however, did not take place until the Vietnam War became a major source of national controversy and debate in the 1960s, exacerbated by the abuses of the Nixon administration, culminating in the Watergate crisis of the early 1970s.

From the late 1960s into the 1970s, Congress questioned or challenged nearly every area of executive policy making involving foreign and defense decisions. It did so through investigations, appropriations, and legislation. At a minimum, legislators aimed to regain a voice in the nation's response to the global community; at a maximum, they desired to make the legislative branch the executive's equal in both foreign and defense policy. While Congress from the late 1960s forward shook off the passivity of the early Cold War years, it never came close to matching presidential power. Legislative influence in foreign and defense policies certainly increased in direct and indirect ways at the expense of the executive. Nonetheless, under particular sets of circumstances, presidents could largely ignore Congress in the pursuit of policies abroad. Such was the case during the first two years of Ronald Reagan's first term and all but the last two years of the George W. Bush administration.

During the Cold War years and after, in sharp contrast with the years preceding them, foreign and defense policies cannot be separated. They are so intertwined and interacting that they must be treated together. This is a complicating situation for Congress and the presidency, and it contributes to the complexity of analyzing the political economy of warfare.

THE COMPLIANT COMMITTEE STAGE

In the years 1945 through 1960, Congress was in the so-called committee stage. Beginning in the early years of the twentieth century, committees dominated the national legislature. Their chairs, determined by seniority, were usually southern Democrats, and they could be virtual autocrats, working in harmony with ranking minority members. They oversaw the crafting of legislation and guided it through both houses of Congress. Responding to overwhelming popular sentiment, Congress passed neutrality legislation in the 1930s and kept a diminished military structure on a very short leash. It was those circumstances that plagued the Roosevelt administration as it maneuvered in the late 1930s and early 1940s to guard national interests in a world that was ultimately engulfed in war. After Pearl Harbor, the president largely had a free hand in conducting the two-front war. At home, however, the administration faced endless challenges in mobilizing the economy. Dating back to the late New Deal years, southern Democrats forged a coalition with Republicans for the purpose of limiting and, where possible, undoing domestic reform. This conservative coalition continued not only during the years of hostility but also into the early Cold War period.[1]

Consistent with the war years, Congress could be unruly and troublesome for the Truman administration and, to a lesser degree, the Eisenhower administration, without significantly limiting the president's ability to formulate and implement foreign and defense policies. Actually, the executive relied on a limited number of major committees to usher its programs through Congress. The Senate Foreign Relations Committee, the House Foreign Affairs Committee, and the Armed Services and Appropriations committees of both houses were among the most important. Powerful figures dominated these committees, such as Senator Arthur Vandenburg (R-MI), Senator Richard Russell (D-GA), Representative Carl Vinson (D-GA), and Representative Clarence Cannon (D-MO). The House and Senate Armed Services and Appropriations committees were also responsible for overseeing the newly created CIA, a heavy responsibility they carried out in a limited way. Later, both houses established their own intelligence committees.[2]

Congress played a role in shaping national security policy immediately after World War II, as exemplified by the National Security Act of 1947. But in the most significant areas, the initiative remained principally with the executive. That was the case with nuclear weapons, the size and mission of the armed forces, and the containment policy aimed at the Soviet Union, including the division of Germany, the Truman Doctrine, the European Recovery Program, and NATO. Committing troops to what became the Korean War without con-

sulting the legislative branch or seeking its approval was the Truman administration's most drastic and daring move. Even then, Congress went along and
provided at least its tacit consent through appropriations, legislation authorizing economic mobilization, and other acts. Only when the war stretched out
and bogged down, national defense budgets skyrocketed, and public dissent
grew did Congress, and particularly Republicans, begin attacking the administration's response to and conduct of the conflict.

The Korean War marks the beginning of massive Cold War defense budgets.
Spending for national security had fallen from World War II highs to $11.8
billion, or 4.5 percent of the gross domestic product (GDP), in 1948. By 1953,
the figure had more than quadrupled to $50.4 billion, or 13.8 percent of GDP;
it would remain close to 10 percent of GDP throughout the decade. Expenditures for national security gradually declined to around 5 percent of GDP by
the mid-1970s but did not drop to the 1948 level until nearly the turn of the
century, only to rise sharply following the September 11, 2001, crisis.[3] Once
the Department of Defense and related spending reversed its postwar decline,
institutional forces—ultimately labeled the military-industrial complex by Eisenhower—began acting to perpetuate national security expenditures.

Congress, which had largely supported the Truman administration's efforts
to limit defense spending and to aim for balanced budgets, went along with
massive, unprecedented "peacetime" military outlays. By the 1950s, the Democratic Party was fully committed to hard-line Cold War policies, and the Republican Party was increasingly defined by its internationalists. Moreover, the
benefits of huge defense expenditures for the economy as a whole, as well as
for regions, states, and localities, were becoming clear. Under such circumstances, both houses of Congress became willing partners with the executive
in keeping defense spending high. Congressional committees tinkered with
DOD and related budgets without substantially altering their basic nature.
Even before the high-technology stage, weapons systems were considered to
be largely beyond congressional competence. The armed services were viewed
as the true experts. At congressional hearings on DOD budgetary requests, dissenters rarely appeared; instead, the nation's legislators heard from military representatives, supportive members of Congress, veterans' groups, defense
manufacturers, and business spokespeople. When conflict occurred, it usually
involved the size and mission of the armed services or funding for weapons
authorization.[4]

It was during these years, in the late 1940s and 1950s, that America's strategic air fleet (under SAC) grew from a few aircraft to 1,850 bombers. In all,
eight different aircraft were involved, ranging from the B-29 Superfortress to
the B-66 Destroyer, and ultimately cost more than $16 billion (equivalent to

$113 billion in 1996 dollars). At the same time, the nuclear arsenal grew in size and sophistication and ultimately included hydrogen as well as atomic explosives. Typical of congressional committees at the time, the Joint Committee on Atomic Energy (created in 1947 and abolished in 1977) acted as executive advocate and failed to pursue or enlighten Congress about the numerous vital issues involving nuclear weaponry and atomic energy.[5]

Toward the end of the period, and especially after the Russians launched *Sputnik* in late 1957, missiles began to be emphasized. The navy started stressing air as well as sea power, first with aircraft carriers and later with missile-launching submarines. In the process, conventional ground forces were downgraded as the Truman administration stressed airpower and the Eisenhower administration relied on massive retaliation and brinkmanship. Eisenhower turned to a strategy based largely on nuclear weapons in a concerted effort to reduce defense budgets and rein in the unending quest for more money on the part of the armed services. This approach caused the administration to come under steady attack, first for a "bomber gap" and later for a "missile gap" vis-à-vis the USSR. All such charges turned out to be misguided, as the president well knew, but the allegations documented his growing concern about a military-industrial complex.

THE BEGINNING OF REFORM

The first signs of reform in Congress appeared during the 1950s.[6] A growing number of liberal, northern Democrats were elected to Congress, particularly to the Senate, and they bristled at the conservative and hierarchical nature of the upper chamber. On foreign and defense policy, they ranged from moderate liberals such as Hubert Humphrey (D-MN) and Frank Church (D-ID) to those further on the Left and mavericks such as Wayne Morse (D-OR), Joseph Clark (D-PA), and Ernest Gruening (D-AK). Focused initially on domestic affairs, this diverse group favored reforming Congress along more open and democratic lines. During the 1950s, however, they lacked the numbers necessary to significantly change congressional operations. Nonetheless, working within existing institutional restraints, they started breaking the pattern of Congress passively rubber-stamping executive initiatives in foreign and defense policy. They began questioning and criticizing executive actions in those areas and made some gradual gains. For example, Humphrey, as chair of the Foreign Relations Committee's Subcommittee on Arms Control, played an instrumental role in creating the Arms Control and Disarmament Agency (ACDA) in 1961. Such action helped prepare the way for the Limited Test-Ban Treaty in 1963.

That same year, Congress revolted against the Kennedy administration's proposed foreign and military aid package, which was often used to support and prop up unsavory developing world regimes. Led by Morse and Gruening, but supported by conservative Democrats and Republicans, the legislature cut requests by more than one-third and restricted future executive latitude. In 1967 the Senate Foreign Relations Committee discovered that the Johnson administration was furtively circumventing congressional monetary and statutory restraints on weapons sales to underdeveloped regions. Congress not only prohibited the practice but also rejected the administration's request for a blank check in upping economic assistance to Latin America.

These acts were more promising departures than major advances. Significant congressional change resulted from the Vietnam War and its consequences. Southeast Asian hostilities provided the breakthrough for those members dedicated to reforming congressional operations, particularly the stranglehold of the committee chairs, and giving the legislative branch a meaningful voice in foreign affairs and national security matters. Contentious hearings on the war by the Senate Foreign Relations Committee in January–February 1966 made manifest that the elite was dividing, along with the Democratic Party, on the poisonously divisive Vietnam conflict. Committee chair J. William Fulbright (D-AR) was emerging as a prominent, leading war critic. He and the committee not only legitimized dissent but also accelerated the Senate's resurgence as a participant in America's response to the world community.

Conflict over the war continued to grow in Congress and the nation during and after 1966, ultimately forcing President Lyndon B. Johnson to decide not to seek reelection in 1968. A bitterly divided Democratic Party denied presidential candidate Humphrey a victory, and by a small measure, Richard M. Nixon became president. After his resignation in 1974, Congress gained unusual and, in many respects, unprecedented power in foreign and national security policy.

Congressional advances were facilitated by reforms of the legislative branch beginning prior to and continuing during the Nixon years. Cumulatively, these changes succeeded in ending the committee stage and ushered in a much more open, democratic, and dynamic, albeit unruly, era. By providing for additional and properly staffed subcommittees, the Legislative Reorganization Act of 1946 created opportunities for some progressive change. This trend produced more results as subcommittees grew in number, stature, and strength over the years. Other modest steps, such as expanding the size of the House Rules Committee, led to a more flexible structure and fed the drive for further change. By 1970, the floodgates for reform had opened. Over time, Congress rigorously strengthened regulations on campaign fund-raising, codified ethics rules, opened committee proceedings, reduced the votes necessary to end filibusters in the Senate, authorized recorded teller votes, severely weakened the House Ways and Means Committee, and, most important, opened committee chairs to caucus votes, thereby diluting seniority rights. Under the new procedures, four powerful House committee chairs were removed in 1974–1975. By the end of the decade, party caucuses and leaders had replaced committee chairs as the principal centers of power in a much more open and accountable system. Practically all these reforms were carried out by the Democratic Party, with some support at critical points from Republicans. Furthermore, changes were always greater in the less tradition-bound House than in the Senate.

Outside developments and pressures assisted and accelerated congressional reforms. Supreme Court decisions and resulting legislation and governmental action on redistricting and voter dilution led to more representative Congresses that also tended to be more reform minded. Additionally, the societal changes occurring in the 1960s and 1970s led to more minorities, women, and other victims of discrimination being elected to Congress.

CONGRESS RESURGENT

In the process of democratizing its structure and operation, Congress was no longer willing to act as the executive's advocate in the critical areas of foreign and defense policies. With widespread distress over the Vietnam War, the Nixon administration's abuses, and operations abroad in general, Congress steadily moved to exercise its intended oversight responsibilities.[7]

Appropriations for the antiballistic missile signaled a new direction for Congress in responding to a major weapons system. Because the missile threatened to trigger another round in the arms race with the USSR, and because it was technically questionable, the Johnson administration held off in seeking funding for the ABM. Amidst growing pressure, the administration requested appropriations of $1.2 billion for the system early in 1968. In a departure from tradition, military critics mounted an intense, informed, and effective challenge to the request. The administration organized a major counteroffensive to beat back the opponents, but ABM's future remained clouded when Johnson's term ended.

Shortly after taking office, the Nixon administration renewed the appropriations request but proposed a modified ABM with a mission different from that of its predecessor. What ensued was a five-month, no-holds-barred battle in the upper house between the principal ABM proponents, represented by the Armed Services Committee, and the opponents, represented by the Disarmament Subcommittee of the Foreign Relations Committee. Stuart Symington (D-MO), who in 1966–1967 had converted from a superhawk to a superdove, was out in front for the opposition. As a former secretary of the air force and an expert on weaponry, the Missouri senator was an invaluable addition to the ranks of ABM critics. Additionally, for the first time, opponents called on scientists and engineers to address the missile's technical value and flaws. The Armed Services Committee restricted its witnesses to ABM supporters. When the final vote took place in August, the opponents lost by one vote. With the House still in the hands of military adherents, the outcome there was never in question.

Despite the final outcome, the showdown over ABM was a moral victory for the opponents. Thereafter, the Nixon administration negotiated SALT I with the Soviet Union, which included the ABM Treaty restricting ABM deployment by both sides. Furthermore, the extended ABM debate stripped away much of the mystery surrounding modern weaponry. Informed and properly advised members of Congress could determine the value of weapons and make intelligent decisions concerning them. The military and defense contractors had no monopoly on the subject. Finally, the DOD could no longer assume congressional approval of its projects. Within and outside the Armed Services and Appropriations committees, dissent had become common, and recommendations were open to challenge and change. Indeed, to guard their turf, the Armed Services committees of both houses had to become much more informed and diligent in their reviews of Pentagon budgets. Their membership was becoming more ideologically diverse and was often willing to criticize specific weapons and spending in general. Also, the Senate Foreign Relations Committee, the Joint Economic Committee, the House Government Operations Committee, the Budget committees of both chambers, and other committees began probing defense spending and operations. Unlike in the past, roll-call votes on defense appropriations became common, especially in the more liberal Senate.

After a hiatus, Southeast Asia became a central battleground between the Nixon administration and Congress. Through hearings and investigations in 1969, the Senate Foreign Relations Committee and a subcommittee uncovered more than a decade of American military involvement, secret wars, and undeclared commitments in Thailand and Laos. The specter of more Vietnams haunted the legislators. Senators Church and John S. Cooper (R-KY) responded by introducing an amendment at the end of 1969 prohibiting American advisers or combat troops from serving in either Thailand or Laos. Following extended debate and attempts to hold off the amendment, the Cooper-Church proposal was adopted by an overwhelming majority. It was the first time during the Cold War that Congress had used its appropriations authority to curb military action. Sensing the antimilitary shift in Congress, the Armed Services and Appropriations committees of both houses cut DOD budgets substantially in both 1969 and 1970. In May 1970 Cooper and Church introduced another amendment to cut off all funding involved with the invasion of neutral Cambodia, which had been ordered by the Nixon administration in April. Despite national outrage and the catastrophes at Kent State University and Jackson State College, the administration managed first to emasculate the second Cooper-Church initiative and then to defeat it. Troops withdrew from Cambodia on July 1, according to Nixon's declared schedule, but matters did not end there. Symington and Harold Hughes (D-IA), members of the Senate Armed Services Committee, discovered in 1972 that the Nixon administration had secretly been bombing Cambodia for a year before the April 1970 incursion and falsifying records to conceal the operations. Hughes all but forced the committee to hold hearings in 1973 that exposed the details of the hidden air war, further eroding the administration's credibility.

With the midterm elections of 1970 further strengthening the "new internationalists," Congress was more willing to challenge the executive directly on Vietnam. In 1971 Congress repealed the Tonkin Gulf Resolution. Going further, between 1971 and 1973 the legislators repeatedly debated and voted on various amendments, often introduced from the floor, designed to end American hostilities in Vietnam or all of Southeast Asia. Late in 1972, after intense and confusing parliamentary maneuvering, the Senate voted to include in a military aid appropriations bill the Case-Church amendment, which would cut off funding for the war by December 31, 1972, if all POWs had been released. When the Senate defeated the bill by a close vote, Congress halted further action on Vietnam, awaiting the outcome of the 1972 election.

Actually, the Nixon administration had regained its foreign policy footing in 1972. The opening to China, peace negotiations in Paris, and detente with the USSR, including SALT I, had shifted the initiative from Congress back to the White House. At around the same time, Senator George McGovern's troubled Democratic campaign for the presidency acted to weaken measurably the congressional antiwar momentum and effectiveness. Moreover, Congress's numerous failed attempts during 1971–1972 to extricate the nation from the Vietnam debacle dramatically demonstrated the legislature's limited options during ongoing hostilities.

Despite Nixon's landslide victory in 1972, followed by the Vietnam peace accords of January 1973, Congress increased its determination to influence and alter foreign and national security policies. Its ability to do so was facilitated by the expanding Watergate crisis in 1973–1974, which first distracted and weakened and ultimately overwhelmed the White House. This reality became clear in mid-1973 when complicated maneuvering in both houses of Congress compelled the president to accept a modified and expanded version of the Cooper-Church amendment that had been defeated in 1971. All military action on the part of the United States would be banned in Cambodia, Laos, and Vietnam after August 15, 1973.

The boldest move was the War Powers Resolution of 1973. Reasserting war powers was a logical progression for a resurgent Congress. In a nonbinding National Commitments Resolution of 1969, the Senate affirmed that extending American obligations abroad required agreement by both the executive and legislative branches. The Case Act of 1972 was more explicit. It required the president to report to Congress within sixty days of execution all international executive and like agreements and commitments. Symington's subcommittee had revealed that through such actions, presidents had secretly committed the nation to using military force in certain circumstances. Jacob Javits (R-NY), the principal author of the War Powers Resolution, insisted on a forthright, not tangential, approach. Although his 1973 resolution was revised, watered down, and left ambiguous at critical points to make it veto proof, it prohibited the president from committing troops without a declaration of war, except to protect the nation's security and citizens. If armed forces were so used, the president had to report such action to Congress within forty-eight hours; he could continue operations beyond sixty days only with congressional authorization. The resolution specifically excluded CIA activities.

During the same time, Congress continued with its piecemeal approach to influencing foreign and defense matters. An Office of Human Rights was created in the State Department, hearings were held to expose activities such as the nation's involvement in the military overthrow of the Allende government in Chile, Pentagon budgets were cut and weapons systems were more closely scrutinized as Armed Services Committee membership became more varied and subcommittees' impact grew, and Congress required more reports from various executive agencies. In 1974 an amendment by Gaylord Nelson (D-WI) and Jonathan Bingham (D-NY) required the State Department to report to Congress all military arms sales abroad exceeding $25 million; Congress then had thirty days to block the sale with a two-house veto. In 1976 the amendment was extended and strengthened substantially by the Arms Export Control Act. Earlier, a 1974 amendment by Thomas Eagleton (D-MO) prohibited further military assistance to Turkey until its troops were removed from Cyprus.

Congress also addressed the critical issue of nuclear proliferation. The Nonproliferation Treaty of 1968, which took effect in 1970, appeared to ease concerns about the spread of nuclear technology, including power plants, processing technology, and fuel. Yet in 1974, Senator Abraham Ribicoff (D-CT), while involved in writing the Energy Resources Act, discovered that export controls were haphazard at best. The United States accounted for over 50 percent of nuclear technology exports. Neither the industry, its congressional supporters, nor the president wanted to subject American trade to strict oversight, an outlook a host of representatives and senators considered exceptionally dangerous. Hence, in 1977 they acted to terminate the Joint Committee on Atomic Energy, which had become an agent of the status quo. Its duties were transferred to more reliable committees. Concerned members of Congress then authored a tough regulatory act, signed into law by President Carter in 1978.

Democratic landslides during the 1974 elections acted as a big boost to congressional foreign and defense policy activists. One of their more important gains was the Budget Reform Act of 1974. Under this act, committees in both houses would work out a comprehensive congressional budget and then had the authority, based on the assistance of task forces, to determine spending ceilings for the numerous committees. The new system was used to cut DOD appropriations.

The pain of Southeast Asia and Vietnam persisted for the new internationalists right up to the end. As the North Vietnamese armies advanced south toward Saigon, Gerald Ford requested in January 1975 military assistance for Vietnam and Cambodia exceeding $500 million. Neither house was willing to act positively on the proposal. By this time, any assistance for Cambodia was totally unacceptable to Congress. Humanitarian aid to South Vietnam and funding for the evacuation of U.S. citizens were accepted as necessary by many, but distrust of the executive had reached such intensity that few were willing to grant the president any discretion. In the spirit of "no more Vietnams," Congress continued to limit executive prerogatives. A 1975 amendment by Thomas Harkin (D-IA), which was supported for different reasons by both liberals and conservatives, banned all assistance to nations that systematically and grossly violated their citizens' civil rights. At the end of 1974, an amendment sponsored by Hughes and Leo Ryan (D-CA) prohibited covert operations unless the president declared them to be crucial for national security, and it required that the Foreign Relations, Foreign Affairs, Armed Services, and other committees be briefed on intelligence activities. Additionally, late in 1975, Congress adopted Dick Clark's (D-IA) amendment to the foreign aid bill, banning covert operations in Angola. Three factions were battling for control of the Portuguese colony, which would gain its independence in mid-1975. Out to prove that Vietnam had not made the United States impotent abroad, the Ford administration had authorized CIA support for favored groups. Intent on avoiding additional Vietnams, the new internationalists pushed through Clark's handiwork.

All these amendments dealt with the issue of intelligence oversight, which Congress had previously been reluctant to address directly. The legislators felt compelled to act after Seymour Hersh revealed at the end of 1974 that the CIA had been engaged in widespread domestic intelligence gathering, which included collecting information on former members of Congress. The Democratic caucus in both houses authorized panels to investigate intelligence operations. From the outset, the House committee was racked by repeated conflicts; its Senate counterpart performed more smoothly. Nonetheless, both inquiries turned up ample information and revelations about the dark and hidden side of American Cold War activities abroad and at home. Both chambers became convinced of the need for closer and more responsible intelligence regulation. Consequently, in mid-1976 the Senate created a Select Committee on Intelligence. A year later, the House followed suit with a Permanent Select Committee on Intelligence. Many would have preferred a joint committee, but differences between the two chambers stood in the way. In 1980 Congress enacted the Intelligence Oversight Act, which modified earlier legislation, established how Congress would monitor intelligence agencies, and legally required the latter to keep legislators informed of their activities. Senate Majority Leader Michael Mansfield (D-MT), along with others, had been pressing for reliable congressional oversight of the vast Cold War intelligence establishment since the 1960s.

RETREAT FROM REFORM

By the time the intelligence committees were in place, the critics of the militarized Cold War had lost their momentum and were being placed on the defensive.[8] The rapid collapse of South Vietnam and a growing sense of confusion and fear about America's international role were having an effect. Within that context, foreign policy subject to often vague congressional rider amendments appeared wanting. The whole thrust of the reformers came under attack from Democrats or former Democrats who were recasting themselves as neoconservatives and calling for a more aggressive stance toward the Soviet Union in behalf of liberal, democratic values. Along different lines, a radical Right was emerging in the Republican Party, with Ronald Reagan, who was seeking the party's presidential nomination, becoming its foremost advocate.

Running as a reformer, Carter had barely edged out a weak and politically wounded Ford in the presidential election of 1976. The outcome strongly signaled the difficulties facing the new internationalists. Congressional elections reinforced the message. While the House remained about the same, some leading Senate revisionists retired or lost their races, and more hard-line anticommunist Republicans joined the chamber. Within this context, the Armed Services Committee continued to rise in influence, while the Foreign Relations Committee resumed its decline. Since Fulbright's departure in January 1975, the latter committee, which had been the leading source of new internationalism, had lost its favored place and clout. That change made the House Foreign Affairs Committee the principal source of congressional influence for policies abroad, a responsibility that was far beyond its capability.

The consequences of the congressional elections soon became evident. The Carter administration faced enormous odds in securing the Senate's approval of Paul Warnke as director of ACDA and lead negotiator for SALT II. Even more troublesome was getting the Panama Canal treaties through the upper house. Pressure was also building in Congress to increase, not maintain or cut, defense spending. Furthermore, revisionist gains of the past came under attack. In 1978 the Eagleton amendment, cutting off military assistance to Turkey over the Cyprus imbroglio, was repealed. In 1980 the Hughes-Ryan amendment was reworked so that CIA covert operations needed to be reported only to the intelligence committees. In the same year, the Budget committees of both houses ceased to be reliable forums for last-ditch stands against increased defense spending.

If the election of 1976 indicated change, the midterm balloting of 1978 proved to be a body blow. Leading new internationalist Dick Clark was defeated by conservative Roger Jepsen (R-IA), a former lieutenant governor who was weak and uninformed and bordered on being a demagogue. Other internationalists chose not to run, and New Jersey Republicans refused to nominate liberal internationalist Clifford Case for reelection. Nationalism and anticommunism were rising to a fever pitch. With the Iran hostage crisis and the Russian invasion of Afghanistan, the Carter administration shelved the troubled and controversial SALT II and turned rather hawkish itself. In 1979 Jeane Kirkpatrick articulated the New Right's attitude on foreign aid. Authoritarian regimes of the Right, she argued, should be differentiated from totalitarian left-wing governments. The former should receive aid as U.S. supporters and to facilitate their purported tendency to evolve into open systems, while the latter must be boycotted as threats to American interests and their own people. Under such guidelines, assistance for Nicaragua's Anastasio Somoza continued despite a well-organized effort to terminate it. In that spirit, the emerging dominant figure on the Foreign Relations Committee was Senator Jesse Helms (R-NC). Clearly, the new internationalists were diminishing in number and were in full retreat.

That reality was more than confirmed by Reagan's victory in the presidential election of 1980, which helped deliver the Senate, by a fifty-three to forty-seven majority, into Republican hands for first time since 1955. Although the Democrats managed to hold on to the House, conservatives also had control there. During the campaign, the president-elect had articulated a program almost exactly the opposite of the international revisionists' in all particulars. Once in office, he and his party proceeded to implement it.

Secretary of Defense Caspar W. Weinberger oversaw a 64 percent increase in defense spending between 1980 and 1983. Although the amounts later tapered off, they continued to grow throughout Reagan's years in office, constituting the most sustained peacetime growth in expenditures for the armed forces in the twentieth century. Since Weinberger exercised no restraints on the services he oversaw, Congress, bolstered by Democratic gains in the House after the 1982 elections, began moving to temper the unchecked buildup. In part, Congress responded to a swing in public opinion. A more than doubling of the national debt between 1980 and 1986, as well as revelations of widespread waste, fraud, profiteering, and other abuses in defense procurement, changed popular thinking about the need for additional increases.

After Reagan's first few years in office, and particularly during his second term, the administration faced a Congress that insisted on having a meaningful voice in foreign and defense matters, as trends in defense budgets indicated. The legislators refused to give up altogether the hard-won gains achieved in the 1960s and 1970s. The trend was further strengthened when the Democrats took control of the Senate in 1986. In that year, for example, Congress enacted the Goldwater-Nichols Defense Reorganization Act, over strong resistance from the executive branch. The law enhanced the authority of the secretary of defense over the various services in general and joint military operations in particular. Other similar reforms followed.

Congress made itself heard most clearly on strategic weapons and especially nuclear armaments. The administration became vulnerable through its often casual references to the use of nuclear weapons and warfare. Consequently, it had to struggle mightily to mobilize its forces first to delay the Nuclear Freeze Resolution in the House and then, when it finally passed in mid-1983, to bury it in the Senate. Nonetheless, Congress insisted that the administration generally follow the arms limitations agreed to in SALT II, negotiate seriously with the USSR on strategic weaponry through existing or other avenues, abide by the ABM Treaty of 1972, set up nuclear risk reduction centers with the Soviet Union (a goal achieved in 1987), and refrain from testing antisatellite weapons, which led the Pentagon to scrap the project in 1988. Through complicated maneuvering, the legislature managed to limit the authorization of MX missiles to fifty and, at least indirectly, to keep the "Midgetman" missile from going forward.

On intervention abroad, military aid, weapons sales, and related policy, executive-legislative relations during the Reagan years were mixed at best. The administration was as determined to oppose communist, radical, and revolutionary challenges in the developing world as it was to beat down the Soviet Union strategically. Between 1981 and 1989 the administration and Congress worked together, with the latter sometimes taking the lead, to assist Afghanistan in driving the Russians out. With the introduction of American troops in Lebanon between 1982 and 1984, Congress pressured a very reluctant Reagan to invoke the War Powers Resolution (WPR). The administration did so in a halfhearted way, and even then a seriously divided Congress had to finesse the law's requirements to win the executive's cooperation. A somewhat similar situation developed during 1987–1988 in the Persian Gulf, when U.S. naval forces expanded to protect Kuwait's oil tankers from attacks growing out of the Iraq-Iran war. Although the administration refused to implement the WPR, it did make periodic reports to legislators.

Middle East meddling ultimately became entangled with messy and controversial policies in Central America. The Reagan administration was determined to beat back guerrilla threats to El Salvador and undo the Sandinista government in Nicaragua. Despite congressional opposition, which was often intense, the Nicaraguan operations went forward. Finally, Congress passed the Edward Boland (D-MA) amendment in 1984, prohibiting any further direct or indirect military assistance to the Contras, who were out to topple the Sandinistas. The administration bypassed the amendment and continued to assist the Contras by using funds from the sale of arms to Iran in exchange for American hostages taken in Lebanon. Additional money came from private American organizations and from friendly governments and was collected by the National Security Council, which was conducting the arms-for-hostages swap. Exposure of these activities in 1987 led to congressional hearings and ultimately criminal prosecutions and convictions. The Reagan administration had not only broken the law but also lied to Congress, failed to report covert activities, and violated its own declared policies.

Other interventions in the developing world never reached the extreme action and acrimony of Central America. In 1983 the Reagan administration sent troops into Grenada, informing Congress after the fact and removing the troops quickly, before challenges could be raised. In 1986 air strikes were launched against Libya to warn against further terrorist acts, but congressional leaders were told only when the planes were already in the air and the operation was nearly completed.

Shortly after taking office, the Reagan administration resumed aid to Argentina and Chile, finding that their civil rights records had improved considerably. After repeated efforts, Reagan finally succeeded in having the Clark amendment repealed in 1985 so that assistance to the administration's favored faction in Angola could be resumed. Moreover, after being kept on a tight leash by the Carter administration, the CIA was allowed to carry out practically unlimited covert operations from the outset, including supplying select weapons to Angola. The administration was also much more willing to engage in questionable arms sales, such as airborne warning and control systems (AWACS), to Saudi Arabia and other Middle Eastern countries. As the practice grew, Congress from 1984 onward began to exercise its authority to block such transactions or require their modification.

Overall, the Reagan years were among the more militarily and internationally aggressive ones of the Cold War era. A friendly and intimidated Congress passively followed the executive's lead for the first two years. Thereafter, as public opinion swung more toward the center, Congress slowly became more active in opposing and then challenging the administration. In doing so, Congress drew on the changes and powers the reformers and new internationalists had worked out in the 1960s and 1970s. The difference in the 1980s, however, was that many of the political and intellectual heavyweights of the earlier period were no longer in Congress. Their absence was sorely felt.

With the international situation changing even more dramatically than the makeup of Congress, American foreign and national security policies entered a period of extended transition, tension, and confusion. The collapse of the Soviet Union between 1989 and 1991 ended the Cold War. The bipolar world became a multipolar one that was increasingly characterized by regional, state, and local strife. The George H. W. Bush administration ultimately negotiated START I and START II with Russia, drastically reducing each side's nuclear warheads and delivery systems. Yet the peace dividend was slow to materialize, particularly as the economy faced a downturn that would have been made worse by significant reductions in military spending. Nearly sixty years of substantial to heavy outlays for national security had made such spending vital to the nation's economic and political systems. A rapid reduction would have created extreme distress. Moreover, America was quickly evolving into the world's foremost arms exporter and depended on such sales to offset its grossly distorted international balance of payments.

Although the Bush administration was unable to formulate or articulate a coherent policy for the nation in the post–Cold War world, it was unwilling to surrender a global reach. It held back a number of congressional initiatives for policies abroad while seeking a proper role for the United States. After a period of vacillating, the administration clumsily invaded Panama at the end of 1989, and it sent troops to Somalia in 1992. However, the Persian Gulf War, not these other minor events, highlighted the Bush administration's global policies. For the president and those who shared his views, America had at last shaken off the stigma of Vietnam. The United States had established that it was relevant to the maintenance of a stable and peaceful world and had regained the confidence needed for such a role. Foreign policy accomplishments notwithstanding, economic woes quickly took priority, leading to Bush's defeat in 1992.

During his eight years in office (1993–2001), Bill Clinton avoided major hostilities, although he engaged in many minor ones. However, defense budgets did not decline significantly. The president moved very cautiously in this area because of his inexperience and an unfriendly military. Until his final years in office, Clinton also approached foreign policy in a hesitant and indecisive way. This quality was evident in his handling of the crises in Somalia and Haiti and the later military intervention in Bosnia and Serbia. The president seemed most comfortable in the role of peacemaker; this was true in Bosnia and even more so in his determined efforts to mediate the Israeli-Palestinian discord.

During Clinton's first two years in office, Democratic Congresses were willing to follow the president's lead in foreign affairs. Thereafter he faced Republican Congresses, for the most part, and encountered ongoing aggravation from the intensely partisan opposing party and particularly from Jesse Helms, chair of the Senate Foreign Relations Committee.

At the outset, although his policies later changed, Clinton tended to share the thinking of the so-called declinists, best articulated by Paul M. Kennedy in *The Rise and Fall of the Great Powers.*[9] Such analysts insisted that America's vast empire and the huge military required to maintain it had led to national decline as a result of neglect of the domestic economy and society (Kennedy's "imperial overstretch"). Certainly, the population at large shared some of these views, as reflected in the public's opposition to long-term military intervention abroad and its absorption in massive problems at home. A much more clearly and intensely articulated outlook came increasingly from the Right in a heightened nationalism. Some nationalists insisted that the United States should turn its back on the world and focus principally on its own interests, a modified isolationism. Others, such as Donald H. Rumsfeld, favored an activist foreign policy carried out by the nation on its own, an aggressive unilateralism. Both groups had a strikingly negative assessment of the United Nations as a bloated, ineffective bureaucracy that was inappropriately answerable to too many developing countries. Their assessment of most allies was not exactly complimentary either.

George W. Bush brought to the White House an extreme neoconservative unilateralism that became more exaggerated and gained a strong measure of public support after the terrorist attacks of September 11, 2001. The administration's policies ultimately led to warfare in Iraq and Afghanistan that bogged down the nation and its military in one of the most volatile regions of the globe.

Although 9/11 certainly played a part, Congress responded very differently to the invasion of Iraq in 2003 than it had to the use of force to drive Iraq out of Kuwait in 1991. The elder Bush had dealt with a strong-willed Democratic Congress; the younger Bush faced not only a Republican Congress but also an exceptionally partisan one that reliably followed his lead. Only with the midterm elections of 2006, in which the Democratic Party took control of both houses of Congress, did a semblance of balance return to the nation's capital.

Even when the new internationalists' influence declined meaningfully beginning in the late 1970s, Congress was unwilling to return to the passivity in foreign and defense matters that had been characteristic of the 1940s through the mid-1960s.[10] Once they regained their proper constitutional role, the nation's legislators were not about to retreat. Throughout the 1960s and 1970s, moreover, they had strengthened immeasurably an institutional structure for holding their own vis-à-vis the executive, particularly in the defense area but including foreign policy as well. Besides the various reforms, practices, and changes specified above, congressional support services had improved greatly in the 1960s and 1970s. The enlarged and improved General Accountability Office and Congressional Research Service and the newly founded Office of Technology Assessment and Congressional Budget Office were especially important.

The nation's legislators could also turn to outside experts for information and analysis, including scientists and technicians and organizations such as the Brookings Institution, the Federation of American Scientists, the Council for a Livable World, and the Center for Defense Information. Most of these sources differed from the Pentagon, but the DOD was supported by the National Strategy Information Center and like societies.

Congress also relied on its own informal resources. Both party caucuses began to provide guidance on foreign and defense policies and to enforce party discipline. More specialized groups included the Democratic Study Group, the Republican Conference, and the bicameral and bipartisan Members of Congress for Peace through Law. Other nonparty caucuses consisted of the National Security Caucus, the Arms Control and Foreign Policy Caucus, and the Military Reform Caucus.

In general, Congress was much better prepared to deal with the complexities of defense and foreign policy in 1980 than it had been in 1960. It was no longer willing to rely on the DOD and elite members of congressional committees to determine action on presidential policies involving war and peace.

EXECUTIVE-LEGISLATIVE CODETERMINATION?

Did the era of congressional reform and activism have a significant impact on the nation's foreign and defense policies?[11] Certainly, it did not constitute a revolution, as a number of scholars and analysts have claimed; an age of codetermination between the executive and legislative branches was not achieved.[12] Depending on various aspects of public affairs, the changes of the 1960s and 1970s had a moderate impact at best; at worst, they were cosmetic. Congress, after all, is a deliberative, not an executive, institution; it does not and cannot lead in complex and demanding areas such as foreign relations and matters of national security. What it can do is limit or influence executive behavior directly through appropriations and legislation and indirectly through investigations, hearings, congressional reports and those it requires from the executive branch, and publicity. Consequently, the legislature's effect on defense and foreign policy must be gauged by analyzing its areas of activity.

There is no question that Congress played a vital role in extricating the nation from the morass of Vietnam that had trapped and paralyzed successive administrations. Congress legitimized dissent against the war, reflected the widespread popular conviction that hostilities must be terminated, and kept up the pressure until American troops were withdrawn and negotiations ended the conflict. After Watergate, Congress ensured that no American action was taken to save the collapsing South Vietnamese regime.

Although the War Powers Resolution was triggered by the Vietnam conflict, it had deep roots in the Cold War's past. Responding to the Korean War and growing American commitments around the globe, often executed without congressional consent, conservative Republicans in the 1950s attempted to curb executive latitude in operations abroad and limit the impact of UN sanctions with an amendment proposed by Senator John Bricker (R-OH).[13] After the defeat of the amendment, Congress returned to a docile role until the advent of the new internationalists in the 1960s and 1970s.

The WPR turned out to be a rather crude instrument for restricting executive war-making powers and reasserting Congress's constitutional authority.[14] Numerous members of Congress have advocated that it be amended or repealed, yet the resolution remains on the books, and it has certainly had an indirect effect. No administration has wanted to recognize and validate the

WPR, but all have felt compelled to comply with it, at least minimally. Another Korean or Vietnam war is highly unlikely.

Although never directly confronting Congress on the constitutionally of the WPR, the Ford and Carter administrations used the ambiguity of the resolution to limit its impact on executive action. Neither administration ever consulted the legislative branch or sought its advice prior to the use of troops. Both presidents cryptically notified Congress after American forces had been used in situations of conflict. Such was the case with the Ford administration after the *Mayaguez* incident and the Southeast Asia evacuations in 1975. The Carter administration followed a similar pattern with the mission to rescue the Iranian hostages. All these episodes were brief, never approaching the sixty-day limit when Congress would have to act for operations to continue. Neither administration went so far as to report the established and ongoing use of U.S. forces in Korea or the airlifts of foreign troops to Zaire.

Congress never mounted a full-scale challenge to Ford or Carter for a number of reasons. At critical points, the WPR is ambiguous. Most basic is the critical matter of enforcing the resolution. Moreover, if Congress is determined to be consulted before armed forces are deployed, it needs to establish a formal consultative body that is readily available to the president. Additionally, Congress tends to hesitate because a substantial number of representatives and senators do not want to assume responsibility for decisions involving hostilities and war. A divided Congress allows the executive branch to interpret the act as it chooses. Yet, prior to the WPR, the president had a relatively free hand in committing armed forces to battlefield conditions; after the WPR, the chief executive has to account to Congress at some point for his action. Beginning in the 1960s, Congress was intent on being included in the full range of foreign policy decisions. The WPR was an important step in that direction.

The real test of the WPR came with the Reagan administration, which was intent on implementing an assertive, aggressive foreign policy. A Republican Senate during the first six years and a rather conservative Democratic House acted to guard the administration's numerous initiatives. The administration invoked the WPR repeatedly, three times alone for Beirut. The resolution should have been activated for Central America but was not. Like its predecessors, the Reagan administration at least minimally complied with the WPR without either validating it or confronting Congress over the resolution's legality.

Grenada and Libya followed the patterns of Ford and Carter. Beirut was a new departure in which Congress used the WPR to force the president to terminate an open-ended commitment that was spinning out of control. In this instance, public opposition to the mission and an upcoming presidential election worked in Congress's favor. Using naval forces in the Persian Gulf fell somewhere between *Mayaguez* and Beirut. Unlike the latter situation, however, the 1987–1988 use of force remained manageable. Since Reagan refused to invoke the WPR for Central America and repeatedly misled Congress about his policies and intent concerning Nicaragua, the legislators turned to other means of reining in the administration.

Despite its interventionist instincts, the Reagan administration used the military in a relatively restrained manner. In part, that stemmed from the administration's own prudence. But the executive was also fully aware that the legislative branch could and would use the WPR or other congressional powers to challenge its action if they became excessively risky or extreme. The Reagan administration was given wider latitude with regard to the WPR for political and ideological reasons, not institutional ones. Republicans and conservative Democrats repeatedly followed Reagan, even at expense of their commitment to Congress's constitutional role in foreign and defense matters. Yet there was always a line that Reagan could not cross with impunity. Congress insisted on upholding its regained authority.

Before the first Gulf War, Bush Sr. secured the endorsement of Congress. The president differed little from his predecessors in terms of his response to the WPR in minor interventions, although American forces participating in UN-sanctioned military operations after the Cold War further complicated the resolution's many legal issues. The Clinton administration's numerous limited interventions generally followed the pattern of those that preceded it. George W. Bush secured the prior support of Congress before initiating military action in both Afghanistan and Iraq. Whether those acts met the requirements of the WPR remain open to question. Whatever the case, the Middle East wars engulfed the nation in quagmires resembling Vietnam, precisely the situation the WPR was intended to prevent. President Barack Obama has followed past patterns concerning Libya. He has ignored calls from Congress to invoke the WPR by insisting that the nation's participation in the NATO-led bombing campaign does not constitute hostilities as envisioned under the resolution.

Before the enactment of the WPR, Congress required that it be notified of all executive agreements. The initiative has been less than successful. The legislature has had difficulty efficiently and effectively cataloging the vast number of pacts, let alone digesting them and properly informing the appropriate members.

Mandating that the intelligence agencies inform Congress of covert operations has been of some significance. Many members of Congress, however, do not want to be informed of covert activities owing to concern about the responsibility that follows. Nonetheless, an informed Congress acts over time to restrain intelligence activities that can range from the questionable to the unwise, not only abroad but also at home.

On arms sales, Congress has had little involvement except in high-profile cases, such as Arab nations seeking to acquire sophisticated weapons. For arms sales in general, the issues are too complex and congressional expertise is too slight to generate any systematic and ongoing review.

In the area of nuclear arms control, Congress's greatest impact has been on what was once considered an almost exclusively executive prerogative. As public pressure mounted to halt the strategic arms race, Congress responded. The battles over ABM, SALT I and II, the nuclear freeze, the MX and Midgetman missiles, and the push to negotiate with the Soviet Union all illustrate the point. Furthermore, since the mid-1970s, Congress has played a vital role in restricting and regulating the proliferation of nuclear technology. Congress can also have negative effects, as was the case when Senator Henry Jackson (D-WA) maneuvered to weaken the SALT negotiations.

Congress's most continuous and enduring role in national security involves reviewing DOD budgets and determining force and command structures. Its impact has been substantial. Congress has both raised and reduced budgets, had a hand in the armed services' relative strength and weaponry, participated in DOD reorganizations, and generally overseen the Pentagon. The major criticism of Congress since the 1970s is that DOD budgets have not declined in a meaningful manner, even after the Cold War ended.

Overall, and despite its substantial limitations, Congress's expanded authority made a positive contribution from the late 1960s through the 1980s. Currently, the future does not look promising unless there is further change. The reforms of past decades began to break down in the 1990s as Congress became increasingly dysfunctional. The erosion has been caused by the unforeseen consequences of an open legislature without established lines of authority. Intense partisanship and scandalmongering cause further deadlock. Outside influences exacerbate these developments, particularly immediate and constant media coverage and unrelenting pressure from multiplying interest groups.[15]

VOTING PATTERNS

Whatever Congress's effect on foreign and national security matters, discerning what influences voting patterns is critical. This subject has been studied extensively for defense spending by numerous scholars.[16] The widespread assumption that defense contracting, or parochialism, plays a major role in how senators and representatives vote on DOD budgets as a whole and on specific weapons in particular does not hold up well. Although there is some correlation between voting patterns and the award of prime contracts, it is tenuous and weak at best. However, prime contractors distribute subcontracts, which can constitute more than 50 percent of awards; these may be divided among as many states as possible in the hope of gaining and maintaining support for weapon systems. However, statistics on subcontracting are not systematically kept, and reliable analysis of the subject suffers as a result.

A much stronger correlation exists among those members of Congress with military or naval facilities in their areas and regions. Unlike contracting, these are very tangible and visible operations, often employing large numbers of nearby residents. Closing such sites could have a dramatic impact that tends to create a pro-military climate. Senators and representatives discount such realities at their political peril. Indeed, since 1965, Congress has attempted to become directly involved in decisions about reducing the size of military and naval bases or closing them entirely. Beginning in 1988, the politically sensitive issue has been handled by a series of bipartisan Defense Base Closure and Realignment Commissions.[17] Although the base realignment and closure (BRAC) approach may have slowed down the pace of partial or total base closure, it has acted to rationalize the process of eliminating excessive army, navy, and air force facilities. The procedures help areas and communities prepare for the shutdowns and determine possible alternative uses for the sites. Members of Congress have also been sheltered from the political fallout of closures by the BRAC system.

Except for highly controversial weapons, such as the ABM, and volatile foreign situations, such as the Panama Canal treaties, members of Congress have a great deal of latitude in defense and foreign policy decisions. Most vote according to their ideology, although party discipline and favors owed to colleagues also play a part. However, as a fundamentally conservative and cautious institution, Congress prefers to act on foreign and defense matters along procedural, as opposed to substantive, lines. Hence, requiring the president to report all executive agreements to Congress uses procedure to control the executive branch through exposure and possible further congressional action. Instead of challenging the executive directly on a particular missile system, Congress can deny funding because the weapon is inconsistent with doctrine. Violation of appropriations rules can also be used very effectively for negative legislative action that avoids substantive issues. In this way, members of Congress are less accountable, and their votes are harder to discern.[18] Therefore, determining with certainty their motives for voting can be difficult.

But there is an even larger truth related to congressional voting and defense budgets. Military spending has become a systemic part of the nation's economic, and hence political, operation. Throughout the 1970s and 1990s, peace dividends never appeared in the expected amounts or durations. Reducing defense spending or even planning for reconversion is difficult at best. DOD budgets have become so sacrosanct, they have become such a vital part of society's functioning and are protected by so many public and private entities, that representatives and senators of both parties are loath to systematically analyze the size and consequences of the spending.

Despite all the progress Congress has made since the 1960s in informing itself about defense and foreign issues, it is still no match for the executive. The DOD, for example, can mobilize nearly endless resources, be they public, semipublic, or private. Its lobbying capacity is mighty. And whereas the DOD is focusing on one area, members of Congress must deal with numerous ones. The scales of political battle are hardly balanced. Moreover, the president has status that no one member of Congress can match.

Nonetheless, the legislative, budgetary, and oversight powers of Congress are formidable, and when they are used properly and are in tune with public opinion, Congress can make a difference. In doing so, Congress can act to balance executive policies in a way that serves the larger interests of the nation. To a substantial degree, that is what took place from the late 1960s through the 1980s. Authority without structure, discipline, balance, and leadership, however, can be ineffective. Such has been the case since the early 1990s.

3
A BIG MILITARY

For the first time in its history, the United States maintained a large permanent military establishment after World War II. Although the Cold War was the principal reason for this development, all the armed services had begun planning during hostilities for the continuation of substantial forces after the war—before American-Soviet relations had become seriously strained. Such plans were generally consistent with the views of President Franklin D. Roosevelt and his successor Harry S. Truman. Facing the reality of a world destroyed, the United States by necessity would assume a major role in reconstructing and reforming the international order. Now more than ever, the nation faced unmatched challenges and opportunities for implementing the twentieth-century elitist quest for the "open door." The free flow of finances, trade, and raw materials would not only further American and world prosperity but also globally advance democratic capitalism modeled after and led by the United States. A U.S.-dominated United Nations could and should play a significant role in achieving a stable, peaceful world order. Nonetheless, military might, maintained or exercised either by the United States on its own or through the UN, was essential to meet threats to international stability and American national security.

Postwar trends affecting policies both at home and abroad resulted in part from wartime trends. World War II marked the ascendancy of the armed forces in the American polity. Directly or indirectly, the War Department and the Navy Department had achieved great, even dominant, influence over the civilian mobilization agencies. More important, with the State Department in relative decline, the military began to assume an important role in the formulation and implementation of American foreign policy. With the Cold War elevating national security to the top priority and leading to a large military establishment, the armed services' wartime ascendancy became a permanent feature of American life.

The military's rise made urgent the twentieth-century interest in unifying the armed services. World War II had glaringly revealed the numerous and serious consequences of interservice rivalry and the lack of coordination. Roosevelt had cobbled together the Joint Chiefs of Staff in early 1942 so that the nation could participate in coalition warfare and make use of joint commands. At best, the JCS's record was mixed. Working through compromise, the joint chiefs reached decisions only when action on their part became imperative. Whenever possible, controversial issues and those lacking unanimous support were dodged or postponed. During the last years of the war in Europe, the army and navy managed to cooperate, but joint or unified commands never worked well in the Pacific. In 1945 the army, navy, and army air forces were all preparing to defeat the tottering Japan on their own.

Unifying the armed services began tentatively in 1947, with a secretary of defense heading a National Military Establishment. In 1949, 1953, 1958, and thereafter, an increasingly strengthened Department of Defense—which replaced the National Military Establishment—centralized control over the army, the navy, and the newly created air force. Although service identification remained, management and operation of the armed forces as a reasonably united whole was carried out by the secretary of defense, assisted by the JCS, acting for the president as commander in chief.

Technological advances in weaponry became an ongoing preoccupation of the military in the Cold War years. That drive resulted in growing ties among the armed forces, scientists and engineers, and defense industries. With the air force leading the way, the services gradually relinquished significant aspects of their weapons research and development (R&D) to nonprofit or private research centers, industries, and universities. More often than not, defense firms directly or indirectly conducted the R&D for the weapons they ultimately manufactured. In the process, the military emerged as a national source of R&D funding.

R&D was only a prelude to weapons output. Massive armed services, increasingly equipped with high-technology weapons, required and created America's first peacetime munitions industry. Once it became apparent that the United States would maintain a comparatively sizable military structure, corporate America, largely under the banner of free, private enterprise, insisted on taking over munitions and related production previously performed by navy yards and army arsenals. In reality, the armed forces needed corporate flexibility, adaptability, and capacity if they wanted to stay on top of ever-changing technological advancements. As with R&D, the air force was out in front. The newest of the military departments had never created a weapons production capacity similar to that of the other services. Instead, it had grown along with and depended on the emerging aircraft industry in the twentieth century to supply its principal weapons. The air arm continued this pattern in the postwar years, but at an accelerated pace and at an increasingly sophisticated technological level. In time, the army and navy followed suit. From these circumstances grew a full-blown military-industrial complex.

In the view of some, huge forces armed with the most advanced weaponry, including nuclear explosives, obviated the need for economic mobilization planning, which the War Department had initiated after World War I and continued in the interwar years with increasing effect. Although such planning was resumed in the late 1940s and 1950s, various military representatives ultimately began to perceive that the existence of large forces prepared for hostilities made the interwar-type of premobilization planning unnecessary.

UNIFICATION

The army led in the drive for unification.[1] Chief of Staff General George C. Marshall was committed to the principle at the war's outset and initiated formal service planning for the postwar period early in 1943. In Marshall's mind, the war amply demonstrated that the army and navy could no longer operate as separate entities, and the air forces' autonomy following hostilities made unified command all the more essential. The chief of staff wanted Congress to commit to the idea of unification before hostilities ceased. He feared a repetition of the interwar years, with the nation turning its back on and neglecting the armed services. That same concern led Marshall to advocate universal military training (UMT). With a vast pool of trained reserve forces, the United States would be prepared for future conflict without incurring the expense of, and possible opposition to, a large standing army.

Reflecting Marshall's thinking, the army supported full-fledged unification. Although concepts and details varied over time, the War Department proposed that a secretary of defense and, under him, a chief of staff of the armed forces would directly manage and command the army, navy, and air force, thus eliminating the separate service secretaries. A body similar to the JCS would assist and advise the secretary and the chief of staff.

Out of respect for Marshall and the army's commitment to the air forces' independence, the air arm supported unification plans and, until March 1945, UMT. Nonetheless, the air forces were convinced that strategic airpower would make them the dominant service in the postwar years. For its part, the navy backed UMT but opposed unification, fearing that its future seemed uncertain and that it could be victimized by an army–air forces alliance. The navy began to mount a meaningful challenge to army advocacy only when James V. Forrestal became secretary of the navy after the April 1944 death of Frank Knox, who had supported unification on army terms.

The army's postwar ambitions for the armed services were largely frustrated. For a host of reasons, including popular opposition and widespread belief that airpower and atomic weapons guarded the nation, Congress never seriously considered UMT; it would go no further than authorizing selective service as needed.[2] Marshall's unification proposals fared somewhat better, but even on this crucial issue, the navy outmaneuvered the army, despite the fact that Truman, unlike the elusive Roosevelt, came out in favor of unification on army terms. Nonetheless, the army did not present its case skillfully, failed to speak consistently with one voice, and encountered congressional and popular concerns about the excessive concentration of military power.

The navy's most effective move was presenting an alternative to Marshall's insistence on the total unification of the armed services. Forrestal had concluded by mid-1945 that the navy could no longer protect its interests by stalling or saying no. He turned to his fellow financier and friend Ferdinand Eberstadt to analyze and make recommendations concerning unification. Eberstadt had assisted the War and Navy departments with World War II mobilization activities, and he had served as a high official in the War Production Board as well. In mid-October 1945, when Congress opened hearings on unification, the navy was able to counter army proposals by putting forward the suggestions of Eberstadt and his study group.

Eberstadt shrewdly shifted the center of focus away from unifying the services and toward coordinating military affairs with the larger and more important issues of overall national policy and security. To facilitate the process, and by playing on the nation's fear of militarism, he proposed federating, rather than consolidating, the armed forces. Nearly two years of negotiations involving the services, the White House, and Congress ultimately reconciled the differing approaches of the army and navy, largely on Navy Department terms.

The National Security Act of 1947 created a National Military Establishment headed by a secretary of defense and consisting of military departments of the army, the navy, and the now autonomous air force. With statutory sanction, the JCS would continue to plan strategy and logistics for the services to carry out. As additional interservice agencies, a Munitions Board and a Research and Development Board would be responsible for industrial mobilization and weapons advancement. A new collection of executive agencies would assist in defining and executing national security policy under which the National Military Establishment would operate. The president, assisted by a National Security Council composed of the chief executive, the secretaries of state and defense, the service secretaries, and others, would determine national policy. A Central Intelligence Agency would oversee intelligence collection and analysis, and a National Security Resources Board would coordinate civilian and military economic mobilization activities.

Serving as the first secretary of defense, Forrestal quickly realized that his and Eberstadt's creation was fundamentally flawed. The secretary was unable to direct his department. He had no staff; with only a few assistants, he could do little more than coordinate the services, whose roles and missions were determined by Congress and by statute, not by the secretary. The secretary could not turn to the JCS to strengthen his hand because the joint chiefs continued to be plagued by weak committee operations; in addition, the NSC was unable to set forth national security guidelines for military policy. Under such circumstances, defining a coherent military doctrine was out of the question. In broad and general terms, Forrestal worked with the services in defining and restricting themselves to primary and secondary missions. At most, these were limited accomplishments. Worn down by the grueling years of World War II service, the hectic tensions after hostilities, and unrelenting pressure from all sides as secretary of defense, a broken Forrestal left office in March 1949 and took his own life shortly thereafter.

Through legislative and executive action between 1949 and 1966, the armed services were unified roughly along the lines spelled out by the War Department during and after World War II. The major steps in this direction were usually preceded by studies and recommendations by various commissions, committees, and boards. At the urging of the Truman administration, Congress amended the National Security Act in 1949 to replace the National Military Establishment with the Department of Defense as an executive agency with a proper staff, to strip the three military departments of their executive status and remove their secretaries from the cabinet and the NSC, and to provide the JCS with a chair who would serve as the principal military adviser to the secretary of defense and the president.[3]

After the Korean War revealed continuing problems with interservice commands, President Dwight D. Eisenhower relied on the tacit consent of Congress in 1953 to centralize DOD control over the military. With his number of assistant secretaries greatly increased, the secretary of defense's operational authority expanded substantially at the expense of both the JCS and the service secretaries. Henceforth, the secretary of defense, not the joint chiefs, would select the service chief to head joint commands, and the service secretaries would be further subordinated to the role of operating managers for the defense secretary. Although the secretary's power grew, these changes left the lines of authority among the president, the secretary of defense, and the military departments vague and confused.

The launching of *Sputnik* in late 1957 spurred the Eisenhower administration to undertake full-fledged reform. Although Congress was unwilling to go as far as the president desired, the changes were profound. With the Department of Defense Reorganization Act of 1958, the chiefs of the services and the service secretaries were removed entirely from the chain of operational command. Henceforth, the chiefs and their services would recruit, equip, and train their members for hostilities and, when so designated, perform supply and logistical functions for unified commands. They no longer had any operational authority per se. The secretary of defense was responsible for all unified and specified commands, including strategy, operations, and force planning. For assistance, he would turn to the JCS as his staff. Moreover, the secretary, based on presidential emergency powers, could transfer and consolidate service activities and functions. Clear and unobstructed lines of authority now ran from the president through the secretary of defense to the field commanders.

Robert S. McNamara's tumultuous years as secretary of defense began in 1961. During his tenure, he pushed to the limits the secretary's domination of the department under the 1958 statute. According to McNamara's thinking, the secretary had the responsibility of developing a defense program that took into account and related "foreign policy, military strategy, defense budgets, and the choice of major weapons and forces."[4] To accomplish such ambitious purposes, he had to have firm control of his department, which he intended to achieve through integrated and centralized management.

Almost immediately the new secretary of defense began to radically reorganize his office for purposes of efficiency and effectiveness. Simultaneously, he oversaw the restructuring of all three military departments along lines approximating those of the Office of the Secretary of Defense. Of particular importance to McNamara were the army and air force technical services and the navy bureaus that handled weapons systems and related supplies and equipment. Proper oversight required that all military department supply systems be functionally structured and reasonably standardized. By August 1962, McNamara had pushed through an army reorganization in which most technical services were phased out and their duties taken over by the Army Materiel Command and other subdivisions based on functional lines. In 1966 a comparable process took place for the navy under what became the Naval Material Command. Prior to McNamara's taking office, the air force had begun to reorganize itself functionally, including the technical services. In 1961 the secretary not only approved the air force's changes but also drew on its experience in perfecting his management reforms, especially those dealing with weapons development and acquisition. Similar organizations facilitated the Defense Department's ability to supervise the armed forces' supply and service operations.

In a host of areas, the department went much further. Late in 1961 McNamara created the Defense Supply Agency, which gradually took over the purchasing of common supplies consumed by the military departments. Starting on a basic level, the agency then expanded its operations to include the most sophisticated equipment and supplies. DOD also assumed control over the military departments' activities involving atomic support, communications, intelligence, contract administration, contract audits, and traffic management and terminal services. In some instances, the centralization had begun before McNamara took office.

Overall, under the no-holds-barred leadership of McNamara, the unification of the armed services that had begun during World War II finally reached culmination. Since technologically advanced and expensive weaponry absorbed so much of the defense budgets and so aggravated interservice rivalry, the decentralized supply, procurement, and service operations that had plagued both the army and the navy throughout the twentieth century and even earlier could no longer be tolerated. Despite great resistance, the secretary of defense managed to implement critical and substantial changes that many officers and civilian executives never expected to see.

McNamara appropriately singled out weapons development as among his highest DOD reform priorities. Prior to World War II, weapons R&D was usually carried out by the supply bureaus, and production often took place in various arsenals, supply depots, and navy yards. The World War II operations of the National Defense Research Committee/Office of Scientific Research and Development and the Manhattan Project significantly affected those practices. After hostilities, all the services created special offices or agencies to ensure ongoing contact with universities and other research centers; they also organized R&D offices for weapons either to oversee bureaus' and their successors' activities or to centralize the efforts under service control. By the mid-1960s, all three military departments had set up similar centralized structures for carrying out R&D duties.

Step by step, the DOD consolidated control of the armed services' R&D operations. The National Security Act of 1947 established a Research and Development Board, which was intended to oversee and coordinate the armed services' R&D budgets, programs, and progress. As part of the ineffective National Military Establishment, this board was all but stillborn.

Subsequent offices proved to be more effective as the DOD and the secretary of defense gained increasing power at the expense of the service secretaries, the military chiefs, and the JCS. The 1958 legislation went even further in centralizing new weapons and weapons systems for all services under a director of defense research and engineering. Although the DOD carried out no R&D itself, all significant projects required its approval and were subject to its oversight. In carrying out these duties, the director of defense research and engineering worked closely with the military departments and appropriate subdivisions of the JCS. In theory, this put an end to the services' practice of claiming the mission for weapons systems they developed, regardless of whether they duplicated the missions of other services or encroached on their roles.

McNamara insisted that all weapons systems be compatible with the nation's foreign policy and with DOD-determined military strategy and defense budgets. Consistent with his leadership style and goals, the secretary of defense relied on sophisticated cost-effectiveness or systems analysis and the planning-programming-budgeting system to maintain firm control of service R&D and weapons production programs. These management methods grew out of the secretary's expanding authority and were used to extend his control over the military departments in general. Nonetheless, the prolonged and bitter TFX controversy, in which the air force and the navy thwarted McNamara's attempt to force a common fighter-bomber on them, forcefully demonstrated the limits of even the most determined and organizationally talented defense secretaries and the services' ability to protect their perceived interests through passive resistance, if not bureaucratic guerrilla warfare.

PRIVATIZATION OF MUNITIONS OUTPUT

The post–World War II private munitions industry leading to the military-industrial complex was not totally unknown to the nation. The outlines of a weapons manufacturing base could be perceived in the building of a modern naval fleet beginning in the late nineteenth century and the emergence of an aircraft industry before, during, and after World War I. But the magnitude and permanence of what evolved after 1945 were both new and profoundly significant.

The army air forces were out in front when it came to practices leading to an MIC.[5] Beginning in the interwar period and accelerating during World War II, the air force obsessively focused on achieving its independence from the army in the postwar years (which it accomplished in 1947). Its pursuit of that goal combined with an even more ambitious assertion that strategic airpower constituted the nation's first and primary line of defense and military strength. The atomic bomb appeared to make the claims of strategic airpower even more effective and lethal. To the degree that they were necessary at all, the army and navy would assume subordinate and supporting roles. Starting during hostilities and continuing after World War II, the air force launched aggressive public relations campaigns in support of its aims. Its shrewd promotion and propaganda exploited the air arm's close association with striking advances in science and technology applicable to warfare. The promise of airpower helped defeat proposals for UMT and gained vital public and congressional support for the maintenance of massive strategic air fleets in the postwar world.

The air force was able to outmaneuver the army and the navy in battles for popular support and official endorsement in part because it was a relatively new military arm, led by comparatively young, vigorous, and determined officers. Uninhibited by traditional military discretion and caution, those officers did not hesitate to take their case to the public and employ tactics that were both daring and ruthless. For example, the air force managed to insert into the official reports of the U.S. Strategic Bombing Survey a bogus report it had written stating, contrary to official findings, that the air force had practically single-handedly defeated Japan through strategic bombing in the last phase of the war.[6]

Moreover, born of technology and always dependent on private industry for the production of aircraft as its principal weapons, the air force, backed by scientists and engineers, readily turned to the manufacturing sector for support. While the air arms of both the army and the navy had R&D facilities for airplanes and related equipment, they never acquired arsenals, navy yards, or similar institutions that could produce their weapons.[7] In 1948 the air force established the first of the Cold War "think tanks," the RAND Corporation. It was an outgrowth of a wartime contract between the army air forces and the Douglas Aircraft Corporation for civilian input on the development of bombers. After hostilities, Project RAND was reorganized as a nonprofit firm, providing the air force with top-level scientists, engineers, and social scientists who otherwise would have been unavailable owing to the low pay and other disadvantages of government employment. RAND was called on to provide advice, studies, and analyses of weapons, strategy, and problems and issues facing the air force in the nuclear age. Besides first-rate civilian talent, RAND provided the air force with well-connected and influential supporters, since it was tied to most of the major aircraft producers. Both the army and the navy soon followed the air force in creating such nonprofits, and the air force established additional institutions to further its role and mission.[8]

After the end of the Second World War, aircraft manufacturers, shipbuilders, and machine-tool makers were among the few industries that favored the existence of large standing armed forces supplied by robust munitions makers. With the rapid demobilization of the armed services between late 1945 and 1950 and economic reconversion, these industries—particularly the aircraft firms—suffered a drastic drop-off in demand.[9] These dire circumstances were quickly reversed with the outbreak of the Korean War in 1950 and the subsequent and rapid buildup of the military under the prescriptions of NSC-68. The revived munitions production was characterized by more than increased quantity; the quality and nature of weaponry were undergoing dramatic changes with advances in jet propulsion, electronics, computers, missiles, atomic explosives, and nuclear power.

The armed services' expansion in the 1950s yielded the nation's first large, permanent, and private munitions industry. By 1966, a formidable scientific-technological-industrial complex was in place. Its base consisted of an extensive R&D system. By then, the armed services relied on 143 DOD laboratories and centers, 350 nonprofit and not-for-profit firms, 300 university research centers, 1,400 industrial enterprises, and a substantial number of private foundations and scientific committees. Industry, ranging from small companies to industrial giants, however, carried out most of the military's R&D. As of 1966, private firms, with large corporations in the lead, accounted for 66 percent of the DOD's R&D budgets. Department installations absorbed around 24 percent, and college, university, and other nonprofits accounted for 9.5 percent.[10] As the Cold War progressed, the actual production of weaponry by prime and subcontracting spread throughout the nation. Increasingly, however, and especially as heavy industry began to decline in the Midwest, defense output concentrated in what one group of scholars has labeled the "Gunbelt": industries, centers, and nonprofits located primarily on the East and West coasts and across the South. Hundreds of thousands of firms, ranging from the smallest to the largest enterprises in America, are involved in the MIC.[11]

From 1950 onward—once it became clear that the nation would maintain relatively large armed services requiring a permanent, substantial, and potentially profitable "peacetime" munitions industry—corporate America insisted that such an enterprise rightfully belonged to it. Stressing the virtues, efficiency, and ideological consistency of private enterprise vis-à-vis government output, industry prodded Congress to act on its behalf. It was backed by influential bodies such as the Hoover Commission. By the end of the 1960s, the once powerful and productive army arsenals and navy yards had been dramatically reduced in number and function. By comparison, the air force, lacking such institutions from its past, continued much as it had before.[12]

Arsenals, supply depots, navy yards, and the like date back to the early nineteenth century, and sometimes earlier. They grew out of the armed services' need for reliable sources of supplies and weaponry in the face of unreliable and often corrupt private contractors. The military's own institutions usually handled these needs during years of peace, turning to private producers only when wartime demand far exceeded what the armed services could produce on their own. Once hostilities ceased, old patterns resumed. However, in the case of the navy, it began to work closely with the shipbuilding, steel, and related industries in the late nineteenth century to build its modern fleets. During the interwar years, the navy distributed contracts among private firms to ensure adequate capacity for continued building in the event of war. From the outset, the army and navy air arms, assisted mightily by agencies such as the National Advisory Committee for Aeronautics, grew along with and depended heavily on the fledgling aircraft industry. With the exception of the situation that developed with the shipbuilding and aircraft firms, no private munitions industry per se existed in the United States prior to around 1950.[13]

With the termination of World War II, all the armed services ended up with a vast array of production facilities built at federal expense from 1940 forward. Although some of these plants were held in reserve, most were sold. With an expanded wartime production base, the navy easily could have handled the building, repairing, and converting of its fleets. Nonetheless, it returned to its prewar practice of sharing a substantial portion of the work with private industry to keep it viable for emergency expansion. Facing reduced demand at home and abroad, and apparently unwilling to make the vast investments required to increase their competitiveness, private shipbuilders turned to the federal government for relief. Insisting that they could build, repair, and convert vessels more efficiently, effectively, and innovatively than the navy yards, they slowly began to gain ground in the 1950s.

The Eisenhower administration and the Republican Party were much more inclined to see the shipbuilders' point of view than the Truman administration and the Democratic Party had been. Communities benefiting from private yards—which outnumbered their naval counterparts—also began lobbying publicly in behalf of their firms. Additionally, as the DOD was increasingly staffed with corporate executives and their allies, who were often from firms involved in or associated with munitions output, it extended its control over the military departments, and industry's position was strengthened even more. Finally, the shipbuilders and related industries argued intensely that in the growing worldwide conflict between the open societies of capitalism and the state-dominated systems of communism, private enterprise must be supported at all costs.

Responding to all these pressures, Congress and the DOD made staged changes from 1962 through the end of the decade. They closed various navy yards, restricted the construction of new ships to private firms, and left the remaining navy facilities to handle a diminishing amount of maintenance work. For the navy, a vital tradition dating back in some cases to the founding of the nation had come to an end.[14]

The army experienced a similar fate. By the interwar years, its Ordnance Department was producing almost all of the service's weapons. After World War II, the army sold off or put in standby status numerous facilities built and acquired during hostilities for the manufacture of powder, vehicles, and various weapons. However, it retained a considerable number of government-owned, privately operated plants to maintain peacetime output for the army. But the Ordnance Department continued to play the central role in designing, developing, and experimentally mass-producing weapons and other items before contracting full production out to private industry.

In the 1950s the Ordnance Department system came under attack for excluding private enterprise, emphasizing government ownership, and perpetuating an inflexible, inefficient, and unimaginative military bureaucracy. With the Eisenhower administration and Congress joining industry's case against the army, the Ordnance Department gave way by cutting back on the role of arsenals in favor of industrial contractors. But Ordnance and the army never succeeded in placating their critics.[15] The case against the arsenals was strengthened when the army engaged in a bitter dispute with the air force in the mid-1950s over developing ballistic missiles. Although the army's Jupiter missile, originating at the Redstone Arsenal in Alabama, got a jump on the air force's Thor missile, handled primarily by private industry, the army was destined to lose. By launching a vicious attack against Redstone and its German (perhaps formerly Nazi) scientists and engineers and the collectivist enterprise they ran, the air force put the army on the defensive. Before the decade was over, the Redstone Arsenal was all but absorbed by the newly established National Aeronautics and Space Administration (NASA), which also managed to take over the army's contractor-operated Jet Propulsion Laboratory in Pasadena, California. Henceforth, the army's role in missile development would be confined to short-range tactical weaponry.[16]

Severely weakened by the missile battle, the arsenal system suffered another major blow during a new controversy over the M14 rifle, officially designated in 1957 to replace the M1 as the standard infantry weapon. For a host of reasons, the M14 proved to be inferior to a privately designed and developed rifle ultimately labeled the M16 and manufactured by the Colt Fire Arms Company. As the Ordnance Department desperately fought for its rifle and to preserve its right to design and select army weapons, Congress, DOD, and industry became increasingly frustrated with continued resistance. (Unlike in the missile imbroglio, in this case the Ordnance Department displayed its worst, not its best, features.)

The Springfield Armory, like the Redstone Arsenal, was engaged in an unwinnable cause. In 1962, McNamara's reforms ended most of the technical services as their roles were functionalized and absorbed by the Army Materiel Command. Before the end of 1967, the secretary of defense had ordered the closing of the Springfield Armory, and that year, the army adopted the M16 as its standard rifle. In actuality, shutting down the armory in such a precipitate fashion ended up harming, rather than advancing, the services' development and production of small arms. Nonetheless, the army's direct role in production was severely cut in favor of private firms. Although the army, like the navy, continued to operate various design, supply, and maintenance facilities, its massive manufacturing operations with roots in America's far distant past were now over.[17]

The air force faced a different situation in the post–World War II years. During hostilities, it had financed more facilities than any of the other armed services. With the vast cutback in purchasing after the war, many firms left the field, and the air force sold or otherwise disposed of a good part of the wartime plant. Nonetheless, it retained a substantial number of facilities, and these were either run by private contractors or held, along with their tools and equipment, in standby capacity. With the Korean War, reserve plants were activated, and another modest round of building and equipping took place, for which Washington footed a significant part of the bill. By the 1950s, well over 50 percent of plants producing for the air arm were government owned and privately operated.

By the mid-1950s, the contradictions of the situation—the air force owned much of the plant and equipment used by private industry to produce its planes—became a sore point for both the aircraft manufacturers and the air arm. After all, the air force was pummeling army arsenals as statist, and industry was insisting that the army and navy surrender their production establishments, which violated the principles of free enterprise. The air force was also anxious to cut down on plant ownership and maintenance costs, which drained its stringent budgets; freed-up funds could then be used for more weaponry and manpower. For its part, industry insisted that allowable profit ratios had to rise if firms were to own the plant and machinery involved in aircraft output. Progress in shifting investment from the air force to industry was slow. Some gains were made in the late 1950s as government plants were disposed of or sold to private firms. Consistent with his response to navy shipyards and army arsenals, McNamara accelerated the selling of facilities and minimized air force investments in new plants and equipment. By the mid-1960s, contractor-owned and -equipped plants supplying the air force may have been more privately than publicly owned.[18]

Privatizing military R&D and production during the Cold War hardly stemmed from ideology or acquisitive instincts alone. The armed forces' deep-seated pre–World War II resistance to innovation as a threat to organization, mission, and morale, along with entrenched bureaucracies, proved to be incompatible with rapid technological change. The services' supply bureaus proceeded deliberately in weapons development and acquisition to temper the tug of technology, to ensure quality, and to guard against the rampant corruption, profiteering, and fraud of the past. Congress exerted its control by insisting on competitive bidding, fixed-price contracts, detailed budgeting, and similar practices. As long as military demand remained limited, budgets small, and industrial change gradual, the system worked. During the war, Congress lifted many if not most of its safeguards and surrendered much of its oversight to allow the armed services to meet emergency conditions. After hostilities, the nation's legislators restored peacetime restrictions.[19]

But the Cold War differed from all previous experience. It went on for nearly half a century and was characterized by an arms race that pushed technological innovation to its limits and included potentially world-destroying nuclear weaponry. The consequences were momentous. Huge, permanent national defense budgets, which included numerous sophisticated R&D projects, were beyond the capability of effective congressional review. As with earlier wars, Congress's oversight of the armed services was drastically compromised, but under different circumstances and for a longer period than had ever been the case in the past.[20]

Meaningful control by both the executive and the legislative branches has never been so essential for restraining weapons-driven DOD budgets and contractor malfeasance, misfeasance, and other abuses. Yet both the president and Congress have become part of the MIC problem rather than its remediation. As a result, the public, not to mention the overall governing system, has never candidly faced the negative consequences of the MIC on the armed services, the economy, and the nation. The general population has remained in the proverbial dark while misinformation is rife and goes unchallenged. Claims that arsenal and navy yard output constitutes a challenge to private ownership, for example, are as farfetched as they are distorting. Contracting for the armed services in the post–World War II world has hardly been an exercise in unfettered competition. Monopsony is not free-market capitalism. The military contractor has become all but a ward of the state, often operating in government-owned and -equipped facilities and enjoying protection against competition and failure through various forms of federal financing and buy-in

practices; these contractors exhibit cost overruns, overstaffing, underperform-
ing or failing weapons systems and products, and all the other characteristics
associated with private firms producing for the armed services. As Seymour
Melman points out in his seminal publications, the nation has developed economic sectors that can no longer compete under conditions of "Pentagon capitalism" and a "permanent war economy." Moreover, the munitions industry
has contaminated the larger economy in which it operates.

ECONOMIC MOBILIZATION

Criticism of DOD contracting notwithstanding, as military forces grew in size
after 1950, became armed with nuclear weaponry, and were backed by a substantial munitions industry, the importance of industrial mobilization receded.[21]
Such was not the case immediately after World War II. The National Security
Act of 1947 provided for a Munitions Board (MB) and a National Security
Resources Board (NSRB). The former, a successor agency to the interwar and
early World War II Army-Navy Munitions Board (ANMB)—deactivated in
1943 but reactivated in 1945—reported to the secretary of defense and was
responsible for planning, preparing, and coordinating the military departments
for participation in a mobilized economy. The latter reported to the president
and was charged with preparing the nation's economy for war mobilization,
including the coordination of civilian and military operations.

The NSRB-MB system never worked well. The duties of the two agencies
were vaguely defined, leading to ongoing conflict between them. Additionally,
as a successor to the ANMB, which had planned for economic mobilization
throughout the interwar years and participated in transforming the economy
for war from 1940 to 1942, the MB had a distinct advantage over the NSRB,
which was starting from scratch. Building on the work of the ANMB, for example, the MB published the first postwar industrial mobilization plan in 1947.
The NSRB's association with the MB cast a military shadow over the entire
economic mobilization planning structure, leading to suspicion of its actions.
Eberstadt's role in the creation of both boards only added to the distrust they
encountered, especially in and about the White House.

Furthermore, the NSRB was hampered in carrying out its responsibilities
by the board's composition. The board's chair was a statutory member of the
National Security Council, but he did not sit in the president's cabinet. The
board itself, consisting of key members of the president's cabinet, held the ultimate authority. In planning for economic mobilization, the board was charged
with using existing executive departments and other appropriate government

agencies to the greatest extent possible. Executive heads balked at planning for or approving any proposals whereby their departments' power might be encroached on during an emergency. As a result, the board members constantly challenged and thwarted the NSRB. The first chair resigned in frustration in December 1948. John R. Steelman, assistant to the president, took over as acting chair and ultimately recommended that the chair assume full authority for the NSRB, with the board's role restricted to an advisory one. This reform was enacted by executive order in May 1950, along with appointment of a new chair. It was preceded in 1949 by a reorganization that placed the board in the Executive Office of the President, ending its independent status.

With the outbreak of the Korean War, Truman first attempted to use the NSRB as a mobilization agency. Once it became clear that the war would stretch out and that substantial mobilization of the economy would become necessary, the president had to adopt a more realistic approach. A staff agency intended to plan for and advise the president on how to harness the economy was unsuited for directing the mobilization process itself.

Based on proposed legislation that the NSRB had written after years of study, Congress enacted the Defense Production Act in September 1950. It provided for a host of mobilization agencies that would perform functions similar to those carried out during World War II. The Truman administration elected to have existing departments, or new divisions of those departments, execute as much of the mobilization as possible. That was particularly so for the Commerce, Interior, Agriculture, and Labor departments. The Office of Defense Mobilization (ODM) was created in December 1950 to oversee all aspects of mobilization through policy making and coordination. To tie the ODM's operations in with the larger war effort and general administration policies, its chair sat in both the cabinet and the National Security Council.

Economic demand for the Korean War was modest compared with that of World War II. Because the conflict was new and different and intensely controversial, the Truman administration's mobilization program was rather disjoined, frequently uncertain, and usually politically tumultuous. Nonetheless, the administration realized significant industrial expansion and widespread prosperity while maintaining relative economic stability.

National defense spending totaled around $13.1 billion in 1950 (approximately 4.4 percent of GDP) and grew to about $50.4 billion in 1953 (approximately 13.2 percent of GDP). The multiplying expenditures did not go toward financing the Korean War alone, of course; they also covered part of the massive buildup at home and abroad in response to general Cold War tensions. After having generally declined from 1946 through 1950, national security budgets remained at a comparatively high level in the following decades. During the Vietnam War, for example, President Lyndon B. Johnson pushed defense spending up to nearly $82 billion (almost 9 percent of GDP) before leaving office. In the absence of any large or prolonged conflict, President Ronald Reagan's escalating defense outlays fell just short of $304 billion in 1989 (5.5 percent of GDP). Numbers of active-duty military personnel also remained relatively high and fluctuated during the Cold War years. All services combined stood at about 1.5 million in 1950; in 1953 and 1968, at the height of the Korean and Vietnam wars, the figures jumped to over 3.5 million. Thereafter, without any major hostilities, the numbers began to drop; the process was accelerated from 1973 on, when the all-volunteer force replaced the selective service system. By 1995, the number of active-duty military personnel had dropped back to just over 1.5 million.

With the Korean War ended, the NSRB returned to its earlier role of planning for future mobilization. During the Eisenhower administration's first year in office, it terminated the MB as part of its first reorganization of the DOD and, as a separate act, combined the NSRB and the ODM into a newly constituted Office of Defense Mobilization. The administration intended to have the reworked ODM both plan for mobilization and oversee economic preparedness for future hostilities, such as maintaining reserve plants, ensuring machine tool availability, stockpiling strategic materials, and the like.

The post–World War II thrust for economic preparedness and mobilization planning, which began in earnest with the creation of the NSRB and the MB in 1947, soon lost its momentum.[22] By 1955, those activities were already beginning to be either de-emphasized or ignored. The air force took the lead in that direction by ceasing to plan, arguing that its forces in being and the deterrence doctrine made planning superfluous. (In a sense, the air force was being consistent with its interwar stance that procuring planes and coordinating activities with the aircraft industry were adequate substitutes for economic mobilization planning.) The strategy of massive retaliation proposed by the Eisenhower administration acted to strengthen the air arm's claim, as did the air force's insistence that strategic bombing and atomic weapons made it the nation's premier military service and first line of defense.

With the air force opting out of planning, industry began to get mixed signals from DOD on the subject. As planning and preparedness measures waned, manufacturers began to lose interest in the projects, insisting that their participation no longer seemed worthwhile. By the time of the Vietnam War, the elaborate measures taken during the 1940s and 1950s to ensure the nation's readiness for quick mobilization had largely fallen victim to declining interest and neglect. For political reasons, the nation fought the Southeast Asian conflict without formal economic controls and regulations, which left a punishing economic legacy. Thereafter, with the military in popular disfavor owing to America's longest war to date and national security budgets tight, mobilization planning and preparedness never regained their post–World War II or Korean War emphasis.

Although military budgets escalated extravagantly during the Reagan administration, the dollars went principally to existing forces, not in anticipation of future hostilities per se, despite lip service about strengthening the industrial base to meet national security challenges. Additionally, the so-called baroque arsenal had become a major preparedness issue. The skyrocketing cost of high-technology, gold-plated weaponry had reached the point where relatively few individual weapons could be manufactured within existing budgets. Maintaining reserve plants for their production was out of the question because of the weaponry's expense, sophistication, and early obsolescence. Preparing for future mobilization in any realistic fashion was out of reach.

All these developments were affected by two larger issues: the short-war–long-war debate, and American deindustrialization. With the advent of nuclear weapons, short-war proponents held that any future war would be brief, ending in one side backing down from a confrontation, the two sides negotiating a settlement, or a nuclear or thermonuclear holocaust. Such being the case, industrial mobilization planning was both a waste of time and irrelevant. Long-war advocates maintained that periods of hostility are usually not short, as World Wars I and II established. Few world leaders would unleash a potential world-destroying nuclear or thermonuclear attack if another alternative existed. Hence, any future war would most likely resemble those of the past, and the United States must be prepared for that probability. Indeed, with most of the nation's defense spending going toward raising, training, and maintaining conventional forces, American policy tacitly endorsed that reality. The United States drifted to a position between these poles. Much of its strategic thinking was along short-war lines, but its forces in being and its spending priorities kept it in a state of reasonable preparedness for conventional conflict.

Deindustrialization, though hardly new and a major concern in some sectors during interwar planning, became of pressing importance beginning in the 1970s. In that decade, the United States began to lose its competitive edge as the leading industrial economy of the world. Smokestack industries began a steep decline in primary metals, automobiles, chemicals, and shipbuilding, along with machine tools and, as the decades wore on, in the high-technology sectors of electronics, biomedical technology, computers, and aerospace. Those industries, and even prosperous manufacturers, increasingly relied on materials, parts, or subassemblies supplied from abroad, or they utilized foreign machinery or production technologies and methods. As a result, imports escalated as exports declined, leading to severe balance-of-payment deficits. In the process, structural unemployment grew significantly, and high-paying blue-collar jobs gave way to lower-paying employment. Inevitably, the nation's pool of skilled workers declined in number and training.

For a short-war scenario, industrial decline meant little. But for a long-war one, it could be very threatening. In key sectors, the nation would be dependent on foreign output of materials, machinery, and high-technology products that might be delayed, in short supply, or even unavailable. In addressing the consequences of deindustrialization, however, popular thinking has focused more on the economy in general than on national security in particular. What has been emphasized is the impact on regions, structural unemployment, declining tax bases, international dependence, and eroding international clout.

These various trends have been reflected in the changing institutional structure relied on by successive administrations to deal with the issue of economic mobilization planning and preparedness. After reworking the ODM in 1953, the Eisenhower administration in 1958 combined that office with another that covered civil defense. Thereafter, both the Kennedy and Nixon administrations went through a series of reorganizations that involved dividing civil defense, mobilization, and emergency planning among a number of existing departments and agencies. Finally, the Carter administration in 1978 consolidated five agencies into one—the Federal Emergency Management Agency (FEMA), which began operating in early 1979 as an independent agency outside the Executive Office. Most of this shuffling took place under the amended and extended Defense Production Act of 1950. FEMA appeared to have all the planning authority specified in the National Security Act of 1947 and the coordinating powers set forth in the Defense Production Act.

If FEMA took up economic mobilization planning and preparedness begun by the MB and the NSRB in 1947 and continued by the ODM in 1953, it was not apparent. Late in December 1980, the Defense Industrial Base Panel of the House Armed Services Committee (the Ichord Panel) issued a report entitled *The Ailing Defense Industrial Base: Unready for Crisis*, in which it graphically detailed why the nation could no longer reliably mobilize its economy for a major crisis. The study confirmed earlier findings based on military mobilization exercises. Although much hand-wringing took place, little was done because the Ichord Panel was, in effect, describing national defense in the context of the nation's larger problem of industrial decline.

Apparently in an effort to back up FEMA, in late 1981 President Reagan formed within the National Security Council the Emergency Mobilization Preparedness Board, made up of senior department and agency officials involved with emergency management. They were to consult on mobilization's potential to benefit the armed forces, protect national interests, and meet other civil emergency preparedness requirements. Such vague charges given to otherwise busy and engaged executives almost ensured inactivity or merely ceremonial responses.

The Mobilization Concepts Development Center, set up in 1982 and situated in the National Defense University, is much more important for industrial mobilization for war. It not only analyzes various mobilization issues but also commissions academic projects, encourages the study of relevant subjects, and identifies social scientists and engineers working in the field and supports their efforts. As a relatively long-standing sister institution, the Industrial College of the Armed Forces (ICAF) also plays an important role in mobilization study. ICAF was created in 1924 as the Army Industrial College in the Office of the Assistant Secretary of War (OASW). It was instrumental in the OASW's industrial mobilization planning during the interwar years; in the post–World War II period, the college resumed those efforts. With passage of the National Security Act of 1947, it continued the emphasis, but from a base that now included all of the armed services. In 1962 the college's mission was modified from studying industrial mobilization to training in logistical management. Nonetheless, economic preparedness remains one of ICAF's areas of interest and productivity.

Returning economic mobilization study and planning to military institutions is consistent with pre–World War II practices. With the National Defense Act of 1920, Congress assigned similar planning to what became the OASW. It did so because the army had caused the most difficulty in mobilizing the economy for the First World War. Members of Congress, executive officials, and businessmen participating in harnessing the economy insisted on such an approach to avoid a similar situation during future emergencies. At the time, few objected to the military planning for mobilization of the civilian economy as well as for itself. Between 1930 and 1939, the OASW published four industrial mobilization plans, the last of which roughly outlined how the World War II economy was mobilized for the extended conflict.

As World War II was drawing to an end, industrial and military elements— which together dominated the War Production Board (WPB)—thwarted the efforts of WPB chair Donald M. Nelson and other economic reformers to implement a WPB-directed reconversion program. Both industry and the military were intent on blocking or reversing New Deal advances in the postwar years. Planning for the civilian economy at the national level in the Cold War and post–Cold War eras would encounter similar resistance.

The National Security Act of 1947, in contrast to the National Defense Act of 1920, separated civilian and military mobilization planning. The intricate system authorized by the statute and its numerous modifications has not worked well. In one form or another, mobilization planning for the armed services has taken place. But civilian mobilization planning has never made much progress. Besides the organizational defects and the question of need, several other reasons help explain why. Civilian agencies are simply not as invested in mobilization planning as are those of the military. Furthermore, any form of national economic planning during and after the Cold War has faced formidable opposition, as was the case at the end of World War II. Moreover, defense spending has become so substantial and consequential that planning for the military can affect the economy in multiple ways. With the impact of deindustrialization, for example, mobilization planning could logically lead in the direction of proposals resembling an industrial policy. Such was the case with the Ichord Panel and later with the Young Commission during the last years of the Reagan administration.

A number of scholars and other analysts maintain, despite all protests to the contrary, that the United States *does* have an industrial policy. But it is an unacknowledged policy carried out by the DOD since around 1950. The department's massive budgets have helped shape vital aspects of America's economic direction by supporting in whole or in part some of the nation's largest industries and firms, heavily influencing R&D policy, helping to alter regional economies, leading in areas such as industrial automation, and siphoning off resources that might otherwise go to investment in civilian industries, infrastructure, health and welfare, and urban planning.

Viewing DOD operations as constituting an industrial policy involves a great paradox. The so-called policy has resulted as much from drift as from design. Unintended consequences have occurred regularly from military procurement and production. And, contrary to the generally accepted intent of an industrial policy or indicative planning, the DOD has acted to weaken rather than strengthen the American economy.

Post–World War II mobilization planning has had a much more uncertain quality than OASW planning during the interwar years. The difference arises in part from the fact that defense spending in the interwar years was so slight that procurement and economic mobilization planning, unlike in the Cold War years, had no actual or potential effect on the economy. Also of importance is the matter of need. The planning of the 1920s and 1930s was of critical importance, while that of the Cold War and after is less so. Indeed, short-war advocates insist that mobilization planning is unnecessary, while long-war adherents maintain that such planning is essential for preparedness. In practice, American policies have emerged somewhere in between the short- and long-war positions, so mobilization planning goes on, although in a more restricted way than in the early years of the Cold War.

CONCLUSION

Between 1945 and the 1960s, a virtually new military came into existence in which the various services were unified under the Department of Defense. This relatively huge military was equipped and armed with weaponry of the most advanced technology, produced primarily by the nation's large and privately owned munitions industry. Both the military and the munitions industry became permanent in nature, and alone and together, the two were unprecedented in American history.

Relations between the two have become so close and interactive that distinguishing between them is not possible in critical areas such as designing, developing, producing, and using equipment and weapons on and off the battlefield; recruiting and training troops and officers; camp and plant management; and related supply and logistical functions. That being the case, military and civilian elites move between the two spheres with relative ease. From these circumstances has arisen the so-called military-industrial complex.

With trillions of dollars involved in national defense and with the military benefiting from the munitions firms' formidable lobbying and promotional efforts, the DOD has come to exercise great influence in the nation's economic and political life and in the formulation and implementation of its national security and foreign policies. Indeed, the military-industry partnership has progressed over the decades to the point of being practically self-perpetuating. Although the Cold War ended years ago, the MIC goes on as before and searches for a rationale to justify its existence. Global military spending comparisons illustrate the point. The nation's military outlays regularly surpass worldwide averages expressed as a percentage of gross national product (GNP). In 1968 U.S. military expenditures were 9.3 percent of GNP, compared with an international average of 7.2 percent; that year, the United States accounted for 38 percent of total global spending. In 1975 the respective figures were 5.9, 6.0 (a rare year), and 25 percent; in 1989, 5.8, 4.6, and 28.7 percent; and in 1993, 4.7, 3.3, and 34.2 percent. Jumping to 2005, estimates of global military expenditures totaled $1 trillion; American spending stood at $520 billion, or 52 percent of the total.[23]

Neither the military nor industry wants to surrender any aspect of their partnership, which is rewarding in terms of power, career, position, prestige, and personal as well as corporate wealth. As with civil-military relations, both parties go out of their way to obscure the realities of their relationship, with the intent of diverting public attention.

4

THE DEFENSE INDUSTRY

The vast and private Cold War munitions industry grew along with the large and permanent military establishment and, like the latter, was a departure in American life. As noted earlier, the army air corps—later the army air forces and then the air force—played a seminal role in the defense industry's emergence.

The air force never acquired facilities comparable to army arsenals or navy yards. During the interwar years, the air corps and its naval counterpart created a number of research, development, and testing centers; some manufacturing capacity; and other related facilities. The numbers, however, were never very great. Private industry pioneered the production of what became the modern airplane. In doing so, it depended heavily, even overwhelmingly, on military procurement, with its demanding specifications and lucrative contracts. Air mail contracts and other federal assistance, including the operations of the National Advisory Committee for Aeronautics, also loomed large in the aircraft industry's rise. In short, substantial and ongoing federal, and particularly military, assistance and regulation were indispensable to the interwar growth and maturation of the aircraft industry.

The demand for aviation during World War II acted to convert a relatively small and scattered collection of aircraft firms into a giant, oligopolistic industry. After hostilities, the air force relied on industry to develop and produce its airplanes. With the introduction of missiles and then space vehicles, electronics and communications firms joined aircraft manufacturers to constitute the high-technology aerospace industry. Exceptionally high levels of R&D—later, testing and evaluation—characterized aerospace, necessitating the employment of large numbers of scientists and engineers. Continuous with interwar and wartime practices, the air force remained convinced that private industry, as opposed to arsenal-type facilities, was best equipped to handle the demands of high-technology weapons. Among other advantages denied to the military and the civil service, corporations had the ability to hire top scientists, engineers, and technicians. Additionally, contractors, subcontractors, labor unions, communities, and members of Congress all acted as an effective lobby for air force procurement and growth. Over time, the army and navy began to adopt the air force's contracting practices. In doing so, they were pressured by corporate America, which was determined to keep massive and ongoing munitions output in private, not public, hands. Although some arsenals and navy yards survived, they did so principally as weapons and equipment laboratories and maintenance and repair centers.

The private defense industry of the Cold War decades and afterward is usually associated with the large corporations of the aerospace industry, where high technology is applied to weaponry on the broadest scale. To a lesser degree, however, the same holds true for nuclear-powered submarines, aircraft carriers, nuclear weapons, radio and communications equipment, and even some combat vehicles such as tanks and armored personnel carriers. Though centered in aerospace, defense spreads across a host of other industries, particularly shipbuilding and wheel- and motor-driven weaponry. Hence, the defense industry varies from others in that it is not identified by product; instead, it consists of all industries contracting with and selling to the Pentagon.

Two outstanding features characterize the defense industry. First, it is not subject to traditional market forces. Most contracts are negotiated between aerospace and other firms and the Department of Defense. Competition is far from the norm. With monopsony facing oligopoly, the outcome could hardly be different. Second, defense is largely a high-tech industry based on extensive R&D, far more than the typical commercial firm. From these circumstances has grown an industry (particularly aerospace) that is highly concentrated, although it has a large and varied subcontracting system. Several other attributes of the private munitions industry are worthy of note. Dating from its origins, aerospace has been relatively stable in terms of entry, existence, and profitability; yet the industry as a whole tends toward instability because of its nearly total dependence on the armed services and their varying levels of demand. Additionally, the defense industry operates primarily away from the major centers of older manufacturing; defense output is geographically centered on the East and West coasts and across the South. Furthermore, since the 1970s, the industry has become increasingly dependent on international sales. Finally, prospects for converting to nonmilitary operations, outside of commercial aircraft and merging with firms producing for civilian markets, are poor and have failed when attempted in the past.

At best, defense firms are a cross between private and public entities; less charitably, they operate under conditions of socialized risks and privatized profits. Under these circumstances, relations between the armed services and the defense companies are close and interactive. The two generally act in harmony, even collusion, because of their shared interests. Together they constitute the powerful center of the military-industrial complex.

AIRCRAFT, AEROSPACE, SHIPBUILDING, AND OTHERS

Even before the conclusion of World War II, the air force took action to ensure that the major aircraft firms would be able to manufacture planes for its projected postwar air fleet.[1] Most of the massive production capacity for aircraft built during hostilities was either financed or owned by the government, and the air force considered it essential that a substantial portion of those facilities and equipment remain available to aircraft companies.

Actually, Defense Plant Corporation financing for the aircraft industry exceeded that for all other areas of manufacturing. In 1939 the value of the industry, including aircraft, engines, parts, and accessories, stood at $114 million. Between 1940 and 1945 facilities expansion totaled $3.9 billion, of which $420 million, or less than 11 percent, was private; the rest was public. As a result, at war's end, many aircraft firms owned no facilities for producing modern military aircraft. To remedy this situation, the air force joined the other services in vastly expanding its ownership of the postwar plant. Overall, the military withheld 149 projects, built or manufactured at a cost of $4.6 billion, from government-financed manufacturing capacity to be sold as surplus property after World War II. (Prewar arsenals and shipyards had a net capital value of $210 million, contrasted with the new acquisitions, which involved some of the "largest and costliest" projects of the war years.[2]) Included in the count were numerous aircraft plants and a great deal of equipment held in reserve to be leased to aircraft firms at a nominal fee.

The massive cancellation of military contracts after the conclusion of hostilities seriously clouded the aircraft industry's future. At the peak of production, contracts had totaled $16 billion; this fell to $1 billion by 1947. Several short-run conditions mitigated the threat. Contract figures included armaments for planes that the industry did not provide, and the automobile industry ceased its aircraft output. Civilian demand also picked up, but that market was saturated by 1948. It was the Korean War that provided major relief to the aircraft industry and also unleashed another round of government-sponsored facility building, but with private industry carrying a greater share of the costs.

The longer-run prosperity of the industry rested with its transition from aircraft to aerospace.[3] In this crucial transformation, the air force also played a significant role. Various aircraft companies and other corporations, such as General Electric, had begun working on missiles as early as 1944. In general, however, aircraft firms hesitated to take up the new line, and the air force had to generate interest in the project. Only after testing of the first hydrogen bomb in 1952 did missile development begin to come into its own. Thereafter, aircraft companies initiated the serious transition to aerospace.

Several key differences set off aerospace from aircraft output. The first is R&D. For aircraft firms, R&D is functional, intended to improve the efficiency of production or the quality of the product. For missiles and spacecraft, R&D is a major and basic function that precedes output or is actually a part of it. Second, electronics are much more important to missiles than to airplanes, accounting for around 13 to 20 percent of the cost of the latter but fully 50 percent of the former. For aircraft firms to navigate the transition to aerospace, they had to create or acquire adequate R&D and electronics capabilities, and the two were usually closely related. Not infrequently, companies either absorbed or merged with smaller firms specializing in these fields. Third, the government accounts for more than 90 percent of aerospace sales involving missiles, rockets, and space vehicles.

Most airframe corporations managed the transition to aerospace. Hence there was significant continuity from the major aircraft manufacturers of World War II to the aerospace industry of the postwar years, including the familiar names of Douglas, Grumman, Lockheed, McDonnell, North American Aviation, and Northrop. A number of electronics companies also entered aerospace as prime contractors, concentrating on missiles. To succeed, they had to reorganize their corporate structures to offer more broadly based electronics systems and to effectively manage large and complex systems. Once again, well-known companies were involved, such as Raytheon, Western Electric, and Minneapolis-Honeywell. Another group of firms specialized in propulsion units for rockets and engines for aircraft, including General Motors, General Electric, Westinghouse, Thickol Chemical, and Hercules Powder.

Prime aerospace contractors are expected to be able to evaluate, supervise, and coordinate the activities of associated contractors and subcontractors in the production and assembly of the final product, now designated a weapons system. Owing to the complexity and size of some projects, however, a new entity has emerged: the systems management firm. The air force initiated the use of such companies in 1954 when it contracted with what later became Thompson-Ramo-Wooldridge (TRW) to oversee the development of the missile program. Later, NASA turned to General Electric and Bellcomm for the Apollo Project. Systems management companies are usually privately owned, but some are nonprofits. They can be involved in evaluating contractor proposals, offering scientific and technical advice, testing equipment and systems, and generally supervising projects. Such firms came into existence because the government lacked adequate skilled personnel to monitor aerospace. Because these firms are usually spin-offs of or associated with aerospace contractors, they attest to Washington's dependence on and close and compromising relations with the aerospace industry.

Unlike aerospace, shipbuilding remains a much more traditional industry in terms of design and construction. In the early 1980s twelve private yards built ships for the navy; fewer firms were available for the construction of specialized vessels. Only one firm, Newport News Shipping and Drydock Company, had the ability to build large aircraft carriers. Furthermore, Newport News and the Electric Boat Company were the only ones capable of constructing nuclear-powered submarines. By around 1980, shipbuilding was a distant third behind aerospace in terms of contract value. Tanks, produced principally by the automobile manufacturers, were even further down the list, although the contract dollar amount increased when other motor-driven weapons systems and vehicles were included.

The defense industry in general, and particularly aerospace, was both relatively stable and highly concentrated for at least twenty years after 1945. These patterns extend back to World War II. Of the eleven major aircraft manufacturers in existence during hostilities—all of which were also present in the interwar years[4]—seven of them, or their merged entities, were among the top twenty DOD contractors in 1958, and six continued in that status up to 1988 and after. According to two careful scholars of the defense industry, six corporations remained on the DOD's list of top ten contractors from 1958 through 1988: McDonnell Douglas, General Dynamics, General Electric, Lockheed, United Technologies, and Boeing. An additional seven companies remained in the top twenty-five during the same period: Raytheon, General Motors (and Hughes Aircraft Company), Westinghouse, Rockwell International, Unisys Defense Systems (and its predecessors Sperry Rand and Burroughs), Textron, (with Avco), and IBM. Six firms have entered the ranks of the top twenty-five since 1966. Most of those disappearing from the top twenty-five have done so through mergers and acquisitions. Only one aircraft firm and one shipbuilding company dropped out of the DOD's top twenty-five in the thirty-year period, along with a few oil, rubber, and chemical companies. All the defense contractors remaining in the top twenty-five are aerospace firms.[5]

NASA contracting, though done on a much smaller scale than that of the Pentagon, is still substantial; however, it does not significantly change this outline. Most top NASA contractors are also leading DOD contractors.

The stability of the defense industry results in part from its concentrated nature. From the late 1950s to the end of the 1980s, the top hundred contracting firms accounted for about 70 percent of overall defense business, the top twenty for around 50 percent, and the leading five for approximately 20 percent. These firms tend to cluster into defense subdivisions. Out front are the airframe companies, such as McDonnell Douglas, Lockheed, and Boeing, which might also include electronics and communications, ships and tanks, and systems management. Another group concentrates on smaller unmanned missiles, as is the case with Martin-Marietta, Raytheon, and Minneapolis-Honeywell. General Electric and like firms deal in propulsion units and aircraft engines. Usually below the level of the top contractors are those specializing in systems integration, such as TRW, and other firms, such as IBM, that handle guidance, control, and communications equipment and instruments. Most of these subdivisions are primarily in aerospace. Since the 1960s, 75 percent of all DOD prime contracts have fallen into seven general categories: aircraft, missiles, electronics and communications, ships, ammunition, tanks, and weapons. Demand shifts among the categories according to changing needs.

In addition to being concentrated, the defense industry comprises some the nation's largest corporations. By 1968, seventy-five of the leading hundred defense contractors were included in the *Fortune* 500, and more than half of *Fortune*'s top fifty firms were defense suppliers. In the late 1980s Boeing, United Technologies, McDonnell Douglas, Rockwell International, and Allied-Signal had made their way to *Fortune*'s top twenty-five, and federal contracts helped keep IBM, General Motors, and General Electric among the leading corporations as measured by the value of their stock.

Defense and space corporations (most operate in both areas) are heavily dependent on government contracts. Between 1985 and 1988, for example, 88 percent of Grumman's sales were to the DOD and NASA. Raytheon and Rockwell International were just above and below the 50 percent mark, respectively. Boeing and Texas Instruments came in at around 25 percent, and TRW at 19 percent. The other nine of the top fifteen in terms of federal dependence were scattered between these extremes. Not included in these calculations are conglomerates and mixed-market firms like Allied-Signal, with military or aerospace divisions that are heavily government dependent. Additionally, subcontracting, which is common among the defense giants, is not included. Also omitted from the calculations are foreign sales, which constitute an ever-increasing portion of defense industry sales. Many of the defense giants rely heavily on sales abroad, which are much more lucrative than their contracts with Washington.

After more than twenty years of comparative stability, the aerospace industry entered turbulent times that continue to the present day. The basic problem stemmed from declining demand and excess production capacity. By the late 1960s, advances in aeronautic and avionic technology had resulted in weapons systems with extraordinarily high costs. That outcome severely limited the armed services' procurement ability. The large-scale orders for combat aircraft, running into multiple thousands, that had begun in 1938 were over, never to return. Orders usually totaled in the hundreds and sometimes fell even lower. Further down the line, obsolete aircraft were not replaced, and dated models were often kept in service indefinitely, with aerospace firms scrambling for contracts to rebuild and upgrade them. Redesigned older aircraft models were even brought back into production as the Pentagon struggled with skyrocketing costs that eroded its buying power. Matters were made worse when defense budgets declined as the Vietnam War began to wind down and competition for weapons exports grew. The end of the Cold War changed the strategic and economic environment, adding greatly to aerospace's problems. By then, total demand could accommodate at most three or four giant firms. Excess national production capacity was made worse by a glut of international aerospace firms.

To the degree that aerospace faced and met the extended crisis, it did so through an ongoing process of restructuring and consolidating. In the 1960s aerospace joined the merger and acquisition movement sweeping through corporate America. McDonnell and Douglas, for example, combined, and the Glen L. Martin Company merged with American Marietta to become Martin-Marietta. A host of other companies were absorbed by nonaviation conglomerates with limited records of success at best. By the late 1960s and into the 1970s, the industry became more consolidated than at any time since the 1930s. Owing to this development, only the largest companies had the ability to handle major weapons and related programs. Thereafter, as demand continued to decline and international competitive pressure mounted, restructuring and consolidating moved forward. The process appeared to plateau in the 1990s, with only three massive aerospace firms remaining, along with a number of lesser companies and those only partially engaged in defense output.

Lockheed was at the top when it merged with Martin-Marietta, its equal, in 1995 to become Lockheed Martin. The corporation completed its consolidation by absorbing the Loral Corporation in 1996. Boeing, the second leading defense contractor, acquired McDonnell Douglas in 1997, after purchasing what was once North American Aviation in 1996. Boeing went on to acquire a division of the Hughes Tool Company in 2000 to enrich its holding of another Hughes subsidiary that McDonnell Douglas had acquired in 1984. In third place was Northrop, which in 1994 bought Grumman to constitute the Northrop Grumman Corporation. Through 2008, the new corporation acquired twenty other firms, including Westinghouse's Radio Division, Ryan Aeronautical Company, Litton Industries, Newport News Shipping, and TRW.

These three top companies, along with other firms, both compete and cooperate in obtaining and completing defense contracts. Joint efforts on demanding and expensive major weapons and equipment systems are not uncommon. Such is currently the case with spin-offs of the Strategic Defense Initiative. American aerospace firms have also considered and experimented with various European and other international production partnerships. For the most part, these efforts have been less than successful. Along different lines, defense subcontracting is both important and problematic. More than 50 percent of the value of prime contracts goes to subcontractors and lower-tier suppliers. Of that amount, about half is taken up by other prime contractor divisions, with the remainder going to medium and small businesses. Although reliable data on subprime participants are hard to come by, most analysts agree on a number of conclusions. Some lower-tier firms are not defense dependent because DOD-related demand is only a part of their market; others are specialty firms heavily or nearly totally reliant on defense or space orders. The latter firms are exceptionally vulnerable. Their existence depends on the flow of Pentagon business and the whims of principal contractors. Unlike the prime contractor, they usually operate on fixed prices and are denied DOD financing, the use of government plants, tolerance of cost overruns and missed delivery dates, and all the other benefits lavished on primes. Furthermore, when contracts become scarce, prime contractors cut back on subcontracting to reduce their dependence on lower-tier firms or to enhance their ability to win DOD awards.

As early as the 1960s, the number of lower-tier firms able and willing to handle defense and space business was shrinking. These diminished numbers are responsible for the principal bottleneck in the weapons field. Companies with alternative markets are increasingly unwilling to tolerate the cumbersome paperwork, rigid and demanding standards, security restraints, delayed and slow payments, and numerous other annoyances involved in dealing with the DOD. Many of the firms dependent on Washington give up on volatile markets, close their doors in down times, or go bankrupt. If qualified firms are unavailable to supply parts, components, and the like, prime contractors must take on the responsibility themselves. As a result, output is slowed, and prices inevitably rise.[6]

Aerospace's size, complexity, and economic importance are compounded many times over by the fact that it is almost entirely a creation of the federal government, and especially the military. Without military procurement, supplemented by air mail contracts, the aircraft industry barely would have survived the interwar years. Massive military procurement and federal investment in plant during World War II made the diminutive aircraft industry into big business. By carefully distributing contracts among selected companies and providing them with production plant and equipment, the air force helped nurse the industry through the traumatic postwar transition to peace, until Korean War demand created an expanding market. Thereafter, the demand for increasingly sophisticated military aircraft and the introduction of missiles, rockets, and space vehicles made the leading aerospace firms among the nation's largest corporations.

RESEARCH AND DEVELOPMENT

Since its origin, a defining characteristic of aerospace has been its emphasis on exploring the limits of high technology. This drive inevitably led to an extraordinary focus on R&D, later expanded to include testing and evaluation. Once again, directly or indirectly, DOD pays for most of the enormous expense involved. With the armed services seeking the most advanced weaponry and the defense industry adapting to that imperative, the sources of demand and supply have interacted to make weapons more sophisticated, more expensive, and fewer in number. When spacecraft and nuclear weapons are added to the equation, the entire R&D factor becomes even more exaggerated.

R&D for aerospace and defense differs greatly from that for civilian industry. Commercial manufacturing spends, on average, around 3 percent of sales on R&D. By comparison, the defense industry average is 10 percent, and it can go well beyond 40 percent. As much as 70 percent of defense R&D is performed by private industry. Indeed, in 1989 one-third of all private industry R&D was federally funded, with the DOD accounting for 82 percent of expenditures. When R&D costs associated with the military aspects of NASA, the Department of Energy, and nonreimbursed R&D expenses of independent industry (coverable by the DOD, based on a percentage of the firm's defense sales) are combined with those of the DOD, fully one-third of the nation's R&D is military related.

Similar to defense contracts, R&D contracts are highly concentrated. In 1987 the top five firms—McDonnell Douglas, Lockheed, Martin-Marietta, Boeing, and Grumman—received more than 32 percent of all R&D contracts. The top ten received nearly 46 percent, and the top twenty, 58 percent. This level of concentration has a number of major consequences. First, R&D helps protect existing firms in the industry by creating a barrier to entry. Facilities and scientific and engineering staff essential for carrying on R&D are very expensive and hard to maintain. Second, R&D contracts are the best way to win follow-on production awards, another practice that maintains the industrial status quo. Rarely does a firm uninvolved in R&D receive a production contract. Third, numerous R&D contracts exist because they are very lucrative for industry in and of themselves, and the armed services are usually open to the promise of better or improved products. Last and most important, much of R&D turns out to be a poor or wasted investment. Huge, bureaucratic corporate structures on the supply side, and even more inflexible administrative systems on the DOD side, act to stifle innovation. Seeking to minimize risk, both sides cautiously favor the improvement of existing weapons over chancier efforts to produce new ones. Over time, the nearly inevitable results are diminishing returns and baroque weaponry.[7]

CONTRACTS

R&D contracts, like most DOD contracts, are negotiated. Indeed, only about 8 percent of defense contracts are advertised and awarded by bids. The rest result from negotiations. Of the 92 percent that fall into this category, around 30 percent are awarded competitively, in that various firms submit proposals and estimated costs, which the DOD uses to select a contractor and establish terms. More than 60 percent of all DOD awards are noncompetitive, involving sole-source firms or follow-on contracts. Within this general framework, the DOD has a variety of fixed-price, incentive, and cost-reimbursable contracts, all of which are used as appropriate. Almost without exception, the DOD assumes the risk for all costs, and the contractor is liable only for profits. Furthermore, nearly all military contracts prioritize quality performance and timely delivery; at best, costs are of secondary significance. The nature of such contractual arrangements makes defense firms more like agents of the DOD rather than business interests serving it. Contracts come to resemble administrative agreements between defense corporations and the Pentagon for the achievement of an agreed-on end, with managerial and detailed processes worked out as required.[8]

PROFITS

In one way or another, all contracts provide for profits.[9] They also include provisions for audits, renegotiations, and the like to limit profits and minimize abuse. With public money and security involved, the focus on returns to defense corporations is fully understandable. How to measure profits and determine whether they are excessive or inadequate remains a matter of ongoing controversy. Most scholars agree that, based on percentage of sales, the profits of defense contractors are low. In the 1970s they averaged around 4.7 percent. This is the preferred measure of the DOD and industry. It makes the former look good in the public eye, and it provides the latter with a rationale for insisting on better terms.

According to analysts outside defense circles, return on investment is a much better and more accurate gauge of profits than is percentage of sales. Relying on a 1976 DOD study, this approach calculated shipbuilding profits at a low of 5.8 percent, missiles at 20 percent, and the average for all defense contracts at 13.5 percent. By comparison, a Federal Trade Commission sampling of 5,000 similar durable goods producers found that profits averaged 10.7 percent. Economist Murray Weidenbaum arrived at figures close to these. For the period 1962–1965, he calculated aerospace profits at 17.5 percent of net worth, compared with 10.6 percent for commercial companies.

Defense profits based on return on investment are more than twice those calculated based on sales because investment levels in the defense industry tend to be exceptionally low. In effect, DOD contracting procedures discourage investment on the part of private firms. With all costs covered and little credit given for new plant and equipment, companies continue to use existing facilities even if they are dated or obsolete. The availability of government-owned plants simply exaggerates the practice. The same is true of DOD progress payments at regular intervals, which ensure contractors adequate working capital, and a host of other policies intended to prop up defense firms regardless of their level of performance or nonperformance.

In truth, however, defense industry profits levels have not been reliably established, and in terms of current practices, they cannot be. This is the case because the DOD does not require firms to report profits on a contract-by-contract basis. Existing studies are based on sampling, audits, and questionnaires that are either open to challenge or subject to varying interpretations. More to the point, corporations can hide profits through various practices, such as shifting commercial expenses to defense accounts, using government plant and equipment for civilian output, or reducing profits by assorted accounting devices. Ferreting out all possible subterfuge is all but impossible and would require time and effort far beyond the value of any return.

From the information available, a fair conclusion is that defense industry profits at least equal those of the commercial manufacturing sector and probably exceed them. This certainly appears to be the case for top-tier companies. The smaller contractors, subcontractors, and suppliers operate on much narrower profit margins, and more than a few face a fight for survival.

Even attempting to compare profits for defense firms with profits for commercial ones is questionable. Most analysts agree that defense is a "nonmarket" industry. "What goes on in the industry," according to Frederic M. Scherer, "cannot be called private enterprise in any conventional sense; it lies instead in the grey area between private and public enterprise." Hence, William L. Baldwin proposes that, as indicated above, contracts are closer to administrative agreements subject to constant adjustment as needed. Richard F. Kaufman is less charitable, contending that Washington finds its interests so intertwined with those of defense firms that it lavishes both subsidies and welfare on them.[10]

A NONCOMPETITIVE INDUSTRY

Whether described in neutral or negative terms, defense contracting practices vary from all competitive norms. This is clear from R&D contracts, cost overruns, late deliveries, gold-plating, poor to failed weapon performance, canceled contracts, follow-on contract awards, and bailouts.

As discussed earlier, R&D is basic to the origins of all weapons systems. R&D contracts are usually awarded competitively, and rivalry for them can be intense because, with few exceptions, they are followed by production contracts if the project goes forward. Even if an R&D contract does not lead to follow-on awards or if one firm loses out to another, R&D turns out to be profitable. The government, either the DOD or NASA, customarily ends up paying all costs. If an R&D award involves fixed costs, a company can write off any cost overruns as overhead on a production contract, or the procurement agency can simply cover overruns. Moreover, there are few if any guidelines for determining legitimate R&D expenses, and government laboratories have been so diminished in number, size, and function that they no longer serve as effective yardsticks for gauging private efforts. Typically, defense contractors, and particularly those heavily involved in R&D, maintain a full and probably excessive complement of well-paid scientists and engineers who are indirectly compensated by the federal government. Based on informal agreements, the DOD and NASA frequently reimburse corporations for "independent research" that is carried out without authorization and may or may not result in defense or related output. In addition to all the other rich benefits of R&D, contractors gain from increased know-how, patent rights, and laboratory equipment, if not entire laboratories.

Government Accountability Office (GAO) studies have established that R&D expenditures are wide open for abuse and have been misused frequently, if not regularly. Whatever the case, R&D for the DOD and NASA carries no risks for the contractor, contrary to commercial practices.[11]

Cost overruns have become a standard part of DOD contracting. Reliable statistics on the subject are hard to come by. The Pentagon does not track or publicize overruns in any systematic way and often attempts to either hide or underestimate the problem. Various studies set the average overrun between 200 and 300 percent, with some as low as 90 percent and others as high as 600 percent or more. With fixed-price contracts, excess costs should be the contractors' responsibility; with negotiated ones, the government usually pays the bill. More often than not, however, Washington ends up covering all or most of the excess expenses.

The cost overrun phenomenon is partly institutional and involves a practice known as *buying in*: the slow buildup of money and effort committed to a weapons system or some other product until the investment is so high that it practically precludes cancellation. The practice begins with overly optimistic estimates concerning performance, cost, and time on the part of both the originating service or agency and the contractor. The air force and its preferred firm, for example, follow this line to gain approval from the DOD, which in turn gains authorization and funding from Congress. With major weapons systems taking five to ten years to develop and many more years to produce, numerous adjustments and changes take place, inevitably driving up costs at all levels.

A principal reality of cost overruns is that the DOD is not genuinely concerned about costs; performance and development and production time are the military's priorities. Under such circumstances, the defense industry is practically encouraged to increase expenses. The problem is exaggerated manyfold by the gross inefficiency resulting from the huge bureaucracies of both the Pentagon and the giant defense corporations. Also involved are duplicated efforts, DOD's and NASA's protection of contractors, and outright corruption. Pinpointing the exact causes of cost overruns is nearly impossible. In part, the difficulty stems from the fact that the DOD does not maintain, nor does it insist that contractors provide, running accounts of the costs of labor, materials, or overhead. Since the DOD does not have such data in usable form, neither does the executive, Congress, or the public.[12]

Delay in the delivery dates of major weapons systems occurs with the same regularity as cost overruns, and for many of the same reasons. One study puts the average delay at two years. Adding to both time delays and cost overruns is a practice known as *gold-plating*, in which weapons technology is pushed to the point of marginal returns. Such results can originate with the procuring agency, the contractors, or both. The practice increases costs and the time needed to develop and produce armaments, but it often adds little of value or even degrades the end product.[13]

The most serious charge leveled at the defense industry is its frequent production of poor to failed weapons systems. In a study published in 1969, Richard A. Stubbing, a Bureau of the Budget defense analyst, reviewed thirteen major aircraft and missile programs with advanced electronics systems that had started in 1955 and cost approximately $40 billion. Ultimately, two of the programs were canceled because they failed to function, two others were phased out after three years as unreliable, and five others also suffered from reliability problems and poor performance. These nine weapons systems had run up a bill of $25 billion. Another 1969 study by the DOD's Office of Systems Analysis reached similar conclusions about various electrical and electronics systems. The problems identified in the 1950s and 1960s continue today, despite numerous changes and attempts at reform.[14]

Once work on a weapons system is under way and significant amounts of money have been committed to it, cancellations are rare. Too many interests have become involved, and the prestige of both the procurement agency and the contractor is at stake. Nonetheless, failed systems or ones that are unable to achieve performance goals have been terminated. This occurred, for example, with General Dynamics' F-111B navy fighter-bomber (or naval TFX) and Lockheed's Cheyenne helicopter. A project can be canceled because of default on the part of the contractor for failure to perform. In such a case, the company can suffer punishing losses. However, the DOD has the option of ending the project for the "convenience" of the government. If this takes place, the corporation is compensated for costs and prorated profits.[15]

In addition to attempting to minimize losses on the part of its favored giant contractors, the DOD awards contracts with an eye to corporate solvency. In several publications, James R. Kurth has labeled the practice "the follow-on imperative." By tracing DOD contracting for major weapons systems between 1960 and 1990 among the principal aerospace companies, including North American Rockwell, Grumman, and Boeing, he established that no production line of any firm was allowed to remain idle for more than a year. Indeed, the corporation usually received a contract for a system similar to one being completed to minimize the stress of taking on a new product. Although a host of other factors can come into play, the follow-on imperative appears to be the most important; design competition can be of lesser significance.[16]

If a major aerospace corporation faces the threat of bankruptcy or some similar calamity, the DOD, the executive, or Congress has the option of bailing out the firm. Such action is drastic and is taken only as a last resort. More modest bailout strategies, or what the industry calls "get well" measures, have already been mentioned, such as cancellation for government convenience rather than contractor default.

The best example of a bailout involves Lockheed and the C-5A cargo plane.

Moreover, this case illustrates almost all the DOD–defense industry practices discussed above, including cost overruns, delivery delays, poor- or nonperforming weapons, and follow-on contracts. The C-5A was intended to facilitate the rapid deployment of American troops and equipment anywhere in the world. It was designed to carry up to 200,000 pounds of cargo, cruise at 600 miles per hour, and take off and land on short and primitive landing strips. Lockheed won the contract in 1965 over Boeing, contrary to the recommendation of the air force's technical committee, because the latter was already flush with orders while the former was in trouble economically.

From beginning to end, the C-5A took on nightmarish proportions for Lockheed and the air force. Cost overruns began early on, but until late in 1968, the air force and the secretary of defense denied to Congress that anything was amiss. Records were also falsified to protect the company and ensure its ability to sell much-needed bonds to finance operations. By 1971, the price of individual planes had increased to three times the original bid, and delivery dates fell further and further behind. To make matters worse, the aircraft fell far below expected performance. Wing defects limited its carrying capacity to 100,000 pounds, flawed engine mounts precluded flying at maximum speed or using unpaved runways, a defective landing gear prevented the plane from descending in a crosswind, and other malfunctions interfered with the C-5A's operational capabilities.

The record was further tarnished by the fact that the air force whistle-blower on the project was ultimately fired, and the air force ignored recommendations from its own evaluation division to cease production of the aircraft. When congressional committees called on the GAO to investigate the C-5A project, it was stonewalled by both Lockheed and the air force. Congress ultimately stepped in and decided to continue production of the aircraft not based on merit but because Lockheed would otherwise face default or bankruptcy. With billions of dollars already invested in the project and no planes delivered yet, Congress, in the words on one senator, was being blackmailed. How could such a calamity be explained to the public? Matters did not stop there. In 1971 Congress underwrote bank loans to Lockheed, and the DOD implemented additional strategies to keep it working on various contracts and receiving others to ensure its solvency. By 1980, the company was back on its feet financially and had risen from second to first place among the largest defense contractors.[17]

In effect, Lockheed, along with the other major aerospace corporations, constituted what the DOD considered its industrial base. As the C-5A project amply demonstrated, the DOD, backed by other executive departments and Congress, would go to extreme lengths to protect these relatively new, private arsenals.

NASA suffered from most of the same contracting problems and abuses experienced by the DOD. Since many of the aerospace and related companies serving the military also acted for the space agency, the outcome was hardly surprising. The space shuttle, for example, was plagued by cost overruns, delayed deliveries, and performance deficiencies.[18]

The negatives of the DOD and NASA, of course, are matched by striking technological positives. This becomes clear when considering ballistic and guided missiles, aircraft of remarkable speed, electronic equipment and weaponry, nuclear-powered and -armed ships and submarines, reconnaissance satellites, and the Global Positioning System (GPS). The same is true of advances in conventional weapons, NASA's Apollo program, and the numerous other space exploration missions. Aerospace and other defense contractors created monuments as well as ruins.[19]

THE GUNBELT

The postwar defense and space industries have fundamentally altered the nation's regional economic patterns and the nature of the manufacturing sector. The most thorough and innovative studies of these critical developments have been done by Ann Markusen and her associates.[20] Their central point is that aerospace production, which constitutes the greatest and most important part of military procurement, occurs outside of the traditional industrial heartland of the Northeast and the Midwest. While American heavy industry, such as the automobile and steel industries, experienced a severe decline in the 1970s and 1980s, military and space electronics, aircraft, spacecraft, and related output underwent rapid, even stunning, growth, albeit subject to the expectable fluctuations of DOD and NASA budgets.

During World War II and continuing through the Korean War, a high percentage of output for the armed services took place in the existing industrial sector, which either converted to war production or divided its efforts between armaments and civilian markets. Beginning in the 1950s and continuing to the present day, a so-called Gunbelt was created by the DOD's ongoing and massive demand for R&D and high-technology weapons, which led to the birth of the aerospace industry. This Gunbelt runs down the West Coast, includes some of the southerly mountain and plains states, sweeps across the South, and extends up the East Coast. Although many Gunbelt regions are sparsely populated, such as the area around Colorado Springs, Colorado, a number of major urban areas are involved, particularly Los Angeles, Boston, Washington, D.C., Seattle, and San Diego.

A number of factors led to the creation of these new armaments centers. The interwar and World War II location (often relocation) of the aircraft industries in these areas, alongside army, navy, and air force bases, laid a foundation for the military's Cold War demand; so did the weapons and related research occurring during and after the Second World War at universities, corporate laboratories, and nonprofit institutions. The air force led the way in the Gunbelt evolution because it lacked its own arsenals and preferred to deal with private corporate structures; in addition, it favored the West for its bases and operations. Of considerable importance is the fact that, after World War II, heavy industries in the midwestern and north-central parts of the country were thoroughly absorbed in consumer and capital output and responded only tepidly to being tied down by military orders. Furthermore, the manufacturing heartland was imbued with a mass-production ethos under huge oligopolistic firms. New England was the exception. Its traditional textile and shoe and boot industries, which were in serious decline, were characterized by the small-batch, high-craft, precision-machining, and innovative approaches to manufacturing practiced by smaller firms. They could therefore adapt more easily to the high technology of the armed services' requirements.

Whereas the armed services found the traditional industrial centers only mildly interested in government contracts, the communities, cities, and regions that would become the Gunbelt enthusiastically welcomed military procurement riches, and their boosters launched campaigns to win favor with the military. Many of these areas also met the armed services' strategic concerns of minimizing exposure to enemy attacks and protecting large population centers. Also of great significance was the fact that with military cost-plus contracting, industry could bypass the age-old concerns about locating plants according to the availability of raw materials, transportation, labor supply, and capital markets. With the DOD covering all costs, the elements of production could be brought to the preferred geographic location of the military and industry. Corporations such as General Motors and General Electric, which only partially relied on military contracting, remained located in traditional manufacturing regions, although they sometimes created branches in Gunbelt areas.

Markusen concludes that Congress as a whole had little influence in the emergence of the Gunbelt. Individual senators and representatives had a voice, but they often reflected community sentiment rather than molding it; or, usually as members of armed services committees, they acted to protect existing military bases, firms, and contracts. Over time, as the Gunbelt grew, the nation's chief executives increasingly came from Gunbelt areas and influenced the location of new bases, the distribution of contracts, and the like. In actuality, though, more important than civilian political leaders in Gunbelt affairs are military officers, Pentagon officials, and industrialists and their advocates.

A striking aspect of the Gunbelt is that it has led to an unprecedented population migration—one that has generally been financed by the DOD. To an unusual degree, this demographic shift has included scientists, engineers, technicians, and skilled labor. With new population centers emerging in sparsely populated areas and small communities burgeoning in the West and the South, many attributes common to large urban areas had to be built or upgraded. That required, in addition to plants and related facilities, infrastructure, housing, schools, medical facilities, social centers, and entertainment sites. Billions of dollars have been spent to transform the Gunbelt to accommodate the migrating millions.

As new urban or suburban areas sprouted and grew, the old manufacturing heartland experienced just the opposite. Its population declined, its plants emptied and deteriorated, and its infrastructure and community institutions fell into decay. The change constituted a waste of created wealth on an enormous scale. To compound the loss, institutions of higher education in these traditional industrial centers educated and trained much of the scientific, engineering, and technical talent required by the Gunbelt, leading to a brain drain of vast and rich proportions. The Cold War military's demand for weapons helped enrich the Gunbelt while bypassing the Rust Belt.

The Gunbelt has had a number of important, positive effects besides its provision of weapons, space vehicles, and other equipment. It has helped even out income levels and standards of living in the South and West, making them comparable to those in the Midwest and Northeast. Additionally, the DOD and NASA have helped create and nurture new high-tech industries and those supplying them.

Defense companies have also been a rich source of employment. At the height of its activity in 1967, aerospace alone was the nation's leading industrial employer, accounting for nearly 1.5 million workers. In 1980 defense-related employment in general constituted 4.7 percent of the labor force. The numbers grow larger when multiplier effects are considered for localities, states, and regions affected in whole or in part by defense operations. Although there are few service workers involved in defense output, skilled blue-collar personnel can be in high demand, and the market for scientists, engineers, and various technicians is outstanding.

Drawbacks have matched or exceeded gains, however. Some of them have already been mentioned, and others need to be considered. The Gunbelt has made the nation's economy more vulnerable. With military and space production concentrated in selected states and regions, those areas are highly susceptible to reduced defense budgets and changed emphases in military procurement. Relatedly, traditional manufacturing regions cannot depend on noncyclical military and space spending to help balance their cyclical downturns. The Gunbelt, in turn, cannot look to the commercial sectors for balance if it is in decline. Consider, for example, that half of all defense employment is concentrated in ten states. Separating defense and space production from traditional manufacturing areas has made both sectors more subject to downturns, without offsetting, complementary forces. The separation has also exaggerated the problem of converting the Gunbelt should the need arise.

Another consequence of the Gunbelt is that its constituents generally act as a potent, built-in lobby and advocate for existing and growing defense expenditures. As populations have shifted to the South and West, these regions have grown increasingly conservative and hawkish.

Not all defense contracting, of course, takes place in the Gunbelt. Various prime contractors are located outside the area, and subcontracting is somewhat less concentrated in the Gunbelt, but not significantly so. States and regions that hardly register on the defense spending scale nonetheless get some spillover from military procurement through subcontracting and the supplying of parts. Rockwell International, for example, drew up maps in the early 1980s to demonstrate that nearly every congressional district contributed in some way to the B-1 bomber. For the most part, the benefits are rather minimal, however. Most subcontracting remains in the Gunbelt for a number of reasons. First, many of the largest firms serve as prime contractors on some projects and subcontractors or associates on others. Hence, a substantial part of subcontracting remains restricted to the giant defense and space firms. Second, subcontractors do not benefit from prime contractors' latitude with regard to costs, location, overruns, and the like. Efficiency of production dictates that subcontractors remain in close proximity to the principal. So too does the prime contractors' ability to terminate subcontracts practically at will, switch to competitors, or take over production in-house.

TRANSNATIONAL OPERATIONS

Foreign sales are of growing importance to the Gunbelt and to the defense and space industries in general.[21] This trend took on increasing significance in the 1970s, with the nation's gradual withdrawal from Vietnam and the declining defense procurement that accompanied it. Measured in constant dollars, DOD arms purchases fell from $44 billion in 1968 to $17 billion in 1975. At the same time, growing international wealth led to heavy demand for high-tech weaponry in Europe and third-world areas. Responding to a vast new market, aerospace firms began adopting transnational characteristics, along the lines of commercial corporations. Given these developments, U.S. sales of military weaponry and equipment shot up astronomically. The nation's export of arms rose from $1.5 billion in 1970 to $12 billion in 1975. During the latter year, the Pentagon bought only $17 billion in weapons. In critical categories, foreign sales predominated. Such was the case with the U.S. Army Missile Command, which purchased 70 percent of its equipment for overseas markets.

Throughout the 1970s, transnational sales kept many of the largest aerospace companies in business. In 1976 eight of the top twenty-five defense firms depended on foreign sources for 25 percent of their sales; in another five, foreign sources accounted for over 15 percent of sales. Northrop's sales abroad constituted 53 percent of its total. The top twenty-five contractors sold 4 percent of their output overseas in 1970; by 1976, that figure had risen to 20 percent. Additionally, foreign sales bring in 2.5 times the returns of domestic ones because of high markups. A significant portion of the arms sold abroad are produced rent-free in government plants and with the use of DOD-owned equipment.

In the 1980s American firms began to experience growing competition from Europe and even some developing countries, such as China. Ever since then, the international arms trade, and aerospace in general, has faced intense and brutal competition. In the 1970s the United States accounted for 79 percent of world aerospace markets; that number fell to 64 percent in 1980 but was pushed back up to 73 percent in 1985 by Ronald Reagan's massive defense spending, only to drop to 62 percent in 1989.

Quantity is only a part of American transnational sales. Quality has taken on vast and consequential importance. Prior to the 1970s, U.S. arms sales abroad were restricted to older-generation weaponry. In the 1970s and after, as a bipolar world transformed into a multipolar one, the United States could remain competitive only by selling its most advanced high-tech military equipment. Developed countries not only produced weapons for themselves but also competed for foreign markets, and oil- and mineral-rich countries in the developing world insisted on setting the purchase terms. Their demands included the very best and latest weapons the United States had to offer. Various buyers may also insist on coproduction agreements, "offset" terms (under which the United States purchases parts or other products to match sales), sophisticated production equipment, and even entire "turnkey" plants for manufacturing the most advanced armaments, along with engineers, technicians, and instructors to train nationals in the management and operation of the facilities and the use of the weapons. Indeed, some oil-rich countries are purchasing American military goods that are more technically sophisticated than those the United States itself uses or can afford. And production lines that are not fully operative here are going abroad to manufacture the most advanced military hardware. At times, American firms selling or assisting customers abroad end up talking with themselves, since they are dealing with their own subsidiary or a foreign division.

Advocacy for transnational operations, which can be intense, comes from both sides of the military-industrial complex. For some aerospace corporations, such as Northrop and Grumman, foreign sales can be a matter of survival; the top twenty-five defense firms are heavily dependent on overseas transactions. The survival and economic viability of the leading defense contractors are matters of great significance to the DOD. These firms constitute both its industrial base and its surge capability. Consequently, the DOD and its support network inside and outside Washington, D.C., both endorse and frequently lead in transnational operations.

The DOD and its predecessors have always had a role in foreign sales, including licensing or approving such transactions and sometimes either initiating or facilitating the efforts. At some point in the late nineteenth or early twentieth century, as modern technology started to transform the tools of war, governments began supplementing, complementing, and ultimately replacing the often notorious arms merchants of earlier times. That certainly became evident in the interwar years and continued during World War II and after. As foreign sales took on increasing importance in the 1970s, the DOD moved from a relatively passive, moderate stance on multinational arms operations to a very active, even aggressive role.

In 1976 Congress required that all foreign sales be carried out through the DOD. Hence, the department would purchase the weapons, equipment, and manufacturing capacity from defense firms and sell them to foreign buyers. The latter were more than pleased with the practice, since Washington was underwriting transactions, providing assistance where necessary, and continuing to be the responsible party for up to thirty years or the life of the product. In its expanded role, the DOD could seek out potential sales, pave the way for their consummation, and act as facilitator to ensure satisfactory buyer-seller relations.

Washington has consistently tried to persuade NATO to standardize its weaponry and equipment, ostensibly to allow the alliance's armed forces to be serviced more efficiently and to enhance its fighting effectiveness. In reality, it is recognized both here and in Europe that the principal motivation is to increase opportunities to sell American military goods and equipment. Additionally and importantly, government credits and commercial bank and Export-Import Bank loans, along with military assistance in the form of weaponry, enhance various foreign sales. Transnational arms operations inevitably have a dark side that compromises national security at home and abroad and raises serious issues of economic, political, and moral consequence. The United States emerged in the post–World War II years as the world's principal arms merchant, with all the opprobrium associated with that label. These sales have led not only to the proliferation of high-tech weapons throughout the world but also to international and regional arms races, and they have undermined efforts to achieve arms limitation and control. In one way or another, the prevalence of weapons enhances the incidence of conflict and hostilities. The United States has ended up supplying the tools of war to both sides, as occurred with Greece and Turkey, Iran and Iraq, and other parts of the developing world. Helping to arm Peru, for example, leads its neighbors Brazil, Argentina, and Chile to increase their war-making potential. In the last decades of the Cold War, foreign transactions directly or indirectly put our most advanced technology in the hands of the USSR and other communist countries and helped supply guerrilla and terrorist operations. And in Afghanistan, American troops faced enemies armed with U.S. weapons. If those antagonistic to the United States gain information about or even weapons incorporating our latest and most effective technology, they can devise defenses against them, reducing or nullifying their impact.

The sale of arms abroad has helped sustain America's defense industry as well as improve the nation's trade balances. Otherwise, the exchange has few redeeming features and is often morally reprehensible. As discussed later, the international production and trade of armaments are growing, not diminishing, in importance and consequence. These practices threaten the security of both the nation and the world. Any solution to the massive threat must take place on an international level. Whether such an approach is possible remains in doubt.

PROSPECTS FOR DIVERSIFICATION AND CONVERSION

Although the USSR collapsed decades ago, defense budgets remain high or grow, and the hunt is on to justify a large military armed with the most sophisticated and lethal weaponry. Rather than resisting this trend, Congress often increases defense budgets and does not properly monitor the DOD and its spending. Within the Gunbelt, support for arms without end can be expected, but the same holds true elsewhere, though to a lesser degree. Industry, finance, organized labor, and both political parties treat national defense and the DOD's voracious budgetary appetite as either sacrosanct or in their best interests. Communities shudder when military bases of any sort are considered for closure and fight mightily to prevent it. The spillover effect, extending to military budgets in general, appears to take place. The entire situation is exaggerated manyfold by the conservative turn the nation has taken, at least in part under Gunbelt influences, producing more hawkish strength in both houses of Congress and in the presidencies of Ronald Reagan and George W. Bush.

There would be less opposition to reducing defense production within industry, labor, communities, and Congress if the prospects for conversion to commercial output were at least within the realm of the possible.[22] Overall, conversion attempts have been abysmal. During defense build-downs in the 1970s, late 1980s, and earlier, large aerospace companies unsuccessfully attempted to convert to commercial production. In the 1970s, for example, Grumman tried buses, refrigerators, solar energy, and other products but was forced to return to aerospace. Diversification through mergers and acquisitions among some giant companies lowered their dependence on government markets. That took place at an accelerated pace in the mid to late 1980s, with Lockheed reducing its military sales from 62 to 41 percent of total sales and Rockwell International going from 65 to 32 percent. In general, however, the results of this approach have varied from fair to poor. Aerospace's only successful escape from defense has been to shift production capacity to commercial aircraft. Boeing and McDonnell Douglas adopted this strategy in the 1980s, with positive outcomes: Boeing's defense dependence dropped from 41 to 19 percent of total sales, and McDonnell Douglas's went from 79 to 55 percent. But this avenue is open only to those companies with extensive and ongoing experience in commercial aircraft, excluding most of the top aerospace corporations such as Rockwell International and Grumman.

Most of the largest defense companies face enormous odds in diversifying, let alone converting. They are saddled with obsolete and specialized equipment, astronomical overhead costs, and high debt levels. They lack the plant, the cost-efficient operations, and the financing necessary to function in competitive civilian markets. Furthermore, the corporate leadership of aerospace and other companies is largely unfit for today's harsh business climates. They have been coddled and spoiled by practically guaranteed cost-plus contracts, government financing, lax performance standards and schedules, and numerous subsidies and welfare protections. Consequently, most major defense contractors elect to remain under the DOD's and NASA's protective wings. They adopt various approaches just to get by: hunkering down during periods of declining defense budgets and insisting that defense markets will grow again, as they always have in the past; seeking safer defense harbors in military markets or niches with assured minimal and ongoing demand; and searching out foreign sales.

When giant contractors are forced to cut back, subcontractors face even tougher times. During build-downs, prime contractors call in subcontracts or reduce the number of small firms they deal with. The same is true of the government. A few small to medium-sized firms have managed to significantly reduce their defense dependence or have converted to civilian markets, but not many. Success usually occurs when civilian output is close to defense production. For both the giants and the smaller firms, however, the increasingly specialized nature of military demand differentiates it drastically from any commercial applications. Hence, like the major firms, the smaller ones respond to threats by holding on more tightly to military business, even though they have much less room for maneuver than do the huge contractors. Few giant firms actually go under because the DOD usually acts to prevent such a loss. Instead, they may be acquired by other firms. This is not the case with small to medium companies. More than a few have simply closed their doors or been taken over for their land value, storage capacity, or some other nondefense purpose.

Successful conversion or diversification depends on careful planning at the federal, state, regional, and local levels. Committees or commissions are needed to analyze and recommend approaches, financing is required for the high costs involved, and the labor force must be retrained and supported during the transition period. Management, labor, and government at all levels must be involved in the vast, long-range task involved.

In some instances, beginning in the 1970s and continuing to the present day, various community, professional, labor, and peace groups have pooled their efforts to convert plants, big and small, facing severe cutbacks or shutdowns. Some congressional, state, and local legislation has supported these projects. None have succeeded. Generally speaking, management has been opposed or only reluctantly involved, labor is often divided, professional advice is not acted on or is subject to critical delays, and government action varies greatly in its effectiveness.

The root of the problem is that the United States—from the local to the federal level—remains committed, despite all doubts and reservations, to America's weapons culture. If and when that commitment wavers or weakens, the DOD and conservative, hawkish administrations can be relied on to crank up the propaganda machine concerning threats to the nation and the security that arms provide. Few voices of protest will be heard from Congress or from mainstream organizations, media, and opinion makers. Until those harsh realities change, converting or diversifying the defense industry will remain academic, with only token, cosmetic efforts on the periphery.

CONCLUSION

The defense industry is critical to the American economy. While spending for the military grew slowly and steadily beginning late in the nineteenth century, it took on massive proportions during World War II and has remained high ever since. Although the MIC resulting from the Cold War buildup achieved notable technological advances and produced and supplied various weapons and equipment of worth, on balance and over time, it has been more of a negative than a positive force. The MIC has been allowed to go beyond meaningful control and regulation. It has given birth to a Gunbelt populated by new or vastly expanded communities and regions in the West and the South. The residents there are conservative and are fully supportive of defense production without end, since, among other motives, that is what sustains their lifestyle. This Gunbelt favored policies that aggravated Cold War tensions and, after the Soviet Union's demise, has looked to other threats to justify continued high levels of military spending.

The defense industry is both a substantial and powerful enclave within the American economy and an intertwined part of it. It is an enclave in that few other corporations have the protections and guarantees that the DOD, NASA, and, to a lesser degree, the Energy Department provide to their contractors. As more than one author has suggested, this arrangement is not market capitalism; it is a curious mixture of public risk and private gain. Yet these characteristics do not extend outside the enclave; in fact, they do not even include all the participants within it. Subcontractors, parts suppliers, and sources of raw or semifinished materials, which play a considerable role and can encompass whole communities and industries, depend to varying degrees on prime contractors, but they do not enjoy the same security. Universities and other nonprofits benefit from defense R&D, but the money is soft and the competitors for it are many. Within the enclave, the workforce, ranging from highly trained scientists to unskilled workers, has little job security. Their communities have no promise of assistance if contracts end and are not replaced or if they move elsewhere.

Hence, a whole host of industries, businesses, professionals, labor forces, communities, and educational and nonprofit organizations within and outside the defense enclave are dependent on defense output without the fail-safe comforts of the giant corporations that hold most of the contracts and reap most of the gain. Support for ever-greater defense budgets is strongest within the Gunbelt, but since the enclave's reach is wide, its values are reflected throughout a good part of the nation, albeit with differing levels of enthusiasm. As long as that reality persists, the MIC and its consequences will endure.

5
"BIG SCIENCE"

World War II ushered in "big science" on a widespread and massive scale. Examples of such science had existed in universities and industries both within the United States and abroad prior to the 1940s, but only in limited ways. Although various authors emphasize different attributes when defining what constitutes big science—that is, large-scale, industrialized science—most agree on a set of common characteristics.[1] These include research conducted in large laboratories with big, sophisticated, and extraordinarily expensive equipment and instruments and research that is carried out by interdisciplinary teams of theoretical and experimental scientists, engineers, technicians, and other staff who emphasize applied as well as basic science. These attributes first appeared in high-energy physics but then spread to other scientific and engineering fields to become the norm.

Big science requires big money. Unlike in the years preceding World War II, universities and philanthropic organizations could no longer come up with the vast financial amounts involved. During and after hostilities, the federal government, and increasingly the military, became the principal patron of big science. As a number of analysts stress, this type of science is hierarchically, even autocratically, organized and operated, and it abounds with the administrators and committees typical of huge bureaucratic systems. Since World War II, the small-scale, principally individual scientific research typical of the earlier university has been largely eclipsed, but not totally eliminated.

The most dramatic and consequential big-science effort of World War II was the Manhattan Engineering District (better known as the Manhattan Project), engaged in producing the world's first atomic bombs. Initially, the National Defense Research Committee (NDRC)/Office of Scientific Research and Development (OSRD) structure oversaw the project, but then the U.S. Army took control. NDRC/OSRD's principal activity involved awarding and monitoring millions of dollars of federal contracts between 1940 and 1945 to many of the nation's top-ranking universities, institutes, and laboratories for research on, and in some cases the development of, various weapons and related equipment. Numerous contracts financed what became big-science projects and forged increasingly close ties among the academy, industry, federal agencies, and the armed services.

The big science of World War II became the dominant scientific mode in the postwar years. With the OSRD being phased out, the military stepped in with the necessary funding, a trend that grew in importance as the Cold War set in and became global. In time, other federal agencies emerged as significant sources of financing for R&D, including the Atomic Energy Commission (AEC), the National Institutes of Health (NIH), the National Science Foundation (NSF), and NASA. As opposed to pre–World War II practices, R&D was no longer carried out primarily by the armed services' in-house facilities or by other government agencies such as the National Advisory Committee for Aeronautics (NACA), NASA's predecessor. Instead, the bulk of it was contracted out to aerospace, electronic, electrical equipment, and other defense industries; universities; federally funded R&D and production centers run by universities or industries; various nonprofit corporations; privately operated laboratories; and the like. Many of these institutions also engaged in big-science approaches of varying magnitude and duration.

Almost from the outset, the nature and consequences of big science generated extreme tension and controversy within the scientific community, between it and the state, and between it and other institutions and groups. The security issue constantly aggravated relations between the army and the scientists at the Manhattan Project. Using the first atomic bomb against Japan initiated agonizing conflict inside and outside scientific circles over the morality and practicality of employing such heinous weapons. The strife over whether to proceed with the hydrogen bomb grew more intense. Although waxing and waning over time, the debate triggered by big science during and after World War II has never been fully quieted. Besides issues related to the morality and practicality of weapons, numerous other weighty matters are involved: federal funding and state and military control of science, security clearances and restrictions that interfere with open research and the free flow of information, and the emphasis on applied over basic research. Also of concern is how military, AEC, and NASA contracts shape existing scientific and engineering fields and create new ones, and whether a military presence on campus taints and distorts the academy.

THE OFFICE OF SCIENTIFIC RESEARCH
AND DEVELOPMENT

The NDRC and OSRD were central to the emergence and operation of big science during World War II. Four men—three prominent, well-placed scientists and one engineer—took the lead in setting up the NDRC in mid-1940. At the head of the group was Vannevar Bush, an electrical engineer who had risen rapidly at the Massachusetts Institute of Technology (MIT), becoming dean of engineering and then vice president of the institute.[2] In 1939 Bush moved to the capital to serve as president of the Carnegie Institution of Washington, and in 1940 he also became chair of NACA.[3] There, Bush joined forces with colleagues and friends in an effort to prepare American science for war. The most important members of this close, elite circle were Bush's mentor Karl T. Compton, MIT president and physicist; James B. Conant, Harvard University president and chemist; and Frank B. Jewett, president of the National Academy of Sciences and of Bell Telephone Laboratories.[4] Together, the four represented all the so-called estates of science, including universities, technical institutes, the federal government, foundations, and industry. With backgrounds in or extensive contacts with the engineering community, Bush and Jewett brought a practical, applied emphasis to the group.

Bush and his associates fully understood that World War I had made industry and science central to any major war effort.[5] While new federal agencies mobilized corporate America in a reasonably successful way, science did not do as well. The National Academy of Sciences and its subdivision the National Research Council enlisted the support of numerous scientists but did not fully utilize their talent, training, and experience. Many branches of both the army and the navy called on scientists for assistance with weapons, medicine, and other war-related activities. However, most scientists lent their services while they were in uniform and subject to military discipline and hierarchy, a situation that tended to limit their accomplishments and violate their scientific sense. Other civilian and military organizations and a number of cabinet departments, such as the Department of Agriculture, carried out science-related projects, as did temporary wartime agencies such as the Naval Consulting Board. What was missing, however, was any source of centralized direction or coordination to ensure that the scientists' contributions were maximized.[6]

After the armistice, wartime scientific activity fell off, but federal agencies such as the Bureau of Mines and the Bureau of Standards continued to grow and improve. More significant, owing to the stimulus of war, industrial research achieved a major breakthrough. The 300 corporate laboratories that existed in 1920 grew to 1,625 by 1929.[7] Another development of great importance occurred in 1915 when Congress created NACA; its members, drawn from both government and private life, were instrumental in advancing aeronautical interests. Unusual for an independent executive body, NACA was directly funded by Congress, and it contracted with universities and others to carry part of its research burden.[8] In one way or another, NACA was associated with nearly all aeronautical progress made during the interwar years.[9]

Scientific activity within universities, the federal government, and industry on the eve of World War II was much further ahead than it had been before World War I. The various estates also interacted more frequently and more broadly. Nonetheless, as before and during the First World War, centralization and coordination among the parts were still missing. Without some form of overall direction, science's potential would again be thwarted, despite the fact that the wartime need for scientists had reached the critical, even indispensable, stage.[10]

Fretting about such a harsh reality, Bush, Compton, Conant, and Jewett were determined to do something about it. Bush took the lead in creating the NDRC, based on four principal ideas. The committee would function under the president and be properly funded to ensure its independence and its ability to act. It would work closely with the armed services in weapons development, and their representatives would serve on the committee. Nonetheless, the NDRC would remain independent so as to avoid military conservatism, parochialism, and rigidity. Additionally, the committee would direct war research through contracts with universities, institutes, and industry, not in its own laboratories. Finally, the NDRC would act to establish some overall direction for and coordination of war research. In finalizing his plans for the committee, Bush used and adapted the NACA model.[11]

Working through presidential adviser Harry Hopkins, Bush met with Franklin D. Roosevelt early in June 1940 and received approval for the NDRC. Bush took over as chair, and Conant, Compton, and Jewett joined army and navy members and others to fill out the committee's ranks. Although it got off to a fast start, the NDRC was restructured after a year of experience revealed a number of serious flaws. First, committee research on military devices had to be developed to the point of production in order to achieve maximal effect. Second, organizing medical research for war demanded attention. Third, wartime scientific research in general required better and firmer coordination.

The OSRD, created by executive order on June 28, 1941, as a replacement for the NDRC, addressed all these weaknesses. As its name indicated, the OSRD's authority included both research and development. The order also created a Committee on Medical Research operating under the OSRD. Most significant, the executive order specifically charged the office with overseeing the mobilization of wartime science and research. Its ability to do so was enhanced by placing the OSRD in the Executive Office of the President and providing for congressional funding. The NDRC, the Committee on Medical Research, and NACA, along with representatives from the army and navy, constituted an advisory council to Bush, who served as OSRD director and spoke with the authority of the president. Moreover, beginning in 1940 and continuing into 1945, Bush and Conant acted as Roosevelt's de facto scientific advisers.[12]

Once war was declared, the OSRD entered its most active period. Spending for fiscal year 1942 jumped to nearly $40 million from a little over $6 million in 1941; it peaked at around $167.5 million for 1945. Total expenditures of NDRC/OSRD exceeded $536 million in June 1946. The bulk of the money went to the thousands of contracts negotiated with universities, institutes, and industry.[13] The OSRD turned to the armed services for most of its activity but reserved the right to determine what to undertake and how to conduct the research, as well as to initiate projects on its own.[14]

Radar became the OSRD's largest and most significant R&D effort. The project was carried out at MIT's newly created Radiation Laboratory. By war's end, the lab had spread out over the campus and had a staff of nearly 4,000, 1,200 of whom were scientists and technicians. This was big science in all its manifestations. Approaching the Radiation Laboratory in size and importance was Johns Hopkins University's Applied Physics Laboratory, concentrating on the proximity fuse. The California Institute of Technology (Cal Tech) was not far behind in its research on jet engines and rockets. Most other contracts fell in the medium to small category and could frequently be handled at a university or some other facility without the extensive recruitment of additional scientists. By 1944, the OSRD had negotiated contracts with more than 300 university and industrial laboratories.[15]

The Manhattan Project exceeded in cost, size, and importance any other wartime program with which the OSRD was associated. Although the office turned control of the project over to the War Department, top officials remained engaged with atomic policy throughout hostilities and into the postwar years. The NDRC assumed responsibility for the Uranium Committee—created in late 1939 to advise the president on fission explosives—shortly after its organization in mid-1940. Once an atomic bomb appeared feasible and a program had been launched to make such a weapon, the NDRC concluded that the enormity, cost, and complexity of the undertaking far exceeded what the committee could or should manage. By slow stages between June 1942 and the early months of 1943, the atomic bomb undertaking was transferred to the Corps of Engineers. Nonetheless, Bush and Conant served on the Top Policy Group, formally chaired by Roosevelt and charged with overseeing atomic policy. In addition, Bush chaired and Conant was a member of the Military Policy Committee to the Manhattan Project, and Bush was part of the Scientific Advisory Committee to General Leslie R. Groves, who headed the project. Bush also chaired the Joint Committee on New Weapons and Equipment, an advisory group to the Joint Chiefs of Staff, and, along with Conant, remained an informal adviser on science to Roosevelt.[16]

The costs for producing the first atomic bombs between 1940 and the end of 1945 totaled approximately $1.9 billion. Major universities across the nation performed the initial research and experiments. Ultimately, the Manhattan Project included two massive production plants at Oak Ridge, Tennessee, and Hanford, Washington, and a new laboratory at Los Alamos, New Mexico. At the height of activity, around 1,400 scientists and technicians served at Los Alamos.[17]

As the Manhattan Project illustrates, the OSRD was involved in, if not the center of, nearly all technological developments and innovations during the war. Its mobilization of scientists, engineers, and technicians goes far in accounting for the agency's success. But Bush's leadership ability also played a vital role. A strong, adept executive, he selected his divisional chiefs with care and gave them wide latitude and reliable support in carrying out their duties. In overcoming resistance from the territorial armed services, he worked with a sympathetic secretary of war and his lieutenants in moving ahead, and he even managed to gain a measure of cooperation from the tyrannical Admiral Ernest J. King. To deflect challenges and resentment, Bush went out of his way to consult and placate the National Academy of Sciences, the National Research Council, engineering societies, NACA, and other scientific centers that the OSRD inevitably overshadowed or subordinated.[18]

Bush and his OSRD colleagues helped transform how science operated while relying on the status quo. Hence, the director consistently stressed that the NDRC and OSRD were temporary wartime agencies, operating through contracts with existing private and public research facilities. The scientific status quo of the time, similar to the NDRC's founding group, was a quintessential elite. From the outset, Bush and associates recruited from and contracted with what they declared to be the nation's best professionals and institutions without regard to state or geography.[19] Consequently, contracts were concentrated in the Northeast and on the West Coast. The top twenty-five universities and institutes received around $334 million in contracts, with MIT, Cal Tech, Harvard, Columbia University, and the University of California leading the way. OSRD leaders ended up awarding major contracts to their own institutions. By comparison, industrial laboratories and corporations were decidedly second, with the top twenty-five contractors winning awards totaling about $102 million. Western Electric Company, Research Construction Company, General Electric Company, and Radio Corporation of America were at the head of the list.[20] Though operating on a no-profit contractual basis, the OSRD adapted its policy when doing so was essential to win industry support, and the same flexibility extended to policies governing patents. Both universities and private laboratories and corporations were treated generously in terms of overhead costs.[21]

By comparison with most other major mobilization agencies, the OSRD's spending of around half a billion dollars appears modest. Yet the office's impact was enormous. Prior to the war, the federal government's direct support of scientific research had been comparatively rare and slight. Almost overnight, seemingly unlimited amounts of money poured into universities from Washington. Although some centers of learning could incorporate the funds without substantial change, others, such as MIT, joined Los Alamos in a headlong pursuit of big science. The postwar world quickly demonstrated that these radically changed circumstances were permanent, not transitory.

THE NATIONAL SCIENCE FOUNDATION

Bush concluded in 1944 that the OSRD should be terminated as soon as hostilities concluded. He held to this position and ultimately implemented it, despite widespread opposition. Various members of the office itself, universities and laboratories holding contracts, the armed services, and, ultimately, the Truman administration all favored continuing the OSRD into the postwar period. Many of those involved insisted that the federal government needed time to sort out its relations with the scientific community. A practical consensus had emerged around the idea of continued federal support for science, although differences abounded over what the policies should be.

The OSRD began cutting back in 1944 and 1945, was shut down at the war's end, and completed termination procedures in 1947. Bush's motives were varied. Once the emergency had passed, he insisted, scientists, engineers, and other staff members would be anxious to return to their peacetime pursuits as quickly as possible. Furthermore, staff members throughout the OSRD had directly or indirectly awarded contracts to their own institutions, possibly violating federal statutes. Efforts to pass legislation exempting OSRD personnel from these laws had failed, and Bush saw a quick end as the best way to head off any legal challenges.

These were only contributing reasons for Bush's action. By forcing a sudden end to the OSRD, his principal aim was to maximize his opportunity to shape a peacetime federal science agency. He took the first major step in that direction by having Roosevelt sign a letter to the OSRD director in November 1944 that Bush had, in effect, written himself. In it, the president instructed Bush to make recommendations about how scientific operations during the war could be carried over into the postwar years for the benefit of society. Relying on a series of elite committees to do the spadework, Bush and his staff combined and edited their contributions. Bush wrote the introduction to what became his report to the president: *Science—The Endless Frontier,* published in July 1945. In it, the OSRD director proposed a legislatively created National Research Foundation to fund research for the natural sciences, medicine, and national defense. The foundation would also award science scholarships and fellowships, as well as formulate national programs for scientific research and education. In this way, civilian scientists would have a major voice in determining science policy at the national level. An initial proposed budget of $33.5 million would grow to $122.5 million within five years.

Bush's push for a National Research Foundation was in part intended to preempt what he viewed as competing efforts from Senator Harley M. Kilgore (D-WV). Heading the War Mobilization Subcommittee of the Senate Military Affairs Committee, Kilgore had held hearings throughout the war years on more effectively mobilizing science and technology. As the end of hostilities approached, the West Virginia senator redirected his attention to the postwar years and what he eventually called a National Science Foundation. Unlike Bush, who was a conservative Republican, Kilgore was an avid New Dealer who favored a strong, active state. The OSRD head and his associates persuaded Kilgore to accept their position on a number of key issues, but the senator would not change his mind on other significant matters concerning science and the state in the postwar years. That being the case, Bush concluded that he and elite scientists must act on their own.[22]

Bush's leadership on science's future turned out to be as wanting as his wartime record was accomplished. He seemed unable to grasp the elemental fact that the political tactics of war would not work during periods of peace. "Even with both ears to the ground," lamented Secretary of Defense James V. Forrestal, Bush did "not hear the rumble of the distant drum."[23] Scientists, he insisted, had to be treated as if they were just short of royalty. Hence, in the bill that Bush all but wrote, the National Research Foundation would be directed by a governing board chosen by the president; however, the board itself would select the director, who would answer to the board, not to the head of state.

Predictably, Bush's bill led to bitter and ongoing conflict. By rushing to have the proposed legislation introduced in Congress, Bush alienated Kilgore, who believed that he and the OSRD chief had agreed to work out a compromise.

The senator retaliated by introducing a competing bill. Actually, the two bills and their sponsors agreed more than they disagreed on the substantive issues. One major difference and some lesser ones existed in the proposed legislation. Kilgore's only nonnegotiable position was that the director of the National Science Foundation had to be selected by and answerable to the president. Differences over patents, the social sciences, the geographic distribution of research funds, and applied as opposed to basic research could all be finessed. Kilgore's position was strengthened by firm support from the Bureau of the Budget, the Office of War Mobilization and Reconversion, and, most significantly, the president.

Although compromise legislation was worked out in 1946 and passed by the Senate, Bush's forces undermined it in the House of Representatives. Bush continued to demand that the foundation remain beyond presidential control, and he appeared to become more inflexible as he lost favor at the White House. When elite scientists managed to have Bush's bill pushed through Congress in 1947, Truman vetoed it. Finally, Congress passed legislation in 1950 creating the National Science Foundation. The enabling statute created an agency weakened even further from that proposed in the compromise bill of 1946.

Kilgore, Bush, and most interested scientists wanted the NSF to be at the center of federal science policy. With the OSRD serving as a nucleus, that was an achievable goal in 1946. By 1950, however, the NSF was little more than an afterthought. Within four years, mission agencies had emerged as dominant: the AEC, created in 1946; the Public Health Service, greatly strengthened when it acquired contracts of the Committee on Medical Research; the Office of Naval Research, set up by Congress in 1946; and other R&D subdivisions of the navy, army, and air force.

The NSF picked up what others had not claimed, principally competitive awards for pure or basic science. In doing so, the foundation was starved for funds. Its first operating budget for fiscal year 1952 totaled only $3.5 million. Funding remained modest throughout the 1950s; it began to grow at a faster pace after the Russians launched *Sputnik* in 1957 and later when the NSF began expanding its research and educational efforts. Only in 1962 did appropriations exceed the $100 million mark.

A curious set of circumstances led to the Office of Naval Research (ONR) becoming the bridge agency between the OSRD and the NSF from 1945 to 1950.[24] Historically, the navy had been more involved with and open to civilian science and scientists than the army had been. Nevertheless, because of its size, leadership, and bureaucratic quirks, the army, not the navy, took the lead in wartime military science. The OSRD, for example, tapped the army to head what became the Manhattan Project, leaving the navy largely squeezed out.

Seeking to regain ground and strengthen its relations with the scientific community, the secretary of the navy created the Office of the Coordinator of
Research and Development in July 1941 and selected Jerome C. Hunsaker, an
MIT professor, former naval officer, and prominent aeronautics pioneer, to
head it. Hunsaker, who represented the navy in the OSRD, coordinated navy
R&D with that of civilian scientists until he resigned in December 1941 to
devote his full efforts to NACA. In staffing his office, Hunsaker recruited a
young and talented group of reserve officers, many of whom held Ph.D.s in
science.

By late 1943, these troubleshooters, or "bird dogs," had outlined a proposal
for keeping the navy scientifically current after the OSRD closed down at the
war's end. A temporary Office of Research and Inventions, set up at Secretary
of the Navy Forrestal's prompting in May 1945, became the statutory Office
of Naval Research in 1946. At the outset, the ONR faced the obstacle of university scientists who were reluctant to participate in military projects involving red tape, security classifications, publication restrictions, and an emphasis
on applied research. To break down the resistance, the office launched a nationwide campaign to convince scientists and universities that it would provide
generous financial support to all areas of pure science, with a minimum of oversight and accounting. Its efforts paid off. With the creation of a civilian organization stalled by the Bush-Kilgore dispute, the ONR stepped in to replace
OSRD funding as the latter agency wrapped up its affairs. Between 1946 and
1950, the ONR awarded almost $125 million (including transfers from other
agencies, such as the AEC) to hundreds of projects involving thousands of scientists and graduate students.[25] During this period, three out of four federal
dollars for basic research came from the ONR. Once the NSF came into being,
though, the ONR had to restrict future awards to those directly relevant to the
navy.

Military funding of civilian science inevitably generated controversy. Late
in 1944 the War and Navy departments worked out a civilian-military arrangement with the National Academy of Sciences to provide scientists with research
funding under academy auspices while a civilian agency was created to replace
the OSRD. Opposed to federal spending that was outside of Washington's control, Bureau of the Budget director Harold D. Smith turned to both Roosevelt
and Truman to nix the scheme.[26] The National Academy of Sciences' willingness to go along with the armed services' proposal is revealing. Conservative
elite scientists adamantly rejected Kilgore's insistence that the NSF be answerable to the president because, they argued, science would be politicized and its
freedom and integrity compromised. Yet many of those same scientists eagerly
embraced the National Academy of Sciences–military approach, as well as that

of the ONR. (More than most, Bush constantly vacillated over the conundrum of scientific research and civilian versus military control.) Physicists and others welcomed the arrangement, for several reasons. During the defense and war years, various scientists had grown accustomed to and comfortable with joining the armed services' operations away from public scrutiny and, in their minds, political pressure. Additionally, the military, unlike some civilian agencies, was flexible and generous about overhead costs, patent rights, auditing procedures, and the like. Finally, many elite scientists shared the military's politically conservative outlook.

But the physical science community did not speak with one voice. For example, the May-Johnson bill to create what became the AEC was written in the War Department and endorsed by Bush, Conant, and the leading Los Alamos physicists. As a carryover controversy regarding whether and how to use the atomic bomb, the young rank-and-file atomic scientists revolted against their elders, lobbied against May-Johnson, organized the Federation of American Scientists, and published the *Bulletin of the Atomic Scientists*. Among their objections were that the bill put the future of nuclear power in military hands, stressed weaponry instead of peaceful use of the atom, and proposed stultifying and draconian security restrictions on all nuclear research.

Teaming up with like-minded members of the Truman administration, the dissenters helped persuade Congress to adopt the McMahon bill instead, providing for civilian control of atomic energy and other favored provisions.[27] Around the same time, Harvard astronomer Harlow Shapley and others in his circle argued that the navy's financing of research threatened science's independence by influencing either subtly or blatantly what went on in the lab. The ONR itself pointed out that navy dollars invested in civilian research paid big dividends by recruiting preparedness advocates among the nation's leading scientists.

On a more practical level, scientists had learned that the expansion of departments, laboratories, or entire institutions financed by military money carried high risks. Cutbacks in funding for whatever reason created crises that forced the academy to make harsh and unwelcome choices. It had to retrench, find alternative funding, or take up R&D projects for military weapons. Universities had already faced such threats as the OSRD began wrapping up operations as the end of hostilities approached. With a civilian research foundation bogged down in Congress, the ONR became a lifeline. The office committed itself to transferring all strictly pure-science projects to an NSF-type agency upon its creation. That shift never occurred in the face of the Korean War and the escalating Cold War. A good part of academia considered that turn of events a godsend. NSF funding was so meager compared with the military's that many if not most ongoing projects would have faced an early end. Lee A. DuBridge, president of Cal Tech, had frequently fretted about the military's potentially corrosive effects on science and lamented that the NSF could not support large research projects. "The California Institute of Technology," he argued, "would go broke very promptly if all of its basic research support were suddenly transferred to the National Science Foundation."[28]

DuBridge indirectly hit on the critical dilemma facing scientists and universities as they entered the postwar world of big science. Despite all the reservations and anxieties about the armed services financing scientific research, turning the funding down was nearly impossible. America's major universities were intensely competitive. Large science projects allowed them to recruit or retain prestigious faculty, attract graduate students, and generally maintain or improve their standing. If Harvard said no to the army, navy, or air force, Berkeley and other academic rivals would be approached. Before the war, MIT had turned to industry for research support, and at Berkeley, Ernest O. Lawrence used both foundation and state awards to finance his cyclotron and recruit a first-rate nuclear physics staff; others likewise combined the two. But money flowing from the armed services was unlike anything academia had ever seen or imagined. Frederick E. Terman rightly pinpointed federal funding as the key to Stanford University's steeplechase to the top. Open-ended choices existed for less competitive universities and colleges below the first tier.[29]

THE MILITARY AND THE ACADEMY

Controversy aside, military financing of scientific research became a major, and for a time dominant, part of the American academic scene. Money flowing from the armed services to the academy fluctuated over time, depending on budgets, Cold War developments, and other variables. What did not vary was the fact that the federal government, including the military, became the principal source of funding for university research, with the largest portion going to science. Federal research financing came mainly from five centers: DOD, AEC, NSF, NIH, and NASA. A significant amount of AEC and NASA R&D spending, and almost all the federally funded R&D centers administered by universities and colleges, can legitimately be lumped together with the DOD. The McMahon bill notwithstanding, the AEC became heavily influenced by the armed services, focusing primarily on nuclear weaponry and following a military path, even in its limited pursuit of peaceful applications of atomic energy. From the outset, the air force played a major role in the operations of NASA.[30]

Defense budgets for R&D consistently accounted for an exceptionally high percentage of Washington's outlays. In 1952 total federal R&D spending was nearly $1.9 billion; defense accounted for $1.7 billion, or 90 percent of the total. These figures remained fairly stable through the 1960s. By 1970, Washington had increased its R&D expenditures to over $15 billion, with the defense proportion dropping to slightly under 82 percent. Within these larger patterns, however, a shift was starting to take place for federally-supported university research. After the launching of *Sputnik* in 1957, Washington began devoting more nondefense resources to university research and to education in general. Of the total federal spending for these categories in 1958, around 60 percent came from defense sources; in 1964 the defense sector's proportion dropped to approximately 50 percent, with other departments and agencies, including the NSF and NIH, accounting for a larger share. This downward trend continued, bottoming out in around 1968. Thereafter, real federal money going to university research remained on a relative plateau into the 1980s. Nonetheless, defense spending as a part of federal funds for university R&D continued to decline, gradually falling to about 44 percent in 1970 and to just over 30 percent in 1980.[31]

The decline in defense-financed university R&D beginning in the late 1950s led to less applied and programmatic research and more pure research supported by Washington. With the major exception of the ONR between 1945 and 1950, most military-sponsored research was of a practical nature. By comparison, the NSF, NIH, and other federal sources stressed basic research. Several important developments accounted for the change.

After *Sputnik*, a national consensus emerged about the need for more basic research either to catch up with the Soviet Union or to stay ahead of it. As the principal centers for fundamental scientific investigation, universities benefited handsomely from rapidly growing nondefense research budgets. While *Sputnik* pulled nondefense research support up, the Vietnam War pushed universities' defense research budgets down. Students vehemently challenged all aspects of a military presence on campus. Additionally, the general public began to view scientists less as dedicated and detached public servants and more as members of a self-serving interest group, if not partners of an increasingly disdained military. The growing disenchantment with the war led Congress to pass the Mansfield amendment in 1969, which prohibited the armed services from financially supporting research that was not directly linked to the military mission.[32]

Most, but not all, scientists preferred that the academy concentrate on basic rather than applied research. With federal support shifting in that direction between 1958 and 1968, academic science experienced what a historical specialist has labeled a "new golden age." Financial change was matched by institutional change. With science and technology transforming the military and warfare at a rapid rate, the president required access to expert scientific advice and analysis. To meet this need, the Truman administration in April 1951 created the Science Advisory Committee as part of the Office of Defense Mobilization, intended to oversee the economics of the Korean War. For a host of reasons, the most important of which was the committee's distance from the White House, it had little or no impact. Shortly after the launching of *Sputnik*, President Eisenhower appointed MIT president James R. Killian Jr. as special assistant to the president for science and technology. Killian chaired an expanded and elevated Science Advisory Committee that was renamed the President's Science Advisory Committee (PSAC). It was located in the Office of the President, with ready access to the chief executive. Killian, the PSAC—which was staffed with the scientific elite—and related advisory groups made their voices heard.[33]

The president's scientific adviser and the PSAC had their greatest influence under Eisenhower and Kennedy. Killian was replaced by George B. Kistiakowsky (unlike Killian, a scientist) in July 1959, and Jerome B. Wiesner (an electrical engineer) became Kennedy's scientific adviser. At the height of its influence, this "scientific establishment" acted as an effective counterweight to the DOD. It reviewed and could influence major high-technology programs at the Pentagon, it tended to favor nuclear test ban treaties and strove to prevent the arms race from getting out of control, and it challenged the idea that military spending necessarily strengthened the economy.[34]

The PSAC and its chair lost power when scientists began differing with President Johnson over defense policy and the Vietnam War. The process of decline vastly accelerated under President Nixon, and in 1973 he disestablished both the office first held by Killian and the PSAC. As the scientific advisory structure waned, both Johnson and Nixon increasingly turned to Pentagon scientists for expert advice. The golden age of academic science was short-lived both financially and institutionally. In mid-1976 Congress authorized the president to set up a scientific advisory structure in the executive branch. Little more than window dressing, the replacement advisers had none of the prestige or influence of the scientists assisting the Eisenhower and Kennedy administrations.[35]

In the midst of change, there was still continuity. Defense and defense-related R&D funds going to universities and colleges both before and after the golden age of science were concentrated in a few departments and specialties, including aeronautical engineering, electrical engineering, computer science, physics, optics, and some other academic areas aimed at specific military problems.[36] Despite the reduced flow of money from the DOD, AEC, and NASA to universities and its concentration in just a few areas, defense spending continued to have a substantial impact on the operation of the academy as a whole, and it acted to create whole new disciplines.

The golden age of academic science highlighted a truth that the earlier security-clearance case involving J. Robert Oppenheimer had painfully revealed: scientists were not a policy-making group. Individually and collectively, they could wield public power only with the support of the state. If the state withdrew its support from scientists or divided over their advice or advocacy, they could lose power and might even be harshly punished. Once scientists moved out of the academy, their greater visibility and influence were matched by much greater vulnerability.[37]

Scientists and academics in general also learned that associating with and depending on defense structures can affect the operation of universities in fundamental and often unwanted ways. Security classifications, restrictions, and clearances, combined with prescribed research goals and severe limits on the free flow of data and ideas, were blatant examples. More subtle and consequential was the impact of the weapons culture on disciplines, departments, and curricula.

With unprecedented amounts of federal money going to higher education on a regular basis, such an outcome was inevitable. When federally funded R&D centers are included, defense dollars in 1980 conservatively accounted for about one-third of university and college research budgets. Though varying according to circumstances, those figures remained fairly steady throughout the Cold War. They went up to a degree during Reagan's years in office and then began a slow decline that continued to the end of the century. Predictably, according to one scholar writing in 1984, "military-oriented technology has been a major preoccupation of much of the nation's research and development efforts for more than four decades."[38]

Military money on campus has always generated tension and dissent, especially as the consequences of such support spread. Whole disciplines—in some instances entire campuses—have been reshaped. The phenomenon is most evident and significant at the nation's premier research universities and institutes, such as the University of California–Berkeley, Stanford, MIT, and Cal Tech, which received most of the support. Following World War II patterns, funds for defense research were concentrated at the top of the academic hierarchy. In 1980, for example, 56 percent of DOD money for academic R&D went to ten universities, with the sciences, engineering, and related fields receiving the most.[39] Every defense dollar spent at these campuses in Berkeley, Palo Alto, Cambridge, and Pasadena has a much greater effect than if it were invested in lesser institutions. These institutions are where the nation's best and brightest students go for both undergraduate and graduate degrees. Their professors are often leading authorities in various fields who have written books that define or redefine their disciplines and are read nationwide. Such was the case with

MIT's Electrical Engineering Department. Strongly influenced by the work and publications associated with the institute's military-financed Research Laboratory of Electronics, the department restructured its curriculum in the early 1950s, moving away from a commercial emphasis on electric power to stress military-oriented and -applied electronics, communications, and electromagnetic and circuit theory. The department coordinated its efforts with counterparts at Berkeley, Stanford, and Cal Tech and with various practicing electrical engineers. The innovative work of these universities was extended and advanced by their undergraduate and graduate students in industry, the academy, and the military.[40]

What took place in electrical engineering at MIT occurred in numerous other fields in America's leading academic centers. Stanford has received a great deal of scholarly attention and well exemplifies the trend.[41] Frederick F. Terman, professor of electrical engineering and later dean of engineering and then provost, led Stanford's rise from the second tier to the first during the Cold War years. Stanford had benefited only marginally from federal R&D spending during World War II. Terman concluded that money from Washington, combined with that from industry, could speed the university's push to preeminence. Accomplishing that end required a clearly defined and executed plan: first, bypass undergraduate education to concentrate on graduate studies, which determined academic excellence; second, stay with "mainstream theory" and avoid unpopular areas of interest; and third, in the drive for first-tier status, aim for distinction in selected areas of strength, not a futile quest for overall eminence.

Stanford's principal area of strength was electronics, Terman's own specialty. By implementing his approach, the university was at or near the top of the field by the mid-1950s. Military money financed a number of laboratories that Terman brought together in 1955 as the Stanford Electronics Laboratories. Reputation and greater resources from federal contracts supported the hiring of additional top-notch faculty. These developments, and the ability to offer generous financial aid, attracted growing numbers of high-quality graduate students. Interaction with industry also grew. A number of Stanford graduates, such as William Hewlett and David Packard, set up what became high-technology companies in the area. During the Korean War, numerous major electrical firms, including General Electric and Sylvania, established branch facilities on the West Coast to meet the escalating demand for military electronics. Small and large firms crowded into Stanford Industrial Park, which was opened in 1951 on university land. A continuous and circular flow of personnel grew among the university, industry, and the military. Stanford faculty acted as consultants to firms and assisted armed services contractors, Stanford graduates were hired by businesses in the industrial park and in the larger Silicon Valley, industrial researchers stayed abreast of the work being done at Stanford Electronics Laboratories and taught at the university, and industry and the military sent students to campus to acquire degrees and update their knowledge and skills. Many of the same faculty who advised industry also traveled to Washington and elsewhere in advisory or executive positions involving defense.

Similar patterns occurred in other Stanford departments, including aeronautical engineering (later the Department of Aeronautics and Astronautics) and its Center for Space Science and Engineering. The Physics Department, increasingly shaped by the Stanford Linear Accelerator Center, also experienced dramatic change, as did metallurgical engineering, which was restructured as materials science (a new academic discipline all but created by the nation's defense system), with the Center for Materials Research in the forefront. Military money played an even larger role in the rapid ascent of Stanford's aeronautics and materials science departments than it did in the case of electronics.

The effect of defense-related funding was not confined to just the sciences and engineering. New fields such as Soviet studies and communications and established ones such as psychology, political science, and other social sciences also benefited from federal contracts and foundation support, particularly if they adopted a behavioralist or quantifying methodology to make their findings appear more "scientific." Most of the humanities and other disciplines, such as economics and geology, which were opposed to or ineligible for governmental patronage, drew the ire of university administrators. Terman insisted that all departments and their faculty make themselves self-supporting through outside contracts. Failing in that goal meant budgetary pressures, hiring and salary restrictions, increased teaching and administrative loads, and changes in leadership.

Almost from the outset, defense-supported research caused disquiet and concern within the sciences and engineering, which received most of the funding. The money was "soft" and could be cut back or reduced on short notice. On a different plane, military research contracts acted to distort teaching as the primary goal of higher education, undermined the quest to explore the unknown and the partially known by emphasizing applied over basic research, and generally subordinated the academy's independence to narrowly focused outside forces interested primarily in weaponry. In the 1960s Stanford's Physics Department was torn by dissension as "traditionalists" fought to prevent the department from being taken over by those devoted to applied and high-energy physics.

Similar conflicts broke out in other Stanford departments and occurred with some regularity throughout academia. Strife over the consequences of the military presence on campus came to a head in the 1960s and early 1970s as students challenging the Vietnam War turned their attention to what they considered to be the compromising and corrupting of higher education. MIT and Stanford, along with Berkeley, Columbia, Wisconsin, and many others, were swept by protest movements that included faculty as well as students. In the process, various military-financed or -dominated research centers and institutes were forced to sever their academic ties and become independent nonprofit institutions. For a time, defense contracting on campus remained controversial and subject to challenge.

After the tumult of the 1960s and 1970s subsided, the academy was largely unchanged. Attempts to convert higher education–affiliated or –associated institutes, laboratories, and centers created for national security, military, and war purposes to those for civilian and peaceful purposes proved futile. The iron triangle of the military, the defense industry, and higher education had been in the making for more than thirty years and was already too entrenched. Neither the funding nor the will existed in ample amounts to take alternative approaches. During the Reagan administration in the 1980s, defense spending soared again, and so did the military's presence on campus.[42]

CONCLUSION

Big government elevated big science to major status during World War II and the Cold War. Washington's extensive involvement in R&D was a departure in and of itself. The fact that the federal government acted principally through the defense establishment in the form of the DOD, the AEC and its successors, and NASA was even more consequential. This constituted militarizing R&D in the United States to a significant degree. Numerous academics viewed the trend with alarm. Only a few, however, walked away from military dollars; others found a way to go along, despite their qualms. Most never quarreled with the system that helped support their research and allowed them to work in various fields on a level that otherwise would have been out of the question. As junior partners, academics had directly and indirectly become part of America's national security or warfare state.

Cold War universities and institutes were larger, better funded, and more prestigious than in the prewar years. The price of the change was extremely high. The academy had become significantly more beholden to the state; it had lost a large measure of autonomy in the fundamental goals of research, publication, and education.

6
OTHER ESTATES

The entire academic community and related professional societies, along with America's major foundations, also felt the impact of the Cold War and the accompanying warfare state in dramatic and consequential ways. Although different, the transformation in these areas was as fundamental as that in the physical sciences, the military, and the defense industry. The emergence of think tanks, featuring "defense intellectuals," illustrates the point. The RAND Corporation of Santa Monica, California, is among the most prominent and influential of such institutions. Research and advisory groups ranging from those that are very specialized to those focusing on national security in general became so numerous and influential in the Cold War years and beyond that they constitute other estates of government.

Think tank is the popularized term for research or R&D firms, centers, and the like. Although such entities specialize in civilian projects, many of the largest and most important ones concentrate on national defense. Think tanks can cover many facets of defense, focusing on specific areas such as air, ground, or naval warfare or tackling subjects such as weapons, psychological warfare, area studies, or strategic, tactical, or logistical issues. They also take a rich variety of forms. All the armed services have R&D units, exemplified by the army's Institute for Land Combat. Outside of the military, think tanks have proliferated at a remarkable rate since World War II. Most depend on federal contracts and financing from the DOD, the AEC, the Department of Energy, the CIA, and NASA. Foundations sometimes supplement the support from federal departments and agencies. Among the nongovernmental entities are those affiliated with universities, such as Johns Hopkins University's Applied Physics Laboratory, dating from World War II, and the Lincoln Laboratory at MIT, established in 1950 as a follow-on of the wartime Radiation Laboratory. Other think tanks are nonprofit corporations. Some think tanks are Federal Contract Research Centers, financed in whole or primarily by one government sponsor. RAND falls into this category, as does the Charles Stark Draper Laboratory.

Defense industry corporations, of course, engage heavily in R&D, along with universities, government-owned facilities for the armed services, the AEC, and other government agencies. These enterprises, however, are usually devoted to weapons. Furthermore, numerous other government departments and entities conduct, finance, or contract for in-house and outside research activities, and various commercial firms are devoted almost exclusively to a wide variety of nondefense research projects. Although they are all seriously involved in research, these efforts generally fall outside the category of what is analyzed here as post–World War II think tanks.

Defense intellectual is also a trendy postwar label for those specializing in national security, strategic and international studies, and related subjects; these individuals are often current or former members of think tanks or are somehow associated with them. This label was not used for individuals working in universities and industries assisting the war effort through contracts with the armed services, the NDRC/OSRD, or the Manhattan Project. Moreover, weapons development prior to and during World War II, with the exception of the air services, was handled largely within the armed services, as were doctrine and policy for strategy, tactics, and logistics. The closest that civilian advisers to the military came to approximating the role of defense intellectuals was in operations research.

Operations research originated in Great Britain during the late 1930s and was put to use in the United States beginning in 1942. Both countries relied on teams of civilian physical scientists, engineers, mathematicians, statisticians, and economists to utilize with optimal efficiency bombers and fighters; new weapons of war such as radar and rockets, antiaircraft guns, and antisubmarine operations; and so forth. Through the modification of existing tactical operations based on quantitative analysis, dramatic improvements could be achieved. Changing the level at which depth charges detonated, for example, resulted in a much higher U-boat "kill" rate. Americans expanded operations research by adding social and behavioral sciences to the analytical mix when assessing issues such as enemy economic strength, weaknesses, and potential bottlenecks in order to guide strategic bombing goals and similar tactical approaches. The army air forces and, to a lesser degree, the navy readily turned to operations research for assistance, while the army used the system primarily for management tools and scheduling methods.[1]

The RAND Corporation grew directly out of operations research projects designed to optimize the bombing of Japan. As the nation's first national defense think tank, it served as a prototype for similar organizations. Although other nations created research institutes of one sort or another, the post–World War II think tank is American in origin. No nation has ever come close to matching the United States in the quantity and variety of such institutions, which numbered well over a thousand in the 1990s.

The major foundations, including the Ford Foundation, the Rockefeller Foundation, and the Carnegie Corporation, are often involved in financing think tanks. At times, they even do so in clandestine and deceptive ways to facilitate sensitive military and intelligence operations. Universities and scholarly societies and organizations also lend their moral support when think-tank activity becomes controversial and divisive. In general, these trends led to an ominous orthodoxy in various academic disciplines that discouraged, even stifled, debate, questioning, and dissent involving national defense. Hence, to a degree, the social sciences and the humanities experienced the same type of tension and fear afflicting the physics community after the intensely divisive AEC security review of J. Robert Oppenheimer.

Although the research, analysis, findings, and recommendations of think tanks affect public policy to varying degrees, these institutions are only advisory. Civilian and military government officials and agencies are free to accept or reject their handiwork. The same was true, of course, of the General Advisory Committee to the AEC; the Office of Special Assistant to the President for Science and Technology (OST) and its companion body, the PSAC; and numerous other agencies in similar positions. Indeed, beginning during the war and continuing at an accelerated pace after hostilities, all the armed services, other national defense agencies, and many of their principal subdivisions set up scientific advisory committees. Over a thousand such groups exist or have existed. One of the more intriguing advisory committees/think tanks is the superelite Jason, created in 1960 by leading physicists and funded by the Defense Department. The work of think tanks and science advisory committees assists and is supplemented by major national defense review panels operating at the highest levels of the federal executive, such as the H. Rowan Gaither Committee of 1957.

With few exceptions, national defense think tanks, advisory groups, and principal review panels turn out to be conservative in nature. They generally accept and support the policies of their civilian or military sponsors. (When that is not the case, they may come under attack, as took place with the General Advisory Committee to the AEC, or they may disappear from the scene, as did the OST and PSAC.) In that sense, these entities became advocates for the Cold War and the warfare state the conflict fed. Hence, even when the positions of think tanks and advisory committees are not accepted, these bodies strengthen the DOD, CIA, AEC, and related agencies by helping them rationalize their existence, justify their policies, and enhance their legitimacy and prestige.

ANTECEDENTS OF THINK TANKS

Entities approximating think tanks are practically as old as the nation itself.[2] The more relevant antecedents of the post–World War II think tanks, however, began to appear in the early twentieth century to address the complexities of industrialism at home and abroad. Such was the case with the Brookings Institution, created in 1916; the National Bureau of Economic Research, established in 1920; the Carnegie Endowment for International Peace, founded in 1910; and distributing organizations such as the Carnegie Corporation (1911), the Rockefeller Foundation (1913), and the Twentieth Century Fund (1919). The voluntary nature of economic mobilization for World War I and the political economy of the 1920s acted as powerful stimuli for private efforts to inform and shape public policies. The most germane and immediate models for the post–World War II national defense think tanks were the wartime NDRC/OSRD and NACA set up in 1915 and after which the World War II agencies were patterned.

Private think tanks designed to facilitate government functions are a peculiarly American phenomenon. Europe, Japan, and other mature industrial nations relied on public, not private, sources for such ends. Basic national characteristics help explain the difference. The strong strains of antistatism, prevalent even as the federal government expanded in the twentieth century, certainly played a part. Furthermore, in the words of Donald T. Critchlow, "the entrepreneurial origins of American philanthropy," along with tax laws favoring the preservation of large fortunes dedicated to public interests, certainly aided the growth of research institutes and civic-minded foundations.[3] Most important, however, was America's conscious and unconscious decision to reject at both the federal and state levels the creation of large, professional, and elite civil service systems like those of Europe and Japan. This crucial absence, resulting in part from antistatism, provided a grand opening for the industrial-financial elite to fill the vacuum in a way that was protective of its interests. America turned to private sources to provide the knowledge and analysis needed to handle the strains of industrialism and emergencies such as war mobilization. By funding researchers and research organizations, economic movers and shakers tapped the professional expertise essential to do so.

In the pre–World War II twentieth century, practically every new think tank was either founded or financed by—usually both—enlightened corporate capitalists. Consequently, in the years before the war, think tanks operated fundamentally as traditionally conservative institutions.

Most of the important Progressive reforms, such as the Federal Trade Commission, the Federal Reserve System, the Tariff Commission, and rudimentary labor and welfare reform, stemmed from the informed economic elite seeking to rationalize the new industrial state and to quell restlessness among rural and urban populations. In this process, think tanks and their personnel, both directly and indirectly, assumed a critical role. Those functions were vastly broadened and deepened with the curious public-private modes of mobilizing the economy for the two world wars. During the latter conflict, the military emerged as a vital and, in some respects, dominant power center. During the Cold War, that reality logically led to the armed services turning away from government arsenals and shipyards and looking to private munitions firms to meet their increasingly high-technology needs and to politically support their continued growth. Just as logically, the military outsourced to private civilian firms research that embraced nearly all disciplines and included a vast array of subjects, both national and international in nature. What the air force, navy, army, and DOD did, the AEC, CIA, NASA, and other national security agencies emulated. The proliferation of post–World War II think tanks, therefore, differed only in quantity and focus, not in nature or function. They emerged from the nation's past and for reasons uniquely American.[4]

THINK TANKS

The RAND Corporation at the outset was a continuation of wartime operations research.[5] General Henry H. Arnold, commanding general of the army air forces, was determined to continue the air arm's close alliance with the scientific and technological community. The use of civilian talent was essential for maintaining the air forces as the primary military service. Arnold was both a visionary and an advocate of overwhelming brute power and destruction in defeating the enemy.

Late in 1944 Arnold tapped Theodore von Karman, a pioneering aerodynamicist at the California Institute of Technology, to study and report on future technology as it would affect the air forces. At around the same time, Edward L. Bowles, science and technology consultant to the War Department and the army, and the Douglas Aircraft Company, already assisting the air forces' operations research against Japan, combined their efforts in exploring various options for continuing scientific and technological aid to the service after the war. These deliberations ultimately led Douglas Aircraft to create a new and separate department designated Project RAND (an acronym for research and development). RAND officially got under way in March 1946, based on an army air forces contract for a study of air arm weaponry appropriate for intercontinental warfare. The contract was exceptional in its very general, open-ended quality and in allowing RAND maximum latitude to reject proposals, initiate studies, determine methodology and time schedules, and work independently, free of all but nominal oversight. Because of the complications and limitations of being part of an aircraft firm engaged in production for the air force, RAND was reorganized as a totally independent nonprofit corporation in 1948.

At the outset, RAND's research staff consisted principally of physical scientists, engineers, mathematicians, and statisticians who focused on futuristic developments, weapons and their uses, and related projects. Before too long, however, the corporation expanded its divisions to include social scientists, with economists and political scientists being of special importance.

Over time, RAND made substantial technological contributions involving airborne reconnaissance and over-horizon radar, nuclear weapons design, computers, hardened silos for missile defense, new materials such as titanium, and space operations, including power systems, heat-resistant nose cones for returning vehicles, and weather and intelligence satellites. Apart from its work in nuclear strategy, RAND is best know for methodological innovations. These include expanding operations research to the much broader and complex systems analysis, program budgeting, cost-effectiveness analysis, linear programming, and war games. The corporation has also funded extensive area and international studies programs, with particular emphasis on the Soviet Union and China.

RAND's reputation is inextricably tied to thinking about the unthinkable: nuclear and thermonuclear warfare—how to prevent it, how to defend against it, and, if necessary, how to fight it. Despite the corporation's technological origins, the social sciences put RAND on the map. Practically every major concept, theory, or proposal involving nuclear weapons—ranging from Bernard Brodie's theories of deterrence and controlled use at the beginning of the new age to Andrew Marshall's and Fred Ikle's coercive strategy and war-winning goals of the Reagan administration—originated with or was refined, validated, or advocated by the RAND Corporation or those associated with it in one way or another. Although RAND had no strategic party line, several key ideas guided its thinking at the outset. First, preventive war or a first strike was not an option. Second, war was a genuine threat for which the nation must be prepared, and deterrence or a balance of terror could be used to hold off a nuclear conflict. Russia could launch a surprise attack, and many believed that such an aggressive move was imminent. As this conviction became more widespread and strategic analysis evolved, opposition to preventive war weakened and was then dropped at the think tank.

The strategic air bases study by Albert J. Wohlstetter and colleagues, carried out for the air force between mid-1951 and early 1953, is among RAND's most significant contributions. It stressed the need to protect Strategic Air Command bases and planes against a first strike by the USSR. With SAC commanders imbued with the doctrine of an overwhelming and, if necessary, surprise attack, or "Sunday punch," against a strategically inferior Russia and its cities, a defensive posture was not emphasized. With time and persuasion, the air force went along with the Wohlstetter recommendations to the extent of addressing vulnerability. Additionally, the study could be used to justify increased budgets for defense and more aircraft to execute a second strike.

Although the overall effect of the strategic air bases study on the air force is open to question, it had a profound impact outside the service. Through his quantitatively based systems analysis, Wohlstetter succeeded in placing "calculated vulnerability" at the center of strategic analysis. What may have been a valid concern at first was eventually transformed "into an infatuation, then an obsession and finally a fetish of sorts."[6]

If the author of the study had been the only victim of this idée fixe, the outcome would have been unfortunate but inconsequential. But it went much further. The concept became received and revered doctrine at RAND, among strategic theorists, and in the policy-making corridors of Washington. For many, no single weapon, no number of weapons, no defensive or offensive strategy would ever be enough to overcome calculated vulnerability. Such was the case regardless of current nuclear policy, be it deterrence, city destruction, counterforce, superiority, sufficiency, mutually assured destruction, or some variation, combination, or new dimension. Numbers could always be used in a way that made America's survival seem to be at risk. A nuclear and thermonuclear arms race without end was the present and the future. Any attempts to limit or control nuclear weapons, their delivery systems, or defenses against them were approached with great caution and were usually opposed because the Soviet Union constituted an ongoing threat and could not be trusted to honor agreements.

RAND took great pride in its commitment to thoroughly rational, objective, hardheaded analysis. Yet the strategic air bases study, which Wohlstetter and associates updated later in the 1950s to account for intercontinental ballistic missiles (ICBMs), relied on air force programs, estimates, and data. Still, influenced to a significant degree by Wohlstetter's work, the Gaither Committee report of November 1957 predicted that the Soviet Union could unleash a devastating ICBM strike on the United States within a few years. Both the Wohlstetter and the Gaither findings rested on a weak statistical foundation. Since the mid-1950s, the CIA and the other armed services had engaged in a spirited debate over what they considered to be the air force's high and exaggerated estimates of the USSR's intercontinental bomber fleet and its ICBM holdings. Russia's *Sputnik* launches beginning in October 1957 intensified the intelligence dispute.

After considerable confusion and discord, the conflicting parties appeared to set the Soviets' ICBM count at somewhere between 50 and 200. By late 1960 the intense and consequential battle was authoritatively settled by satellite surveillance, following earlier U-2 intelligence. The USSR had a total of only four ICBMs, all closely bunched together in the open, unprepared to launch, and easily knocked out by conventional explosives. The purported "missile gap," like the "bomber gap" preceding it, was not even close to the truth. The adversary was still far behind, not far ahead of, the United States.

According to Daniel Ellsberg, who was a RAND strategist before joining the DOD under Secretary Robert S. McNamara, RAND never accepted the revelation of Russia's missile inferiority or the fact that the air force's fundamentally flawed statistics had deceived the think tank. He and others in the Kennedy defense structure concluded that their work at RAND had gone beyond the unrealistic and into the realm of fantasy. In analyzing the thoughts of Herman Kahn, another RAND theorist, and particularly his 1960 volume *On Thermonuclear War*, Fred Kaplan points out: "Kahn was more extreme in his tone and views than many of his RAND colleagues. But he was only pushing the strategic postulates, the analytic techniques, the underlying world view of RAND conventional wisdom to their logical limits. He was the ultimate creature and creation of the rational life at RAND, the desperate, at times fervid effort to find, as Kahn phrased it, 'more reasonable forms of using violence.'"[7]

If Kahn cast RAND strategic thought in its harshest light, Vietnam made a mockery of the corporation's claim to objectivity. RAND members directly participated in various intelligence operations, such as interrogating prisoners, defectors, and others; assessing cultures, attitudes, and responses of the North and South Vietnamese and related peoples; and conducting studies for and making recommendations to the military. Both in Vietnam and in the United States, RAND specialists devised and propagated rationales for past, present, and future tactics and strategies. Indeed, McNamara's policy of rational, graduated escalation to end the war through negotiations on American terms was based directly on the concepts of RAND theorists. Toward the end, even some at the think tank grew silent or turned against the conflict. But others, like Kahn, remained steadfast. Whatever the stance, the Vietnam War revealed that those at RAND were not the detached, value-free analysts they purported to be; they were cold warriors, hawks, and, in some cases, active participants. In that respect, the war discredited both the theorists and their theories.

These realities before and after the Vietnam War encouraged some members to leave the corporation. Nonetheless, few doubted RAND's ability to attract personnel. For those who wanted an academic environment without the burdens of teaching and committee work, RAND was very attractive: the colleagues were first rate, latitude was wide, salaries and benefits were excellent, research topics could be stimulating, and assistance and equipment for carrying them out were beyond compare. The promise of power and influence was the principal lure for many. Their contributions could end up in the offices of the president, the secretaries of defense or state, or the heads of the armed services; they could have a meaningful role in shaping national or international policies; and they could rub shoulders with the high and the mighty. If warfare and topics related to it were appealing, RAND was hard to beat. It always had many more high-grade applicants than it could accommodate.

In time, RAND broadened its research base as air force funding was cut back or failed to grow sufficiently. Maintaining adequate income required the corporation to begin diversifying in 1959. Ultimately, it did substantial work for the Office of the Secretary of Defense, other air force units outside of Project RAND, the AEC, NASA, the NSF, the NIH, and other government agencies. By the early 1960s, Project RAND still accounted for 68 percent of RAND's budget, but that was a drop from 95 percent prior to diversification.

RAND's diversification became more dramatic and consequential in the late 1960s as the think tank took on increasing amounts of civilian research. By 1970, Project RAND had fallen to 50 percent of the corporation's funding, while civilian projects had grown to 35 percent. This transition was essential for survival. The heady days of defense and space innovation supported by expanding military budgets were over, along with the glittering reign of strategic theorists. Defense projects tended more toward the mundane and workaday. Moreover, the armed services were performing more of their own research, and numerous think tanks now competed for outsourced projects. Meanwhile, neglected civilian problems grew in urgency, demanding attention. RAND's roster came to include health, medicine, and medical care; urban decay and the general crisis facing cities and states; education; crime; the environment; and, ultimately, at the beginning of the new century, projects abroad, especially in the Middle East. The list was nearly endless. Unlike defense contracts, however, the projects tended to be small and often underfunded. The scramble for funds was time-consuming and continuous. Still, whereas RAND was once a prime example of distorted national priorities, with public resources flowing lavishly to the military while the civil sector languished, the corporation in the late 1960s began efforts to balance the scales in its own functions.

RAND played a critical role in setting up several other think tanks. It did so to protect its long-term research mission. Growing out of air force projects, the corporation established a System Development Division in the early 1950s, devoted to carrying out systems projects for the air force, training the service's personnel, and handling rush requests. By the mid-1950s, the division had twice as many employees as the remainder of RAND, threatening the Santa Monica institution's nature. Corporate leaders worked out a solution whereby the division was spun off as a separate nonprofit at the end of 1957, the System Development Corporation (SDC). RAND provided leadership and guidance, but by early 1961, SDC had severed practically all ties, and the new think tank stood alone.

In 1964 SDC ended its affiliation with the air force owing to congressional pressure and the desire to compete for other contracts. In 1969 it converted from a nonprofit to a profit-making corporation. Over time, SDC became one of the leading international software and systems companies, stressing computer programming, automation, and new technology. Highly profitable, the firm established numerous offices of varying sizes in the United States and abroad. SDC also achieved a record of solid, reliable performance, avoiding the cost overruns and product deficiencies of other defense contractors. By 1970, 80 percent of its contracts were with the military, ranging from the top to the bottom of the DOD's and the armed services' structures. Like RAND, SDC diversified by expanding into the civilian realm, including the areas of health, water and air pollution, law enforcement, transportation, education, and other fields; in 1970 this accounted for the other 20 percent of its work.[8]

RAND's role in founding Analytical Services Incorporated (ANSER) differed from its role in SDC. In 1951 the air force created the position of director of development planning to evaluate weapons, plan R&D, and perform related functions. The director's office never worked well, regardless of whether research was performed in-house or contracted out. The air force leaned on RAND to take over the operation, but again, the corporation feared distorting its mission. Instead, RAND prevailed on the air force to allow it to set up and virtually run ANSER as an independent nonprofit in 1958. By January 1961 the new think tank was on its own, with only a couple of RAND executives on the board of directors. Unlike SDC, ANSER stayed true to its origins. It remained a comparatively small nonprofit working only for the air force on the development of advanced weapons systems, recommendations on force size, weapons retirement, space, new materials, and various "rush" assignments. Nearly all of ANSER's output is shrouded in secrecy, and the firm maintains a very low profile.[9]

Although neither a spin-off nor a ward of RAND, the Hudson Institute owed its inspiration to the Santa Monica think tank.[10] Herman Kahn and Max

Singer created the small research firm in 1961, shortly after Kahn left RAND. The iconoclastic, irreverent Kahn dominated the institute through the strength of his quirky personality. At the outset, 80 percent of Hudson's income came from the military, but by 1970, that had been reduced to 50 percent. In 1968 the think tank was removed from the list of Federal Contract Research Centers because of its eccentric behavior. Nonetheless, Hudson was still welcome in DOD circles, and Kahn even had a temporary office in the Pentagon for a time in 1970. Although Hudson performed projects related to Vietnam and ABMs for the armed forces, it preferred subjects such as nuclear warfare and weapons of the future. In the civilian area, it has undertaken a drug abuse study for the State of New York, other research work for the City of New York, and development projects in Latin America and Africa. But again, huge amorphous subjects are what stirs the think tank's blood. The Hudson Institute remains, like Kahn himself, an enigma. Is its output to be taken seriously or dismissed as an outrageous, ingenious put-on?

The Research Analysis Corporation (RAC) of McLean, Virginia, is the army's most important think tank and the one closest to RAND in nature.[11] Established in 1961, RAC actually began in 1948 as the Operations Research Office at Johns Hopkins University. The office performed hundreds of projects for the army, such as those involving the service's use of tactical nuclear weapons and psychological warfare programs, and it created a number of operations research groups within the army. In 1961 the army severed ties with the university over policy differences with the office's director and reorganized it as the independent RAC. Although somewhat smaller than RAND, RAC also carries out projects on weapons systems, technology, tactics and strategy, management techniques, and political studies, and it claims to be the very best at war-gaming and military modeling. RAC is diversifying into civilian areas, but it is not as far along in that regard as its Santa Monica counterpart.

The Institute for Defense Analyses (IDA), a nonprofit located close to the Pentagon, ranks at the very top of military think tanks.[12] Its studies and recommendations are intended for the principal policy makers and strategists, particularly the secretary of defense and the Joint Chiefs of Staff. Most of its work is secret, and the rest is at least restricted. IDA was created in 1956 to help settle conflict among the three services over the assignment of new weapons systems. Since then, it gradually expanded to include most of the critical issues facing the DOD and the Pentagon. Initially sponsored by a consortium of twelve universities (including MIT, Cal Tech, University of California–Berkeley, Columbia, and Princeton), IDA had to sever those ties in 1968 because of student protests. Nonetheless, researchers and university officials continue to serve on the IDA board of trustees as individuals rather than institutional representatives. Hence, among defense-oriented think tanks, IDA still has the most prestigious academic affiliations.

IDA's work covers weapons evaluation, tactics and strategy, counterinsurgency, and international and economic studies, among others. The institute also handles rush, emergency projects on battlefield weapons and matters of national security. Negative findings on vital issues such as the ABM are carefully guarded from public view. IDA also performs some analyses for various civilian agencies, along the lines of improving U.S. Postal Service efficiency and the Justice Department's crime-fighting efforts.

IDA's relations with Congress are rocky at best. Under claims of security, the nation's legislators have been denied access to reports on critical issues such as Vietnam. Reviewing IDA's operations in 1966, the House Armed Services Committee revealed the institute's freewheeling ways. The think tank spent as it chose, purchased equipment without proper approval, stashed away profits, kept an independent fund at public expense for research unauthorized by Congress, and provided exorbitant salaries and benefits to its staff. These disclosures led to some reforms, but they appear to have been superficial in nature. No follow-up investigations have taken place, and IDA continues to function in the protective shadows of secrecy.

Jason is the most intriguing entity included in IDA's structure. After *Sputnik*, a number of elite academic physicists explored how they could assist national defense. Various endeavors along these lines led to the formal creation in January 1960 of Jason, a name from Greek mythology. Of the hundred or so members over the years, almost half have been elected to the National Academy of Sciences, at least eleven hold Nobel Prizes, and all are or were members of the nation's top university or institute science departments or were trained there. The group prides itself on including only the very best. Some of its early members included Val Fitch, Murray Gell-Mann, Marvin Goldberger, Charles Townes, and Kenneth Watson.

The Jason group roughly followed the pattern of so-called summer studies that began in 1948 and continued into the 1960s. The armed services contracted with groups of academics in the Cambridge, Massachusetts, area—eventually broadened to include those from industry and the government—to study and advise on problems and issues during the summer months, when most faculty were free. For example, Projects Charles and Harlwell, both begun in 1950, focused on continental air defense for the air force and antisubmarine warfare for the navy. Once Jason was under way, thirty to sixty physicists would meet during the summer, preceded by short meetings in the spring and others in fall and winter, to focus on some of the principal national defense issues facing the nation. Topics included ABM defense, nuclear test detection, Southeast Asian insurgency, use of tactical nuclear weapons in Vietnam, what became McNamara's proposed barrier between North and South Vietnam, the MX basing system, the Strategic Defense Initiative, biological warfare defense, post–Cold War nuclear weapons reduction and stockpiling, and the urban battlefield. Summer meetings originally alternated annually between the East and West coasts, but beginning in the mid-1980s, they were held regularly at La Jolla, California.

Jason was financed by the Advanced Research Projects Agency (ARPA)—later renamed the Defense Advanced Research Projects Agency (DARPA)—set up in the Office of the Secretary of Defense during 1958 to pursue innovative research outside the range of the three services. The group was placed under the jurisdiction of IDA, but, other than administrative functions, it is unclear how much authority IDA or ARPA exercised over Jason, since the organization insists on maximum independence in all its operations. Nonetheless, Jason members in key positions provided close and protective ties between that group and ARPA and IDA.

The first half of the 1960s constituted Jason's golden years. Thereafter, the Vietnam War created tension and division within the organization. In 1971 the Pentagon Papers revealed the existence of the group, and other publications named some of its members—up until then, a secret. (A full roster of Jason membership remains unavailable to this day.) The proud, often arrogant Jasons became targets of attack and derision among their antiwar colleagues and the student protest movement, particularly at Berkeley and Columbia. Additionally, in the late 1960s and into the 1970s, ARPA/DARPA moved Jason from the jurisdiction of IDA to the Stanford Research Institute as part of an effort to persuade the group to broaden the range of its members and change its mode of operations. In that way, it could handle subjects involving computers, semiconductors, and such. In time, Jason did diversify its membership to include mathematicians, chemists, electrical engineers, computer scientists, biologists, oceanographers, and astronomers. It also contracted with other agencies to lessen DARPA's hold, although the latter remained its principal source of income. Its new sponsors included the navy (the largest), the CIA, NASA, the NSF, and what became the Department of Energy. Around the same time, Jason also began doing work in some civilian areas, such as climate studies, adaptive optics, and human DNA.

Although Jason marked its forty-fifth year in 2005, the future of the group appears uncertain. It prefers to work in the defense area, but competition from in-house and outside research facilities is great, and the same is true in nondefense fields. Additionally, Jason's prestige and influence have declined substantially; its analyses no longer go to the top levels of government. This decline has occurred within the general context of Washington turning its back on independent-minded scientists. Furthermore, in half a century, Jason and the academic community have changed dramatically, breaking down the cohesion that encouraged a sense of community and esprit. If the group survives, it will be different from that put together in 1960.

The Aerospace Corporation of El Segundo, California, is the largest defense think tank, contracting principally with the air force.[13] It is a systems management and engineering firm involved with major weapons and space projects. Over the years, Aerospace has developed, overseen, and acted to improve missiles, missile boosters, spacecraft and booster reliability programs, and communication satellites.

Almost from the outset, Aerospace has been the subject of controversy, if not scandal. It is a spin-off of the Ramo-Wooldridge Corporation, which, when organized in 1953, consisted of just a few people. In 1954 the air force awarded Ramo-Wooldridge a contract under which it became the acting systems engineering and technical director of the Atlas, Titan, and Thor missile projects. Within months, Ramo-Wooldridge expanded massively and, in a 1958 merger, became TRW. With that development, Simon Ramo and Dean Wooldridge parlayed their investments of less than $7,000 into more than $3 million apiece. The two went on to become powerful multimillionaires as TRW became a leading corporation at home and abroad. For a time, the firm was among the top fifty government contractors. TRW's astronomical expansion was made possible by political favoritism and government contracting largesse.

Aerospace was set up in 1960 as a nonprofit to quiet growing private and public protest over the air force's compromised relations with TRW. The new corporation took over a TRW subsidiary's responsibilities in the missile field. An investigation in 1959 by the House Government Operations Committee had laid bare the special treatment, conflict of interest, and abuse of government contracting and taxing practices that led to TRW's spectacular profits and growth. These revelations resulted in the creation of Aerospace, but it continued to be mired in questionable activities. Hearings in 1965 by the Subcommittee for Special Investigations of the House Armed Services Committee established widespread corporate violations and air force neglect. The corporation purchased real estate without air force approval, violated its contract by withholding for unspecified purposes $15.5 million paid for research, and refused to account to the air force for fee expenditures. Aerospace also ignored contract provisions by spending millions on advertisement and promotion. Furthermore, the firm was lax in security matters and paid its executives and employees exceptionally high salaries and provided equally lavish perquisites. For its part, the air force spent generously, even recklessly, on Aerospace and appeared to avoid policing it or moving to address the corporation's numerous abuses. As a result of congressional censure and legislation, some reforms resulted, but their overall effect was slight.

The MITRE Corporation is another large think tank that gets most of its business from the military, particularly the air force. Created in 1958 by MIT to take over projects too large or not suited for an educational institution, MITRE eventually severed all ties with the institute. It was reorganized as a private corporation with numerous offices in the United States and some abroad that specialized in developing systems for communications, communication satellites, air defense, and radar detection. The corporation also oversaw the creation of the AWACS. By 1970, 20 percent of MITRE's contracts were with civilian contractors, and it sought to expand along these lines. The corporation pursues high-technology solutions to pressing problems in the areas of education, health, transportation, law enforcement, and the like.[14]

The Human Resources Research Office (HUMRRO) is different from most other think tanks, in that it is staffed principally with psychologists. It is among the largest behavioral science groups of its type. Originally organized in 1951 by the army at George Washington University, the service cut HUMRRO's university ties in 1969 because of student protests, moved the think tank to Alexandria, Virginia, and reorganized it as a nonprofit corporation. HUMRRO works in the field of "psychotechnology" or, more explicitly, human engineering. It studies how best to condition troops for nuclear warfare and to withstand stress. The think tank also emphasizes the soldier's role as part of a weapons system, not just as a member of an amorphous group. Additionally, HUMRRO prepares manuals, texts, lesson plans, and electronic devices to make training more efficient and effective.[15]

The Logistics Management Institute, by comparison, is much smaller and more limited in its reach. Created in 1961 by the DOD and with the approval of Secretary McNamara, the institute advises the secretary of defense on procurement, storage, and maintenance. It covers a broad field, ranging from the simplest cookware to the most sophisticated accounting methods, to ensure that the department is getting the most for its massive expenditures.[16]

The Navy Department relies on fewer outside think tanks than does the air force or even the army. That stems in part from the navy's numerous in-house research facilities. Nonetheless, the service does use the private sector. Its most important outside research source is the Center for Naval Analysis, which acts for the navy in a similar fashion as RAND does for the air force and RAC for the army.

There are a host of large and important think tanks, along with many more mid- to small-sized ones. Among the biggest of these is MIT's Lincoln Laboratory. In addition, there are a number of basically commercial research firms that do defense work, including the Stanford Research Institute.

ACADEMIC PROGRAMS FOR STRATEGIC
AND DEFENSE STUDIES

Defense think tanks have both benefited from and contributed to the academy. The benefits have come principally from the numerous faculty who joined these research groups, either temporarily or permanently, providing them with expertise as well as prestige and credibility. For their part, think tanks played an important role in introducing and helping to create programs for strategic and defense studies at a number of universities. Prior to World War II, the systematic analysis of strategy, tactics, and logistics, to the degree that it occurred, was performed within the armed services and by various academics, journalists, and freelance writers focusing on military history. The overwhelming impact of World War II and the Cold War, including their global reach, ideological intensity, technological sophistication, and nuclear weaponry, created the urgent need to study national security policies and practices.

The RAND Corporation played a significant role in both developing and propagating defense studies. In the 1950s and 1960s the corporation funded Defense Policy Seminars at leading universities and institutes such as Columbia, Princeton, the University of Chicago, and MIT. It also set up graduate fellowship programs related to defense in the physical sciences, economics, international studies, and similar fields for students at Berkeley, Harvard, Yale, and other institutions of higher learning. Graduate study could be followed by work at RAND. Such was the case with Daniel Ellsberg, first at Harvard and then in Santa Monica.[17]

In time, many top-level universities established their own programs, centers, and institutes devoted to national defense or subjects relevant to it.[18] Yale was out front in this regard. The university had created the Institute for International Studies in 1935; recruited a quality faculty, ultimately led by Frederick S. Dunn; and, as World War II drew to a close, began attracting a number of young scholars with strategic interests, such as Bernard Brodie, William T. R. Fox, and William W. Kaufmann. Institute members increasingly sought to shape national defense policy through publications and government appointments—preferably both. Their ambitions were frustrated by A. Whitney Griswold, Yale's new president, who took office in 1950. As an academic conservative, he insisted that the institute turn away from activism in favor of traditional scholarly, historically based goals. Refusing to follow Griswold's dictates, most institute members bolted from New Haven in 1951 for a warm reception at Princeton, Yale's Ivy League competitor.

To accommodate the fresh arrivals, Princeton turned its back on Wilsonian idealism and the quest for peace through international law by establishing its new Center for International Studies, where the muscular realism of strategic studies reigned. Moreover, the center forged close ties with RAND, and a number of faculty members joined the Santa Monica think tank or acted as consultants for it. Indeed, according to Bruce Kuklick, "The university assisted in making RAND-style security studies respectable in the more traditional academic world."[19]

The University of Chicago experienced some of the same turmoil that stirred Yale and Princeton. Quincy Wright of the Department of International Relations, famed for his epochal study of war, had trained in the interwar years a generation of scholars who later became prominent in strategic studies, including Brodie and Fox. During and immediately after World War II, Wright, though hardly an idealistic dreamer, looked to the United Nations to resolve the growing tensions between East and West. This view played a role in thwarting his attempts from 1945 to 1951 to set up an Institute on World Affairs (or some such title). Instead, university president Robert Hutchins gave Hans Morgenthau, the hardheaded realist, the green light to create the Center for the Study of American Foreign Policy in 1950.

Johns Hopkins University also faced conflict. Its long-established but modest Walter Hines Page School of International Relations was threatened early in 1950 when its director, Owen Lattimore (who advised Washington on Asian policy and criticized its approach to China), came under attack by Senator Joseph R. McCarthy (R-WI). In 1952 the Carnegie Corporation cut off funding for the strapped research facility. The university responded by granting Lattimore a leave to handle the charges leveled against him, and in 1953 it closed the school.

The Page School was, in effect, replaced by the already existing School of Advanced International Studies (SAIS), founded in 1943 in Washington, D.C., by Paul H. Nitze and Christian Herter. Anchored by a board of trustees consisting of leading diplomats and corporate executives, SAIS devoted itself to furthering foreign investments and improving understanding between business and government. Although it granted degrees, the school's academic credentials were thin at best. In 1950, under a three-way agreement among Johns Hopkins, SAIS, and the Carnegie Corporation, the school become part of the university, with a broadened scholarly and research base in addition to substantial financing by Carnegie. Decades passed before SAIS gained any genuine academic heft. Nonetheless, it won respect in the nation's capital for its powerful political and economic connections and as a way station for those taking up government service. That was the case with Nitze himself, who in the 1950s took a leading role in shaping the reorganized school.

Columbia University proceeded along lines similar to its Ivy League counterparts. Toward the end of World War II, it began breathing new life into the somnolent School of International Affairs. When Dwight D. Eisenhower became president of the university in 1948, he accelerated the process and took initial steps toward creating the Institute of War and Peace Studies. He wanted the institute to concentrate on how best to meet the demands of national defense while still ensuring the basic health of the economy. When Eisenhower temporarily left Columbia for NATO, Grayson Kirk took charge of shaping the institute, loaded its board of trustees with diplomats and businessmen, and set it on a course of tying scholarly efforts to the practical world of policy formulation. The addition of academics such as William T. R. Fox, who deserted Yale for Columbia in 1951 and served as director of the institute, emphasized the new strategic realism. Among other things, Fox headed the Social Science Research Council's Committee on National Security Research and ultimately recruited a network of like-minded faculty.

Most of the academic institutes, schools, and centers were inspired by the Cold War, in that they focused on a world rent by East-West strife and did so from a realistic perspective. The growing conflict was central to Washington and, increasingly, the nation. That being the case, ample funding for international and area studies was readily available from the government, foundations, and other sources. By supporting faculty research and publications; interacting with RAND, the Social Science Research Council, and other such organizations; providing academic homes for those moving in and out of government; and training students in crucial subjects, the various institutes played an important part in formulating and executing America's Cold War policies. Throughout the 1950s a high percentage of declared federal funding for the social sciences involved national security. Undeclared financing channeled through foundations and like institutions reinforced the pattern.

The closest link between the Cold War and the behavioral sciences and the humanities involved area studies. In a meaningful sense, these studies were extensions of the World War II operations of the Office of Strategic Services (OSS), the CIA's predecessor. Shortly after the conclusion of hostilities, William J. Donovan, wartime OSS director, and John Paton Davies and George F. Kennan, both from the State Department, originated foreign area studies. Although a principal goal of such programs was to enhance intelligence, the originators concluded that the government's role had to be concealed for the purpose of claiming objectivity and detachment. Hence, funding for the projects came principally from the major foundations, particularly the Ford Foundation, the Carnegie Corporation, the Rockefeller Foundation, and, to a lesser degree, the Russell Sage Foundation. Ford played the largest role. Early in 1951 the Ford Foundation created a behavioral science program based on the advocacy of the State Department, the armed services, and the CIA and as an outgrowth of Project Troy (described later). H. Rowan Gaither, the foundation's president, headed the effort, assisted by members of RAND and the military's Research and Development Board. During World War II, Gaither had been the business manager of MIT's Radiation Laboratory. In 1947–1948 he had provided the legal know-how for separating RAND from Douglas Aircraft Corporation and reorganizing it as a nonprofit. Thereafter, he served as the think tank's chairman of the board of trustees until his death in 1961. Between 1953 and 1966 the Ford Foundation made grants of $270 million to thirty-four universities for area and language studies.[20]

Columbia and Harvard founded the first area study programs. In setting up and directing these centers, professors and administrators worked closely not only with intelligence agencies but also with the State Department and leading foundations. Most directors of and participants in area study groups had backgrounds in the OSS or other intelligence agencies and military or related service. They helped forge close ties among universities, foundations, and the state. Many executives and members of these area study programs were leading figures in their respective behavioral sciences and humanities disciplines. As a result, faculty at Columbia, Harvard, and other universities exercised exceptional power and influence over the creation, operation, and direction of area studies.[21]

At Columbia, Philip Mosely, professor of political science, was the mover and shaker.[22] In 1946 the OSS transferred its Soviet Division to Columbia, and it became the foundation for the university's Russian Research Institute, which Mosely directed. From the late 1940s until his retirement in the early 1970s, Mosely was perpetually involved with secret and classified government agencies and projects; he headed the Council on Foreign Relations between 1952 and 1956, was a high-profile leader of the American Political Science Association, and was especially active in the functions of the Ford Foundation. All evidence points to the fact that the Russian Research Institute emerged virtually as an extension or appendage of the CIA and other intelligence units.

Mosely's involvement with the Ford Foundation and the Social Science Research Council is of particular importance. Mosely played a leading role in setting up the Ford Foundation's area study programs in the early 1950s and remained involved in foundation affairs into the 1960s. Periodic meetings were held to work out procedures for area studies. Participants included representatives from the CIA, the State Department, and the Social Science Research Council. Prominent scholars in various specialties, such as Russia and the Slavic regions, Asia, and the Near East, also joined the meetings. Available records indicate that the CIA was authorized to reject research proposals and those carrying them out. Individuals of questionable ideology, including supporters of Henry A. Wallace's Progressive Party, were generally considered out of bounds. Even liberal academics such as Arthur M. Schlesinger Jr. were viewed suspiciously by some. Most likely, undeclared CIA background checks were done on administrators, authors, and others participating in Ford Foundation projects.

From the foundation's "country studies," according to Bruce Cumings, came "some of the most important works later published in the field of comparative politics."[23] These include Lucian Pye's analyses of Malaya and Burma, Dankwart Rustow and Robert Ward on Japan and Turkey, Richard Pipes on the "Moslems" of Soviet Central Asia, and later work on China.

Harvard followed, and perhaps exceeded, the Columbia pattern.[24] The university organized its Russian Research Center in 1947 at the urging of the Carnegie Corporation, which was responding to recommendations from the army. The latter wanted a Russian studies program modeled after that of the OSS. In both setting up and administering the center, Carnegie and Harvard worked closely with the CIA, the Federal Bureau of Investigation (FBI), the armed services, and the State Department. The foundation provided initial funding for the Russian Research Center, and when the center worked out to its satisfaction, Carnegie followed up with a five-year grant program. Government agencies had a major voice in the center's operations, had access to its work, and exerted some direct and indirect control over faculty and personnel. With the support and cooperation of university president James B. Conant and, apparently, provost Paul H. Buck, the FBI kept a close eye on the center, investigated its participants, and benefited from various voluntary and planted informers, including faculty members Henry Kissinger and William Y. Elliott. Anthropologist Clyde K. M. Kluckhohn directed the Russian Research Center from the outset. Sociologist Talcott Parsons was also a founding member. Kluckhohn had served in the OSS during the war, and he and Parsons were familiar with intelligence-related scholarship. They, along with colleagues in their respective fields, prominent political scientists, psychologists, and other social or behavioral scientists, constituted a cohesive group of academics who had a great deal of power in shaping decisions within their profession. They could influence, if not determine, who was hired, retained, and promoted; what was published; and who received grants. With such clout, they were able to mold the area studies movement in the nation along the lines first laid down by Columbia and Harvard and later expanded among a host of universities to include Asian, Middle Eastern, African, and Latin American studies.

International studies developed simultaneously and side by side with area studies. As indicated earlier, some existing international institutes took on new life after World War II and refocused their efforts and approaches to address American Cold War needs. New research centers also came into being, and MIT's Center for International Studies (CENIS) was one of the most important ones. CENIS grew directly out of Project Troy. The latter was an extended study carried out at MIT in 1950–1951 by leading academics from MIT, Harvard, and other universities and various specialists. It concentrated on the means and methods for disseminating Western "truth" or propaganda behind the Iron Curtain. Financed by the Office of Naval Research and staffed by those acceptable to both the military and the CIA, Project Troy officially reported to the State Department. In actuality, Troy went beyond its charges to address the larger issues of combating the Cold War on the nonmilitary front and determining how academics—scientists, social scientists, and historians—could contribute to that goal through ongoing cooperation with foreign policy and intelligence bureaucracies.[25]

CENIS was founded in 1952 under the directorship of Max F. Millikan, son of physicist and Nobel laureate Robert A. Millikan.[26] An economist, Max Millikan served as chief of European economic intelligence in the State Department shortly after World War II. He then became assistant director of the CIA in 1951, and from 1952 until his death in 1969, he directed CENIS. At the outset, the center was all but an extension of the CIA, which, along with foundations, financed its operations, had a voice in hiring, and assigned it projects. In effect, through CENIS, the CIA had access to prominent and accomplished social scientists who did not want to work directly for the agency. At the end of the 1950s, members of CENIS, along with MIT and government sources, considered making the National Security Council CENIS's sponsor to avoid the embarrassment of CIA exposure and to improve the opportunities for foundation financing.

CENIS was characterized by interdisciplinary study and analysis among economists, political scientists, sociologists, anthropologists, psychologists, and communications specialists. Although it proposed and advocated theory, the center stressed pragmatic research aimed at national policy problems and policies. CENIS initially concentrated on Russia and China. Among its central interests, however, was providing guidelines for "developing" or "modernizing" the turbulent underdeveloped world along moderate, Western, capitalist lines. To do so, insurgency in general, and communist-inspired rebellion in particular, had to be defeated, most likely by coercive means involving the military as the most modernized of underdeveloped countries' institutions.

CENIS scholars indicated that the United States might have to take an active part in restoring stability and instilling the "right" values required for development. This would provide the mass respect for authority essential for modernization. These ideas were set forth and examined in the influential publications of Lucian Pye, Walt W. Rostow, and others at CENIS, including Ithiel de Sola Pool, Max Millikan, and Daniel Lerner. The application of such policies was demonstrated vigorously and ruthlessly in Indonesia from 1957 to 1965, ultimately resulting in the overthrow of President Sukarno in favor of the regime of General Suharto. Along similar lines, the CIA's Phoenix program in Vietnam, in which operatives killed 20,000 to 40,000 (depending on the source) national rebels in an attempt to end the insurgency, was largely based on sociological and communications theories worked out at CENIS. Rostow, first as deputy special national security adviser in the Kennedy administration, later as chair of the State Department's Policy Planning Staff, and finally as Lyndon B. Johnson's national security adviser, had the unequaled opportunity to apply his ideas on a grand and extended scale in Vietnam. Despite the disaster those ideas helped produce, one of the brightest stars of CENIS never backed away from them.

As a think tank, CENIS had no monopoly on counterinsurgency theory. In the early 1960s, Project Camelot, which highlighted counterrevolutionary strategies pursued by behavioral scientists, resulted in a major scandal.[27] The project was undertaken by the Special Operations Research Organization (SORO), casually affiliated with American University. In 1963 the army contracted with SORO to devise a social science model for predicting and controlling revolution in the developing world. Camelot focused on Latin America and was to be carried out by an interdisciplinary research team that included cultural anthropologists and sociologists, but with a strong psychologist contingent. Prominent behavioral scientists acted as advisers for the project, and it had the support of the National Academy of Sciences. While attempting to use deception to enlist the support and assistance of Chilean scholars, an inept Camelot consultant ended up revealing the true nature of the project. Vociferous protests in Chile, throughout Latin America, and in the larger world community, combined with embarrassment and dissent at home, led the secretary of defense to cancel Project Camelot and implement reforms intended to prevent another such diplomatic and academic blunder.

Despite the uproar Camelot caused, SORO and other think tanks continued to pursue the applied research in Latin America in general (specifically, in Brazil and Peru) and in Vietnam. After the protests subsided, SORO changed its name to the Center for Research in Social Sciences (CRESS) and ultimately ended its tenuous affiliation with American University. In 1968 CRESS published a three-volume study that constituted a storehouse of information on fifty-seven twentieth-century insurgencies that could be utilized for the more effective planning of counterinsurgency campaigns. Forty-five experts from fourteen universities contributed to this massive work.

Ironically, Camelot's most lethal legacy may have affected Chile. CIA involvement in the 1973 coup against President Salvador Allende's government by the military regime of General Augusto Pinochet appears to have stemmed at least in part from conclusions reached by Abt Associates of Cambridge, Massachusetts. Charles Abt had acted as a consultant for Camelot. In 1965 the DOD's Advanced Research Projects Agency contracted with Apt to, in effect, computerize the goals of predicting and controlling "internal wars"—similar to what Camelot had attempted to do in a less technological way. In applying the computerized game to Chile, the program concluded that the elected president could be assassinated without destabilizing the country. Whether Abt's work influenced the Nixon administration in any way cannot be documented.

Significantly, Camelot did not discredit or besmirch in any meaningful way the behavioral sciences. After an investigation and hearings, Congress concluded that the means and ends of Camelot were both necessary and laudable, but they should have been carried out by the Department of State, not the Department of Defense. Most behavioral and social science organizations, such as the American Psychological Association, also supported their disciplines' work with the state on national security and Cold War conflict. Indeed, those participating in SORO- or CRESS-type projects insisted that their objectivity and neutrality were in no way compromised or distorted, even when contracting with the armed services in what could only be described as highly politicized and ideologically loaded projects. Instead, many behavioral and social scientists and their organizations looked on such policy-oriented work as validation that they had achieved analytical and predictive tools that were as accurate and useful as those of meteorologists. No matter where they stood, however, social scientists overwhelmingly favored the flow of money from the federal government to support their work.

Beginning with Camelot and growing as the decade wore on, some social scientists, particularly cultural anthropologists, became increasingly disturbed about the ethics of contractual study for the state and especially for the military. Could bias be screened out when subsequent contracts depended, implicitly if not explicitly, on findings and recommendations that were satisfactory to the contractor? By even agreeing to work on such projects, was not scholarly neutrality being surrendered or compromised? What took place during the Cold War was, in many ways, a continuation of psychological warfare during the "Good War," when the ends seemed to morally justify the means. Margaret Mead wondered whether World War II had seduced many scholars and, in the process, eroded trust, ethics, and standards. Could social scientists continue to devote their expertise to a state that assassinated elected leaders and overthrew elected governments in behalf of authoritarian and dictatorial regimes? Or one that waged war in Vietnam? Noam Chomsky ultimately concluded that scholars of the Camelot mode had become a repressive "secular priesthood" intended "to ensure that the people's voice speaks the right words," contrary to Pool's praise for them as "mandarins of the future."[28]

Counterinsurgency studies such as Camelot proliferated from 1961 on, after the Kennedy administration took office. Rejecting the Eisenhower administration's strategy of massive retaliation in favor of one stressing flexible response, the new administration began building up conventional forces and creating special units to deal with guerrilla and irregular warfare in Latin America, Asia, Africa, and the Middle East. Success depended on basic knowledge about these peoples, cultures, and societies in the developing world, which led to a reliance on the knowledge and methods of the behavioral sciences and especially psychology, cultural anthropology, and sociology.

Since the Kennedy administration drew so heavily on academics and lacked confidence in the Pentagon's ability to respond creatively to threats posed by insurgency in the developing world, McNamara's office turned to universities and nonprofit think tanks for guidance. With funds readily available, numerous campuses and new or existing think tanks welcomed the opportunity to take up the cause of counterinsurgency.[29]

In one way or another, practically every major university and numerous lesser ones, working alone or in conjunction with think tanks or industry, joined the effort. This has already been made clear in the cases of MIT, Princeton, IDA, and George Washington University. A few other universities fill out the picture even more. The University of Michigan became extensively involved in America's counterrevolutionary activities aimed at the underdeveloped world.[30] Michigan was among the twelve universities that collectively sponsored, organized, and oversaw IDA. University professors, acting for the Agency for International Development (AID), led in the organization of the Academic Advisory Committee on Thailand in 1966, following their preliminary assessments of guerrilla operations in that country. The committee was later centered at the University of California–Los Angeles. It was supposed to coordinate and centralize the gathering of information on Thailand from universities, foundations, and other sources that could assist the development and counterinsurgency efforts of AID and the U.S. Operations Mission in Thailand.

A furor arose in 1970 when it was learned that the Academic Advisory Committee on Thailand had been organizing conferences and panels aimed at assisting antiguerrilla efforts without informing participants of that fact and even disguising its own identity in these activities. According to Michael Klare, the committee was only one of many groups tapping unsuspecting scholars for research and publications desired by the Pentagon. "Members of these committees," Klare states, "—most of whom can boast flawless university accreditation—can be found at every academic meeting and symposium, collecting intelligence on the scholarly output of their colleagues."[31]

Beginning in 1962 and continuing until student protests in the late 1960s and early 1970s led to change, Michigan's Institute of Science and Technology was actively engaged in devising military counterinsurgency measures. Working either alone or in collaboration with Cornell University's Aeronautical Laboratory and the Atlantic Research Corporation, the institute researched, developed, and perfected infrared surveillance systems for detecting guerrillas in Thailand and counterinfiltration technology for Vietnam. Under Project Agile, Michigan tested its infrared aerial technology in 1966 and trained Royal Thai soldiers in its use both in Ann Arbor and in Bangkok.

By comparison, Michigan turned its back on efforts to reduce Cold War animosities. In the mid-1950s members of the Michigan faculty, including political scientist Harold Lasswell, psychologist Herbert Kelman, economist Kenneth Boulding, and mathematician Anatol Rapport, founded the *Journal of Conflict Resolution*, aimed at taking an interdisciplinary approach to the avoidance of war. Associating peace studies with leftist politics, the Michigan Political Science Department refused to sponsor the journal. When some of the same faculty joined others in establishing the Center for Research on Conflict Resolution later in the 1950s, they again ran into hostility. In time, the whole effort collapsed. Unable to secure adequate funding, the center closed its doors in 1971, and the journal moved to Yale to emphasize a quantitative approach to international affairs.

Michigan State also became deeply involved in Southeast Asian counterrevolutionary efforts.[32] In 1955 the university received a contract from AID's predecessor to assist in reforming the Ngo Dinh Diem regime's police and palace guard. To carry out the mission, Michigan State organized a thirty-three-member advisory division of the Michigan State University Group (MSUG). Over four years, the group made good progress in overhauling Diem's decaying systems. In 1957 MSUG helped institute a National Identity Registration

Program involving photographs, fingerprints, and biographical data centrally cataloged and filed for all inhabitants of South Vietnam older than fifteen. Those without such papers were designated Vietcong and treated accordingly. In actuality, though, MSUG served as a cover for CIA operatives in Vietnam. A similar situation took place in Laos in the late 1960s and early 1970s, but with AID as the front group. Nonetheless, MSUG was not solely a front. Later in the 1960s, for example, Professor Leslie Fishel, who headed MSUG for a time, carried out extensive research financed by AID on South Vietnamese elites, with the intent of identifying those compatible with the West.

Few academic institutions remained aloof from active Cold War participation. That was the case, for example, with Paul F. Lazarsfeld's widely respected Bureau of Applied Social Research at Columbia, founded in 1940. After World War II, over 75 percent of the bureau's financing came from the government. In 1949–1950 its finances were so shaky and its debt so high that its future appeared uncertain. Government work rescued the bureau. It contracted to do projects on subjects such as the social as opposed to the physical effects of nuclear attack, the management of tactical nuclear war, psychological warfare in the Middle East and the USSR, and LSD as a tool of interrogation and recruitment of political defectors. The Bureau of Applied Social Research also joined CENIS in 1958 to cosponsor the publication of a critically influential volume on development theory and the Middle East that reflected U.S. and British propaganda and official lines rather than detached and knowledgeable scholarship.[33]

Hadley Cantril's Institute for International Social Research at Princeton also relied on government money for more than 75 percent of its budgets after World War II. Indeed, Christopher Simpson points out that "at least six of the most important U.S. centers of postwar communication research [including Lazarsfeld's and Cantril's operations] grew up as de facto adjuncts of government psychological warfare programs." The State Department, for example, secretly and illegally contracted with the National Opinion Research Center for polling to assist it in lobbying Congress on behalf of Cold War policies. "In another case," Simpson states, "the CIA clandestinely underwrote American University's Bureau of Social Science Research studies of torture—there is no other word for it—of prisoners of war." He concludes, "In sum, it is unlikely that mass communication research could have emerged in anything like its present form without constant transfusions of money for the leading lights in the field from U.S. military, intelligence, and propaganda agencies."[34]

Many prominent participants in the postwar fields of public relations, mass communication, and the social sciences, along with foundation executives, constituted a band of brothers and sisters. They had served together in various army psychological warfare units, the OSS, the Office of War Information, and a number of other domestically focused communications groups. After hostilities, these veterans acted as a network of interlocking groups informally organized according to their specialties or fields of interest. Network members could rely on one another to open doors in business, government, and academia for career opportunities and advancement.

By participating in post–World War II defense think tanks, academic centers, and other programs, many wartime activists became cold warriors, ranging from extreme hawks to low-key pragmatists. During the 1930s and throughout World War II, most of them appeared to be liberals. Although some seemed comfortable with the proposed or executed violence of Cold War struggles, others insisted that their endeavors in the sociology of knowledge, national character, and intelligence findings offered nonviolent alternatives to achieve desired goals in the developed and underdeveloped worlds. Such claims involved more than a modest measure of illusion. Their studies and findings in most cases were not detached assessments; rather, they were consciously or unconsciously designed to please the sponsoring agency, which, to varying degrees and differing levels, was devoted to employing violence. Nonetheless, the participants could be fairly certain that their research results would go unchallenged, especially throughout the enforced conformity, rampant suspicions, and witch hunts of the 1950s and into the 1960s. Dissenters faced professional ostracism at best, harassment from the FBI and CIA at the worst. Some academic participants, as was the case with Daniel Lerner, insisted that qualified scholars and experts were patriotically obliged to assist in furthering the state's national security.

Not all institutes and centers dealing with national security became involved in counterinsurgency in the mode of RAND and the Michigan universities. Nonetheless, they could still have a Cold War orientation. Such was the case with Harvard's Kennedy School of Government, established in stages beginning in 1964 in honor of the fallen president. Although the school quickly emerged as the premier center for the study of American foreign policy and implementation, it was not a place of great objectivity and detachment. A principal goal was analyzing and enlightening Washington decision making, and many faculty members were Washington insiders who had RAND affiliations and had served in the Kennedy and Johnson administrations.[35]

DEFENSE REVIEW PANELS

Over time, the contributions of the various institutes, centers, and schools of warfare and foreign policy were supplemented by the findings of review panels, blue-ribbon commissions, and other like bodies. Such committees were large in number and ranged from the very specific to the exceptionally general. A brief look at four of them well illustrates their nature: the Air Policy (Finletter) Commission (1947–1948); the Technological Capabilities (Killian) Panel (1954–1955); the Security Resources Panel (Gaither Committee) of the Science Advisory Committee of the Office of Defense Mobilization (1957); and the Foster Panel (1972–1974). All but the first were composed of either familiar names or those from established private or public Cold War institutions.

In 1947–1948 the nation was still in the process of demobilizing from World War II. The Defense Department had just been established, and the numerous strategy and foreign policy centers and think tanks were just getting under way. Truman appointed the blue-ribbon commission chaired by Thomas K. Finletter during the summer of 1947 to advise him on the role of civilian and military aviation in national defense. Finletter had served as special assistant to the secretary of state during World War II and as a consultant on the United Nations. Other members included George P. Baker, a Harvard economist who had served on the Civil Aeronautics Board from 1940 to 1942; Palmer Hoot, publisher of the *Denver Post*; John A. McCone, an engineer and business executive; and Arthur D. Whiteside, chairman of Dun and Bradstreet and a member of the War Production Board.

Extensive hearings held during the year convinced the commission that airpower constituted the nation's first line of defense, particularly now that atomic weaponry was involved. But the commission found itself in the middle of a raw and brutal struggle between the air force and the navy over the virtues of land-based bombers versus seagoing aircraft carriers. In a report presented to the president late in December 1947 and made available to the public in January 1948, Finletter and his group argued that the airpower of both services was essential. Nonetheless, they favored the air force over the navy, recommending that it be built up to a minimum strength of seventy groups.[36]

By the time of the Killian Panel, dramatic changes had taken place. The Cold War had become intense, the Korean War had been fought, both the United States and the USSR were armed with nuclear and thermonuclear weapons, and defense budgets had more than tripled in less than four years. Hence, unlike the Finletter Commission, the Killian Panel was made up of those knowledgeable about or specializing in military matters, not respected civilian leaders lacking backgrounds in defense and warfare.

James R. Killian Jr. was president of MIT. He selected as his deputy director James B. Fisk, deputy director of the Bell Telephone Laboratories. Other members of the panel's steering committee included Marshall G. Holloway, Los Alamos Scientific Laboratory; Leland J. Haworth, Brookhaven National

Laboratory; Edwin H. Land, Polaroid Corporation; Lee A. DuBridge, Cal Tech; James H. Doolittle, Shell Oil Company; and James B. Baxter III, Williams College. Robert C. Sprague, Sprague Electric Company, acted as special consultant, and high-ranking officers from the army, navy, and air force served as a military advisory committee. Around forty scientists and engineers constituted the professional staff.

The Killian Panel was charged with addressing the nation's vulnerability to surprise attack. In doing so, it was to review, analyze, and report on continental defense, striking power, and intelligence, as well as provide supporting studies of communications and technical manpower. After five months of work, it reported to the president in February 1955. In a calm, balanced way, the Killian Panel favored all possible technological advances in intelligence to discern Soviet progress and intentions and to provide advance warning of an attack. It also supported strengthened communications systems that would make the Strategic Air Command less vulnerable and thus improve America's retaliatory powers. The panel stressed the need for crash programs to make intercontinental and intermediate-range missiles operational. Killian and his associates additionally recommended taking whatever steps necessary to introduce or improve technology and weaponry that would enhance national security.[37]

Despite the fact that the Killian Panel's report had a significant impact and accelerated the nation's defensive and offensive military preparations in nearly all areas, another ambitious preparedness review took place less than three years later with the so-called Gaither Committee. Actually, the committee's initial charge was rather modest. It was to evaluate a proposal for providing blast and fallout shelters over an eight-year period at a cost of over $32 billion. Based on outside advice and on its own initiative, the committee elected to expand its scope to cover the nation's offensive and defensive ability to cope with nuclear or thermonuclear war.

H. Rowan Gaither chaired the 1957 committee, with Robert C. Sprague as his deputy and James B. Baxter III, former deputy defense secretary William C. Foster, Jerome B. Wiesner of MIT, and others specializing in civil defense, economics, and science serving as committee members. Edward P. Oliver, a RAND engineer, was chosen as technical adviser. An illustrious advisory group of past public officials, military officers, and business leaders added to the committee's aura. The day-to-day work was carried out by a research staff of seventy-one scientists, economists, weapons experts, and former and current public officials. RAND's influence on the committee was great, since Gaither sought the think tank's advice on how to proceed, and more than a few of the committee's members, consultants, advisers, and staff came from or were associated with the Santa Monica organization.

When Gaither was hospitalized with cancer shortly after deliberations began during the summer of 1957, Sprague and Foster took over as cochairs. By October, the committee had largely concluded its review when the entire nation was startled by the Russians' launching of *Sputnik*. That event and its military implications generated an intense sense of urgency in the committee. Committee members were convinced that the Eisenhower administration had to be pushed, even bludgeoned, into acting with vigor and haste to enhance national security.

The Gaither Committee's findings and recommendations were based on various staff reports that Sprague and Baxter summarized. Baxter did most of the writing, but he brought in staff member Paul H. Nitze to assist in the final draft. Characteristically, the latter had bulled his way into becoming a de facto member of the committee. As already demonstrated by NSC-68, Nitze had the ability to succinctly and harshly convert concern into abject fear, even despair. The former State Department official used those skills to make the Gaither Committee's report energetic and compelling; nuance and qualification gave way to certainty and stark declaration.

The Gaither Committee presented its findings and recommendations to the president early in November 1957. Stressing the increasing economic and military might of the USSR and its growing threat to the United States, including the possibility of a devastating surprise strike, the Gaither Committee recommended steps to keep SAC on ready alert to guard against a sneak attack, a speedup in making intercontinental and intermediate-range missiles available and multiplying manyfold the number deployed, and increasing the nation's ability to fight limited wars. The committee also warned that Russia was probably ahead of America in missile development and that catching up, staying even, or surpassing the enemy would not be easy. Less urgently, the committee supported a national fallout shelter program. Altogether, Gaither and his colleagues favored increasing defense expenditures by over $44 billion in a five-year period, with more than $19 billion for strategic and conventional military purposes and somewhat more than $25 billion for civil defense.

What did not appear in the Gaither Committee report by either statement or implication was what Sprague had learned on his own about SAC and its apparent vulnerability to a Soviet attack. The SAC commander, General Curtis E. LeMay, had never appeared fazed by Wohlstetter's, RAND's, and numerous other private and public sources' worry that SAC could be knocked out with relative ease under the right circumstances. When pressed, LeMay explained why. America's U-2 spy plane flights, originating in 1956, kept Washington informed of significant Russian military moves. Should the USSR begin amassing its bombers for a major attack, SAC would launch a devastating air strike on the enemy's forces. In doing so, LeMay declared, SAC would disregard official war plans authored by the Joint Chiefs of Staff and approved by the president.[38]

The Foster Panel, appointed late in 1971, was to recommend whether McNamara's strategic doctrine of mutually assured destruction should be replaced with a counterforce strategy—a flexible nuclear war–fighting doctrine initially targeting the enemy's military capabilities. Counterforce was a doctrine that had originated with RAND and had been popular in the 1950s and 1960s; it was first adopted and then rejected by McNamara. With weapons and related technology constantly improving, particularly the introduction of multiple independently targeted reentry vehicles (MIRVs), nuclear engagements short of full-scale atomic warfare once again appeared feasible. Nonetheless, the reintroduction of counterforce generated controversy that needed to be addressed and resolved—hence the new panel.

Unlike study groups of the past, this one was largely composed of those within the DOD. John S. Foster Jr., a nuclear scientist, directed Defense Research and Engineering. Air force General Jasper Welch served as executive secretary. The head of the Systems Analysis Office and two of his principal assistants, along with a member of the State Department's Policy Planning Staff, were the other workhorses. Representatives from the Joint Chiefs of Staff and other offices participated on an irregular basis.

After nearly eighteen months of analysis and consideration, the Foster Panel came out in favor of counterforce, but resistance in Washington policy-making circles persisted. The breakthrough came in January 1974 when James R. Schlesinger, Nixon's new secretary of defense and former RAND authority on strategic issues, unexpectedly announced publicly that counterforce was now the radically revised strategic doctrine of the United States. As in the past, trying to apply the policy led to nearly insurmountable obstacles. "In a crunch, nobody could quite figure out how to translate the theory into practice," notes Fred Kaplan. "It was the perennial dilemma: how to plan a nuclear attack that was large enough to have a terrifying impact but small enough to be recognized unambiguously as a limited strike."[39]

The review and recommendations of all advisory bodies cast varying degrees of light on the national defense system, as the four panels considered above make clear. Of the four, the Gaither Committee is the most important and revealing, for several reasons. First, Sprague allowed the committee's report to become a slanted call to arms, even though he had gained inside information indicating that the Soviet threat was exaggerated. The armed services, intelligence agencies, and RAND-type institutes generally shared the view that the USSR intended to wipe the United States off the map, and this had become an article of faith for strong defense advocates like Sprague. Evidence to the contrary went ignored; ideology and politics replaced objectivity and detachment. Second, and along the same lines, the Gaither report paved the way for charges of a "missile gap" (to replace the discredited claims of a "bomber gap") that could be used against those calling for some restraint, as the election of 1960 so dramatically demonstrated. Leaking the report served the purposes of those who were convinced of the need for more crash defense efforts and of the Democrats, who were interested in an exploitable campaign issue. Third, LeMay's claims about SAC's role in the face of an impending Soviet attack raised the critical issue of civilian control of the military in the most vital area of atomic warfare.

Finally, Eisenhower's basic rejection of the Gaither report and Secretary of State John Foster Dulles's angry attack on it turned out to be extremely consequential. These acts led to press leaks. But much more important, they began the process whereby influential scientists such as Jerome Wiesner, Herbert F. York, and Spurgeon M. Keeny Jr., who had previously shared the extreme views of Edward Teller, turned against the nuclear arms race. Support for the report had been unanimous in the Gaither Committee, but many of the participating scientists had suppressed their growing reservations. After the committee presented its report to Eisenhower, he ultimately observed: "You can't have this kind of [nuclear] war. There just aren't enough bulldozers to scrape the bodies off the streets." The president's opposition validated the doubts of Wiesner and others. They began to realize that there were no technological safeguards that could protect civilization once an atomic war was unleashed. The only hope rested with nuclear arms limitations, restraints, and reductions negotiated between the United States and the USSR. After the White House meeting, the president approached York and several other scientists with an offer: "Why don't you fellows help me with the nuclear test ban? Everybody in the Pentagon is against it."[40] In less than a month, Eisenhower had appointed Killian as his special assistant for science and technology and as chairman of the President's Science Advisory Committee, whose members included many of the scientists participating in the Gaither Committee. A critical corner had been turned. No longer would the nuclear arms race go forward without meaningful challenge.

CONCLUSION

Think tanks, strategy intellectuals, and academic centers, institutes, and schools devoted to national defense and to area and international studies were the cerebral counterparts of defense contractors. Just as the latter largely replaced or supplemented arsenals and shipyards, think-tank-type organizations partly replaced or supplemented the armed services' schools, institutes, and centers devoted to tactics, strategy, logistics, and specialties such as communications and irregular warfare. These basically new entities, like the postwar munitions industry, resulted from the nation's first large and permanent military altered by extraordinarily rapid scientific and technological change. Similar to the defense industry, the Cold War think tanks and schools originated during World War II, principally to conduct operations research. Hence, in his farewell address, Eisenhower simultaneously warned against a "military-industrial complex" and a "scientific technological elite," covering "research" that had become "formalized, complex, and costly."[41]

Eisenhower sounded the alarm about an emerging warfare state that threatened democracy and society at home and the stability of the international order. The Cold War defense industry had broken down the distinction between military and civilian producers; national security centers were erasing the lines between the armed forces and civilian institutions in determining defense policy. Civilian and military systems were combining in a way that affected and reshaped fundamental aspects of American life.

On a more circumscribed plane, for the armed services, the advantages of the new institutions were many. Through private and university-affiliated research centers, they tapped much of the nation's best scientific, behavioral sciences, and humanities talent. Many academics were unwilling to serve in national security and related agencies for a host of reasons, but they would do so indirectly through research institutions. Most universities and think tanks welcomed and pursued the vast flow of federal money, most of which came from the military, and the numerous opportunities it presented.

On the darker side, think tanks of whatever type allowed the national defense establishment to conduct research and operations away from public view and with little accountability, as was the intent of Project Camelot. Russian studies at Columbia, Harvard, and elsewhere provided a sense of respectability and objectivity to American Cold War policies in general and to the seamier side of implementing those policies in particular. Furthermore, like the defense industry, the other estates acted as numerous well-placed and effective lobbies for the Cold War establishment.

Think tanks also helped put the executive and legislative branches of government at a disadvantage vis-à-vis the armed forces, intelligence, the AEC and its successors, and NASA. Directly or indirectly, advisory groups could assist in preparing their sponsoring agencies' justifications for projects and budgets. Since neither their superiors nor national legislators had the expertise or the head start of the proposing agencies, the latter usually got their way. Such was the case, for example, in the 1950s and 1960s in the battles fought over the ABM. In the midst of the conflict, MIT's Wiesner observed that Congress required an "anti-RAND" research source to provide it with independent evaluations of Pentagon proposals.[42] Conversely, Nixon complicated his political battles on behalf of the Safeguard ABM and the supersonic transport by both bypassing OST and PSAC and refusing to set up scientific advisory boards. That denied the administration the necessary technical and scientific input and encouraged scientists to unite against the proposals. Otherwise, they might have either supported the president or remained neutral.[43]

For a time, the same situation existed for the DOD and the executive branch in dealing with the air force. H. L. Nieburg explains why:

> The Air Force during the 1950's exerted a powerful influence in the National Security Council and on the Joint Chiefs of Staff. It was supported by RAND's closely reasoned, firmly documented technical papers, embellished with mathematical symbols and the impenetrable armor plate of tables and graphs spun out by giant computers whose tireless peregrinations could barely be followed, much less disputed. RAND served its patron well, building elaborate steel cobwebs of obfuscation in support of Air Force positions in the critical disputes concerning strategy, weapon systems, mission assignments, and budget allocations.

By bringing key RAND members into his office, McNamara quickly disarmed the air force in that regard.[44]

Even the armed services and other government patrons of think tanks shared critics' concern about insufficient policing of these institutions. Some could take maverick turns, as was the case with the Hudson Institute and Jason; they could prove to be uncooperative in filing required reports and financial statements, they could do shoddy work, and they could and did seek other government contracts and civilian clients, which adversely affected their primary sponsor. Oversight of think tanks by the contracting agencies, the federal executive, or Congress ranged from adequate to minimal. Throughout the Cold War years, there were only two general reviews of private research centers. Daniel E. Bell, director of the Bureau of the Budget, headed the first study in 1962 as part of a larger investigation of government procurement and contracting, with a special emphasis on R&D. In 1969 the GAO carried out the other inquiry. Although both sources reached similar findings and recommendations, the Bell report was the more thorough and penetrating of the two.

The Bureau of the Budget group found that the public interest was not being sufficiently protected and was often abused when the armed forces, intelligence services, and other government agencies turned to private sources to facilitate public policy, particularly in the critical area of national security. To reverse and reform that condition, Bell and his colleagues recommended that public-sector salaries involving R&D be raised and those of private firms be lowered and regulated. Such steps, along with more flexible and less bureaucratic regulations, including institutional innovations similar to those of public corporations, would reduce private think tanks' ability to draw off high-quality public employees. Also, these changes could encourage the expansion and creation of internal government research centers, thereby reducing dependence on private ones. To the degree private research corporations and nonprofits continued to operate, Bell and his colleagues advised that they must be subject to much greater oversight, regulation, and control. Private sources had vital roles in shaping public policy, often with only nominal supervision and legal accountability. Under such conditions, corporate or nonprofit welfare could be maximized not only at public expense but also in a way that was threatening to national interests. Effective oversight required Washington to centralize control over and coordinate the use of private think tanks by the government.

The work of the Bureau of the Budget and the GAO was supplemented from time to time by congressional investigations, some of which were mentioned earlier. In general, however, Congress knows little about private think tanks and spends relatively little time and effort investigating them. As a result, congressional inquiries and proposed reforms usually go nowhere, and little follow-up occurs. The same was true for the Bell and GAO reports. Little change occurred. Some advances took place among the armed services in terms of strengthening existing internal think tanks and institutes or creating new ones. The army and navy, with long and strong traditions of arsenals, laboratories, and R&D centers, usually welcomed the opportunity to return to past practices. The air force, NASA, and others without such experience moved reluctantly and often only ceremonially in that direction.[45]

A more basic critique of think tanks and the various institutes, centers, and schools is that most of them turned out to be hard-line Cold War advocates. Since contracts, grants, and money flowed from the national security establishment, that outcome is hardly surprising. Nonetheless, that basic reality stripped the research and advisory groups of the objectivity essential for providing reliable information and analysis.

The matter of objectivity was further complicated by research groups' tendency to rely on measurable analytical techniques. Unlike World War II operations research, which involved truly measurable and limited problems, analyzing Soviet intentions and insurgency in the developing world dealt with unmeasurable ideological considerations, political issues, and international relations of the most subjective nature. Attempting to approach these extraordinarily complex matters quantitatively and technologically opened the door to distortion, illusion, or sometimes nonsense. Wohlstetter's strategic air bases study, for example, was based on quantitative systems analysis. This was true for a good part of RAND's research output as well. No historical analysis, context, or insight guided Wohlstetter's or RAND's strategic studies. Russia was reduced to numbers and game theories; it was not approached as a country, a society, and a culture with a past and a present that suggested how it would respond in the future.

RAND, of course, was not alone in its views of the USSR, but the approach of Wohlstetter and others strongly influenced America's strategic response to the "enemy" and the potentially lethal atomic arms race it fed. But the RAND assessment of the Soviet Union, with the usual variations both right and left, characterized most of mainstream academia and particularly those think tanks, institutes, centers, and schools directly or indirectly involved in Cold War affairs. Had the Soviet Union been assessed as a defensive, vulnerable nation, U.S.-USSR relations might have been very different, and there may have been the opportunity for gradual, relatively peaceful change.

Deborah W. Larson trenchantly points out that most of the principal Cold War strategists were not from the military but were civilians, such as Brodie, Kaufmann, Wohlstetter, and Kissinger. Largely excluded were military and diplomatic historians and Sovietologists. These are the very specialists who could have provided the missing context to the nation's Cold War military strategy. In rejecting the findings and recommendations of the Gaither Committee, which closely followed Wohlstetter's conclusions, President Eisenhower insisted that wars seldom if ever start suddenly or with a surprise attack. They are preceded by growing and heightened tensions that signal potential hostilities unless change takes place.

If think tanks and Cold War academics were lacking in their analysis of the central adversary, they were equally deficient in responding to the developing world at the periphery. In its scholarship, theories, and activities involving underdeveloped countries, CENIS, for example, stressed the threat of insurgency and the necessity of countering it with force—maintaining order usually through military or military-backed rule. Stability would then prepare the way for development and modernization through an understanding and manipulation of the political culture. Whether justifying existing practices or formulating new ones, these theories supported America's repeated and ongoing misguided approaches to Asia, Latin America, Africa, and the Middle East, which involved the toppling of distrusted governments, political and military intervention, and extended wars.[46]

The emergence of think tanks and academic centers, institutes, and schools indicated the enormous impact of the Cold War on American society. Washington required the services of the other estates to carry out its global ambitions and meet its national security demands. Increasing numbers of Americans and their institutions were involved in and affected by the nation's foreign and defense policies. Although most of the other estates supported the warfare state, that was not true for all. The PSAC, chaired by the special assistant to the president for science and technology, for example, consistently attempted to temper the nuclear arms race.

7
WEAPONS

With the onset of the Cold War, the United States began a fundamental transition from the traditional armaments of World War II to the high-technology weaponry of the late twentieth and twenty-first centuries. Nuclear weapons have been at the forefront of the nation's military strategy, and the air force has been in the lead with its bombers, missiles, and other aircraft. In time, the navy's nuclear-powered and -armed submarines added to the strategic might of the United States. The army was limited to tactical nuclear weapons, which both the air force and the navy also put into service. For all the armed services, conventional military platforms such as aircraft, ships, and tanks have also been electronically and otherwise upgraded, along with the advanced tools of war they mount.

Despite the collapse of the Soviet Union in 1989–1991, America's public-private defense industry has continued to produce at a high rate weapons of great sophistication and cost. An important outcome is the nation's emergence as the world's principal exporter of high-tech weapons to both developed and developing countries. This practice began before the Cold War's end but accelerated thereafter. Arms exports and global production arrangements became necessary to sustain an overbuilt munitions industry facing reduced demand at home and intensifying competition abroad.

Throughout the Cold War, American weaponry, especially high-tech aircraft and missiles, was clearly superior to that of the Soviet Union and its allies. After the Cold War, no other nation or combination of nations, friend or foe, matched the magnitude of the United States' defense output. In its ongoing quest for higher-performing aircraft, missiles, ships, tanks, and the like, America competed with itself, not with either its enemies or its allies. The course of arms production, therefore, was driven more by political, economic, and power considerations than by those of national security, a basic manifestation of the military-industrial complex.

FROM WORLD WAR II TO
HIGH-TECHNOLOGY WEAPONRY

American military forces fought the Korean War largely with updated versions of World War II weapons. The only major exceptions were jet fighters and helicopters, which had been introduced in a minor way during the earlier conflict. Jet-propelled heavy bombers came later. The Strategic Air Command, created in 1946, went through an extended transition involving piston and jet engines until 1955, when the all-jet, long-range B-52s became operational and, in updated versions, remained the SAC's basic strategic bomber. By 1957, navy aircraft carriers were equipped with the final form of jet-powered nuclear attack bombers.[1]

Missiles, however, were the weapons of the future. Based on Allied rocket developments during World War II, and benefiting enormously from German wartime experience and personnel in the field, all three armed services were engaged in guided ballistic missile programs by the early 1950s. The Soviets' *Sputnik* launch in late 1957 acted as an urgent spur to what had been a somewhat leisurely pursuit. By then, the air force had gained control of long-range missiles, the army was confined to short-range tactical missiles, and the navy struggled to stake out a nuclear role for itself.

Sputnik and thermonuclear advances—yielding lighter payloads in nuclear warheads and reducing the demands on guidance systems because of enhanced lethality—set the air force on a crash program to make operational an ICBM. In 1967 the United States had in place 1,000 solid-propellant Minutemen and 54 storable liquid-propellant ICBMs in hardened underground silos and prepared for immediate launching.

Meanwhile, the navy made its first major steps in nuclear propulsion. With the submarine *Nautilus* in 1954, the nation and the world had its first nuclear-powered vessel. By 1980, the navy was well on the way to having its entire submarine fleet propelled by nuclear power. For reasons of economy, only a relatively few surface ships were so equipped. The navy also experimented with conventional and nuclear-armed rockets and missiles in the 1950s. Its major breakthrough, however, occurred in 1960 with Polaris: the first solid-propellant intermediate-range ballistic missile (IRBM), carried by a nuclear-powered submarine that could launch its payload while submerged. By 1967, forty-one such vessels existed, each armed with sixteen missiles. Subsequently, the Poseidon and Trident systems improved on their predecessors.[2]

In the late 1960s the United States' strategic nuclear triad consisted of SAC's long-range bombers, land-based ICBMs, and submarine-mounted IRBMs.

Together and separately, the three systems could deliver devastating, if not totally obliterating, attacks or counterattacks against any aggressor.

Aircraft, and especially tactical aircraft, continued to be a critical component of America's military might. The jet engine made the 1950s one of the most exciting and productive decades in aeronautical history. Aircraft flew faster, higher, and farther than ever before. Record after record was set and then quickly exceeded. By the decade's end, the meaningful boundaries of combat aircraft had largely been reached.[3] At about the same time, the aircraft industry had begun the critical transformation to aerospace. A careful scholar of the aircraft industry defines *aerospace* as generally encompassing the "development and production of manned and unmanned aircraft, missiles, propulsion systems, space vehicles, and associated electronics."[4] The far-reaching transition required aircraft firms to either acquire or develop the capability of working in the new areas, and it led to the inclusion of nonaircraft companies in the aerospace field, as was the case with General Electric, Honeywell, and Raytheon, among others.[5]

With the introduction and development of the jet engine and the growing sophistication of aerospace technology, the cost of combat aircraft escalated wildly. As they were engineered for ever-greater speed, jet engines became increasingly intricate, and airframes had to be redesigned and strengthened with expensive materials such as titanium and beryllium to withstand the enormous stress, pressures, and temperatures of supersonic flight. Moreover, fighter aircraft now displayed advanced avionics, including radar, computers, and fire control systems for smart missiles. All these advances added dramatically to the cost, weight, and complexity of the airplane.

In the late 1970s the air force's tactical air squadrons, consisting of fighters, attack bombers, reconnaissance planes, and the like, accounted for up to one-quarter of the overall defense budget. In the early 1960s tactical air had absorbed around 20 percent of air force spending; by 1980, that figure had jumped to 40 percent. A DOD analyst in 1971 calculated that the cost of a top-line American fighter plane had risen in constant dollars by a factor of 100 between 1945 and 1970. Extending that analysis, fighter aircraft avionics had jumped from around $3,000 to $2.5 million, and engines from $40,000 to $2 million. The F-15 air force fighter of the mid-1970s cost approximately $15 million to $25 million, depending on how expenses are figured, compared with the F-4 of the 1960s, which came in at half the price. With such spiraling costs, the air force's ability to acquire the two planes was cut in half.[6]

Although fighters such as the F-15 were rated the very best in the world, the DOD's "Lightweight Fighter Mafia" challenged their combat effectiveness. Members of this so-called Mafia included Pierre M. Sprey, a trained engineer and statistician who moved from the aircraft industry to become a DOD analyst in the early 1960s; John Boyd, an air force major who became the service's leading theorist of air combat; and Ernest Riccioni, an air force colonel who was trained as an engineer, served as a test pilot, and later worked in aerospace. Throughout the 1960s and after, this group compiled studies to support their contention that the growing cost, speed, sophistication, size, and weight of fighters degraded, rather than advanced, their potential combat performance. What mattered most, insisted Sprey and his colleagues, was the pilot's ability to surprise opponents, the capacity to maximize the number of planes in the air, and an aircraft's maneuverability and lethality. According to the Mafia, fighters such as the F-4 and its successors had become so expensive to buy and to operate that pilots were denied adequate training, and fewer planes were available for combat. These problems were compounded by the lessened durability and reliability of the fighters. Their complexity resulted in frequent breakdowns, requiring longer periods for expensive repairs by more highly trained technicians, thereby reducing even further the number of aircraft ready for combat. Moreover, the size, weight, and elaborate avionics of the planes all acted to make their presence more evident to the enemy, decreasing opportunities for surprise and maneuverability. Finally, the intricacy of missiles and other weaponry could undermine lethality because of their demanding nature and repeated malfunctions. A Korean War fighter pilot, Boyd established that the highly regarded F-86 consistently outfought the Russian MIG-15, which was much superior to the American plane by conventional standards, because the F-86 met all the criteria for exceptional aerial combat. It was lighter, smaller, more maneuverable, more lethal, and simpler in design.[7]

The Lightweight Fighter Mafia had some influence in designing and producing the F-15 and even greater input for the F-16. However, the Mafia was always fighting a losing battle. Since World War II, military aviation planning doctrine dictated that aerial superiority depended on speed and electronic sophistication. Despite the unmatched qualities of the F-15 and F-16, the air force later insisted on further upgrades with the F-22, projected to cost $161 million (in current dollars) and intended to meet the threat of USSR advances, even though that empire was defunct. Late in 1998 budget restrictions forced a reduction in the number of F-22s to be procured from 438 to 339. After that, the Joint Strike Fighter, or the F-35, was scheduled for production; it was intended to top all that had preceded it, meeting the multiple needs of the air force, navy, and marines at an estimated cost of over $300 billion (in current dollars) for 2,978 planes. At the end of 2008 the F-35, like the F-22, was experiencing serious problems in terms of price, performance, and delivery dates.[8]

Despite the push to add new planes, the air force actually has a surplus of fighters. Late in the twentieth century, the service's inventory of first-line fighters totaled 7,500. Yet only around 2,000 served in active units. The others were relegated to various forms of inactive service. Mock aerial encounters, which are held annually for training purposes, are inordinately expensive. An F-15 costs nearly $5,000 an hour to fly; an F-16, around $2,500. Even then, such exercises have a somewhat surreal character, with the Soviet Union, relying on MIGs and Russian tactics, posing as the enemy long after the end of the Cold War.[9]

Another factor driving the air force is its desire to maintain its identity as a service devoted to manned aircraft. For tactical purposes, its role is secure, but it could be challenged or compromised by missiles in the strategic area. Beginning in 1957 and becoming urgent in 1965, the air force insisted that it was necessary to update SAC. The command was composed of around 300 B-52 bombers, which had been built between 1955 and 1962, and the smaller FB-111s, which totaled around 60. B-52s are relatively slow and noisy, with limited maneuverability and burdened with avionics that make them vulnerable. They have become obsolete in terms of successfully delivering their nuclear payloads against the Soviet Union. With ballistic missiles and the advent of cruise missiles, widespread doubts arose about the need for strategic bombers. Nonetheless, the air force insisted on the importance of the nuclear-armed bomber as a critical part of the nation's strategic triad.

To begin modernizing SAC, the air force proposed what became the B-1 supersonic bomber, and it awarded a contract in 1970 for around 240 planes at a cost of $15 billion to $19 billion. From the outset, Rockwell International encountered severe problems with the bomber in terms of cost, performance, and deadlines. When neither the air force nor the company could conceal the growing troubles plaguing the plane, opposition became fierce, and the B-1 was raised as a campaign issue in the presidential elections of 1972 and 1976. By then, anticipated costs had escalated to as high as $100 million per unit. Finally, President Carter terminated the B-1 program in 1977. In 1981 President Reagan, as part of his massive military buildup, reinstated a revised bomber (the B-1B) and authorized 100 of the planes at an estimated overall cost of $20 billion, or somewhere around $200 million per plane (in current dollars). Acquisition costs turned out to be nearly $280 million. That same year, Reagan also authorized the procurement of 132 B-2 bombers, scheduled to be active by around 1990. After being rushed into service ahead of the B-2, the B-1B became operational in 1986.

The B-2 had stealth characteristics, allowing it to attack the USSR without being detected by radar and without the need for fighter escort. With a capacity of eighty 500-pound bombs, the B-2 stealth aircraft is a very lethal flying machine. However, like the B-1, it faced constant difficulties involving performance, delays, costs, and strategic rationale. Indeed, with both the B-1 and the B-2, the air force felt compelled to modify the planes' purpose and mission based on changing circumstances. The Soviet Union collapsed before the B-2 came into service in 1994, making the task increasingly challenging. Additionally, the B-2 cost an astonishing $2.15 billion per plane. Facing such realities, the air force cut production numbers to seventy-five; in 1992 President Bush reduced that number to twenty.

Overall, as with fighters, the air force now has more strategic bombers than it can keep in active service. Refitted for conventional instead of nuclear bombs, B-1Bs have no discernible role. A number of them have crashed, and twenty-seven are now in storage. The B-2 is also a bomber in limbo. Nonetheless, the air force looks forward to further expanding its strategic bomber force.[10]

The army suffers from the same glut of weapons and equipment as the air force. While visiting Fort Hood, Texas, journalist William Greider was driven through miles of storage yards for M-1 tanks, Bradley fighting vehicles, Humvees, heavy trucks, and heavy equipment transports. Comparable to the F-15, F-16, and F-22 fighters, the seventy-ton M-1 Abrams tank is an exceptional weapon, especially when it has been upgraded electronically as an M-1A. However, like air force fighters and bombers, only 2,100 of the army's 11,000 tanks are operational with combat divisions. The remainder are in varying forms of reserve and storage. Moreover, actual training with the Abrams tank is prohibitively expensive. It costs $2,000 an hour to run the multimillion-dollar fighting vehicle. To save funds, M-1s are moved by heavy transports if they must go more than three miles.

Expenditures are also kept down by training troops on Abrams tank simulators, using Cold War–era Soviet weapons, satellite weapons, terrain, and tactics as portrayed on dated videos of a simulated battlefield. Updated videos would be too expensive to make and would not properly represent potential enemies.

The army disposed of about 6,000 surplus tanks in the 1990s. They were given to other countries, sold for a fraction of their worth, donated to museums and public displays, and even used as salvage to make artificial barrier reefs. Such practices were cheaper than destroying or storing them. A 1997 study established that the same occurred on a massive scale for armor, artillery, helicopters, and other equipment. Although these models were usually older, many of them had been procured or reconditioned at the cost of billions of dollars during the Reagan buildup of the 1980s and were still usable. By reducing its weapons inventories, the army not only saved funds but also created opportunities to purchase replacements. The air force and navy adopted a similar approach in dealing with "excess" aircraft and ships.[11]

The navy, like the air force and the army, has turned to high technology in its ships and vessels. This is certainly the case with nuclear-powered submarines armed with strategic missiles. To a lesser degree, this holds true for ships of war in general. A valid question is whether it is wise to continue building aircraft carriers. Two of the latest ones, the *Harry S. Truman* and the *Ronald Reagan*, cost in the vicinity of $4.5 billion and $5 billion, respectively. The *George H. W. Bush*, a nuclear-powered, Nimitz-class carrier, was officially launched in January 2009 and came in at a price of $6.2 billion. The need for additional carriers is questionable, and in the case of limited or broader conflict, they constitute an inviting target for missile attacks.

For all their sophistication in weaponry, detection capacity, operating ability, and the like, modern combat ships are inordinately expensive to build and operate. The Arleigh Burke–class destroyer, for example, costs nearly $900 million to build and over $13 million a year to operate. In addition to other weaponry, the destroyer is armed with ninety various missiles. The crew, in port and on the seas, trains largely through videos and similar media-type simulation devices. A major mission of the destroyer, as is the case with most other naval ships, is training men for operations, maintenance, and battle. Indeed, the repeated cycle of training is a principal function of all the military services.

Perhaps more so than most other services, the navy finds it difficult to allow its ships to remain idle or in storage. Their heavy electronic components will quickly deteriorate if they are not regularly used, serviced, and maintained. Hence, officers and crews cannot be reduced below a certain level without either eliminating ships or devising some means to keep them functional without being fully manned.[12]

As noted, for the Korean conflict, the United States basically relied on World War II weapons and a strategy of attrition. During the Vietnam War, however, the technological transformation of military weapons and equipment was already well along and evident in all the services. Through radio, microwave, tropospheric, and satellite systems, headquarters, battlefield commanders, and the nation's capital could all communicate with one another, making centralized command and control of warfare more efficient than ever before. Ground and aerial radar, along with infrared, electronic, and other sensors connected to central information centers and analyzed by computers, enhanced intelligence operations to previously unknown levels. Vastly improved helicopters played a much more active and critical role in Vietnam compared with Korea. They acted as aerial attack, communication, and command systems and provided an efficient and effective way to transport troops, supplies, and equipment and to evacuate casualties rapidly.

High-tech F-4 jet fighters and those of the navy dominated the skies, armed with Sidewinder, Sparrow, and other missiles. Early versions of so-called smart bombs, along with various types of guided missiles, also debuted in Vietnam. Both afloat and in the air, the high-tech navy was fully active in the Southeast Asian conflict. Perhaps the most dramatic innovation in Vietnam was Secretary of Defense Robert S. McNamara's "electronic fence," designed to cut off North Vietnam's infiltration of South Vietnam and thus lessen or terminate the costly and ineffective bombing of the former.

Many of the new and advanced tools of war proved to be wanting, unworkable, or even dangerous to their users. Such was the case with the Sheridan tank. Its engine, electronic components, and other parts caused ongoing problems; the guns, principally the main one, and ammunition were unreliable and created conditions hazardous to the crews, some of whom considered the tank to be a death trap. The Falcon missile ended up having a kill record of 7 percent, not the 99 percent claimed by its sponsors, and the Sparrow was not much better. Indeed, the smart weapons often proved to be disappointing. In general, the more sophisticated and complex the weapon and equipment, the more prone they were to malfunction and breakdown. Service, repair, and replacement, often requiring highly skilled technicians, took inordinate amounts of time, drove up costs, and sidelined the weaponry for long periods. The biggest failure, however, was the electronic fence. Predictably, the North Vietnamese and Vietcong just went around the various barriers.[13]

The loss of the war itself, of course, was the most jarring blow to the armed services and the nation. An underdeveloped nation of largely peasant people relied on maneuver, stealth, and guerrilla operations to hold off America's massive and technologically enriched war of attrition. Under the right circumstances, ideas, commitment, and morale could overcome sophisticated brute strength.

A REVOLUTION IN MILITARY AFFAIRS

The outcome in Vietnam propelled the American armed services to push even further along the path of high-technology weaponry. By the 1980s and 1990s, many asserted that a new stage in military affairs had begun. Jacques S. Gansler, a defense industry expert and insider, proposes that attrition warfare has given way to "information-based warfare" characterized by "real-time, all-weather intelligence; dramatically improved command and control; unmanned, precision-guided, brilliant weapons; and nullification of the enemy's information systems."[14] In pursuing this line of analysis, the author points to the use of reconnaissance satellites and advanced aircraft intelligence systems to guide land, air, and sea operations and track enemy positions and activity; night-vision devices; and satellite-based GPS. These approaches have allowed the military to use its smart weapons more effectively. Unlike in Vietnam, however, where new technology was used in a random, hit-or-miss fashion, the new information-based warfare maximizes effects by integrating all the advances into a fully coherent whole.

What Gansler labels information-based warfare others call electronic or digitalized warfare, a revolution (or transformation) in military affairs, or Force XXI. Designation notwithstanding, most analysts point to 1991's Operation Desert Storm as an indication of what information-based warfare can achieve. The United States was constantly aware of where its forces and the Iraqi forces were, and with the ability to destroy the enemy's command, control, communication, and intelligence systems, the United States and its allies swiftly subdued Iraq while suffering only a minimal casualty rate. During the conflict, precision-guided cruise and other missiles, often fired from hundreds of miles away, were used with devastating effect.

Throughout the 1990s the army attempted to go even further with what became known as Force XXI. It aimed for a comprehensively digitalized battlefield in which all combat elements would be electronically linked, including tanks, mobile rocket launchers, unmanned aerial vehicles, ground-based precision-guided missiles and other weapons, and even foot soldiers. Proponents argued that with all forces sharing common information and a battle map that showed complete, critical data, the less advanced armies of the enemy would quickly be wiped out by Force XXI. After years of effort, field-testing, and mock battles, the ambitious project was abandoned as impractical and electronically unattainable.

Even Operation Desert Storm was not the nearly flawless campaign touted by high-tech enthusiasts. The GAO estimates that the accuracy rate of the precision bombing during the conflict was only about 45 percent, not the 85 percent initially claimed by the Pentagon. Furthermore, the attacks launched by the Bush administration in 2003 against Afghanistan and Iraq have become prolonged, challenging conflicts resembling the stalemate and quagmire of Vietnam. The Middle Eastern wars have more than tarnished the triumphal claims for information-based warfare.

In addition to its limitations, digitalized warfare is inordinately expensive. Besides all the electronic weapons and equipment involved, the armed services, supported by the defense industry, insist on the continual upgrading of the conventional military platforms, such as tanks, aircraft, and ships, that mount and transport the advanced tools of war. The nation is already beyond the point of being able to afford the defense system it has, without pursuing additional futuristic military goals that are long on cost and short on promise. Indeed, as DOD budgets continue to rise, combat-ready forces in all the services continue to decline in number and increase in age.[15]

NUCLEAR WEAPONS

Nuclear weapons were always central to America's Cold War military posture, particularly in the strategic area but also in the tactical and even theater areas. At the heart of this approach was the nuclear triad consisting of nuclear bombers, land-based missiles, and sea-based missiles. Until the late 1950s the SAC, made up of air force nuclear bombers, was the principal arm of the strategic force. Thereafter, with the introduction of operational missiles, the navy and army were included in the strategic force; this development also expanded the reach of the air force.

Shortly after the end of World War II, the nation resumed production of nuclear, and later thermonuclear, bombs. It did so for a number of reasons. As tension grew between the United States and the USSR in 1946 and the Cold War began in earnest in 1947, Washington moved to build up its military forces. With strong public and congressional opposition to large and expensive conventional forces and a lack of interest in universal military training, airpower was pushed by the air force and various political elements as a relatively inexpensive and very effective alternative. Such reasoning was bolstered by the nation's nuclear monopoly, which, it was assumed, would make the Soviet Union more pliable during the emerging conflict between the East and the West. Most of the conjecture about atomic weaponry proved to be questionable or wrong. The USSR grew more rigid and, within a few years, acquired nuclear weapons of its own. And, with the United States leading the way, the two world powers engaged in an extensive and deadly arms race.[16]

Nuclear weapons turned out to be unimaginably expensive, both on their own and in comparison to conventional armaments. According to the most thorough study of the subject, between 1940 and 1996 the United States spent a minimum of $5.5 trillion (in 1996 dollars) on nuclear weapons programs, including their development, production, and deployment and plans for their use and defense; by 2005, the figure had reached $7.5 trillion (in 2006 dollars), according to a more recent analysis. In total, the nation manufactured more than 70,000 nuclear weapons, which were deployed at different times and for varying purposes; the overall estimated costs of these weapons constituted 29 percent of total defense spending, placed at $18.7 trillion between 1940 and 1990. Up to 1998, the United States was still spending $35 billion annually on nuclear weapons. In unadjusted dollars, the figure for fiscal year 2008 was a minimum of $52.4 billion.

Although nuclear armaments have been reduced considerably since the Cold War ended, in the late 1990s the United States and Russia still retained approximately 10,000 warheads apiece. As of April 2007, it was estimated that the United States had 5,736 warheads, mostly strategic and a few tactical; Russia had 7,200, believed to be split about evenly between strategic and tactical. The two nations are believed to have 26,000 warheads between them, with the excess numbers in responsive reserve. The accuracy of these calculations was validated when the Obama administration released official figures on the United States' nuclear arms stockpile in May 2010: in 1967 the nation possessed 31,255 warheads; the number had dropped to 10,903 in 1997 and 5,709 in 2007; as of 2009, the figure stood at 5,113. According to the *Bulletin of Atomic Scientists*, the international nuclear weapons inventory in 2009 totaled approximately 23,360.[17]

The air force has always been the primary service for the deployment of nuclear weapons. Starting with the World War II–modified B-29, SAC has procured nearly 4,700 nuclear-capable bombers since the late 1940s; this number involves fourteen different types of planes, twelve of which became operational. The B-70 and the B-1A (virtually the same plane) never reached that stage, and the B-1B and B-2 are of dubious value.

Beginning in 1959 and continuing to the present, nuclear-armed ICBMs have been dominant in the air force's strategic mission. This occurred as missiles became increasingly accurate and lethal, leading to the MIRV. Over time, the air force acquired nine different types of ICBMs, totaling 3,160 in number. Beginning in the early 1950s, the air force also brought into service a large fleet of nuclear-armed or nuclear-capable tactical weapons, including tactical fighters, fighter-bombers, air-to-air missiles, and ground-launched cruise missiles. By the mid-1980s, the service counted some 2,900 such weapons in its tactical arsenal.[18]

Next to the air force, the navy has had the most important strategic nuclear role. Its principal weapon in this regard is the nuclear-propelled submarine, armed with sea-launched ballistic missiles (SLBMs). Deployment began in 1960. Since then, nuclear submarines have consistently been upgraded, along with four successive missile systems. The number of these submarines never exceeded forty-one; that number dropped to eighteen after the end of the Cold War and stands at fourteen today. From 1960 to near the end of the twentieth century, the navy procured a total of 2,975 SLBMs. Like the air force, the navy also acquired various tactical nuclear-capable aircraft and related weapons, some of which were deployed for only short periods. They included fighter-bombers, land-based antisubmarine warfare patrol planes, helicopters, various other aircraft, attack submarines, and surface combat vessels. Moreover, the navy relied on sea-to-air missiles, sea-launched cruise missiles, bombs and torpedoes, and rounds for big guns. By 1984, the navy had close to 3,000 tactical nuclear weapons.[19]

The army was largely restricted to tactical nuclear weapons and, similar to the navy, various army weapons had short lives. Its atomic armaments started to become operational in the 1950s and included nuclear rounds for artillery and recoilless rifles, surface-to-surface missiles, surface-to-air missiles, IRBMs, and atomic demolition munitions. In 1984 the ground forces' nuclear armaments included around 10,000 warheads, artillery rounds, and other weapons.[20]

Besides those weapons already mentioned, one or more of the services has employed medium-range ballistic missiles, IRBMs, cruise missiles, advanced cruise missiles, and surface-to-ground ABMs. Many of these nuclear weapons were short-lived. The fascination with and drive for nuclearization, especially in the tactical area, peaked sometime in the mid-1960s. The armed services found it increasingly difficult to justify such armaments. Some senior military officers argued that these weapons were inappropriate and drew funds from conventional usage.[21]

Such analyses went further and deeper for the strategic area. In 1966 the nation's nuclear stockpile reached its zenith of 36,000 warheads and bombs (the DOD figure for 1967 is 31,255). Both civilian and military personnel argued that deterrence required only minimal, not maximal, nuclear strategic weaponry. This was the path followed by both France and China. As early as 1960, General Maxwell D. Taylor claimed that a couple hundred well-handled missiles and a small number of bombers would suffice. Jerome Wiesner, President Kennedy's science adviser, basically agreed. After conducting a study, Kennedy's Bureau of the Budget concluded that any more than 450 missiles would be all but meaningless, and this was before the introduction of MIRVs. Since that time, numerous civilian organizations and groups and high-ranking civilian and military officials and officers have voiced similar views and have even proposed the total elimination of nuclear weapons.[22]

Dating from the 1940s, the United States has stressed maximum output of nuclear weaponry and the maintenance of nuclear superiority. These goals have led to a backwards process of matching strategic targeting to existing or proposed weapons, not vice versa. In the early 1950s, for example, SAC targeted seventy sites in an all-out war with the Soviet Union; by 1957, as the stockpile grew, targets reached 3,261 and kept increasing. The vast accumulation of nuclear weapons had as much or more to do with interservice rivalry; economics; politics; geopolitics; inadequate, distorted, or corrupted intelligence;

ideology; obsessions; fantasies; and various other goals as with national security.[23]

The outcome of the buildup was potentially cataclysmic. Up until 1960, each of the three services planned its own targeting under the nominal coordination of the JCS. Duplication of targeting was common, which not only wasted resources but also threatened the goals, lives, and weaponry of the three services. To correct the situation, Eisenhower insisted in 1960 on the preparation of a single integrated operational plan (SIOP). The planning took place at SAC headquarters under the leadership of the air force, the principal and most aggressive strategic service. Regardless of whether strategy emphasized attacking cities or command centers and military installations, the air force from the 1940s onward focused on using America's entire nuclear arsenal to inflict maximal destruction on the USSR and, to a lesser degree, China and other identified enemies. Even after the Cold War, that goal remained central to the SIOP. Perhaps growing out of air force advocacy, the critical SIOP document has been so closely guarded that authorized civilian policy makers have had difficulty obtaining access to its details. According to DOD estimates, a full-blown nuclear attack by the United States, and assuming no retaliatory blow, would result in around 285 million deaths. Civilian specialists, expanding military calculations based only on blast effects to include fire, radiation, and other expectable hazards, place the figure closer to 1 billion. Mass fires, or firestorms, alone are estimated to exceed by two to five times the damage caused by the blasts.[24]

Size and targeting of nuclear forces aside, both the United States and the USSR realized that a relatively small number of strategic nuclear weapons would be capable of crippling their ability to respond to a nuclear attack. Consequently, the two adversaries kept their strategic forces on a launch-on-warning status, which gave the U.S. president three to four minutes for decision making. Various civilian and military officials, advisers, experts, and others insisted on even greater security through a first strike.[25]

Although a preventive attack never became official policy, the authority to use nuclear weapons was delegated to head off a surprise attack on the homeland. In 1956, 1957, and 1960, President Eisenhower authorized appropriate commanders to use nuclear weapons under specified circumstances and generally expanded military control over the nuclear arsenal. Some army field commanders down to the battalion level or lower could order the use of tactical nuclear weapons. The United States was slow in implementing locks on strategic nuclear weapons. The Carter administration widely distributed unlock codes among the armed services to increase security.

Earlier, some high-ranking officers, especially among the air force, had indicated that they would unleash a major nuclear attack under certain circumstances, with or without Washington's consent. The notion that only the president can authorize the use of nuclear weapons through the "black box" or the "football" is closer to fiction than reality; the idea was intended to reassure a concerned public. Under the best of circumstances, the chief of state would have a few minutes to make such a momentous decision; more likely, he would face an unfolding catastrophe.[26]

Deterrence could work with a degree of assurance if the major adversaries limited themselves to a minimum, verifiable number of nuclear weapons. In rejecting the Soviet Union's numerous offers to initiate arms control, the United States resisted or complicated the approach. Only the determined and resourceful leadership of Mikhail S. Gorbachev began the process of disarmament in the waning years of the Cold War. The one fully reliable way to prevent nuclear warfare is to rid the world of such weapons. Manufacturing nuclear armaments beyond any point of reason, the United States and USSR managed to avoid setting off a holocaust through careful and wise leadership, various safeguards, and luck.[27]

ARMS PROLIFERATION

The proliferation of high-technology weapons has emerged as a critical issue for the United States. Between 1980 and 1990, the global arms trade totaled nearly $700 billion, with well over $500 billion going to developing nations. By the mid-1990s, America accounted for 50 to 60 percent of international arms sales. Ironically, worldwide arms proliferation grew after the termination of the Cold War, and today the world faces the enormous hazards associated with the globalization of arms development, production, marketing, and sales through corporations taking on multinational proportions.[28]

From the onset of the Cold War, the United States has been at the center of arms exports, and today it leads the way in all major types of modern weapons systems. These realities evolved over a period of around sixty years.

After the founding of NATO, the United States provided or sold to its European allies a wide range of modern weapons throughout the 1950s. By the early 1960s, however, NATO nations had established or rebuilt their own weapons industries and began seeking to reduce their dependence on America. Although European arms did not match those of the United States in terms of quality or range, Great Britain, France, West Germany, and others advanced their output by acquiring the right to produce parts and components for American weapons they purchased; more significantly, the United States arranged for licensed production of major weapons systems in Europe. What began in Europe spread to America's Asian allies and friends, especially Japan, but also South Korea, Taiwan, and lesser powers. By following these practices, the United States aimed to strengthen NATO militarily, advance its cohesion, and improve its weapons commonality. Similar goals held for Asia.

By the mid to late 1960s, England, France, West Germany, and other European countries began to engage in the coproduction of arms, especially in the aerospace area, through joint companies, new international corporations, and other collaborative arrangements. By doing so, they sought to reduce defense spending, upgrade technology, and broaden the base of their national and collective weapons manufacture. Although a great deal of their progress relied on America's technological prowess, European weapons fabrication in a number of fields rivaled that of the United States by the 1980s.

Dating back to the 1960s, European nations collectively sought to maximize arms exports, which ultimately accounted for about one-third of their output. As the quality and variety of their products improved, European international sales came to include some of the most modern and sophisticated weaponry available. Importing nations were located around the globe and included some nations boycotted by the United States. Based on American sales and various shared production practices, Asian countries also began to develop weapons industries, as did developed and developing countries in the Western Cold War camp.[29]

From the 1980s onward, and based on American and European production and export practices, developing countries had the opportunity to acquire a practically unlimited range of weaponry. More than a few of these countries went on to produce modern weapons not only for themselves but also for foreign sales. In doing so, they added to the world's arms manufacturing capacity, which increased proliferation even further. Although not accounting for a significant percentage of global production, arms production and export by developing areas was still problematic. Moreover, by acquiring and producing armaments, these nations frequently diverted revenue from programs for social gain, failed to promote economic growth, propped up abusive and dictatorial regimes, and increased the likelihood of hostilities. In general, the practice had numerous drawbacks and practically no advantages.

What was true for the West also took place in the East, with the Soviet Union out in front. Indeed, by the late 1980s, the USSR was among the leading international arms exporters. Once the Cold War ended, the United States, Europe, Russia, various Asian nations, and other developed and developing countries encountered the economic stress of a vastly overextended weapons plant facing stable or declining worldwide demand and rising costs. Such circumstances intensified competition among the major arms-producing nations, especially the United States and those in Europe. As a result, leverage in the international armaments market shifted from the seller to the buyer. Virtually any nation, splinter group, minority element, and political or economic force, no matter how unstable or unworthy, could acquire weapons if it could afford to pay for them. Ironically, and in its own twisted way, arms proliferation surged with the breakdown of the bipolar world. Under these changed circumstances, centralization through alliances and coherence gave way to decentralization, with growing uncertainty and chaos.

Until the early 1990s, U.S. arms sales and numerous technology and production accords were usually related to national security. Thereafter, the preservation of the weapons industry took on growing, even preeminent, importance. The economic health of the industry depended on new markets and lowered costs. Under stress before the 1990s, weapons firms had pushed domestic consolidation as far as possible. Now they looked abroad to solve their growing problems. This strategy was generally supported by the Defense Department and the national security establishment as a necessary means of maintaining a reliable weapons industry base.[30]

After the 1991 Persian Gulf War, the Bush administration emphasized weapons exports while publicly insisting to its critics at home and abroad that it was trying to restrict destabilizing and irresponsible international arms operations. In actuality, the administration's policies exploited the growing demand for U.S. weapons resulting from their impressive performance during the brief Gulf War. Along these lines, the State Department set up a new center to promote the global sales and business operations of American defense companies. It also instructed its embassies to support these efforts. Additionally, the administration offered financial assistance to potential buyers and reimbursed arms firms for expenses incurred in marketing and sales enterprises abroad. At the outset, Washington concentrated on the Middle East, but its activities eventually included Asia and other regions.

These modified policies were justified as essential for protecting national interests at home and abroad and, more by action than by declared intent, for stimulating the economy. In pursuing these goals, the Bush administration grew increasingly bold. It began to suggest that the United States follow the lead of other nations in treating the armaments trade as if it were commercial exchange. Because the country had no need for and could not afford additional advanced aircraft, missiles, tanks, helicopters, and the like, the administration sanctioned their continued production solely for foreign markets. To facilitate the process, weapons firms modified their output to better serve global customers.[31]

The Clinton administration first followed and then went beyond Bush's policies. After an extended study, the administration issued Presidential Directive 41 (PD41) in February 1995. It instructed all relevant departments to promote the sale of American weapons abroad and, for the first time, officially made economic impact a consideration in arms transfers. Earlier, a high State Department official had informed Congress that the policy would embrace "marketing, export financing, and internationalization of U.S. defense procurement."[32]

In June 1994, before PD41 was issued, Secretary of Defense William J. Perry and Under Secretary John M. Deutch instituted what came to be called the Perry-Deutch initiative. The doctrine aimed at broadening cooperation throughout the West in the development and production of military weapons and equipment by stressing dual-use technology and products. With that goal in mind, the armed services were instructed to modify acquisition procedures by pushing to the utmost the integration of commercial and military technology in the design and fabrication of weapons and equipment.

Perry and Deutch, along with Jacques S. Gansler, insisted that foreign weapons sales alone could not take up the slack from declining domestic demand. The future health of the industry depended on breaking down the domestic barriers between commercial and military output. In general, they pointed out, civilian industry displayed superior innovative capabilities. Tapping such wealth on as wide a basis as possible would make military goods better and cheaper. Fully 60 percent of all military products could be provided by commercial firms. Highly specialized weapons such as advanced aircraft, submarines, tanks, and the like would have to be reserved for the military sector. Nonetheless, the separate industrial sector that had emerged since World War II, with its unique and demanding specifications, gross inefficiencies, and numerous other liabilities, had to be restructured and more closely related to the civilian economy.

Such an approach had a number of benefits. First, U.S. military output could compete more effectively abroad. Additionally, American firms could more readily combine manufacturing operations with foreign corporations, principally those in Europe, but also in Asia. Finally, according to Perry and his associates, civilian participation in military output was the most practical way to penetrate foreign markets, obtain desired technology, and increase demand. In Perry's terms, the cooperative endeavor would be carried out among a "circle of friends" consisting of trusted allies who were reasonable, responsible, and reliable.[33]

Combined operations with overseas firms increased during the Clinton years, but so did sales reminiscent of the Bush administration. With ideological and strategic restraints weakened or lifted after the Cold War, American weapons firms could more easily broaden their reach. Moreover, they could depend on the encouragement, support, and assistance of the Pentagon and Washington in general. The American push to include Poland, Hungry, and the Czech Republic in NATO, for example, was motivated to a significant degree by the quest for new arms markets. It was clearly the aim of the U.S. Committee to Expand NATO, a promotional organization of the defense industry and foreign policy leaders.

The success of U.S. weapons sales to the former Warsaw Pact nations had repercussions far beyond eastern Europe. NATO nations resented American firms' intrusion into what they considered their turf. Moreover, with the United States and NATO countries rushing to sell arms in eastern Europe, independent republics that had once been part of the USSR were pushed out of their former markets. Consequently, they began dumping obsolete and inferior Soviet aircraft and other armaments on the world market at fire-sale prices. Some of these weapons ended up in Latin America. American defense firms used this outcome to pressure the Clinton administration into lifting the informal embargo on such sales in the region. Once American companies became active, European corporations joined in the chase. As a result, an arms race ensued that South American nations did not need and could not afford. From 1992 to 1998, defense spending across Latin America jumped by 35 percent or more. More broadly, whereas the USSR had once been a leader among arms exporters, Russia had great difficulty competing for buyers in developed and developing countries. In response, the economically and industrially distressed country looked to peripheral areas or even "rogue" regimes, such as Iraq and North Korea, as tempting markets. These were countries that the United States and others had tried to isolate through trade restrictions.

Of even greater concern, high-technology products involved in international exchange could end up accelerating nuclear arms competition and proliferation. Although the picture is still clouded, the Loral Corporation and Hughes Electronics gained Washington's permission, with the DOD dissenting, to have China launch their commercial satellites. This arrangement leaked or threatened to leak highly sophisticated American missile know-how to the Chinese military. India protested that the American agreement resulted in China's sharing nuclear missile technology with Pakistan. Whatever the case, India added the incident to its list of regional threats that led it to conduct a series of underground nuclear tests in May 1998. Several weeks later, Pakistan responded in kind.

Arms firms and their advocates insist that their international sales activities are not furthering conflict; rather, they are promoting security and stability. Besides, if Americans refused to export their products, other less discriminating sources would do so. Industry leaders also maintain that selling advanced aircraft, such as the F-15 and F-16, abroad does not adversely affect national security. The United States could quickly come out with an even more sophisticated plane, as it did with the F-22 fighter. Indeed, industry spokesmen proposed exporting F-22s even before the combat aircraft was operational at home. A host of reasons were offered for doing so; one reason the industry left out was to justify R&D and production of a supposedly better aircraft—specifically, the Joint Strike Fighter.[34]

Before the Clinton administration stressed international cooperation as official policy to address weapons producers' many woes, the industry had begun reaching beyond U.S. borders in an effort to globalize. Such activity took on serious proportions during the early to mid-1980s. Until then, collaborative efforts had been steady but modest throughout most of the Cold War years. Calculated in five-year periods, international weapons program start-ups throughout the 1960s and 1970s were 25 or less for each period; they jumped to 60 during 1981–1985; and in the next ten years, they skyrocketed to over 200 in total. About 75 percent of the collaboration was intra-European and transatlantic; the remainder involved Europe-Asia, U.S.-Asia, intra-Asian, and other arrangements. The change was fast and dramatic. In 1970 collaborative international output of major arms was occurring on a minor scale; by 1995, it had become commonplace.

The growing internationalization during the 1980s was carried out principally through agreements between or among corporations, not governments. Up until the 1980s, governments in the United States, Europe, Asia, and elsewhere had arranged and overseen cooperative weapons agreements. Thereafter, government involvement rose only slightly and then plateaued. Private firms initiated the surge in internationalization. Large arms firms negotiated cross-border agreements ranging from the purchase of parts or components for a weapons system to licensed output and assembly, technology transfers (including staff and specifications), and coproduction and joint production agreements; others went further, negotiating partial or total mergers and acquisitions.

The shift from government-led to corporate-driven international weapons operations is of the greatest importance. Under government direction, cooperative transactions were pursued primarily for the purpose of national security and were carefully regulated. Under the direction of private sources, globalization increasingly stressed industrial welfare and proceeded largely free of oversight. A similar trend took place with arms exports. Prior to the 1980s, most American trade was conducted through the strict and controlled procedures of government agencies, and these transactions were designated foreign military sales. From the early 1980s on, direct commercial sales rose rapidly and at times matched or exceeded the level of foreign military sales. The change resulted when Washington opened the door to corporate arms exports by substantially loosening government regulation.

Just as the United States figuratively unleashed weapons firms to negotiate foreign sales, it proceeded in a similar way for international collaborative efforts. Indeed, Washington encouraged all forms of cooperation, including mergers and acquisitions, unless the most sensitive technology might be threatened or highly undesirable nations were involved. For example, between 1988 and 1992, the federal government's Committee on Foreign Investments in the United States reviewed more than 700 proposals for foreign firms to engage in collaborative activities with American companies; it rejected only one. In fiscal year 1993 the Defense Authorization Act prohibited only government-owned foreign firms from acquiring large U.S. arms companies.

In loosening or lifting restrictions on the globalization of arms production and trade, Washington was responding to pressure from the weapons industry, for the most part. Corporate and defense association spokesmen insisted that government controls and bureaucratic processes were limiting their exports and transnational operations. Toward the end of the Cold War and after, these arguments took on greater weight and increasingly coincided with the view of various civilian and military officials.

From experience, the United States and other nations learned that systematized international collaboration on arms production, along the lines of NATO countries overseeing such projects, was difficult at best. Military requirements and government operations can differ greatly among nations. Numerous pressure groups within countries can act to complicate, interrupt, or thwart such ventures. Progress depends on the corporate world, assisted or overseen by government.[35]

The worldwide burgeoning of the arms trade and foreign weapons partnerships actually began under Ronald Reagan. Though his administration did not officially endorse these practices, its emphasis on an arms buildup acted to ease restraints and prompt America's active participation. The Bush administration continued its predecessor's encouragement of international weapons operations, but it stressed more directly the goal of achieving military balance, particularly in the volatile Middle East after the Persian Gulf War. Although it was not clearly articulated, the Bush administration also relied on weapons sales and output to stimulate the economy. Building on Reagan and Bush policies, the Clinton administration aimed higher. It sought to maximize and rationalize international weapons sales and collaborative efforts by integrating civilian and military technology and connecting the West's military industrial sectors.

Additionally, and more directly than any former presidency, the Clinton administration underscored the importance of the arms industry to the strength and prosperity of the economy.[36]

Under these three administrations, America's Cold War arms policies began to come full circle. The high-technology arsenal built to meet the Cold War threat continued to expand its global reach and sophistication after the threat had ceased to exist. The activity was not confined to the developed world but included developing regions as well. In the process, weapons proliferation took place at an unprecedented level and came to include the potential to deliver nuclear weapons, along with other armaments of mass destruction, by aircraft and missiles and even to manufacture them.

With the twentieth century giving way to the twenty-first, the American weapons industry and those of other nations started to take on some of the attributes of the commercial multinational firms proliferating in the United States during the 1960s and after. Like the multinationals, pluses are matched with grave minuses. International collaboration acts to weaken government control over an industry that the American state created and sustained during a good part of the twentieth century and that is critical to national security. As forms of globalization advance, weapons firms' loyalty to and identity with the nation-state become increasingly tenuous. Furthermore, unlike the commercial sector of the world economy, international collaboration in the military armaments sector can adversely affect national and world security. Corporations focus on their own well-being, regardless of whether it coincides with national or international interests.[37]

If the United States and the world community ever face a truly multinational weapons complex, they could be dealing with behemoths that hold the fate of civilization in their hands. Should hostilities break out, combatants could encounter their own weapons on the field of battle, as the United States did in Iraq during 1991, obtained from European sources. Worse yet, internationalized arms merchants beyond the reach of any governmental authority could potentially play nations off against each other for their own benefit. Led by the United States, the post–World War II world appears to have become virtually addicted in a careless, deluded, or desperate way to a globe armed beyond all reason and one that continually grows more dangerous.[38]

8
NATIONAL SECURITY AND THE ECONOMY

The multiple trillions of dollars expended for national defense since 1945 have fundamentally impacted the nation's economy. Related to that spending—and made possible if not encouraged by America's Cold War global reach, including the nation's military presence and imprint—the corporate community expanded its international operations throughout the developed and underdeveloped world to previously unknown levels. In doing so, industrial America de-emphasized its long-term dedication to improving the efficiency, quality, and range of national output for the short-term pursuit of maximizing profits. It took this drastic turn partly because of the outstanding production record of World War II, the enormous wealth and benefits generated by mobilizing the wartime economy, and the United States' position as virtually the only robust industrial and financial system in an otherwise incapacitated world.

For their part, the armed services' lavish Cold War budgets led to the creation of wholly new or modified high-technology industries to provide the fighting forces with sophisticated, futuristic weapons. The research, development, and production of advanced arms and equipment absorbed a high proportion of the nation's scientists, engineers, and technologists. Moreover, nearly all the new and constantly changing weaponry was produced under circumstances that invited escalating costs and declining quality.

The changed nature of the output in civilian and military spheres is related and interacting; the nation appears to have lost the will, ability, and capacity to achieve consistent quality production. Furthermore, and of great significance, the so-called military spin-off of promising new technology has been marginal at best. In the electronics industry, for example, the armed services' contribution was in the development stage, not the invention or discovery stage. Additionally, military output was, for the most part, unsuited for civilian markets without extensive redesigning and reengineering. Focusing on civilian uses for electronics, Japan and western Europe captured most consumer markets by exploiting American inventions and discoveries.

Based on past achievements and some continuing innovation, the United States experienced an economic golden age from 1945 into the 1960s. Thereafter, as allies and former enemies rebuilt their economies and began to contest American economic dominance in nearly every sphere, the nation was unequal to the challenge. Losing markets abroad and at home, within fifteen years, inferior and costly products weakened, shrank, or wiped out numerous manufacturing sectors in many regions of the nation. Prosperity and the quality of life fell victim to stagflation, adverse balances of trade and payments, and growing and extreme dependence on foreign borrowing.

A corporate financial system that stressed profits over production and defense budgets that drained America's coffers and its creative talent without strengthening the economy have badly damaged the nation. For most of the late twentieth century and into the twenty-first, the American industrial economy has been in a state of decline. The U.S. standard of living has eroded, and its infrastructure and basic social services suffer from serious neglect. Other than arms, its exports consist principally of agricultural goods and raw materials, along with computer software and hardware, services, and entertainment, while imports of manufactured goods increase. Despite budgets in the hundreds of billions, America's armed forces have been significantly weakened. Weapons tend to be old and wanting, and servicemen and -women are frequently unprepared for and poorly led during the irregular military challenges they face. The proclaimed (often self-proclaimed) world hegemon lacks both the economic and the military power essential for maintaining its dominance. As things stand, conditions will continue to decline, not stabilize or improve, unless there is far-reaching change.

Before addressing the direct effects of national defense spending on the economy, the post–World War II economy and its transformation must be analyzed. In that way, the costs and consequences of the national security state can be assessed within the proper context.

LAVISH PROSPERITY IN THE EARLY COLD WAR YEARS

Steadily improving industrial productivity was key to American prosperity during most of the nineteenth and twentieth centuries. By 1870, the nation matched Europe in technology; by 1945, it had become envied as the world's premier industrial economy. Between 1950 and 1969, annual productivity growth averaged 2.5 percent; for manufacturing, the figure was 3.35 percent.[1]

Increasing in efficiency and variety, machine tools gave entrepreneurial industrial managers the ability to improve production while minimizing costs. These conditions allowed wages to rise steadily without an equivalent increase in prices. From 1939 to 1947, for example, hourly industrial wages rose 95 percent, while machine-tool costs increased only 39 percent. Although this period involved the unusual circumstances accompanying World War II, these figures reflected the general pattern for the late nineteenth century and most of the twentieth. Wages that were consistently the highest in the international community were vital to upward mobility and the promise of American life. They were achieved through management's investment in advanced capital goods and the reorganization of plants to maximize the opportunities of modified or new production methods.[2]

Entering the twentieth century, the United States was well on its way to becoming the world's leading economy. Although the United States was still an international net debtor in 1914, by 1919, the First World War had increased its industrial strength, and it had become the world's leading net creditor by a substantial measure. In that position, the United States maintained a favorable balance of trade through 1970, regularly exporting more goods and services than it imported. From 1971 on, however (with the exception of a few years), the nation began running up consistently growing negative trade balances, particularly in manufactured goods. In 1985, for the first time since World War I, it also became an international net debtor again, soon owing trillions of dollars.[3]

Before the decline that began in around 1965, the nation experienced exceptionally positive economic conditions.[4] Mobilization for World War II, which began in the late 1930s and included widespread support for allies, finally ended the Great Depression and pushed the economy to new heights. After the dislocation of reconversion in 1945 and 1946, peacetime prosperity prevailed. When the economy began a downturn in the late 1940s, demand related to the Korean War brought back economic growth. In the first half of the 1960s, the economy appeared to be entering a period of nearly perfect conditions. Steady economic expansion took place within a context of rising wages and reasonably steady prices. Escalating spending for the Vietnam War ended the illusion of good times and introduced the nation to stagflation. When the Nixon administration floated the dollar in 1971, it ended the 1944 Bretton Woods agreement pegging international exchange rates to the dollar—an arrangement that had been economically beneficial to the United States both at home and abroad.

The United States' postwar prosperity and economic growth were based on both continuing and unusual conditions. As in the past, productivity steadily improved, averaging 2.5 percent during the 1950s, while inflation remained at approximately 2.2 percent and unemployment at 4.5 percent. The major difference was that for the first two decades after the termination of hostilities, the United States was the only fully intact industrial power with ample financial resources. Under such conditions, American dollars and products flowed into the international community—particularly western Europe and Japan, but also the developing world—in massive amounts.

In retrospect, the two postwar decades were the global high point of the American economic system. Thereafter, decline and disequilibrium set in. Two major developments operated to undermine the continuing progress and stability of the economy. The corporate system turned to maximizing profits through new and elevated levels of consolidation and manipulation instead of the slower and harder process of improving products and productivity. At the same time, the nation began expanding its military system to meet Cold War challenges and to police and oversee an expanding empire. The emerging national security state absorbed enormous resources and energy, claiming more than half the federal budget and diverting funds from the civilian sector. These developments, along with the growing national conservatism of the 1970s, marked the beginning of public neglect of infrastructure, medical care, education, and a host of other needs.

Moreover, and of enormous importance, the Department of Defense became a primary source for the development of solid-state electronics. Whereas most of industrial America was uninterested or unwilling to invest adequately in adapting electronics from military uses to civilian purposes, Japan and western Europe seized the vast and promising opportunity. As a result, America was largely elbowed out of a new, expanding civilian industry for which it had provided most of the basic inventions and discoveries. Years later, however, American firms achieved a dominant role in computer software, hardware design, and Internet services.

America's economic decline did not begin primarily from unanticipated outside forces. Instead, the new postwar direction of its corporate and financial leaders and the pursuit of empire backed by military might were conscious choices of the American power elite. Significant signs of economic trouble became clear around 1965. In the period 1960–1964, industrial productivity increased, on average, around 3.0 percent annually; by 1975–1979, it fell to 1.2 percent; and by the first half of the 1980s, it dropped to 0.74 percent. For those industries that survived, future progress in product and process was slight at best, and at times, productivity slipped into the negative category. Although the economy grew again in the 1990s, the expansion was not based on the necessary structural change.

Looking back, industrial advances in product and process had taken place between 1945 and 1960, frequently earlier. In the immediate postwar period, the innovative standouts were antibiotics, solid-state electronics, television, plastics, pesticides, and nuclear power. Most industries, however, relied on economies of scale to realize productivity increases. Plants grew in size, and equipment became larger and faster, but neither process nor product basically improved. As long as demand grew at home and abroad—which was certainly the case for most of the years between 1945 and 1965 and, in many instances, for periods thereafter—the approach worked. Changing markets and conditions set definite limits to the strategy, however. That was particularly the case starting around 1965, when western Europe and Japan began to compete successfully with the United States in consumer and producer durables and other products. They did so in their own countries, in other nations, and on American soil. With war-torn industrial countries back on their productive feet, the virtually competitor-free postwar world had ended for America.

ECONOMIC DECLINE

A number of industries soon faced meaningful competition from imports. Such was the case with footwear, apparel, textiles, steel, and, in time, automobiles. Steel and autos stand out in this regard; among smaller industries, machine tools and machinery are of great importance.

Although the steel industry faced definite challenges from abroad, along with rising costs and declining domestic demand, its principal problems stemmed from management.[5] The industry neglected R&D, as well as its plant and equipment. Additionally, labor relations were poor, and market awareness was little better. Management emphasized short-run profits, not steel's long-run prospects. This reality is well illustrated by the industry's response to technological transformations in the postwar years. Three basic advances in steelmaking took place after 1945. During World War II, Austria and Switzerland developed the basic oxygen furnace and continuous casting. The first process became operational in 1949 and replaced the cumbersome and costly open-hearth furnace; beginning in 1960, the second cut out soaking pits, reheating operations, and other steps. The third innovation was direct reduction, which eliminated the blast furnace and pig iron stages, taking iron ore directly to steel. Westinghouse developed the plasma-melt process as one of the most promising systems for direct reduction. Separately and together, these three innovations greatly reduced capital costs, significantly increased productivity and efficiency, offered vast savings in energy and labor, eliminated much waste, served environmental purposes, and added to the industry's flexibility. The huge, expensive, integrated plant could be replaced or supplemented by smaller facilities, or so-called minimills.

The American steel industry knew of but generally ignored these three technological breakthroughs. It went forward with an extensive expansion in the early 1950s based on the open-hearth furnace, dating back to the late nineteenth century, although it was now larger to exploit economies of scale. According to a 1980 study by the congressional Office of Technology Assessment, steel managers believed it was cheaper to buy proven technology than to gamble on the costs and risks of innovation. With such an attitude, the new technology was developed without regard for American processes and requirements, which had to be addressed later. In addition, competitors—in this case, foreign firms—had a critical head start. In time, American steelmakers began adapting the basic oxygen furnace and continuous casting for their plants; they remained less open to direct reduction. Nonetheless, U.S. firms consistently lagged behind most foreign producers in updating their facilities.

In actuality, steel firms appeared to be more interested in abandoning the industry through diversification than in modernizing their plant. To help finance the strategy, steelmakers maximized the sale of stock by keeping profits and dividends as high as possible. That goal was achieved by neglecting the plant, implementing other cost-cutting measures, and shutting down the least efficient facilities, as occurred on a major scale in the late 1970s. Additionally, the industry relied on various federal financial concessions, including tax relief, accelerated plant depreciation, and the like. In 1978 U.S. Steel remained among the large steel producers, accounting for around 20 percent of the domestic market. By that time, 44 percent of the corporation's worldwide assets were outside the steel industry. Continuing to diversify, U.S. Steel acquired a controlling share of Marathon Oil Company stock in 1982 for $6 billion; other holdings involved indirect investments in foreign steel competitors. Yet U.S. Steel had the largest group of obsolete plants in the industry. Although U.S. Steel is among the more extreme examples of a corporation undermining its own business, most big steel producers had similar records. Such maneuvering inevitably led to a loss of market share. The nation became a net importer of steel sometime around 1960. Despite quotas and other restrictions, imports totaled about 20 percent of domestic consumption in 1984, and the figure kept rising.

Unlike steel, the automobile represented America's glamour industry and was an important agent for reshaping the nation's social relations. "No single product . . . has ever so dominated the imagination of the population, or the base of a national economy, as did the car."[6] Detroit's assembly lines were the world's most accomplished and complex.[7] The industry turned out 11.1 million cars, trucks, and buses in 1965. In one way or another, approximately one in six Americans owed his or her job to the auto companies. Motor City had an iron grip on the domestic market and exported heavily. It did so by turning out vehicles three times more efficiently than Europe, selling its product at the lowest prices, and paying its workers the highest wages worldwide.

The overwhelming dominance lasted for no more than twenty-five years. Imports were insignificant in the 1950s and picked up only somewhat in the 1960s. By the late 1970s, however, imports, especially from Japan, had taken over 25 percent of the market and were approaching one-third by the mid-1980s. Washington imposed quotas and other import restrictions beginning in 1981 and also bailed out Chrysler Corporation. Chrysler declared bankruptcy in 2009, despite mammoth federal loans that also kept General Motors afloat.

Detroit's fundamental problem is that its attention and resources have been focused on maximizing productivity through improving, refining, and quickening the assembly line with bigger, better, and faster equipment, including automation and, in some cases, robots. The fixation on output blended in with a nearly ideological commitment to large, powerful, spacious cars. Under these imperatives, productivity and profits are increased by the uninterrupted flow of the same or comparable parts, components, subassemblies, and vehicles. Accordingly, the auto firms have been manufacturing a similar product since the 1920s. Different firms have stylistic signatures, market similar cars under a variety of brand names, and offer cosmetic adaptations in annual model changes. Innovations such as power assists and automatic transmissions were significant departures from the norm, with the latter and other advances coming from outside the industry. Genuine change became difficult—almost impossible—with the intense concentration on established products and processes. That led Detroit to fight tenaciously against change and to accept only reluctantly all safety measures, improvements in fuel efficiency, pollution controls, and other proposed modifications. Car companies sometimes appeared contemptuous of technology and the public. Their contempt extended to blue-collar workers and their union, the United Automobile Workers (UAW). Dehumanized by the relentless assembly line and increasingly hostile managers, labor's loyalty eroded, with damaging effects on product quality.

By the late 1960s to early 1970s, American cars had lost their luster. Increasing numbers of Americans considered them too big and expensive and poorly designed and built. Relatively small, less expensive imports that featured fuel efficiency and quality design and construction became attractive alternatives, made all the more desirable by the Middle East oil crisis of 1973. Before the 1970s ended, Detroit's downward spiral was well under way.

The automobile firms responded to the challenges in a number of ways. After a considerable delay, some tried to match the Japanese and European products, without much success. Motor City had become trapped by its own culture: small cars tended to suffer from dismal design and poor quality. General Motors led in building plants in union-hostile states to escape the UAW and reduce labor costs. Employee layoffs and plant shutdowns became rampant in the late 1970s and after.

More and more, the car companies looked to solutions beyond U.S. borders. They had been investing abroad on a growing scale since 1950, and the process speeded up as markets at home diminished. By the end of the 1970s, 54.5 percent of the Ford Motor Company's assets involved foreign holdings; for Chrysler, the figure was 30.9 percent; and for General Motors, 26.1 percent. Increasingly, an American car, as such, did not exist. Parts, components, subassemblies, and entire vehicles came from foreign subsidiaries, joint ventures, or contracts in Europe, Asia, Latin America, and elsewhere. Arrangements could be structured in such a way that American laws, union contracts, regulations, and taxes were avoided or attenuated. Management control could be nearly absolute. This reality was well demonstrated by the Ford Fiesta—the so-called world car—introduced in 1976. It was designed and developed in Europe and assembled in three European countries from components made throughout Europe and the United States. The successor Escort had parts made or assembled in sixteen countries on three continents. With scattered and parallel production plants and multisourcing, union pressure and strikes could be thwarted. Playing off one city, state, or region against another had escalated to bidding wars among competing nations.

Try as they might, however, the automobile companies could not escape their own management strategies. Markets continued to shrink at home, and their foreign operations had helped create competing industries around the globe. Indeed, foreign auto firms established full-scale plants in the United States. Late in the twentieth century, excess production facilities threatened countries throughout the world and worsened the crisis of American auto firms, which were fighting just to survive.

Machine tools, in a sense, are more important to manufacturing than either steel or vehicles: they are the seed-corn industry of any advanced economic system.[8] America's machine-tool industry dates back to the early nineteenth century; it made possible interchangeable parts, leading to mass production. After the Civil War and continuing for about a century, the United States replaced England as the premier producer and was world renowned for innovative, high-quality, reliable, and affordable machines. In 1940, after the doldrums of the Great Depression, the machine-tool industry began an exceptional twenty-five-year period of flush times. Then, from 1965 on, the machine-tool industry, like steel and autos, began to decline. By 1978, for the first time in its history, the United States was importing more machine tools than it was exporting. Imports grew to approximately 25 percent of domestic demand by 1980, and the numbers kept rising.

The industry fell on hard times because of its unwillingness to innovate and invest. Similar to the steel and auto industries, it appeared to lose the drive and creativity that had kept it on top for so long. Once western Europe, Japan, and even Russia had attained postwar economic viability, they began to manufacture and refine standardized and modularized machine tools. Selected parts of the intricate machines were rationalized, and the machines as a whole were manufactured in modules, or subassemblies, that could be quickly put together in various ways to meet different specifications. These redesigned machines could also be rearranged in plants to serve different purposes or organized and reorganized as production centers. Parts and modules could be mass-produced, inventories built up, and orders filled expeditiously. Delivery took place in weeks, not the months or years that customized work required; at the same time, quality remained high, and prices dropped as productivity rose substantially.

So-called numerical control was another significant technological advance. It was sponsored by the U.S. Air Force and devised by technologists at MIT in the 1950s, with the advice of machine-tool industry executives. The end result was various machine tools operated by computer programs; they were used to shape multiple large workpieces for high-performance aircraft with precision, speed, and reliability. Developed and produced largely without regard to cost—simpler, cheaper, and more reliable alternatives were bypassed—the numerical-control machines were so expensive that by 1978, only 6 percent of aerospace contractors purchased them, along with about 2 percent of nondefense companies. However, the Japanese and western Europeans managed to produce affordable numerical-control products and located or created markets for them, as they did for their machine tools in general.

The automobile companies—the machine-tool firms' biggest customers—forced the industry to standardize and modularize machines for Detroit by threatening to produce their own. For most producers, auto plants were the exception to industry executives' general insistence that market volatility simply precluded mass production. Customized output, practically handicraft in nature, was the only approach that made sense. Such attitudes led to the industry dividing roughly in two. The majority of firms were medium to small in size. For those that managed to avoid acquisition, bankruptcy, downsizing, or closure, production proceeded at a deliberate pace, relying on dated, often antiquated, machinery. For some of the larger companies, military contracts could yield lavish returns even with aging equipment, unless the DOD paid for modernization. Industry divisions and differences aside, machine-tool prices skyrocketed after 1965 because of shrinking markets, falling productivity levels, or the rising costs of defense and space contracting. These circumstances restricted demand even further at home and squeezed U.S. products out of additional sales abroad.

As with steel and cars, profits from machine tools were increasingly invested abroad after the mid-1960s. American firms used their foreign subsidiaries to service foreign clients, provide components for output at home, or send entire machines (carrying company labels) to the United States for domestic sale. Some corporations worked out joint ventures with Japan or Europe or acted as other countries' agents, marketing their machines in the United States. Such arrangements could be very profitable, but the price was high: the United States' virtual loss of a critical industry.

The loss affected the entire economy, but especially the machinery industry and the corporations it supplied. General machine companies and their clients depended on American industries to equip their plants; only as a last and desperate act would they turn to foreign suppliers. As a result, machinery and manufacturing companies' own tools aged, and their output declined in quality and quantity. Textile machine makers, along with those for many other industries, all but disappeared, forcing the product manufacturers that survived to rely on imports. In the new and endlessly promising electronics industry, American commercial firms could not compete effectively in circuit board and chip production. The high-precision machines required for such output were unavailable or had been preempted by defense and space contractors that were not concerned about costs. Thus, another field pioneered by Americans was allowed to be commercially developed and dominated by foreign competitors.

DEINDUSTRIALIZATION

What occurred in steel, automobiles, machine tools, and general machinery took place in varying degrees throughout the nation.[9] Localities, states, and regions in most parts of the country were deindustrialized, with often devastating consequences for labor, communities, support services, businesses, and governments. And, more often than not, the destruction was not creative in a Schumpeterian sense: precious little new enterprise arose from the ashes.

The reasons for the broader industrial decline have been touched on in the preceding analysis of specific industries. The unmatched success of the American economy from 1945 through 1965 and beyond goes far in explaining the fall that followed. After World War II, America's manufacturers had ideal, enviable market conditions. Mass wartime savings and deferred consumption created vast, pulsating markets at home; opportunities abroad were every bit as great. In a world destroyed and distressed, the United States accounted for more than 50 percent of international output capacity. It also served as world creditor. As agreed at Bretton Woods in 1944, global economic operations revolved around the dollar, backed up by the American-dominated International Monetary Fund and the so-called World Bank. Later, the General Agreement on Tariffs and Trade furthered international economic operations. All these circumstances, agreements, and agencies facilitated the global reach of American corporations.

Demand for American goods knew no bounds. Nearly every sector of the economy was well prepared to exploit the exceptional, practically unprecedented, opportunities. Industry stood out in that regard. A large part of its plant and equipment had been expanded, renewed, and updated, largely at government expense through huge wartime building programs; facilities and equipment were later sold to private owners for a fraction of their worth. Washington also devised generous financing measures to assist corporate growth, offered accelerated amortization and tax credits, provided reconversion planning and assistance, and so forth.

With an unmatched industrial plant and demand that apparently had no limits, American corporate confidence soared as seldom, if ever, before. The only adjustment, if necessary, was a bigger plant and larger and faster equipment for delivering more. American economic leaders had everything to teach the world and little to learn from it. Corporate leaders had become so confident that they were willing (some more reluctantly than others) to negotiate a social contract with their barely respected trade-union rivals. Labor would receive high wages and generous fringe benefits in exchange for their leaders managing and disciplining the workforce in a way that maintained industrial peace, a pattern similar to that seen during World War II. Collective bargaining would be restricted to pay, other benefits, and working conditions. Management's prerogatives on corporate structure, plant, equipment, location, organization, product, operations, investment, profits, and the like would remain inviolate.

The labor peace that ensued facilitated corporate America's uninterrupted focus on markets at home and abroad. On a new scale, that meant investing abroad. In 1950 direct foreign investment by American firms totaled $11.8 billion; by 1980, it had soared to $200 billion. Of the latter figure, about 40 percent was in manufacturing, 30 percent in petroleum, and 30 percent in other fields. Moreover, foreign investments absorbed increasing amounts of companies' expenditures for plant and equipment. In the period 1957–1961, corporations devoted the equivalent of 12 percent of domestic outlays on foreign operations; from 1967 to 1970, that amount was 21 percent. In 1970 American multinational corporations had assets abroad that equaled approximately 26.1 percent of domestic manufacturing capital. In 1979, among the largest multinationals, foreign investments accounted for, on average, 37 percent of their total assets. For Gillette, the figure was 60.6 percent; for Goodyear, 42.7 percent; for Bendix, 31 percent; for Procter and Gamble, 24 percent; for RCA, 15.1 percent; and for Westinghouse, 9.3 percent. After-tax profits of corporate foreign operations stood at 10 percent in the early 1950s, grew to 20 percent in the early 1970s, and, for the 100 largest corporations and banks, totaled around 33.3 percent of overall profits near the end of the 1970s.

Two critical developments made such worldwide operations feasible. First were breakthroughs in transportation and communications, including jet aircraft, telex, computers, and satellite communication links. In time, multinational giants set up their own exclusive high-technology communications systems, free from the direction of other sources. From a central headquarters in the United States, it became possible to set up and conduct, control, and monitor business, industrial, and financial transactions all over the globe reliably and almost instantly. Second, the concentration of financial resources essential for functioning on such a vast, heretofore unaccustomed, scale was made possible by the consolidation of industrial power in the hands of a relatively few massive corporate structures.

These new worldwide, self-contained production systems not only supplied producers and consumers in developed and underdeveloped regions but also changed the patterns of American trade. In 1970 nearly three-quarters of U.S. exports and close to half of all imports were carried out among American multinational conglomerates and their foreign subsidiaries. The Bulova Watch Company, for example, had watch movements manufactured in Switzerland; they were then shipped to Pago Pago in American Samoa for assembly and then on to the United States for sale. Company president Harry P. Henshel observed, "We are able to beat the foreign competition because we are the foreign competition."[10]

When investing abroad, American firms concentrated principally on western Europe, to some degree on Japan, and increasingly on the less developed regions of Asia and Latin America. Multinationals also began selling or licensing patents, production agreements, and know-how for their products, subcomponents, and parts, and they frequently did so at subpar prices. Intentionally or inadvertently, they helped create the foreign competitors that later challenged and in some cases overwhelmed them.

Corporations manufacturing automobiles, machine tools, and machinery can be classified as multinational; steel corporations fall into the conglomerate category, in which firms invest in or acquire American assets outside their industry. Some firms fall into both categories. Multinational conglomerates are not atypical, as evidenced by U.S. Steel and numerous other corporations. Whatever the situation, conglomerates, like multinationals, took on new levels of activity and importance in the postwar period. During the 1920s and into the 1940s, most mergers and acquisitions were of the horizontal and vertical varieties, with the latter predominating. Conglomerate activity never constituted more than 21 percent of total consolidations between 1926 and 1947. The first fully integrated conglomerate was Textron, which, between 1943 and 1980, acquired and sold more than 100 firms in industries ranging from textiles to aerospace to pens. In the early 1950s, however, almost 49 percent of mergers involved conglomerates, and by 1966–1968, the figure had jumped to nearly 82 percent.

Profits were clearly the driving force for the frantic pace of conglomerate growth. Concerns about product quality, the labor force, and communities were secondary, if they were considered in corporate strategizing at all. The consequences for localities, states, the nation, the economy, and the society as a whole could be dire. One of the principal advantages of the conglomerate structure is flexibility. Divisions or subsidiaries can be treated in differing ways to maximize the organizing corporation's bottom line.

In the early 1970s the prominent Boston Consulting Group (BCG), once affiliated with Harvard's Graduate School of Business Administration, set forth a strategy for conglomerates to maximize profits. They should get rid of "dogs," or companies that required reinvestment to remain profitable. "Cash cows," or mature companies with high market shares but slow growth rates, should be "milked." In doing so, outlays should be restricted to the minimum to keep plants running, and maximum profits should be drained off for conglomerate operations or new acquisitions. Youngstown Sheet and Tube Company of Ohio, the nation's eighth largest steel company, stands out in this regard. It was acquired by the Lykes Corporation in 1969, steadily milked, and then shut down in 1977. Next, BCG advised conglomerates to invest in "problem children" with low market shares but rapid growth rates. Last, the high-growth, high-share "stars" should be given a free hand, with the expectation of enriching the mother corporation in the future. Business schools in general may not have followed BCG's recommendations exactly, but many stressed conglomerate strategy for short-term cash maximization and paid little attention to manufacturing operations and production.

Conglomerates vary in their strategies, but several characteristics and patterns stand out. Bureaucracies proliferate in this type of corporate structure. Between 1950 and 1980, overhead personnel, including managers, staff, and others, grew from 18 to 30 percent of the total number of manufacturing employees. Some of the expansion began before conglomerates became the rage, as corporate management was seeking to strengthen its control. By necessity, conglomerates require more personnel to manage and keep tabs on their multiple parts. For that reason, during a slowdown, central headquarters lays off blue-collar workers at a higher rate than white-collar employees, since managerial control is the priority. However, a price is paid. Growing bureaucracies increase costs and reduce labor productivity, frequently in a very substantial way.

On paper, conglomerates inaccurately accounted for a substantial number of new businesses and industrial firms. During the 1970s, 410 of the nation's largest manufacturers—most of the *Fortune* 500—acquired existing firms instead of building new facilities. Nonetheless, those transactions were recorded as new firms. More than 12,000 plants were involved, although the figure grew to 17,000 after additional sales, transfers, and the like were included. Of those 12,000 firms, only one-seventh were expanded. Acquisitions and sales were hardly restricted to the *Fortune* list. Many large corporations engaged in the practice. Conglomerates therefore tend to lower labor productivity and reduce the number of manufacturing firms. Even foreign investors, for the most part, are acquiring existing plants rather than building new ones.

Conglomerates have multiplied manyfold the responsibilities and authority of management. No executive or group of executives can possibly understand, let alone master, the operating procedures of such a vast and varied collection of subsidiaries or divisions. The situation is exaggerated by the high rate of turnover among top-level executives specializing in short-term profit maximization. Among newly hired college recruits, 50 percent will move on within five years. What has eased management's burden, yet encouraged the turbulence, is a clearly defined major end: profitability, or the so-called cash box. This principle guides decisions on buying, selling, and evaluating divisions and subsidiaries. The goal of profitability can yield positive results, including turning around mismanaged companies, investing (perhaps heavily) in BCG's "problem children," or giving free rein to the "stars" that can prosper in secure circumstances.

But just as frequently, the results are negative. Mistakes occur, and management decisions may be questionable, wrong, or even terribly inept. Dire consequences can follow. Many profitable companies of long standing have been badly damaged, sold, or shut down under conglomerate control. The central office, for example, might set profit goals for subsidiaries as high as 22 percent annually, which few units can meet, leading to a subsidiary's sale or the termination of executives. Old management might be replaced by a new team with little or no experience in the product lines involved. With few exceptions, the predictable outcome is the upending of the company. The same result could occur if the conglomerate imposes unwise or inappropriate methods in the areas of marketing, customer relations, accounting, employee relations, security, or ties with suppliers and subcontractors. Under such circumstances, costs can escalate, production drop, customers and clients fall away, and other disruptions befall a once efficient plant. For accounting purposes, corporate headquarters can also charge its own expenses or those of other acquired companies to subsidiaries, distorting profitability. In one way or another, for good or bad, one corporation or company taking over another almost always leads to change for the acquired firm.

Under conglomerate structures, pressures within the subsidiary holdings can reach nearly intolerable levels, with untoward consequences. Central management wields real or imagined tyrannical power aided by telecommunications, computers, and other high-tech devices, as well as by the ubiquitous quarterly report, backed at times by daily, weekly, or monthly supplements. These short-run measures can dictate executive success, continued employment, highly valued bonuses, and the future of the unit. Management at all levels can be driven to unsound, unprofessional, or even criminal behavior by the unrelieved stress of unending evaluations and demands.

"Creative accounting" may not have originated with conglomerates, but it became a common practice among many of them in the drive to improve the appearance of corporate performance, enhance stock sales, and fill the cash box. In hard times, such as the 1970s, temptations in that direction grew intense. More extreme behavior occurred as well. Executives of 1,043 corporations were included in a 1980 study of illegal behavior. Among these executives, 117 were found guilty or pleaded no contest to criminal charges other than those related to illegal accounting practices. Included were toxic dumping and maintaining forms of peonage among illegal Latino immigrants in commercial agricultural operations in the South and Southwest. Among aerospace executives, bribing foreign officials to obtain sales was repeatedly reported.

The existing statistical studies indicate that conglomerates wipe out more industrial firms and jobs than they create. In New England between 1969 and 1976, plant closings were rampant, eliminating 1.4 million jobs. Conglomerates accounted for 15 percent of the shutdowns but 50 percent of the unemployment, meaning that they were responsible for the largest firm failures. When substantial plants, as opposed to small businesses, close down, they have a great reverse-multiplier effect. Suppliers, subcontractors, and commercial, professional, and community service providers are adversely affected. Due to such conditions, the impact of closures expands severalfold. Data suggest that what occurred in New England is a fair guide to what has taken place throughout the nation.

Conglomerates also tend to reduce the economy's competitiveness by driving up prices and reducing labor productivity. Additionally, the hundreds of billions of dollars these giant corporations require in credit lines and cash reserves for ongoing acquisitions can act to elevate lending rates. As a result, credit for smaller firms can be more expensive or even out of reach. Such an outcome can feed inflationary pressures and adversely affect the nation's economic viability.

The profit quest also put an end to corporate America's social contract with organized labor. The contract was originally worked out at a time when corporate profits were high and the future looked bright. The real rate of return on corporate operations averaged 15.5 percent in the early 1960s. By the end of the decade, when western Europe and Japan became competitive, the figure had dropped to 12.7 percent. As the challenge continued to grow, earnings fell to 10.1 percent in the early 1970s and to 10 percent in 1975, staying at that level or declining further in subsequent years. Reduced returns on investment and a clouded economic future led corporate America to unilaterally abandon its informal pact with unions and to declare war on America's modest welfare state. Under President Reagan, those goals were significantly advanced.

In voiding the social contract, management devised approaches to break unions' hold that were subtle and sophisticated compared with the crude and violent ways of the past. Multinational and conglomerate corporate structures proved highly useful in that regard. Plants and entire industries could be moved from labor-friendly to antilabor locales and, if necessary, to more congenial regions abroad. Such was the case on a massive scale beginning in the 1970s. In 1965, for example, Litton Industries acquired the Royal Typewriter Company. Facing labor challenges, Litton moved all plants abroad, acting with stealth and without notice or benefits of any kind to its employees. A leading firm in the industry thus disappeared from American soil in just a few years.

Even without relocation, unions at home and abroad were placed in a weakened, almost submissive collective-bargaining situation when corporations adopted the tactic of using alternative producers and multiple suppliers. Union resistance could simply be bypassed by arranging bidding wars among companies, states, regions, and even nations. The antilabor onslaught was more than successful. Unions had represented about one out of three manufacturing employees in the 1950s; by the later decades of the twentieth century, they were down to just a third of that level. Membership was increasingly concentrated among service and government employees, with unions in the manufacturing sector often forced to engage in givebacks.

The attack on labor had an intensity that bordered on class warfare. Typically, the antagonism was from the top down, not the bottom up. Blue-collar resentments were generally workplace, not class, related. The broad-scale, often shrill attack on welfare revealed the tone. In the case of labor, industry wanted to go further than wiping out unions; it wanted to build visible walls to distinguish management from the workforce. In 1947 the ratio of managers to workers was 22 to 100; by 1977, it had just about doubled to 43 to 100. Management was tightening its control, becoming more evident, and distancing itself from its charges. Moreover, as productivity dropped, competitiveness declined, and plants and industries shut down, management income skyrocketed, both in isolation and compared with that of labor. All these moves were no doubt intended to motivate management in a corporate system increasingly dedicated to short-run profit making. Still, class antagonism hovered over corporate operations, in place of the real or feigned harmony of the golden years. The animosity certainly facilitated the making of harsh decisions fixated on the cash box, without regard to the impact on workers, communities, or government financing and services at all levels.

Washington encouraged multinational corporations and conglomerates in both passive and active ways. Passively, it usually proceeded with great caution or avoided using the antitrust laws. Actively, the federal government rewarded consolidation through credits and tax breaks, investment incentives, export rewards, import restrictions, and guidance, support, and protection for operations outside the nation's borders. Conglomerate growth was supported out of the mistaken conviction that it would create more and better job opportunities. Multinational corporations were seen as strengthening the nation's institutions and economy, increasing the American presence abroad, assisting the growth of friendly developing nations, and generally aiding America's diplomacy, geopolitical goals, and national security.

Both multinational and conglomerate structures and activity increased as the American economy faced growing competition from abroad. Advocates of multinationals, including those operating as conglomerates, insist that the global reach was and is defensive in nature and helps reduce the nation's unemployment by absorbing or assisting failing firms or industries and those struggling to get under way. Additionally, corporations expanding at home and going abroad create alternative employment opportunities in finance, man-

agement, information and communication systems, and clerical work and as
suppliers of various sorts. From another direction, some scholars insist that the
creative destruction brought about or accelerated by multinationals and conglomerates is essential if America is to move on and regenerate economically.
Both arguments have been analyzed by other scholars and found to be questionable, wanting, or wrong.

THE LOST OPPORTUNITY OF HIGH TECHNOLOGY

If the nation needed to get rid of more "sunset" industries, surely electronics
was the "sunrise" industry to nurture.[11] By drift as much as by design, the nation
initially allowed the military to lead in developing the new field, to the detriment of commercial manufacturing. Drawing on American innovations, Japan
and, to a lesser degree, Europe became the major producers of electronic consumer and producer goods. The United States later made a comeback based
principally on a host of start-ups following a new corporate strategy.

In terms of so-called high technology, with the exception of some parts for
radar and aircraft, the armed services can claim no credit for discoveries or
inventions. Their contribution has stemmed from assisting industries marketing new products by providing massive "first user" demand. All the principal
discoveries were made by commercial firms.

The transistor, unveiled in late 1947 by American Telephone & Telegraph's
(AT&T's) Bell Telephone Laboratories, was the initial and principal innovation
triggering the electronics revolution. Out of concern that the military would
declare the breakthrough to be classified, Bell held off revealing its secrets to
the armed services until the discovery had become public knowledge, ensuring
AT&T's opportunity to develop it for civilian uses. In 1954, however, as part
of an antitrust suit, AT&T had to license and release its patents relating to the
device, creating a vital opening for other firms. The successive steps from transistor to semiconductor to integrated circuit, or microchip, were made by relatively small, innovative firms such as Texas Instruments, Fairchild
Semiconductor, Mostek, and Intel. Large and established firms producing
radios and television sets had just invested heavily in new plant and equipment
for vacuum tubes and wanted to recoup their investment before considering
electronic possibilities.

In terms of actually developing solid-state electronics, the military's contribution was both substantial and vital during the late 1950s and early 1960s.
All the armed services were adopting a new generation of weaponry, including
missiles, satellites, aircraft, ships, land vehicles, and communications and infor-

mation systems. Computers, from the simplest to the most complex, soon became standard equipment. Electronics were central to the military's new age. Hence, all the services and the DOD not only financed R&D projects readily and generously but also assisted advances in electronics through steady and growing procurement. The military's high demand greatly assisted the advances pursued by firms such as Texas Instruments.

Once integrated circuits reached the mass production phase and became standardized and inexpensive, they began transforming consumer and producer products and production. Over time, chips made affordable word processors, personal computers, heating and cooling equipment, and telecommunications systems, along with factory machines and operations and any item, service, or process to which electronic chips could be profitably applied. By the late 1960s and 1970s, civilian demand and products surpassed military procurement in quantity and, in a sense, quality. Electronics became the fastest expanding major American industry. By 1975, sales had reached nearly $44 billion and were growing annually by billions of dollars.

But troubling signs with regard to U.S. dominance started to appear by the mid-1970s. In the 1960s Japan had begun exporting consumer electronic products based on transistors and semiconductors. By 1974, the Asian nation initiated foreign sales in integrated circuits for computers and other industrial uses, and soon thereafter it entered the sophisticated field of high-powered memory chips, which dictate the speed and capacity of random-access memory (RAM). The "chip wars" were under way. Until well into the 1970s, American firms had a virtual world monopoly on microchips. Japan's big break came in 1978, when American firms could not meet the high demand for the advanced memory chips required by the latest IBM computer. Quickly capturing 40 percent of the market, the Asian rival led the drive for skyrocketing RAM, powered by memory chips of once unimagined capacity.

By the early 1980s, the chip wars had been settled in Japan's favor. And that was just the beginning. American companies were making fewer and fewer of the electronic consumer and producer goods sold in the United States. Many "U.S." products, if not actually manufactured in Asia or Europe, included imported parts, components, and subassemblies. Some carried American brand names but little else. Such was the case with computerized machine tools and other plant and office equipment. Most radios, television sets, telecommunications and photographic equipment, copiers, calculators, watches and clocks, tape recorders, video devices, and many other electronic products came from abroad. Large manufacturers such as General Electric had diversified at home and abroad or had become sizable military contractors.

For the first time, America experienced a high-technology trade deficit in

1986. Most of what was imported was based on inventions, discoveries, and innovations originating in the United States. The nation's promising sunrise industry appeared to have reached the sunset stage within just a few decades. Part of the reason why can be laid at the doorstep of corporate America. In the fields of both producer and consumer goods, large, established manufacturers for various reasons failed to seize the vast opportunities electronics offered. Hence, Bell's pioneering accomplishment was taken up principally by smaller firms and start-ups for the further innovation and development required. Those companies had to depend on the great interest and growing demand of the armed services to sustain their progress. That development pushed electronic growth in a narrow and limited direction. The military aimed for arms superiority; Japan and western Europe emphasized economic growth.

The profit-maximizing orientation of post–World War II corporate America also acted to impair the progress of electronics. Major companies in industries that would benefit the most from solid-state circuitry had become risk averse, turning to investments that promised short-run profits rather than those that would deliver returns only in the long run. Even electronics firms appeared to fall prey to the shortsighted pursuit of profits. By comparison, Japanese companies bought American integrated circuit technology, output tools, and machinery to guide their chip production efforts. When American firms realized that they could not penetrate Japan's markets, they granted Japanese companies access to their patents in exchange for royalties, further accelerating their progress. By the late 1960s, 10 percent or more of Japanese microchip output revenue was going to U.S. firms.

The adverse circumstances the industry faced, though serious, were hardly overwhelming. From the outset, the principal drawback was military domination. Short-run benefits notwithstanding, the long-run consequences were extremely harmful for a number of reasons. The DOD and its services concentrated on supporting applied, not basic, research. For electronics, that meant developing existing technology instead of seeking to expand the depth and breadth of fundamental knowledge. Most significant inventions and discoveries grow out of basic work. That was true of Bell's transistor. This helps explain why military-funded R&D yields so few patents. Based on this lack of patents, combined with declining discoveries in the civilian sector, America's inventiveness deteriorated at an alarming rate. Using international comparisons, the nation's "patent balance" fell 30 percent between 1966 and 1973. More concretely, with only about 500 major innovations, the United States' lead over Japan and western Europe fell from 82 to 55 percent from the late 1950s to mid-1960s. A similar record existed with regard to American patents filed in other nations and those countries' patents filed in the United States.

The armed services have a mixed record at best when it comes to guiding research in the right direction. In the drive to miniaturize electronic components, the Army Signal Corps' work with RCA, the air force's pursuit of ambitious goals with Westinghouse, and the navy's experimentation involving "thin film" all failed to yield the desired results. Several conditions explain, at least in part, the military's shortcomings. The officers in charge of projects may not adequately understand the technology. Also of importance is the armed services' preference for contracting with large, established companies. Such corporations generally favor the use of existing practices over the search for better and alternative approaches; relatively new, small firms are much more likely to stress innovation, as evidenced in numerous new and established industries.

Of critical importance is the fact that most military technology has little or no commercial application. This reality is exaggerated as the armed services' weaponry and equipment grow more sophisticated and more specialized and become overdesigned and gold-plated. The technology used in missiles, rockets, stealth aircraft, projects such as SDI, guidance systems for smart weapons, electronic warfare, and night-vision devices is largely irrelevant for producer or consumer use. These weapons and tools are manufactured with little attention to cost, are customized rather than standardized for mass production, are often highly unreliable, require frequent repair and maintenance by trained specialists, and are not user-friendly.

Furthermore, defense contractors employ about one-third of the nation's scientists and engineers, many of whom are among the best in their fields. This denies civilian electronics firms—along with numerous other industries—the crucial services of these individuals at a time when adequately trained and qualified technologists are in increasingly short supply. Along the same lines, massive DOD budgets directly and indirectly act to restrict civilian investment capital, increase production costs, and adversely affect the economy owing to the inefficiency, and even incompetence, characteristic of military contractors' spending.

Finally, as is common for the armed forces, contractors are burdened with secrecy, bureaucracy, and ongoing red tape. Such conditions violate the basic principles of scientific inquiry, impede the development of technology through shared information and cooperation among companies and interested parties, and inhibit the entry of new contractors in favor of those already used.

In short, the vaunted spin-off of military electronics is an illusion. The principal contribution of the armed services and the DOD to advances in electronics came indirectly as a first user and a quantity procurer. Other than that, the military has been a major hindrance to America's progress in the field of electronics. For any military spin-off to occur, output has to be extensively redesigned—

practically reinvented—to meet civilian consumer and producer markets. Thorough reworking is required to standardize and mass-produce reasonably priced, reliable, durable, quality items that are user-friendly. For example, radar had to go through this demanding process before it became applicable to civilian purposes such as navigational guides and traffic control devices. Progress along these essential lines for civilian application has occurred on only a limited basis in the United States. The major corporations such as RCA, General Electric, and Westinghouse were occupied as DOD contractors or reluctant to commit to the long-term investment required.

Japan proved that civilian companies could master the electronics field and prosper, without military assistance. Japan took what it could from American progress and then went forward. With some government assistance, cooperation among government agencies and corporations, and guidance from a consortium of interested official and commercial parties, Japan willingly invested time, money, and intense effort and took a commanding lead in consumer and producer electronic products. A critical characteristic of Japan's success was adopting and then improving on America's corporate organizational and structural operations. Unlike Americans' insistence on maintaining rigid distinctions between salaried and hourly workers, the Japanese devised a system for integrating management and shop-floor labor into a process of ongoing, companywide organizational learning. To a lesser degree, western Europe also became a world competitor in solid-state electronics. Besides the United States, Great Britain is the only other major industrial nation suffering a significant decline in the civilian high-tech area. There, as here, military domination has distorted and stunted advances in civilian electronics.

While the United States was being challenged from abroad in numerous industries during the 1970s and 1980s, a resurgence was taking place in the information and communications technology (ICT) industries. This would usher in what William Lazonick has labeled the "new economic business model" (NEBM), as opposed to the old one (OEBM).[12] The latter characterized the years from 1945 into the 1980s, when the United States experienced exceptional economic conditions. High profits from stable and steady economic growth allowed corporations to offer both management and labor lifelong employment with good salaries and high hourly pay plus fringe benefits. The wealth generated by the system was shared in a reasonably equitable way and promised future generations lives of security and comfort. This was the basis for the new American middle and upper-middle classes and above.

The NEBM has taken away that promise. Stable economic growth has been replaced by boom and bust cycles, lifetime employment has given way to erratic and unpredictable patterns with uncertain compensation and declining benefits, and wealth distribution has become inequitable. Corporate shareholders and chief executive officers (CEOs) receive a grossly disproportionate share of the wealth. The working population is denied its fair share in multiple ways, as is the public through declining corporate and capital gains taxes. In many ways, labor and government have contributed more to the economic growth of the system than have corporate shareholders. Indeed, Lazonick argues that the federal government in the twentieth century was the world's most active developmental state. Whatever the case, the NEBM has fundamentally undermined the economic vibrancy and growth potential of the OEBM.

What eventually became the NEBM started back in the late 1950s with the establishment of solid-state electronics start-ups such as Fairchild Semiconductor. Quickly thereafter, a host of new firms were founded in the 1960s, and even greater numbers appeared in 1970s and 1980s; the trend peaked in the 1990s with the so-called Internet boom, which continues in the twenty-first century. The various firms have clustered in places such as Silicon Valley around Stanford University and Route 128 in the Boston area. This grouping has facilitated a process of intense organizational learning among firms, which complemented the R&D occurring within companies by exceptionally talented and trained personnel sharing varied skills.

IBM, an OEBM corporation, played an important role in the emergence of the ICT industries. In the early 1980s the firm shifted its major focus to the micro- or personal computer and in short order dominated the global market. In doing so, the company scrapped its reliance on proprietary technology in favor of cross-licensing and strategic alliances with other high-tech firms. Along these lines, IBM relied on Intel's microprocessor and Microsoft's operating system. It also outsourced the manufacturing of computers to a firm specializing in electronics production. Thereafter, IBM shifted its emphasis from R&D to product development.

IBM's transformation into the leading producer of personal computers also ended its renowned practice of guaranteeing all employees lifetime jobs with generous salaries, pay, and benefits. These policies were phased out in the 1990s. Besides reducing the number of employees, IBM turned increasingly toward younger, more recently educated personnel who had experience in the emerging high-tech fields. Older employees familiar with the past reliance on proprietary technology became much less valued. Permanence of the workforce, which had characterized the OEBM, was being replaced by interfirm mobility and flexibility.

Although somewhat later than IBM, Hewlett-Packard, another OEBM company, also basically transformed its operations to the standards of an open system. Other older firms such as AT&T made the same or similar changes.

The new Silicon Valley and Route 128 start-ups faced challenges that older companies such as IBM did not. Of immediate concern was finances, which venture capital solved. The risk involved was greatly attenuated in 1971 by the creation of the National Association of Securities Dealers Automated Quotations (NASDAQ), which was much less exacting in its listing requirements than the New York Stock Exchange. Within a few years after founding, start-ups such as Intel had made their initial public offerings. That allowed their financial supporters to recoup their investments. The availability of stock also provided the ICT start-ups with a means of attracting the professional, technical, and administrative personnel essential for their success. Employee stock options proved to be effective in convincing talented individuals to leave the security of OEBM corporations for uncertain but potentially lucrative employment with NEBM companies. Once established and under way, ICT employment patterns stressed younger workers with experience in the latest technology and a tendency to move from one high-tech firm to another.

Silicon Valley also turned to Asia for employees. As early as the 1960s and 1970s, ICT companies began outsourcing the production of semiconductors, circuit boards, and like components to India, China, and other Asian countries. The practice had a number of benefits. It lowered the price of marketed products while training Asian labor in high-tech production. In later years, experienced employees and university-educated personnel immigrated to the United States for employment and experience. As a relatively cheap, dependent source of labor, these immigrants increased the pool of employees and helped keep the level of compensation in the industry down. Globalization of investment and labor became attributes initiated by the NEBM companies.

Unlike the OEBM corporations, NEBM firms have not engaged in widespread diversification. Instead, the various companies have concentrated on improving and expanding output in their specialties. Microsoft and Oracle Corporation, for example, concentrate on operating systems and software; Cisco Systems and Dell focus on equipment manufacturing and hardware design; and Yahoo!, Google, and Facebook specialize in Internet operations.

After issuing stock, high-tech firms seldom paid dividends for years, even decades, and then only in limited amounts. Earnings were reinvested in the growth of the company. The strategy proved to be prudent. In the 1980s and first half of the 1990s, stock prices steadily rose as products improved and prices dropped. In the second half of the 1990s, however, the Internet boom fed speculation, and stock prices careened upward. With the advent of the new century, ICT corporations began manipulating their stock prices through the steady repurchase of their own stock to sustain or raise prices. The buyback process has taken place at the expense of dividends, R&D, and improved and expanded employment policies. Furthermore, it has acted to enrich CEOs and employees selling stock options.

Stock repurchases have spread from the ICT sector to include a good part of the corporate community, and they involve trillions of dollars. Besides the high-tech firms, the practice has become particularly widespread among the giant oil firms, pharmaceutical companies, and many of the banks that were chiefly responsible for the financial meltdown beginning in 2007. The rampant repurchase of stock has led to what Lazonick calls the "financialization" of the corporate structure—that is, the evaluation of corporate performance based on the price of stock and, therefore, shareholder earnings. The financialization actually began with the heightened conglomerate movement of the 1960s, when corporate earnings took precedence over company management. In pursuing this strategy, CEOs have exhausted company reserves and even eaten into capital. Dividends have been drastically reduced, the payment of outstanding debt deferred, and R&D budgets curtailed. Moreover, stock buybacks involve a glaring conflict of interest because they help enrich the CEOs authorizing them.

Under the OEBM, regular and reasonable dividend payments encouraged stockholders to retain their shares. Repurchasing stock—the standard NEBM approach—leads to stockholders selling their shares to reap the rewards of rising prices. Stock market stability, consequently, has given way to volatility. This outcome reflects the badly skewed distribution of corporate resources taking place with the NEBM. The passive stockholders have become the principal beneficiaries at the expense of the more active workforce and the public. Indeed, by practically draining coffers to manipulate stock prices, corporate executives have reduced their firms' ability to deal effectively with crises and competitive challenges. Of critical significance, they have also reduced the innovative capabilities of their companies.

Besides weakening the corporate system, the NEBM is principally responsible for the growing economic inequality in the nation. Employment opportunities and remuneration have been declining for decades. The government's ability to act in ways to serve the public has also been significantly squeezed. Since the early 1980s, corporations—often with high-tech firms in the lead—have successfully lobbied to lower corporate and capital gain taxes under the banner of furthering economic growth. And, while reducing their own R&D, business groups call on Washington to invest more in alternative energy sources, high-tech advances, and other areas of potential economic growth. The federal government continues to pursue its developmental role, but its ability to do so has been considerably limited by reduced revenue.

The faltering of the OEBM beginning in the late 1960s and the advent of many of the worst features of the NEBM have resulted in declining prospects for the American working population. Increasing numbers have had to turn to the rapidly growing service sector for employment in fields such as finance, marketing, sales, real estate, health care, education, food preparation, and janitorial services. Such a trend threatens the status and income of many of those in the blue- and white-collar middle class, to say nothing of the lower-class working population. All these developments have led to a precarious economy with a clouded future. With economic conditions continuing to weaken, the political structure and the social system in general have become more stressed and brittle, further darkening the outlook for the future.

EXPLAINING AMERICA'S ECONOMIC DESCENT

In seeking to explain America's declining industrial productivity and international competitiveness, economists, corporate managers, journalists, and other analysts beginning in the late 1960s put forth a number of possibilities. These included excessive government spending and regulation, high wages and benefits, the strength of the dollar, Organization of Petroleum Exporting Companies (OPEC) boycotts of the 1970s, unfair foreign business and trade practices, the comparative advantage and postwar plant of western Europe and Japan, and, more recently, technological transformation and globalization. Military spending and short-run, profit-maximizing corporate strategies seldom entered the mainstream analysis; to consider either was to run afoul of marketplace economic theory or generally accepted beliefs. Most assumed that spending for World War II put a final end to the Great Depression and that heavy federal outlays for national security and the Korean War beginning in 1949 revived the sagging postwar economy. As additions to the GDP, economic orthodoxy considered military production the equivalent of civilian activity.

Dissenters were few and seldom heard. Marxists looked on armed services outlays as either an essential tool of imperialism or a palliative stimulus that did not compete with the private sector. Either way, in their eyes, military spending was a desperate tactic pursued to save a faltering, doomed capitalist system.

Opposition to the Vietnam War and its economic consequences gained a hearing and earned growing support for the critics of unrestrained military spending. A collection of academics, labeled the "economic depletionists," offered a fresh and persuasive analytical approach.[13] Trained as economists, political economists, or engineers and in business and management (many had experience in some or all of these fields), they contended that decades of lavish military outlays had played a major role in undermining the American economy.

Out in front was Seymour Melman, who published *The Permanent War Economy: American Capitalism in Decline* in 1974.[14] Based on years of research, this seminal volume sets forth a blistering analysis of the warfare state's economic consequences. Rejecting both the orthodox and Marxist economic analyses, Melman maintains that military spending neither stimulates nor adds to the strength of the economy; instead, the outlay saps economic vitality and, analytically, should not be included in the GDP because it fails to benefit either consumption or production.

According to Melman, defense contracting constitutes a form of state capitalism, operating outside the boundaries of the larger civilian economy, free from market pressures, and characterized by inefficiency, waste, and corruption. The outcome is a logical result of a contracting system that guarantees profits and follow-on contracts, covers all costs, invites cost overruns and missed deadlines, wallows in a numbing bureaucracy, benefits procurer and contractor alike, and, results aside, remains unanswerable to any source of meaningful authority. With multiple trillions of dollars and tens of thousands of contractors and subcontractors involved throughout the nation, the effect on the economy is destructive. Together, the DOD and military-related parts of NASA and the Department of Energy (DOE) absorb one-third of the nation's scientists and engineers. These institutions influence the nature of technical education, hoard capital and resources, drive up prices, and add to the growing national deficit. Of critical significance for Melman is that the inefficiency and incompetence of the military-industrial sector inevitably spread out to affect, directly and indirectly, most functions of the civilian economy. The consequences of the military's economic operations, according to the author, go far in explaining America's Cold War economic decline.

In a 1983 publication, *Profits without Production*, Melman sharpens his analysis and expands it to include "managerialism": the short-term, profit-maximizing characteristic of corporate giants in the post–World War II years.[15] In seeking to explain this fundamental transition, the author points to the outstanding production record of World War II. With a large part of the world dependent on America's economic might and looking to the United States as a model for the future, the nation's corporate elite assumed that it had attained a pinnacle of power and influence that was beyond challenge and reach. Such thinking was both encouraged and supported by major scholars, other molders of public opinion, and public officials.

David Riesman, Daniel Bell, John Kenneth Galbraith, and others propounded on the postindustrial society in which the problems of production had been solved and abundance was available for all. The nation was entering the information, knowledge, and service stage shaped by high technology. Low-technology output would be handled abroad by less advanced countries as America luxuriated in its opulence and expanding opportunities for leisure.

Schools of business administration both reflected and influenced the spread of managerialism. Such institutions and the master of business administration (MBA) degrees they conferred were relatively insignificant before World War II. After the conflict they grew in number and importance, with a twelvefold increase in MBAs awarded between 1960 and 1981. The majority of graduates specialized in general management, with increasing numbers focusing on finance, marketing, and sales. Production and manufacturing, or operations management, barely registered as fields of interest. From the most prestigious institutions, such as Harvard's Graduate School of Business Administration, to the more ordinary ones, instruction emphasized short-term profit maximization. Within the corporate structure, top managers increasingly had backgrounds in finance, law, and accounting; engineers and others with technical training simultaneously became fewer in the management ranks.

Managerialism also left its mark on engineering schools. But in this case, the new corporate orientation crossed paths with defense contracting.[16] Throughout the 1960s and 1970s, the DOD, DOE, and NASA heavily funded R&D in science and engineering, with distinguished universities and institutes receiving the most support. Rich federal funding for military-oriented engineering guided faculty and students toward electronics, aeronautics, and space-related specializations, often in very narrow ways. Military and space agencies emphasized cutting-edge R&D and production, and their contractors provided the best reimbursement and benefits. Furthermore, new specialties, such as "engineering science," became available, intended to prepare prospective engineers for the scientific research required by defense and space contractors. At the same time, civilian product design and output were de-emphasized, even denigrated, as low-grade challenges that could be learned on the job. So-called value engineering all but disappeared. This critically important subject, which stresses the necessity of designing and producing goods in the simplest, sturdiest, most reliable, and least costly way, had once been required of most engineering students. But because much, if not most, of the work at the DOD, DOE, and NASA placed a low priority on such attributes, these characteristics came to be considered irrelevant or frivolous.

These trends in engineering education affected both defense and commercial manufacturing. Hence, when Japan and western Europe began surpassing the United States in consumer and producer goods in the mid-1960s, the nation still took comfort in the notion that it would continue to dominate the high end of technological output while surrendering the low end to competitors. When commercial rivals soon took over those markets as well, the post-war promise of an American economic utopia became a cruel joke.

Lloyd J. Dumas, a professor of economics and political economy and Melman's former colleague at Columbia University, proposes a macroeconomic model for understanding the nation's dire economic difficulties in his 1986 publication *The Overburdened Economy: Uncovering the Causes of Chronic Unemployment, Inflation, and National Decline.*[17] Like Melman, he agrees that only transactions advancing productivity should be included in the GDP. Those that do so in the manufacturing and service sectors Dumas labels as contributive; those that do not, he places in the noncontributive category. In the latter category he distinguishes between neutral and distractive. The first consists of contributive output that is devalued by unnecessary costs such as excessive investment in plant and equipment, labor featherbedding, and, most important, bureaucratic expansion and multiplying levels of management. Distractive activity absorbs resources without adding to consumption or production in any way.

America's postwar economic "decay," according to Dumas, results from declining contributive output and rising neutral and distractive enterprise. As corporate managements' goals shifted from long to short term, firms downgraded the importance of productivity. Instead, managers pursued profit maximization through strategic maneuver and manipulation in which conglomerate and multinational organizational structures predominated. In the process, neutral activity abounded as management and bureaucracy grew to acquire and oversee industrial and business empires at home and abroad.

The most devastating blow to America's economic viability, in Dumas's assessment, has come from the sustained, distractive Pentagon budgets measured in the trillions of dollars. For decades, the armed services have drained America's human and physical resources without any positive return and have had a destructive effect on the nation's economic, political, and social system. Until DOD spending is brought under control, the United States has no prospect of regeneration and faces continuing economic decline.

John E. Ullmann, a professor of management and quantitative methods, with degrees in civic, mechanical, and industrial engineering, is another distinguished scholar of economic depletionism.[18] Strongly influenced by Melman and widely published, his in-depth analysis of numerous industries and technologies is enriched by extensive hands-on experience and field work.

After the telling critiques of Melman, Dumas, Ullmann, and many other like-minded scholars, along with journalists and other critics, the attempts to understand and explain America's economic decline generally became much more balanced, insightful, and inward as well as outward focused.[19] A good example is the blue-ribbon Young Commission, created in 1986 by President Reagan to outmaneuver Democratic advocates calling for an industrial policy. The high-powered group headed by John A. Young, president and CEO of Hewlett-Packard, disappointed the administration when it stopped short of recommending an industrial policy and insisted that the federal government lead a broad-based effort to reverse the nation's deteriorating economic fortunes.

The operations of the military-industrial complex constitute an industrial policy, but they are more destructive than they are constructive. Economic mobilization for World War I, the National Recovery Administration of the 1930s, and harnessing the economy for the Second World War, the Cold War, and after established that no form of economic planning is possible in America unless the corporate and financial communities lead or dominate the effort. When the economic elite's power is combined with that of the military, the two constitute an economic partnership that is detrimental to larger national interests. Under such circumstances, and in contrast with most other advanced industrial countries, an industrial policy for peace or war holds little promise for reversing the nation's economic decline.[20]

ORIGINS OF THE MILITARY-INDUSTRIAL COMPLEX

The role of national security spending and corporate managerialism in eroding the economy can be traced back further than the postwar years. Doing so establishes the critical point that the armed services and the corporate community were not operating in separate spheres but were instead interacting in ways that protected their mutual interests, at the expense of the economy and society as a whole. The basis for such an alliance was laid in the late nineteenth century.[21]

The building of a modern navy in the 1880s drew together the shipbuilding, steel, and related industries on a new and permanent basis. By the time of World War I, the experience had given the navy reasonably good preparation to join corporate America in participating in federal agencies for mobilizing the economy. That was not the case with the army, which was still mired in its decentralized, turf-conscious, bureaucratic ways. As the most powerful government department involved in working out a system to harness the economy, the War Department's inflexibility came close to derailing the whole World War I mobilization effort. Under intense pressure from Congress and business, the Woodrow Wilson administration subordinated the War Department's authority in the economic realm to civilian sources, largely corporate and financial in nature. Order was then reestablished in the mobilization effort.

To avoid repeating the experience in the event of another conflict, Congress authorized the War Department to initiate procurement and industrial mobilization planning during the interwar years. Military institutions, eventually including the navy, undertook such planning, assisted by World War I mobilizers and a host of economic, professional, legal, and other organizations. The end results were the industrial mobilization plans of 1930, 1933, 1936, and 1939. A concerted attempt to implement the last plan late in 1939, after the outbreak of war in Europe, was thwarted by the Franklin D. Roosevelt administration. Reform elements and excluded labor, agriculture, and consumer groups vehemently opposed the 1939 plan because it proposed to place the wartime economy largely under the control of industrial, financial, and business elites and the armed services. To prepare the economy for possible hostilities, Roosevelt relied on a series of makeshift mobilization agencies between 1940 and 1942. Once the United States entered the conflict, the administration created the War Production Board and, by slow stages, implemented the industrialization mobilization plan of 1939.

Due to the interwar planning and extensive contacts made throughout the economy, the War and Navy departments were better prepared for economic mobilization than was the business community. Between 1940 and 1943, while New Deal economists and other officials devised the means of harnessing the economic system, the military acted to protect corporate and financial institutions from the encroaching power of Washington. It did so to ensure the cooperation of industrial America, which was indispensable to the armed forces' supply and procurement operations. Moreover, various New Deal reformers sought to impose firm control over the armed forces, matching the control they sought over the corporate system. By standing together, the two power groups could maintain maximal independence.

Under these circumstances, the outlines of the postwar military-industrial complex took shape. New Deal reforms and reformers were subordinated, and the influence of labor, consumers, and smaller business was marginalized. With management's backing, the military determined its own level of demand, with waste, duplication, and unnecessary weapons and supplies accounting for as much as one-quarter to one-third of the military's total wartime demand. For their part, large corporations received most military contracts, and there was minimal concern about concentrated market power, geographic balance, available workforce, congested areas, or the welfare of small to medium-sized businesses. Contractors also received billions of dollars of new, expanded, or modified plants and equipment at government expense or at bargain-basement prices through federal funding programs and generous interpretations of the tax laws. Predictably, profit rates reached lavish levels.

Corporate and business interests were intent on using wartime production to refurbish their depression-tarnished image. They were also determined to reverse New Deal advances, or at least block further progress along those lines. Besides securing reliable sources for weapons, equipment, and supplies during hostilities, the armed services would require backing for the relatively large forces they expected to maintain after the war ended. Business and corporate support would be essential for a successful outcome in the anticipated postwar struggles over the size and role of the military.

Throughout the war years, the corporate and military communities demonstrated that by working together they could thwart any program that threatened their combined interests. This reality became manifest in the defeat of reformers and others inside and outside of government who favored a progressive, government-guided reconversion process. During the many wartime power struggles, the armed services relied on the legitimate and contrived use of military necessity and troop welfare to settle conflicts in their favor, and in ways supportive of their corporate allies.

After the conclusion of World War II, only the aircraft, shipbuilding, and machine-tool industries sought continued output for the military. Without high levels of military production, their economic prospects looked grim. By contrast, the corporate and business world in general was anxious to resume normal civilian production for the enormous domestic and international markets that awaited them. Nonetheless, the corporate and military communities had explored a range of shared interests that would prove to be critical in the postwar world.

During the conflict, the armed forces experienced a range of power and authority in formulating domestic and foreign policies that was unprecedented. For its part, the corporate community benefited bountifully from over five years of government-induced prosperity during which demand soared, plant and equipment vastly expanded, and profits multiplied without undo stress on management's part. Similar conditions of practically effortless plenty followed the war's termination. For both the military and industry, warfare or its equivalent proved to be an empowering and enriching event. Wars hot and cold drew the two spheres together in what the Special Senate Committee Investigating the Munitions Industry (the Nye Committee) years earlier had labeled an "unhealthy alliance" and what postwar generations have called a military-industrial complex, a national security state, or a warfare state.

THE FALSE PROMISE OF UTOPIAN ECONOMICS

Labels aside, warfare and its consequences have become enemies of reform. That outcome is misfortune enough. Even worse, the national security state of the Cold War and after has had adverse effects on most aspects of American civilization. Its unaltered continuance threatens the viability of the republic. The warfare state's current legacy validates this dire assertion.

Since the 1970s, the economy has grown more slowly than in the three decades after the end of World War II and perhaps more slowly than ever before in American history.[22] Blaming the dismal record on excessive government spending and regulation, conservatives insisted that regeneration could take place with "market-based solutions" and deregulation. These policies were first implemented in earnest with the presidency of Ronald Reagan (1981–1989). The results were more than contradictory. While social spending and the agencies implementing it were cut back or eliminated, military expenditures skyrocketed, federal taxes were drastically reduced, and growing government outlays were financed by borrowing, principally from countries running persistent trade surpluses with the United States. Laws and regulations designed to protect the public interest were laxly enforced or repealed, and the way was prepared for the privatization of a host of public services, ranging from street cleaning to military supply operations.

So-called Reaganomics had mixed results. A severe recession was followed by modest prosperity based on massive deficits. Reagan's successor, George H. W. Bush (1989–1993), adopted a milder version of the same approach. William J. Clinton (1993–2001), while endorsing the notion of a less active federal government, implemented more balanced policies and even left office with a federal budget surplus. Exaggerated Reaganomics became the unwavering dogma of the George W. Bush administration (2001–2009).

Instead of addressing the distorting effects of managerialism and uncontrolled military spending on the economy, the Reagan administration evaded them. In doing so, it instituted a pattern of the nation living beyond its means through accumulating debt. From the 1980s through the first decade of the twenty-first century, the federal debt doubled from one-third to nearly two-thirds of GDP; household debt more than doubled, from 50 cents to $1.20 on every dollar of family income. Businesses, banks, and other institutions followed suit.

Cheap and poorly monitored credit and credit leveraging pushed a high-consuming yet faltering economy forward. Washington downgraded or abdicated its roles in regulating and maintaining economic stability. The Treasury Department, Federal Reserve, Securities and Exchange Commission, and other agencies responsible for overseeing banks, financial institutions, and the stock market all performed poorly. Unregulated financial operations such as hedge funds made matters worse, as did financial concoctions such as collateralized debt obligations, which defied any reasonable risk assessment. By 2006, 80 percent of all lending took place in unregulated sectors of the economy—known as the "shadow banking system"—compared with 25 percent in the 1980s.

George Soros maintains that, under Reagan, a "superbubble" began to grow. It not only made the economy highly vulnerable to a momentous crash but also acted to disguise the economic system's serious and growing structural defects. The savings and loan collapse of the late 1980s and later financial crises that were successfully contained convinced policy makers that debt-fed prosperity was sustainable. Such beliefs led to new levels of irresponsibility, corruption, conflict of interest, and criminality, ultimately producing the subprime mortgage binge. The entire system began to fall apart in mid-2007, setting off the worst economic crisis the nation has faced since the Great Depression. In just over a year, $13 trillion of estimated household wealth, around 20 percent of the total, vanished.

The economic benefits of reduced taxes, debt-financed prosperity, deregulation, and privatization went principally to the upper classes. Their taxes fell the most, their opportunities for gain multiplied, and penalties for tax avoidance were slight or unenforced. Beginning in the late 1960s, compensation for top managers in manufacturing, banking, and finance reached new heights that were unrelated to performance. Compensation for chief executives in 1969 was approximately 30 times that of the average worker; by 2007, CEO salaries had soared to 300 times that of workers. The major burden fell on the blue- and white-collar working classes. Between 1945 and 1973, the average family income in inflation-adjusted dollars doubled. Since then, even families with two workers have experienced modest gains, while those with only one employee have made even less.

To make matters worse, the public and private social safety net has frayed badly. Pension programs, when they exist, are increasingly based on defined contributions rather than benefits. Employer-financed health care programs are also disappearing or requiring greater employee contributions at a time when insurance premiums are continually escalating. Minimum-wage rates remain low and coverage inadequate, and unemployment compensation is short in duration and meager in amount. Welfare programs have instituted more stringent eligibility requirements and less generous benefits. Further stress arises from the escalating cost of living, badly performing public education systems, increasing costs for higher education, and mortgage payments that claim a bigger slice of total family income.

Under such circumstances, growing numbers of families cannot save for retirement, cannot pay for their children's higher education, and cannot prepare for emergencies. Debt and its costs multiply, pushing more and more families closer to defaulting on their obligations. All these conditions tend to be exaggerated for the growing number of one-parent families. Some of the financial distress is caused by individuals who are careless about handling money or willfully live beyond their means, but most people are simply overwhelmed by conditions beyond their control.

A comparison with the wealthy countries of the Organization for Economic Cooperation and Development (OECD) boldly underlines the point. For these nations, the public-sector share of GDP averages around 40 percent. For the United States, federal, state, and local government spending approximates 30 percent, the lowest among the wealthy countries. Most of the OECD nations have public health and assistance programs, generous unemployment benefits, retraining systems, retirement income and care plans, and the like. Their citizens pay higher taxes for these services, but much less public spending goes to the military, and the general public is protected against the vagaries of the economy. As a result, the richest nation in the world has the worst record among similar countries in terms of income and wealth inequality, workload, poverty, infant mortality, life expectancy, divorce rate, crime, and incarceration. Moreover, a number of developed nations have a better record than the United States in upward mobility, especially for those born into poverty.

Much of the squalor stems from the corruption of empire and the ruinous national security spending it absorbs. Conditions are made much worse by corporate conglomerates, multinational firms, and companies in the ICT industries that stress managerialism and financialization strategies over the interests of the economy and the nation as a whole.

THE RISING COSTS AND DECLINING QUALITY OF AMERICA'S MILITARY

With the economy tanking, the defense budget continues to climb.[23] By 2007–2008, in inflation-adjusted dollars, it had reached the highest level since the end of World War II. Nonetheless, all the armed services are in a major state of decline. The army has fewer fighting brigades than before, needs to repair and replace its worn-out and destroyed equipment after years of grueling combat in the Middle East, and has additional plans for updates and changes that will require hundreds of billions of dollars. A navy battle fleet that consisted of 568 ships in 1987 has shrunk to 279. Like the army, the navy has vast and superexpensive blueprints for future growth. The air force too has elaborate modernization projects, but it faces the more immediate problem of its aging tactical aircraft. The average age of its existing fighter/attack plane exceeds twenty years, versus the service's goal of ten years in the 1980s and early 1990s. Costs, technical problems, and delays involving the F-22 largely (but not solely) account for the tactical aircraft crunch, and conditions will not improve with the F-35. The F-22 ultimately cost more than $400 million per unit; the final cost of the F-35 will be even higher.

The military in general has never accepted the need to restructure its forces for fourth-generation warfare—the irregular type of warfare carried out by nationalist, religious, ethnic, tribal, and similar groups unleashed by the end of the bipolar Cold War and the relative declining power of states. Such conflicts border on being unwinnable, since their warriors win by not losing. Hence, they should be avoided when possible and always approached with caution. However, according to various military analysts, the nation's armed services never collectively progressed beyond the massive, lethally armed, centrally controlled fighting forces, made possible by the industrial revolution, that dominated from the late nineteenth century forward. This second-generation warfare differs from the first-generation warfare that was prevalent before the industrial revolution allowed the full maturation of firearms. It also varies from the third-generation warfare introduced by Germany in World War I and fully perfected during World War II, which stressed maneuver to overcome the enemy's superior numbers and firepower.

Atomic weapons ended the possibility of any future clash among the major powers being characterized by second- and third-generation warfare. Yet the United States remains committed to a second-generation-type military, despite its rising costs and diminishing strength. How and under what circumstances the challenges of fourth-generation warfare will be defined and met remain unclear, if it indeed occurs. Certainly, second-generation warfare is the wrong approach, as indicated by the experiences of Vietnam, Iraq, and Afghanistan. At a minimum, an electronically enhanced army relying on massive firepower will be of limited use. For the navy, a greater emphasis on green- and brownwater capabilities, instead of blue, is called for. The air force would do well to drastically downgrade the emphasis on strategic bombing or its equivalent and shift attention to the tactical aircraft favored by the "Lightweight Fighter Mafia." Yet it is gearing up for a new long-range, nuclear-capable, stealth bomber that can operate with or without a pilot. The air force has in mind a fleet of eighty to a hundred such planes.[24]

As matters currently stand, the prospects of any adaptations for fourth-generation warfare are remote at best. The expenditure of multiple trillions of dollars over six decades has produced a bipartisan defense establishment that includes the defense industry, the Pentagon, the White House, Congress, and think tanks. It forcefully resists change and, according to Winslow T. Wheeler, "does not know—or apparently care—what it is doing."[25] Much of what takes place in the name of national security remains unknown or unexplained to the public. Wheeler goes on to show, for example, that the Bush administration's 2009 defense budget of $518.3 billion, unveiled in February 2008, did not include costs for the wars being fought in Iraq and Afghanistan; nor did it cover vast amounts of additional spending for national security. When all the expenditures were totaled, including, at best, only about half the costs of the two wars, a more realistic figure would be closer to $863.7 billion.

The condition of military hardware continues to be scandalous. A Defense Science Board Task Force on Development Test and Evaluation found that between 1997 and 2006, 70 percent of army systems had failed to meet reliability requirements. Nonetheless, many of the programs proceeded to production and deployment to the troops. The task force found that similar situations existed for the other services. In additional reports issued between 2001 and 2006, the Pentagon concluded that 50 percent of twenty-eight systems were operationally unsuitable or had major suitability deficiencies. Unreliable and unsuitable weapons, equipment, and supplies bog down combat logistics and negatively affect operations.

With major weapons systems such as aircraft, ships, and tanks, costs rise, production numbers decline, schedules go unmet, and performance often suffers. The principal cause of this production breakdown is not DOD rules and regulations or oversight by agencies within the DOD, such as the Defense Contract Management Agency, or those on the outside, such as the GAO. For decades, blue-ribbon committees have been reviewing and analyzing Pentagon acquisitions. Franklin C. Spinney has spent a good part of his professional life investigating the source of defense procurement failure and explaining his findings to Congress and to Washington defense circles. All these efforts have produced numerous findings and recommendations, yet little changes. The DOD acquisition structure, from program managers to senior officers and their advisers, ignores or fails to implement basic reforms that are generally agreed to be essential.

As briefly outlined earlier, the problem begins with what is called "buying in" or "front-end loading" in the planning for new weapons systems. More often than not, technical and operational specifications are high risk or even unattainable. Yet these advanced and untried weapons are scheduled to be delivered rapidly and cheaply. No independent assessments, let alone prototypes, are offered to back up the claims. The planning approach is aimed solely at gaining the approval of the DOD and Congress. Once that is accomplished—and it usually happens, despite past performance records—a system's future support is secured by "political engineering." Contracts to fabricate systems and components are distributed to as many states and congressional districts as possible. Manufacturers impress upon senators and representatives the importance of the investment and the jobs involved.

With numbers in Congress "locked in" and the program advancing, the make-believe world of defense acquisitions is set aside. Reality becomes manifest, and a familiar cycle begins. Technical problems arise, necessitating the reconsideration of requirements, system redesigns, the working out of fixes, retrofitting, and repeated tests. Schedules can be stretched up to thirty years, and costs can balloon to as much as three times the initial estimate. Production goals are then arbitrarily reduced to keep overall program outlays within the budget range. With fewer new weapons produced, inventory is threatened. This leads to keeping greater numbers of older weapons in service at increasing expense. At the same time, operating funds are raided to support continued production of the replacement system. Less money is available to maintain and repair both the old and the new weapons. Critically, training is also reduced. To further complicate matters, operating goals are seldom met, and weapons and equipment are plagued by shortcomings ranging from minor flaws to total system failures.

With variations of this scenario taking place over decades and encompassing all the services, the end results are predictable. The American military shrinks, ages, and becomes less ready, all at a steadily climbing cost. Yet the services go forward without meaningful oversight from the DOD or Congress. With rare exceptions, public and private officials are not punished or even held responsible. Indeed, practically no one is willing to admit to mistakes, misjudgments, or inappropriate leadership.

Breaking this terribly destructive Pentagon pattern requires fundamental reform. Chances for change within the DOD are remote. During the last twenty years or so, the department and the services, backed by Congress, have eliminated the technical competence needed to shape and execute budgets and acquisitions programs. Initiative and competence must come from the outside.

No progress can be made without first launching a total audit of the DOD. The department is incapable of informing Congress or the executive how its appropriations are spent; at best, it has some estimates. For acquisitions, the DOD relies on contractors to keep its books, to the degree books are kept at all. It fabricates figures to give the appearance that its accounts are properly balanced and then relies on these fanciful numbers to determine new spending requirements. Additionally, the DOD and its subdivisions cannot accurately track their own property, including supplies going to the troops in Iraq and Afghanistan. As a result, the department has been making vital decisions in an informational vacuum filled by fictional, unreliable, and biased data. What is done today is not informed by what was done in the past or what is likely in the future.

This harsh reality is well known to the DOD inspector general and the GAO. Even George W. Bush's Office of Management and Budget recognized that the DOD was one of the worst-run agencies of the federal government. More recently, the alarming state of the DOD has come to the attention of President Barack Obama's National Commission on Fiscal Responsibility and Reform. Senator Thomas A. Coburn (R-OK), cochair of the commission's panel on discretionary spending, has enlightened his colleagues to some of the realities outlined above and, along with other recommendations, has proposed that defense budgets be frozen until the DOD can pass an audit.[26]

A knowledgeable group of analysts from or associated with the Center for Defense Information (CDI) insists that after a DOD audit, critical department functions should be placed under the direction of an independent panel or commission of outside professional experts appointed by the president and Congress. To be effective, the panel members must be free of all compromising ties. The commission would be charged with implementing and overseeing basic changes in DOD operations that are well known and long overdue.[27] The CDI group's proposal for achieving DOD reform is drastic and probably politically unrealistic. Nonetheless, it is a measure of the urgent concern among involved and informed professionals, all of whom have decades of experience in the various areas of national security. Repeated efforts of the past to rectify Pentagon limitations and failures have had little success.[28]

CONCLUSION

The deindustrialization of America has added to the nation's difficulties in controlling defense spending and managing the multiple challenges presented by the military-industrial complex. The defense sector is one of the few remaining industries that provides blue-collar employment that pays well and offers attractive fringe benefits; as such, it has strong support. The armed services and defense contractors can depend on the backing of the working population, unions, communities, and regions. Responding to constituents' concern and pressure, members of Congress generally support military appropriations and defense contractors' interests.

Positive prospects for converting military output to civilian purposes might have lessened support for defense spending. By the time various big and small defense firms began considering or experimenting with conversion to commercial products, however, deindustrialization was already well under way. That reality tended to discourage such endeavors and lessen the chances of success. In an ironic and unfortunate way, industrial America and the military and its contractors have interacted in a fashion detrimental to the larger interests of the nation as a whole.

9
THE POLITICAL ECONOMY
OF THE COLD WAR

From its colonial origins to the present day, the United States has repeatedly mobilized for and fought wars of short and long duration. Yet it was never in the grips of a military-industrial complex until the Cold War, with outlines of such a structure evident during World War II. To understand why this is the case requires turning to the stages of warfare and the four factors shaping the political economy of warfare set forth earlier.

THE MILITARY-INDUSTRIAL COMPLEX

The existence of a MIC requires a major, extended conflict during an industrial stage of warfare in which there is a strong industrial economy, a vigorous national government, a modernized and active military, and specialized, sophisticated weapons systems. By 1939–1940, these essential conditions were in place, leading to an industrial-military alliance dominating mobilization of the World War II economy. The Cold War led to a permanent, though modified, form of economic mobilization that has continued for more than six decades. Such a situation is new in the American experience.

Unlike after World War I, the United States never fully demobilized after the conclusion of the Second World War. The extended conflict left a legacy of widespread destruction, and it weakened or shattered colonial empires around the globe. Future international stability depended on a massive effort of rebuilding and restructuring. As the world's premier nation, the United States would play a major role in reconstruction. Indeed, American statesmen looked on a devastated world order as an unequaled opportunity to shape the world along the lines of democratic capitalism based on the concept of the open door. American intentions, however, faced a challenge from the USSR. Having played a decisive role in defeating Nazi Germany, the Soviet Union would be key to any postwar European settlement. Russia was occupying the major nations of central and eastern Europe, and it had other territorial ambitions around its borders. Moreover, the USSR could be seen as constituting a communist threat to the tottering colonial world.

The United States hoped to rely principally on its overwhelming economic power in achieving its post–World War II international goals. Nonetheless, a modest military was critical for the challenges of a war-torn world. All the armed services had begun planning for their postwar structures and roles during hostilities. Additionally, the Joint Chiefs of Staff and the State Department had acquired territory for military bases strategically located throughout the world. The armed services could still be kept relatively small by relying on airpower and the nation's nuclear monopoly.

These policies began to appear inadequate as American-Russian relations deteriorated after 1947 and the Cold War became a reality. Dramatic change took place in 1949 and 1950. The Soviet Union acquired atomic weaponry, China fell to communist control, proposals for restructuring western Europe stalled, and the Korean War broke out. Under NSC-68, the United States expanded its military strength in all categories and increased economic and military assistance to western Europe. American Cold War policies had now become militarized.

Even before the extensive military expansion in the early 1950s, the armed services had acquired unprecedented power and influence in the formulation and implementation of American foreign and national security policies. This development stemmed from the State Department's relative decline; World War II practices; the armed forces' occupation of and presence in Europe, Asia, and colonial areas; and the military's importance in the expanding conflict with the Soviet Union. The unification of the armed services and the ongoing reform of the Department of Defense also added to the military's strength.

The power and reach of the DOD were further enhanced in the 1950s by its increasing size and budgets and by the emergence of a substantial private munitions industry. Once a large, permanent military became a postwar reality, the army and navy followed the air force's lead in turning to private industry for manufacturing their weapons systems. In the process, army arsenals and navy shipyards were downgraded or closed. Private industry initiated the move for change and ultimately gained the support of the executive, members of Congress, and the DOD as more of its top officials came from industry and finance. For the first time in its history, the United States had a large standing military and a private munitions industry to support it during years of relative peace.

At the outset, the Cold War defense industry was centered among airframe companies. When jet engines and solid-state electronics began transforming weaponry, these corporations modified and expanded their operations to become aerospace firms, stressing a high level of R&D. Aerospace also included a number of companies specializing in electronics, communications, systems management, and the production of engines and propulsion units for aircraft, rockets, and missiles. In addition to the military, NASA relied heavily on aerospace. The more traditional industries included shipbuilding and the automobile makers, which manufactured motor-driven weaponry such as tanks. Although the air force led the way in the application of electronics to its weapon systems, the army and navy also relied on the new technology to transform their armaments. At the height of its output, the defense industry included a number of America's largest, wealthiest corporations and thousands of medium- and small-sized firms and subcontractors.

Based in part on prewar and World War II developments, the defense industry became concentrated principally in a "Gunbelt" that ran down the East and West coasts, across the South, and into parts of the Southwest. The industry's location led to a massive population migration to these areas, especially the South and West. Gunbelt areas tended to be politically conservative and strongly favored America's Cold War and national security policies.

"Big science"—or large-scale industrial science—was critical to both the Cold War military and the defense industry. The practice of big science originated among universities and industries in the interwar years, and it was vastly accelerated by the Second World War. During hostilities, the National Defense Research Committee and the Office of Scientific Research and Development recruited and organized physical scientists, mathematicians, engineers, and technicians from major universities, institutes, and private research laboratories for the purpose of improving weapons. Carried out principally at leading universities and institutes, these R&D projects made major contributions to the tools of war, including radar, the proximity fuse, jet engines and rockets, and, most important, the atomic bomb. Operations research also assisted the armed forces in the use of new technology and the better application of existing weapons.

All the armed forces in the post–World War II years were anxious to retain the advice and assistance of scientists and other specialists. With the delay in creating the National Science Foundation after World War II, the armed services came forward and provided institutions of higher learning with general, open-ended research grants to assist their transition to peace as wartime funding was cut off. Thereafter, with the air force in the lead, the services negotiated specific grants and contracts with universities and institutes for R&D projects directly and indirectly related to weaponry, equipment, and more general national security projects. During the most intense years of the Cold War, the national security establishment—including the DOD, the AEC (later the DOE), NASA, and various federal research centers—accounted for as much as 80 to 90 percent of Washington's outlays for R&D flowing to higher education. Universities and institutes relied on the defense sector during most of the Cold War for about one-third of their total research funds.

Once defense budgets began to grow rapidly in the 1950s, the defense industry became a rich source of employment for physical scientists, mathematicians, engineers, and technicians, along with skilled and semiskilled workers. That was particularly the case when solid-state electronics led to the transformation of weapons and equipment. In time, the defense sector employed one-third of the nation's pool of scientists and engineers, who were often of the highest caliber. Universities, in turn, began steering their students toward the defense industry because of its challenging and stimulating environment and lucrative compensation. For their part, the armed services, related agencies, and defense firms awarded grants and contracts to the academic departments that best served their purposes. In the process, defense requirements helped expand existing fields of study or created new ones.

All the military services also had an elaborate structure of R&D offices, centers, and laboratories. These facilities were overseen by the services or by the Office of the Secretary of Defense. Relations between military and civilian research groups were often close, and all the armed forces and the DOD relied on a large collection of civilian advisory committees and boards to assist their operations.

Besides scientists and those in related fields, a host of other academics became directly involved in national security functions. They did so through the organization of defense think tanks and like institutions. Among think tanks, the RAND Corporation was one of the first and most well known. Created to assist the air force in fulfilling its mission, RAND emphasized analytical approaches such as systems analysis, nuclear strategy, and a host of other topics of its own or the air force's choosing. Though initially employing principally physical scientists, in time, the think tank incorporated those from other scientific fields, the social and behavioral sciences, and the humanities. RAND was only one of many think tanks or defense R&D organizations advising and serving the military. Their activities covered weapons, tactics, strategy, logistics, communications systems, counterinsurgency, troop training, and an entire range of other subjects of importance to the DOD and the armed forces.

Related to defense think tanks were university-based or -affiliated programs, centers, schools, and institutes performing research, preparing reports, and publishing studies on American foreign and national security policies. Although the armed services were interested in and helped found and finance some of these groups, the CIA and the State Department, assisted by the Ford Foundation and others, usually took a leading role. Indeed, some of these centers were like extensions of the World War II Office of Strategic Services. That was the case with Columbia University's Russian Research Institute, Harvard University's Russian Research Center, and MIT's Center for International Studies. The last center was an interdisciplinary program concerned principally with the most effective method of modernizing countries of the developing world. Other area or international studies programs concentrated on Asia, the Middle East, Africa, and Latin America. Nearly all the principal communications research organizations, such as Paul F. Lazarfeld's Bureau of Applied Social Research at Columbia, performed analyses for defense, intelligence, and foreign policy administrations.

The University of Michigan and Michigan State University, along with various other university-based or -affiliated research groups and think tanks, went beyond research and publication to become involved in counterinsurgency, counterinfiltration, and development activities. For the Michigan universities, operations took place in Thailand and Vietnam under the direction of the CIA, the Agency for International Development, and the military.

Many of those taking part in research and advisory groups had participated in World War II intelligence, psychological warfare, and propaganda agencies. Many were also prominent, respected, and high-achieving members of their various academic disciplines, and they often served as officers and leaders in scholarly and academic organizations. As a group, they included those exercising significant power and influence both inside and outside the academy.

In addition to study centers and think tanks, the armed forces, particularly the army, used specialized private corporations to perform military functions. A few think tanks in the early Cold War years assisted the services in training functions, but they were nonprofit organizations. Profit-making companies came into use in the 1970s and grew rapidly during and after the 1990s. At first, they did routine plant operations; later, they began training foreign troops. In time, civilian firms, such as the Vinnell Corporation, built and maintained military facilities at home and abroad, serviced and repaired high-technology weapons, provided security functions, handled troop training and doctrine, ran Reserve Officers' Training Corps programs and recruitment centers, and performed a number of other basic military functions. The CIA also used private corporations in carrying out most intelligence and security duties. Blackwater USA was the agency's most prominent contractor before it changed its name.

The defense industry, think tanks, university-based or -affiliated groups, civilian advisory committees, and privately owned firms performing military functions constituted a formidable collection of institutions. They highlighted as never before the breakdown of the barriers between military and civilian, public and private institutions. The institutional transition began in the late nineteenth century with the building of a modern naval fleet, it advanced with economic mobilization for World War I, and it came to maturity with economic mobilization for World War II and the ensuing Cold War. These civilian groups not only assisted in formulating and executing national security policies but also acted as a powerful lobby for the Cold War and a large military. At the center of the civilian war cohort were the defense industry and universities and institutes. Along with the armed forces, they constituted the essence of what President Dwight D. Eisenhower labeled the military-industrial complex.

During the Cold War and beyond, Congress has had a varied influence on national security policies. In the committee period, extending from the 1940s into the early 1960s, Congress usually followed the executive's lead and provided the armed services with an important public platform for explaining and justifying their requirements. Moreover, beginning before and continuing during the Cold War, various members of Congress established close and protective relations with the armed forces and the DOD. In the 1960s and 1970s the legislative branch significantly changed. A reformed and democratized Congress began moving to rein in the DOD and to challenge presidential foreign and national security policy making as well. Although the national legislature became much more conservative in the 1980s, it still acted to restrain the Reagan administration's more extreme defense and foreign policies. Congress became increasingly partisan beginning in the 1990s, greatly weakening legislators' ability to influence policies outside of American borders and those involving defense as well. However, as the dire economic consequences of deindustrialization expanded after the 1970s, Congress grew more determined to protect the jobs and economic stimulus the defense industry provides. That practice has grown so extreme that Congress has voted to increase defense budgets and to continue weapons systems and programs opposed by the president and the DOD.

Congress's response to defense budgets raises the larger issue of the effect of military spending on the economy. Expenditures for World War II put an end to the Great Depression. Similarly, outlays for the Korean War and the growing tensions of the Cold War pulled the nation out of the post–World War II economic downturn and helped usher in nearly two decades of prosperity. These results led to the belief that defense spending served as an economic stimulus. As long as the American economy grew and prospered in the 1950s and 1960s, DOD budgets generally continued to be viewed in a positive way. With the stagflation of the 1970s, a more critical analysis proposed that defense spending acted to undermine rather than strengthen the economy.

The new critique took on added significance and gained greater attention because it addressed the critical issue of America's industrial decline. The world's leading industrial and financial power since the early years of the twentieth century began to experience economic difficulties after the mid-1960s. In 1971 the United States had an unfavorable balance of trade, and in 1985 it became a net international debtor. By 2010, the nation's long-term debt slightly exceeded its GDP. Basic change in the industrial community played a major part in America's eroding economy. Flush from wartime profits and massive postwar markets at home and abroad, corporate America began to turn away from its past emphasis on introducing new products and increasing productivity. Instead, industry began to focus on short-run profit maximization through the pursuit of conglomerates and multinational corporations. Established industries were neglected, abandoned, or rendered unable to compete. By the 1970s, industrial sectors of the Midwest and Northeast began to suffer from the ravages of deindustrialization. The later promise of economic renewal from the growth of the information and communication sector was dashed when those industries turned to financialization strategies for enriching the few, not the many.

MIC critics such as Seymour Melman combined the consequences of corporate profit-seeking to the detriment of production and the operations of the defense industry to explain the nation's economic plight. Although firms producing for the DOD, DOE, and NASA made notable advances in the manufacture of aircraft, missiles, satellites, nuclear weapons, and a host of other armaments, their overall production record was far from impressive. As a form of state capitalism, the defense sector was freed from practically all competitive market pressures. Under those circumstances, the industry became characterized by inefficiency, waste, and corruption; defense contractors too often turned out defective or failed weapons and equipment. Over time, massive expenditures for defense have had a very deleterious effect on the economy. These outlays have led to the hoarding of capital and human resources, especially among scientists and engineers, and to the diverting of public assistance from civilian enterprises. Of crucial significance, according to numerous critics, DOD budgets have distorted public priorities and spending, denying adequate attention and resources to infrastructure, education, medical care, and other public services and interests.

The military itself ends up being victimized. The skyrocketing costs of high-technology weapons systems have absorbed increasing portions of DOD budgets. As a consequence, basic weapons systems have declined in number and aged, and critical training functions have been cut back. Preparedness levels have inevitably declined. Furthermore, the high-technology weaponry is often inappropriate for the military challenges presented by the irregular warfare of the developing world.

Except for during the wars in Iraq and Afghanistan beginning in 2003, defense expenditures were at their highest levels in the 1950s and 1960s—the golden decades of America's postwar prosperity. The lavish military spending, as Eisenhower feared and Nixon insisted, may not have been wise or necessary, but it could be managed in the short run because of the nation's enormous economic strength. In the long run, however, such vast and abusive outlays were bound to cause grave problems for the nation's economy and society.

When the effects of corporate America's turn to profit maximization and financialization became fully evident, unchecked defense budgets became nearly intolerable in economic terms. Ignoring that reality, and unwilling or unable to change the course of foreign policy, significantly reduce DOD expenditures, or restructure the economy's operations, America's political leadership allowed the nation to drift toward further decline.

Beginning with the Reagan administration and continuing with the administrations of Bush Sr. and Clinton, Washington began to look abroad in an attempt to deal in part with the problems of eroding economic growth, unfavorable balances of trade, and the threatened viability of the consolidated defense industry due to declining demand at home and abroad. Reagan and his successors encouraged and assisted American defense firms in increasing their exports and investments in the international arms trade. This enterprise involved both the developed and the underdeveloped world. In the process, the United States participated in the proliferation of armaments that indirectly involved weapons of mass destruction. Additionally, as the world's principal producer and exporter of weaponry, the United States increased the possibility of creating a multinational arms complex. Such a complex could lead to more threats and damage abroad than the MIC has caused at home.

More immediately, the George W. Bush administration gravely aggravated the nation's foreign and domestic problems with its neoconservative policies. Wars in Iraq and Afghanistan have pushed defense budgets up to near those of 1946 (in adjusted dollars). Those conflicts nearly doubled the nation's long-term debt, and they will ultimately cost trillions of dollars. Simultaneously, by weakening economic regulations, the administration helped create the conditions that led to the devastating economic recession that began in 2007. The early years of the twenty-first century have multiplied America's dysfunctions and have made the nation even less prepared to deal with them than was the case in the late decades of the twentieth century.

PERSPECTIVES ON THE
MILITARY-INDUSTRIAL COMPLEX

In analyzing the MIC of the Cold War and post–Cold War decades, five important points stand out.

First, never before in the industrial stage of warfare (nor in most of the preindustrial and transitional stages) have foreign and defense policies been so closely related and interacting. These policies make much more sense when considered within the context of each other.

Second, although entwined, American Cold War foreign policy determined national security demands, not vice versa. Defense requirements, in turn, created the circumstances for the growth of the MIC. Once in place, the warfare cohort acted to support and strengthen Cold War policies and their continued militarization. Moreover, over time, the MIC has become so entrenched in the economic, political, and social lives of the nation that it is nearly impossible to downgrade, let alone root out.

Third, the MIC did not simply emerge during the Cold War. It resulted from an evolutionary process that began in the late nineteenth century and continued in the twentieth century. On the eve of World War II, most of the institutional adjustments essential for a MIC to exist had taken place. Mobilizing the economy for the Second World War acted to further refine what became the complex's policies and procedures. Thereafter, any sizable military requiring technologically advanced armaments and specialized equipment would necessitate some form of economic mobilization. Such circumstances almost inevitably led to a warfare complex.

The institutional adjustments required to meet the demands of modern warfare were triggered late in the nineteenth century by the transformative effects of the industrial revolution on weaponry. This fundamental change first affected the navy. Building a modern naval fleet featuring steel, armor, steam, and up-to-date ordnance required a newly assembled team of federal officials, naval officers, and industrialists. In differing forms, such a team remained in place permanently to assist the navy in carrying out the essential modernizing process. As a result, the navy was prepared for the Spanish-American War and performed well during those hostilities.

Such was not the case with the army. Unlike the navy, it had not begun to modernize. As a result, the army performed badly in a number of critical areas during the conflict with Spain. After hostilities, and similar to the navy, civilian officials stepped in to help the land forces initiate the modernizing process. Secretary of War Elihu Root led the effort in the early twentieth century with

his basic reforms involving command and control of the army, systemized officer training, and an altered National Guard.

The limited range of the Root reforms and, more seriously, their indifferent
implementation meant that the War Department and the army were still unprepared for the much greater challenges of the First World War. Unlike the limited
Spanish-American War, World War I, as the first fully modern war, required
economic planning. Otherwise, the stability of a mature industrial economy
could not be maintained to produce the enormous quantity required and meet
the specialized demands of the war. Army rigidity prevented economic mobilization efforts from progressing properly. The service's obstruction became so
great that the army came close to losing its supply operations.

Through a gradual process of trial and error beginning in 1915, a number
of civilian organizations worked out a process for mobilizing the economy. It
was finalized between mid-1917 and early 1918 with creation and refinement
of the War Industries Board. Because it had limited authority, the board operated largely through voluntary cooperation. Although the WIB determined
policy, central to its operations were subdivisions called Commodity Committees and War Service Committees. Under guidelines from the WIB, Commodity Committees, advised by War Service Committees, provided
information about and determined policy for all relevant commodities, such as
steel, rubber, copper, and textiles. Commodity Committees were staffed by
those representing the government; War Service Committees were organized,
controlled, and financed by the industries and businesses being regulated.

The WIB supposedly separated public from private interests, but that claim
was more fiction than fact. As it operated, the board was a massive form of
industrial self-regulation. From top to bottom, the WIB was staffed with dol-
lar-a-year men principally from industry, finance, law, and trade associations.
The Commodity Committees and War Service Committees functioned, in
effect, as combined entities, not separate ones. Ceremony notwithstanding,
conflicts of interest were rife. The WIB was a more organized form of the less
structured government-business regulatory alliance that had emerged during
the Progressive Era as a method for controlling and stabilizing a mature industrial system.

The WIB had devised the means for organizing supply in a mobilized economy. But the system could not function unless demand was similarly organized
and integrated into or coordinated with the board's operations. Civilian
demand and that of other wartime agencies, including the navy, complied with
that need. This was not the case with the army, however. The army was the single largest claimant on the wartime economy, and its decentralized, uncoordi-
nated supply structure acted to undermine WIB operations. The board could

do little to correct the situation because it had only implied powers, compared with the War Department's statutory authority. Without basic change, the economic mobilization program ground to a halt, and the economy was badly disrupted by the end of 1917.

To meet the crisis, Congress initiated action to have army procurement and related functions taken over by a civilian ministry of supply. Reluctant to undertake such a radical departure, President Woodrow Wilson worked out a more modest solution. He strengthened the WIB and forced the army to centralize its supply system, pattern it after the board, and coordinate and partially integrate its supply functions with and into the board. With these sweeping changes, the mobilization program was revitalized. At the war's end, it was performing reasonably well, although a great deal of refinement was still essential. Nonetheless, mobilizing the economy for the First World War laid the foundations for harnessing the World War II economy and the operations of the MIC of the Cold War years.

To ensure that the army did not disrupt future wartime economic planning, Congress in 1920 created the Office of the Assistant Secretary of War to carry out procurement and industrial mobilization planning. During the interwar years, the planning was assisted by World War I mobilization officials, trade associations leaders, engineers and their institutions, and representatives from the nation's industries, businesses, and legal and financial firms. In the 1930s the OASW, assisted by the Army-Navy Munitions Board, which was organized in 1922, published industrial mobilization plans in 1930, 1933, 1936, and 1939. These blueprints set forth how the economy should be mobilized for hostilities. Each successive plan came closer to duplicating the WIB of World War I. The 1939 plan, in concept if not in fact, set forth how the World War II economy was in fact mobilized.

When war broke out in Europe in 1939, President Franklin D. Roosevelt moved cautiously in initiating economic mobilization through a series of broadly representative organizations with limited powers. Once the United States entered hostilities in late 1941, the president created the War Production Board. The WPB was a much-improved version of the World War I WIB. From 1940 through 1942, New Dealers, enlightened businessmen, academics, and various economists, political economists, and statisticians led in harnessing the economy. They were the principal advocates for setting high production goals, converting the economy, and increasing output; they were also out front in devising regulatory policies and controls to push the economy to the utmost while still maintaining stability.

In sharp contrast to the First World War, and based on wartime and interwar mobilization developments, the armed services were better prepared than industry to participate in industrial mobilization. Manufacturers were both distracted and on the defensive. Absorbed in burgeoning civilian markets, industrialists responded only halfheartedly to the early mobilization agencies. Moreover, the decade of depression and New Deal reforms had significantly sapped business confidence.

With New Dealers driving to centralize control of economic mobilization in the executive branch, the War Department, with some support from the Navy Department, moved to protect the interests of industry and the armed services. Both departments were headed by high-powered attorneys, Wall Street financiers, and other elites. Once the WPB was working effectively, the military combined its power with that of industry to take control of the board. New Deal elements and those opposing the industrial-military alliance, along with representatives of civilian supply, organized labor, small business, and agriculture, were all downgraded in or eliminated from the WPB. The industrial-military alliance ran the board for the benefit of both parties and often at the expense of others. Military requirements and corporate gains were excessive; civilian supply, services, and facilities were kept needlessly and harmfully low; military and industrial practices created unnecessary labor shortages; small business was underutilized; and reconversion programs to ease the transition to peacetime were blocked. During the ongoing policy battles that racked the WPB, the military legitimately or expediently used troop welfare or strategic necessity to settle conflicts in a manner favorable to itself or to industry.

Despite widespread claims to the contrary, the United States' wartime production record was not exceptional. Based on the prewar level of productivity and the size of the workforce, the nation's output was about where it should have been. Had it become necessary, the nation could have produced, without great strain, 10 to 20 percent more than it did.

The fourth important point in analyzing the MIC involves the limited nature of America's civil service system. Unlike most industrialized nations of Europe, Japan, and elsewhere, the United States has not created at the national level an elite, professional, and expandable civil service system. As a result, when the federal government began to expand in the late nineteenth and early twentieth centuries to stabilize and legitimize a mature industrial economy, it did so by working out a government-business regulatory partnership with the corporate and financial communities. Washington did so because the economic establishment had the power to protect its interests and the personnel and expertise required to carry out regulatory functions. Moreover, business and the opportunities it promised to the public were a vital part of the American ideology.

Progressive Era reforms, therefore, were moderate at best. New Deal reforms went much further because the crisis facing the Roosevelt administration was much more severe. Nonetheless, the administration's principal priority was economic recovery, with massive welfare programs and economic regulation used to buy time to save the economic system and ensure its future viability. The government-business regulatory partnership that was basic to the political economy of both the Progressive Era and the New Deal political economy set the parameters for mobilizing the twentieth-century economy for war. From the outset, the WIB's organizers recognized that any successful mobilization system had to be based on the structure of the economy, and it had to utilize the knowledge and experience of businessmen.

As has been clearly established, the main obstacle to World War I economic mobilization was the War Department and the army. The armed services' mobilization functions constitute the fifth and final point in analyzing the MIC. The military's role in American society has been both diverse and rich. For a good part of the nineteenth century, the armed services were integrated with, rather than removed from, civilian society. Together, the U.S. Military Academy, created in 1802, and the U.S. Naval Academy, established in 1845, are the closest the nation has come to having a national university. From these academies, the officer corps of both services emerged as the basis for an elite, professional, and expandable civil service system that the nation otherwise lacked. When not focused on national security or involved in hostilities, both the army and the navy carried out a wide range of essentially civilian responsibilities along the lines of internal improvements and diplomatic affairs.

In the late nineteenth century, however, the military services entered a period of greater isolation as they became absorbed in the intense process of professionalization. Distracted and remote from civilian society, the armed forces failed to grasp that industrialization was creating conditions in which military and civilian functions could no longer be compartmentalized in terms of weaponry. The navy learned that vital reality with the building of a modern fleet in the late nineteenth century. With no comparable experience, and despite reform efforts, the army remained in the proverbial dark. As a consequence, the army was unready for World War I, and it disrupted the attempts of civilian agencies to harness the economy for hostilities.

The Wilson administration forced the army to adapt its structure and mode of operation to the WIB because, in a mobilized economy, the armed services had to maintain control of procurement. A civilian-controlled munitions ministry was out of the question. Without a professional civil service system, the staff for such a ministry would have to resemble that which ran the WIB. Consistent with the government-business regulatory partnership, industrialists, financiers, and businessmen were the only ones with the knowledge, experience, and power to do so. Placing billions of dollars of military contracts directly into industry's hands would have been politically intolerable. Vehement protests against the massive and gross conflict of interests would have arisen inside and outside Congress. Mobilization paralysis and economic havoc would have ensued. The ceremony, if not the reality, of separating demand from supply had to be maintained.

Economic mobilization for World War I and interwar mobilization planning convinced the army of what was required for modern, industrialized warfare. Once that took place, the military proved to be an invaluable partner of industry, as the industry-military alliance of World War II mobilization indicated. That alliance continued to exist at a very diminished level after the conclusion of World War II. It then grew in size, structure, and importance with the outbreak of the Korean War and the heightened tensions of the Cold War. Since the immediate impact of the semimobilization on the population was not that great, protest levels remained low. Moreover, the Cold War's ideological intensity, its comprehensive nature, and the nuclear arms race it fed all appeared to make the militarization of foreign policy necessary to the public. In his farewell address of 1961, President Eisenhower sounded an early alarm about the threats of the "military-industrial complex," combined with a "scientific-technological elite." Even the president's warning did not generate a great deal of agitation. Widespread and growing protests began only with the student revolt of the 1960s and the ongoing Vietnam War.

FORCES SHAPING THE MILITARY-INDUSTRIAL COMPLEX

In assessing the forces shaping the political economy of the Cold War and beyond, all four factors stand out in differing ways, although the power of the presidency predominates. The first factor, the maturity and strength of the economy, remained critical in both positive and negative ways. From 1945 to 1970, American prosperity was so great that the nation could meet the high costs of defense and foreign policy without any difficulty. Thereafter, the weakening of the economy and the decline of manufacturing began to create problems. These difficulties continued to mount over the decades until, in the early years of the twenty-first century, they have become matters of major consequence.

In terms of the second factor—the size, strength, and scope of the federal government—the Cold War acted to strengthen the presidency. The executive branch largely determines foreign policy and the national security structure for executing it. Congress has a role and, under certain circumstances, can significantly influence both foreign and defense policies, but the president usually remains in the lead.

Civil-military relations, the third factor, changed dramatically. The armed services' size, budgets, and importance enormously increased their power in the operation of the federal government. Support from an influential civilian war cohort enhanced the military's clout all the more. The armed forces' influence grew to the point where even the vastly strengthened presidency found it necessary, at times, to bargain with the military over defense policy and, at least indirectly, foreign policy as well.

More than at any other time in American history, the sophistication of weaponry—the fourth and last factor—was a major driving force in shaping the political economy of warfare. This trend began during World War II with advances such as radar and, most significantly, nuclear weapons. After hostilities, scientists, engineers, and technicians became virtual partners with industry and the military in an ongoing process of transforming weaponry, especially after the introduction of solid-state electronics. The escalating costs of high-technology armaments and equipment began to strain DOD budgets to the point of limiting the availability of basic weapons and funds for their proper repair and maintenance, as well as adversely impacting the training of servicemen and -women. In large part, the runaway expenses of high-technology weapons are the result of the long-term, deep-seated, and widespread misfeasance and malfeasance in the armed forces' and the defense industry's contractual relations.

NOTES

CHAPTER ONE. THE PRESIDENCY

1. Andrew Roberts, *Masters and Commanders: How Four Titans Won the War in the West, 1941–1945* (New York: HarperCollins, 2009), 565. Russia's predominant role in defeating Nazi Germany is a major, though not adequately developed, theme of Roberts's analysis. See also Tony Judt, *Postwar: A History of Europe since 1945* (New York: Penguin, 2005), 13–164.

2. Secondary sources on the Cold War are nearly overwhelming in quantity. The following analysis of the Truman administration's foreign policy is based primarily on revisionist scholarship. The seminal volume of the so-called Wisconsin School is William Appleman Williams, *The Tragedy of American Diplomacy* (Cleveland, OH: World Publishing, 1959). Several bibliographic essays set forth the differing interpretive approaches to twentieth-century American policy reasonably well: Daniel M. Smith, "Rise to Great World Power, 1865–1918," and Gaddis Smith, "The United States in World Affairs since 1945," in *The Reinterpretation of American History and Culture*, ed. William H. Cartwright and Richard L. Watson Jr. (Washington, DC: National Council for the Social Studies, 1973), 443–464, 543–554; Walter LaFeber, "Liberty and Power: U.S. Diplomatic History, 1750–1945," in *The New American History*, rev. and expanded ed., ed. Eric Foner (Philadelphia: Temple University Press, 1997), 375–394; Erez Manela, "The United States in the World," in *American History Now*, ed. Eric Foner and Lisa McGirr (Philadelphia: Temple University Press, 2011), 201–220. The most recent and thorough revisionist accounts of the Truman administration and the Cold War are by Melvyn P. Leffler: *A Preponderance of Power: National Security, the Truman Administration, and the Cold War* (Stanford, CA: Stanford University Press, 1992), and *The Specter of Communism: The United States and the Origins of the Cold War, 1917–1953* (New York: Hill and Wang, 1994). The bibliographies include most of the relevant sources, including works with differing interpretations. I draw heavily from Leffler's volumes.

See also Ronald Steel, *Pax Americana: The Cold War Empire the United States Acquired by Accident—And How It Led from Isolation to Global Intervention* (New York: Viking, 1967); Herbert F. York, *Race to Oblivion: A Participant's View of the Arms Race* (New York: Simon and Schuster, 1970); Richard J. Barnet, *Roots of War: The Men and Institutions behind U.S. Foreign Policy* (New York: Atheneum, 1972); J. Samuel Walker, *Henry A. Wallace and American Foreign Policy* (Westport, CT: Greenwood, 1976); Robert L. Messer, *The End of an Alliance: James F. Byrnes, Roosevelt, Truman, and the Ori-*

gins of the Cold War (Chapel Hill: University of North Carolina Press, 1982); Stephen E. Ambrose, *Rise to Globalism: American Foreign Policy since 1938*, rev. ed. (New York: Penguin, 1983); Robert A. Pollard, *Economic Security and the Origins of the Cold War, 1945–1950* (New York: Columbia University Press, 1985); Walter Isaacson and Evan Thomas, *The Wise Men: Six Friends and the World They Made: Acheson, Bohlen, Harriman, Kennan, Lovett, McCloy* (New York: Simon and Schuster, 1986); Forrest Pogue, *George C. Marshall: Statesman, 1945–1949* (New York: Viking, 1987); Walter L. Hixson, *George F. Kennan: Cold War Iconoclast* (New York: Columbia University Press, 1989); John Mueller, *Retreat from Doomsday: The Obsolescence of Major War* (New York: Basic Books, 1989); John Prados, *Keeper of the Keys: A History of the National Security Council from Truman to Bush* (New York: William Morrow, 1991), 27–56; Alonzo L. Hamby, *Man of the People: A Life of Harry S. Truman* (New York: Oxford University Press, 1995), chaps. 19, 20, 22, 23, 29–31, epilogue; Michael S. Sherry, *In the Shadow of War: The United States since the 1930s* (New Haven, CT: Yale University Press, 1995); John Lewis Gaddis, *We Now Know: Rethinking Cold War History* (New York: Oxford University Press, 1997); Michael J. Hogan, *A Cross of Iron: Harry S. Truman and the Origins of the National Security State, 1945–1954* (New York: Cambridge University Press, 1998); Michael Kort, *The Columbia Guide to the Cold War* (New York: Columbia University Press, 1998); Arnold A. Offner, *Another Such Victory: President Truman and the Cold War, 1945–1953* (Stanford, CA: Stanford University Press, 2002); Chalmers Johnson, *The Sorrows of Empire: Militarism, Secrecy, and the End of the Republic* (New York: Metropolitan Books, 2004), 151–216; Dale R. Herspring, *The Pentagon and the Presidency: Civil-Military Relations from FDR to George W. Bush* (Lawrence: University Press of Kansas, 2005), 52–84; Keith D. McFarland and David L. Roll, *Louis Johnson and the Arming of America: The Roosevelt and Truman Years* (Bloomington: Indiana University Press, 2005); David J. Rothkopf, *Running the World: The Inside Story of the National Security Council and the Architects of American Power* (New York: Public Affairs, 2005), 3–62; Robert L. Beisner, *Dean Acheson: A Life in the Cold War* (New York: Oxford University Press, 2006); Michael Lind, *The American Way of Strategy* (New York: Oxford University Press, 2006); Jeffrey A. Engel, *Cold War at 30,000 Feet: The Anglo-American Fight for Aviation Supremacy* (Cambridge, MA: Harvard University Press, 2007); Kenneth J. Hagan and Ian J. Bickerton, *Unintended Consequences: The United States at War* (London: Reaktion Books, 2007), 118–193; Wilson D. Miscamble, *From Roosevelt to Truman: Potsdam, Hiroshima, and the Cold War* (New York: Cambridge University Press, 2007); Geoffrey Perret, *Commander in Chief: How Truman, Johnson, and Bush Turned a Presidential Power into a Threat to America's Future* (New York: Farrar, Straus and Giroux, 2007), 3–175; Marc Gallicchio, *The Scramble for Asia: U.S. Military Power in the Aftermath of the Pacific War* (Lanham, MD: Rowman and Littlefield, 2008); Eric Hobsbawn, *On Empire: America, War, and Global Supremacy* (New York: Pantheon Books, 2008); Christopher D. O'Sullivan, *Sumner Welles, Postwar Planning, and the Quest for a New World Order, 1937–1943* (New York: Columbia University Press, 2008); Gordon S. Barrass, *The Great Cold War: A Journey through the Hall of Mirrors* (Stanford, CA: Stanford University Press, 2009); Campbell Craig and Fredrik Logevall, *America's Cold War: The Politics of Insecurity* (Cambridge, MA: Belknap Press, 2009); Nicholas Thompson, *The Hawk and the Dove: Paul Nitze, George Kennan, and the History of the Cold War* (New York: Henry Holt, 2009); Richard H. Immerman, *Empire for Liberty: A History of American Imperialism from Benjamin Franklin to Paul*

Wolfowitz (Princeton, NJ: Princeton University Press, 2010); Norrin M. Ripsman and T. V. Paul, *Globalization and the National Security State* (New York: Oxford University Press, 2010); Julian E. Zelizer, *Arsenal of Democracy: The Politics of National Security—From World War II to the War on Terrorism* (New York: Basic Books, 2010); Robert P. Saldin, *War, the American State, and Politics since 1898* (New York: Cambridge University Press, 2011); and John Tirman, *The Deaths of Others: The Fate of Civilians in America's Wars* (New York: Oxford University Press, 2011).

Robert H. Ferrell, *Harry S. Truman and the Cold War Revisionists* (Columbia: University of Missouri Press, 2006), provides a harsh assessment of revisionism. He also briefly reviews the biographical treatment of Truman from the early years to the present. Ferrell has published a number of volumes on Truman and his administration. Geoffrey Wheatcroft, "The Voice of Unconventional Wisdom," *New York Review of Books*, November 11, 2010, 50–52, presents an excellent, insightful, and laudatory essay on William Pfaff's ongoing Cold War and post–Cold War analysis in a review of Pfaff's latest volume: *The Irony of Manifest Destiny: The Tragedy of America's Foreign Policy* (New York: Walker, 2010).

3. U.S. Bureau of the Census, *Historical Statistics of the United States, Colonial Times to 1970*, 2 pts. (Washington, DC: Bureau of the Census, 1975), 1141; R. Elberton Smith, *The Army and Economic Mobilization* (Washington, DC: Office of the Chief of Military History, 1959), 4–7; Doris M. Condit, *The Test of War, 1950–1953* (Washington, DC: Historical Office, Office of the Secretary of Defense, 1988), 500.

4. NSC-68 is reproduced in Ernest R. May, ed., *American Cold War Strategy: Interpreting NSC 68* (Boston: Bedford Books, 1993), 23–82; quotation, 78. The volume also includes numerous commentaries on the document. For Nitze, see David Callahan, *Dangerous Capabilities: Paul Nitze and the Cold War* (New York: HarperCollins, 1990). See also Robert D. Schulzinger, *The Wise Men of Foreign Affairs: The History of the Council of Foreign Relations* (New York: Columbia University Press, 1984), 113–143.

5. Secondary sources on the Korean War include David Rees, *Korea: The Limited War* (New York: St. Martin's Press, 1964); Leslie A. Rose, *Roots of Tragedy: The United States and the Struggle for Asia, 1945–1953* (Westport, CT: Greenwood, 1976); Bruce Cumings, *The Origins of the Korean War: Liberation and the Emergence of Separate Regimes, 1945–1947* (Princeton, NJ: Princeton University Press, 1981), and *The Origins of the Korean War: The Roaring of the Cataract, 1947–1950* (Princeton, NJ: Princeton University Press, 1990); Joseph C. Goulden, *Korea: The Untold Story of the War* (New York: Times Books, 1982); Burton I. Kaufman, *The Korean War: Challenges in Crisis, Credibility, and Command* (New York: Alfred A. Knopf, 1986); Clay Blair, *The Forgotten War: America in Korea, 1950–1953* (New York: Times Books, 1987); Terrence J. Gough, *U.S. Army Mobilization and Logistics in the Korean War: A Research Approach* (Washington, DC: Center of Military History, 1987); Max Hastings, *The Korean War* (New York: Simon and Schuster, 1987); Condit, *Test of War*; Paul G. Pierpaoli Jr., *Truman and Korea: The Political Culture of the Early Cold War* (Columbia: University of Missouri Press, 1999); William Stueck, *Rethinking the Korean War: A New Diplomatic and Strategic History* (Princeton, NJ: Princeton University Press, 2002). Kaufman's volume has an excellent bibliographic essay, and Stueck's endnotes are helpful.

6. Condit, *Test of War*, 500; Bureau of the Census, *Historical Statistics*, 1140.

7. Gregg Herken, *The Winning Weapon: The Atomic Bomb in the Cold War, 1945–1950* (New York: Vintage, 1982), 319–321. See also Gregg Herken, *Brotherhood*

of the Bomb: The Tangled Lives and Loyalties of Robert Oppenheimer, Ernest Lawrence, and Edward Teller (New York: Henry Holt, 2002), 129, 131–135, 149–153; Kai Bird and Martin J. Sherwin, *American Prometheus: The Triumph and Tragedy of J. Robert Oppenheimer* (New York: Alfred A. Knopf, 2005), 179–180, 268–276, 286–289, 290–303, 324–328, 422; and Priscilla J. McMillan, *The Ruin of J. Robert Oppenheimer and the Birth of the Modern Arms Race* (New York: Viking, 2005), 57–61.

8. For Eisenhower revisionism, see Robert A. Devine, *Eisenhower and the Cold War* (New York: Oxford University Press, 1981); Fred I. Greenstein, *The Hidden-Hand Presidency: Eisenhower as Leader* (New York: Basic Books, 1982); and Stephen E. Ambrose, *Eisenhower*, vol. 2, *The President* (New York: Simon and Schuster, 1984). See also Richard H. Immerman, "Confessions of an Eisenhower Revisionist: An Agonizing Reappraisal," *Diplomatic History* 14 (Summer 1990): 319–342; Richard H. Immerman, "Introduction," in *John Foster Dulles and the Diplomacy of the Cold War*, ed. Richard H. Immerman (Princeton, NJ: Princeton University Press, 1990), 7–8n19; and Stephen G. Rabe, "Eisenhower Revisionism: A Decade of Scholarship," *Diplomatic History* 17 (Winter 1993): 97–115. Despite charges of plagiarism and unreliable documentation, I, along with other scholars, still find Ambrose's publications to be useful.

9. Prados, *Keeper of the Keys*, 57–95; Rothkopf, *Running the World*, 61–79.

10. As more document collections are opened, Dulles's years as secretary of state are in the process of being reappraised. No consensus has yet emerged. For reference to standard sources on Dulles and tentative revisionist assessments, see the numerous essays in Immerman, ed., *John Foster Dulles*.

11. Ambrose, *Eisenhower*, 215–217, 328, 354–375, 402–404, 511, 515–521, 524–526; Rolf Steininger, "John Foster Dulles, the European Defense Community, and the German Question," and Hans-Jurgen Grabbe, "Konrad Adenauer, John Foster Dulles, and West German–American Relations," in Immerman, ed., *John Foster Dulles*, 79–108, 109–132; Tim Weiner, *Legacy of Ashes: The History of the CIA* (New York: Doubleday, 2007), 123–135; David M. Barrett, *The CIA and Congress: The Untold Story from Truman to Kennedy* (Lawrence: University Press of Kansas, 2005), 251–261.

12. See note 5 above. See also Richard M. Leighton, *Strategy, Money, and the New Look, 1953–1956* (Washington, DC: Historical Office, Office of the Secretary of Defense, 2001), 1–4. For the most recent volume covering most parts of the developing world, and including a fine and extensive bibliography, see Kathryn C. Statler and Andrew L. Johns, eds., *The Eisenhower Administration, the Third World, and the Globalization of the Cold War* (Lanham, MD: Rowman and Littlefield, 2006).

13. George C. Herring, *America's Longest War: The United States and Vietnam, 1950–1975*, 2nd ed. (New York: Alfred A. Knopf, 1986), 3–72; George C. Herring, "'A Good Stout Effort': John Foster Dulles and the Indochina Crisis, 1954–1955," in Immerman, ed., *John Foster Dulles*, 213–233; Marilyn B. Young, *The Vietnam Wars, 1945–1990* (New York: HarperCollins, 1991), 1–78; Leighton, *Strategy, Money, and the New Look*, 517–550; Robert J. Watson, *Into the Missile Age, 1956–1960* (Washington, DC: Historical Office, Office of the Secretary of Defense, 1997), 640–656. Herring's volume has a thorough bibliographic essay that is updated by his other cited work.

14. Ambrose, *Eisenhower*, 47–49, 212–214, 231–245, 482–485; Nancy Bernhoff Tucker, "John Foster Dulles and the Taiwan Roots of the 'Two China' Policy," in Immerman, ed., *John Foster Dulles*, 235–262; Leighton, *Strategy, Money, and the New Look*, 359,

363–365, 500–501; Watson, *Into the Missile Age*, 219–242; Schulzinger, *Wise Men of Foreign Affairs*, 177–193.

15. Robert R. Bowie and Richard M. Immerman, *Waging Peace: How Eisenhower Shaped an Enduring Cold-War Strategy* (New York: Oxford University Press, 1998), 214, 217–221; Weiner, *Legacy of Ashes*, 81–92; Ambrose, *Eisenhower*, 109–112, 129–130.

16. Watson, *Into the Missile Age*, 47–72, 206–219, 240–242; Ambrose, *Eisenhower*, 314–316, 328–334, 338–340, 350–374, 462–467, 469–475; Wm. Roger Lewis, "Dulles, Suez, and the British," in Immerman, *John Foster Dulles*, 133–158.

17. Weiner, *Legacy of Ashes*, 93–104, 155–158, 160–162, 164–166; Barrett, *CIA and Congress*, 161–170, 425–449; Watson, *Into the Missile Age*, 762–768; Ambrose, *Eisenhower*, 192–197, 464, 504–507, 526–527, 554–558, 582–584; Stephen G. Rabe, *Eisenhower in Latin America: The Foreign Policy of Anticommunism* (Chapel Hill: University of North Carolina Press, 1988); Stephen G. Rabe, "Dulles, Latin America, and Cold War Anticommunism," in Immerman, *John Foster Dulles*, 159–187.

18. Bowie and Immerman, *Waging Peace*, 222–259; Ambrose, *Eisenhower*, 91–96, 131–135, 145–151, 247–269, 489–496, 513–526, 532–545, 551–553, 561–580; John Lewis Gaddis, "The Unexpected John Foster Dulles: Nuclear Weapons, Communism, and the Russians," in Immerman, *John Foster Dulles*, 47–77; Watson, *Into the Missile Age*, 683–730; Prados, *Keeper of the Keys*, 68, 91; Klaus Larres and Kenneth Osgood, eds., *The Cold War after Stalin's Death: A Missed Opportunity for Peace?* (Lanham, MD: Rowman and Littlefield, 2006); Weiner, *Legacy of Ashes*, 112–114, 158–160; Barrett, *CIA and Congress*, 373–422.

19. Bureau of the Census, *Historical Statistics*, 1114; Herspring, *Pentagon and the Presidency*, 90.

20. Gerald Clarfield, *Security with Solvency: Dwight D. Eisenhower and the Shaping of the American Military Establishment* (Westport, CT: Praeger, 1999)—the author is particularly good on the DOD reorganizations of 1953 and 1958; Herspring, *Pentagon and the Presidency*, 85–117; Richard A. Aliano, "American Defense Policy from Eisenhower to Kennedy: The Politics of Changing Military Requirements , 1957–1961" (Ph.D. diss., City University of New York, 1973); Leighton, *Strategy, Money, and the New Look*, 21–43; Watson, *Into the Missile Age*, 243–291. The Leighton and Watson volumes include detailed accounts of the annual struggles over DOD budgets among the services and between them and the White House. A more abbreviated analysis is offered by Ambrose, *Eisenhower*. On the DOD organization and reorganizations, see also chapter 3.

21. Stephen I. Schwartz, ed., *Atomic Audit: The Costs and Consequences of U.S. Nuclear Weapons since 1940* (Washington, DC: Brookings Institution Press, 1998), 151–168; Watson, *Into the Missile Age*, 445–471; Ambrose, *Eisenhower*, 224–225, 229, 259, 405–406; Andrew Preston, *The War Council: McGeorge Bundy, the NSC, and Vietnam* (Cambridge, MA: Harvard University Press, 2006), 56.

22. All these themes are covered in the relevant pages of Weiner, *Legacy of Ashes,* and Barrett, *CIA and Congress*. See also Loch K. Johnson, *America's Secret Power: The CIA in a Democratic Society* (New York: Oxford University Press, 1989); Amy B. Zegart, *Flawed by Design: The Evolution of the CIA, JCS, and NSC* (Stanford, CA: Stanford University Press, 1999); John Prados, *Safe for Democracy: The Secret Wars of the CIA*

(Chicago: Ivan R. Dee, 2006); John Prados, "Intelligence for Empire," in *The Long War: A New History of U.S. National Security Policy since World War II*, ed. Andrew J. Bacevich (New York: Columbia University Press, 2007), 302–334; Athan Theoharis, *The Quest for Absolute Security: The Failed Relations among U.S. Intelligence Agencies* (Chicago: Ivan R. Dee, 2007); Michael Holzman, *James Jesus Angleton, the CIA, and the Craft of Counterintelligence* (Amherst: University of Massachusetts Press, 2008); and Hugh Wilford, *The Mighty Wurlitzer: How the CIA Played America* (Cambridge, MA: Harvard University Press, 2008).

23. The analysis of the Kennedy administration is based on these sources: Charles J. Hitch and Roland N. McKean, *The Economics of Defense in the Nuclear Age* (Cambridge, MA: Harvard University Press, 1960); Robert J. Art, *The TFX Decision: McNamara and the Military* (Boston: Little, Brown, 1968); Bureau of the Census, *Historical Statistics*, 1114; Herbert S. Parmet, *JFK: The Presidency of John F. Kennedy* (New York: Dial Press, 1983); Schulzinger, *Wise Men of Foreign Affairs*, 165–207; McGeorge Bundy, *Danger and Survival: Choices about the Bomb in the First Fifty Years* (New York: Random House, 1988), 350–516; Herring, *America's Longest War*; Thomas G. Paterson, ed., *Kennedy's Quest for Victory: American Foreign Policy, 1961–1963* (New York: Oxford University Press, 1989); Michael R. Beschloss, *The Crisis Years: Kennedy and Khrushchev, 1960–1963* (New York: HarperCollins, 1991); James N. Giglio, *The Presidency of John F. Kennedy* (Lawrence: University Press of Kansas, 1991); Prados, *Keeper of the Keys*, 97–132; Thomas C. Reeves, *A Question of Character: A Life of John F. Kennedy* (New York: Free Press, 1991); Young, *Vietnam Wars*; Richard Reeves, *President Kennedy: Profile of Power* (New York: Simon and Schuster, 1993); Deborah Shapley, *Promise and Power: The Life and Times of Robert McNamara* (Boston: Little, Brown, 1993), 77–265; Richard N. Lebow and Janice G. Stein, *We All Lost the Cold War* (Princeton, NJ: Princeton University Press, 1994), 3–145; Zegart, *Flawed by Design*; Lawrence Freedman, *Kennedy's Wars: Berlin, Cuba, Laos, and Vietnam* (New York: Oxford University Press, 2000); Robert Dallek, *An Unfinished Life: John F. Kennedy, 1917–1963* (Boston: Little, Brown, 2003); Christopher A. Preble, *John F. Kennedy and the Missile Gap* (De Kalb: Northern Illinois University Press, 2004); Barrett, *CIA and Congress*, 423–463; Herspring, *Pentagon and the Presidency*, 118–149; Rothkopf, *Running the World*, 80–96; Lawrence S. Kaplan, Ronald D. Landa, and Edward J. Drea, *The McNamara Ascendancy, 1961–1965* (Washington, DC: Historical Office, Office of the Secretary of Defense, 2006); Preston, *War Council*; Weiner, *Legacy of Ashes*, 171–235; Michael Dobbs, *One Minute to Midnight: Kennedy, Khrushchev, and Castro on the Brink of Nuclear War* (New York: Alfred A. Knopf, 2008); Gordon M. Goldstein, *Lessons in Disaster: McGeorge Bundy and the Path to War in Vietnam* (New York: Henry Holt, 2008); and David Milne, *America's Rasputin: Walt Rostow and the Vietnam War* (New York: Hill and Wang, 2008). Giglio, *Presidency of John F. Kennedy*, has an excellent bibliographic essay that can be supplemented by more recent publications cited here.

24. Center for Strategic Studies, *Economic Impact of the Vietnam War* (Washington, DC: Georgetown University, Center for Strategic Studies, 1967); Bureau of the Census, *Historical Statistics*, 1114; Larry Berman, *Planning a Tragedy: The Americanization of the War in Vietnam* (New York: Norton, 1982); Larry Berman, *Lyndon Johnson's War: The Road to Stalemate in Vietnam* (New York: Norton, 1989); Vaughn D. Bornet, *The Presidency of Lyndon B. Johnson* (Lawrence: University Press of Kansas, 1983); Schulzinger, *Wise Men of Foreign Affairs*, 165–207; Herring, *America's Longest War*; Prados, *Keeper*

of the Keys, 133–260; Young, *Vietnam Wars*; Shapley, *Promise and Power*, 269–615; Gary R. Hess, "The Unending Debate: Historians and the Vietnam War," *Diplomatic History* 18 (Spring 1994): 239–264; H. W. Brands, *The Wages of Globalism: Lyndon Johnson and the Limits of American Power* (New York: Oxford University Press, 1995); H. W. Brands, ed., *The Foreign Policies of Lyndon Johnson: Beyond Vietnam* (College Station: Texas A&M University Press, 1999); Michael H. Hunt, *Lyndon Johnson's War: America's Cold War Crusade in Vietnam, 1945–1968* (New York: Hill and Wang, 1996); Robert Dallek, *Flawed Giant: Lyndon Johnson and His Times, 1961–1973* (New York: Oxford University Press, 1998); Zegart, *Flawed by Design*; Lloyd C. Gardner and Ted Gittinger, eds., *The Search for Peace in Vietnam, 1964–1968* (College Station: Texas A&M University Press, 2004); Herspring, *Pentagon and the Presidency*, 150–183; "Form: Vietnam in Historical Thinking," *Pacific Historical Review* 74 (August 2005): 409–456; Rothkopf, *Running the World*, 96–107; Preston, *War Council*, 131–248; Kaplan, Landa, and Drea, *McNamara Ascendancy*; Mark Moyar, *Triumph Forsaken: The Vietnam War, 1954–1965* (New York: Cambridge University Press, 2006); Randall B. Woods, *LBJ: Architect of American Ambition* (New York: Free Press, 2006); David L. Anderson and John Ernst, eds., *The War that Never Ends: New Perspectives on the Vietnam War* (Lexington: University Press of Kentucky, 2007); Perret, *Commander in Chief*, 176–298; Weiner, *Legacy of Ashes*, 236–288; Milne, *America's Rasputin*; Gregory A. Daddid, *No Sure Victory: Measuring U.S. Effectiveness and Progress in the Vietnam Era* (New York: Oxford University Press, 2011).

25. William Shawcross, *Sideshow: Kissinger, Nixon and the Destruction of Cambodia* (New York: Simon and Schuster, 1979); Seymour M. Hersh, *The Price of Power: Kissinger in the Nixon White House* (New York: Summit Books, 1983); Schulzinger, *Wise Men of Foreign Affairs*, 209–242; Stephen E. Ambrose, *Nixon*, vol. 2, *The Triumph of a Politician, 1962–1972*, and vol. 3, *Ruin and Recovery, 1973–1990* (New York: Simon and Schuster, 1989–1991); Roger Morris, *Richard Milhous Nixon: The Rise of an American Politician* (New York: Henry Holt, 1990); Herbert S. Parmet, *Richard Nixon and His America* (Boston: Little, Brown, 1990); Prados, *Keeper of the Keys*, 261–353; Young, *Vietnam Wars*; Walter Isaacson, *Kissinger: A Biography* (New York: Simon and Schuster, 1992); William C. Berman, *America's Right Turn: From Nixon to Bush* (Baltimore: Johns Hopkins University Press, 1994), 1–36; Raymond L. Garthoff, *Detente and Confrontation: American-Soviet Relations from Nixon to Reagan*, rev. ed. (Washington, DC: Brookings Institution, 1994); Lebow and Stein, *We All Lost the Cold War*, 147–288; Allan R. Millett and Peter Maslowski, *The Common Defense: A Military History of the United States of America*, rev. ed. (New York: Free Press, 1994), 589–601, 656; Terry Terriff, *The Nixon Administration and the Making of U.S. Nuclear Strategy* (Ithaca, NY: Cornell University Press, 1995); Zegart, *Flawed by Design*; Robert M. Collins, *More: The Politics of Economic Growth in Postwar America* (New York: Oxford University Press, 2000), 98–131; Larry Berman, *No Peace, No Honor: Nixon, Kissinger, and Betrayal in Vietnam* (New York: Free Press, 2001); Christopher Hitchens, *The Trial of Henry Kissinger* (London: Verso, 2001); Richard Reeves, *President Nixon: Alone in the White House* (New York: Simon and Schuster, 2001); Richard C. Thornton, *The Nixon-Kissinger Years: Reshaping America's Foreign Policy* (St. Paul, MN: Paragon House, 2001); Herspring, *Pentagon and the Presidency*, 184–216; Rothkopf, *Running the World*, 108–152; Susan B. Carter et al., eds., *Historical Statistics of the United States: Earliest Times to the Present*, 5 vols. (New York: Cambridge University Press, 2006), 5:353–356,

367–368; Preston, *War Council*, 236–248; Yafeng Xia, *Negotiating with the Enemy: U.S.-China Talks during the Cold War, 1949–1972* (Bloomington: Indiana University Press, 2006); Robert Dallek, *Nixon and Kissinger: Partners in Power* (New York: HarperCollins, 2007); Edwin A. Martini, *Invisible Enemies: The American War on Vietnam, 1975–2000* (Amherst: University of Massachusetts Press, 2007); Arnold A. Offner, "Liberation or Dominance? The Ideology of U.S. National Security Policy," in Bacevich, *The Long War*, 1–52; Jeremi Suri, *Henry Kissinger and the American Century* (Cambridge, MA: Belknap, 2007); Weiner, *Legacy of Ashes*, 291–334; Rick Perlstein, *Nixonland: The Rise of a President and the Fracturing of America* (New York: Scribner, 2008); Bruce J. Schulman and Julian E. Zelizer, eds., *Rightward Bound: Making America Conservative in the 1970s* (Cambridge, MA: Harvard University Press, 2008); Asaf Siniver, *Nixon, Kissinger, and U.S. Foreign Policy Making* (New York: Cambridge University Press, 2008).

26. Many of the sources cited in note 25 also deal with the Ford administration. This is particularly true of the works by Isaacson, Garthoff, Prados, Rothkopf, Herspring, and Weiner.

27. The following analysis of the Carter administration's national security and foreign policies is based on these sources: Fred Halliday, *The Making of the Second Cold War* (London: Verso, 1983); Schulzinger, *Wise Men of Foreign Affairs*, 209–254; Garthoff, *Detente and Confrontation*, 623–1180; Gaddis Smith, *Morality, Reason, and Power: American Diplomacy in the Carter Years* (New York: Hill and Wang, 1986); Prados, *Keeper of the Keys*, 379–445; Millett and Maslowski, *For the Common Defense*, 655–656; Thomas J. McCormick, *America's Half-Century: United States Foreign Policy in the Cold War and After*, 2nd ed. (Baltimore: Johns Hopkins University Press, 1995), 191–215; Peter G. Bourne, *Jimmy Carter: A Comprehensive Biography from Plains to Postpresidency* (New York: Scribner, 1997); Berman, *America's Right Turn*, 37–59; Zegart, *Flawed by Design*; Herspring, *Pentagon and the Presidency*, 237–264; James T. Patterson, *Restless Giant: The United States from Watergate to Bush v. Gore* (New York: Oxford University Press, 2005), 13–151; Rothkopf, *Running the World*, 157–209; Odd A. Westad, *The Global Cold War: Third World Intervention and the Making of Our Times* (New York: Cambridge University Press, 2005); Carter et al., eds., *Historical Statistics*, 5:353–356, 367–368; Burton I. Kaufman and Scott Kaufman, *The Presidency of James Earl Carter, Jr.*, 2nd rev. ed. (Lawrence: University Press of Kansas, 2006)—the volume has an excellent and up-to-date bibliography; Preston, *War Council*, 245; Melvyn P. Leffler, *For the Soul of Mankind: The United States, the Soviet Union, and the Cold War* (New York: Hill and Wang, 2007), 234–337; Weiner, *Legacy of Ashes*, 357–374; Scott Kaufman, *Plans Unraveled: The Foreign Policy of the Carter Administration* (De Kalb: Northern Illinois University Press, 2008); Julian E. Zelizer, *Jimmy Carter* (New York: Times Books, 2010).

28. The following analysis of the Reagan administration's national security and foreign policies is based on the following sources: Robert Scheer, *With Enough Shovels: Reagan, Bush and Nuclear War* (New York: Random House, 1982); Halliday, *Making of the Second Cold War*; Robert Dallek, *Ronald Reagan: The Politics of Symbolism* (Cambridge, MA: Harvard University Press, 1984); John Tirman, ed., *The Fallacy of Star Wars: Based on Studies Conducted by the Union of Concerned Scientists* (New York: Vintage, 1984); Stephen J. Cimbala, ed., *The Reagan Defense Program: An Interim Assessment* (Wilmington, DE: Scholarly Resources, 1986); Anthony S. Campagna, *U.S. National Economic Policy, 1917–1985* (Westport, CT: Praeger, 1987); Michael T. Klare and Peter Kornbluh, eds., *Low Intensity Warfare: Counterinsurgency, Proinsurgency, and*

Antiterrorism in the Eighties (New York: Pantheon, 1987); Douglas C. Waller, *Congress and the Nuclear Freeze: An Inside Look at the Politics of a Mass Movement* (Amherst: University of Massachusetts Press, 1987); H. Bruce Franklin, *War Stars: The Superweapon and the American Imagination* (New York: Oxford University Press, 1988); Strobe Talbott, *The Master of the Game: Paul Nitze and the Nuclear Peace* (New York: Alfred A. Knopf, 1988), 162–394; Lou Cannon, *President Reagan: The Role of a Lifetime* (New York: Public Affairs, 1991); Prados, *Keeper of the Keys*, 447–547; John Lewis Gaddis, *The United States and the End of the Cold War: Implications, Reconsiderations, Provocations* (New York: Oxford University Press, 1992); Daniel Wirls, *Buildup: The Politics of Defense in the Reagan Era* (Ithaca, NY: Cornell University Press, 1992); Raymond L. Garthoff, *The Great Transition: American-Soviet Relations and the End of the Cold War* (Washington, DC: Brookings Institution, 1994); Lebow and Stein, *We All Lost the Cold War*, 289–376; Millett and Maslowski, *For the Common Defense*, 655–656; McCormick, *America's Half-Century*, 216–236; Berman, *America's Right Turn*, 85–143; Zegart, *Flawed by Design*; Frances Fitzgerald, *Way Out There in the Blue: Reagan, Star Wars and the End of the Cold War* (New York: Simon and Schuster, 2000); James R. Locher III, *Victory on the Potomac: The Goldwater-Nichols Act Unifies the Pentagon* (College Station: Texas A&M University Press, 2002); Richard D. Burns and Lester N. Brune, *The Quest for Missile Defenses, 1944–2003* (Claremont, CA: Regina Books, 2003); Herspring, *Pentagon and the Presidency*, 265–296; Patterson, *Restless Giant*, 152–217; Richard Reeves, *President Reagan, the Triumph of Imagination* (New York: Simon and Schuster, 2005); Rothkopf, *Running the World*, 210–259; Westad, *Global Cold War*, 331–407; Carter et al., eds., *Historical Statistics*, 5:367–368; Thomas W. Evans, *The Education of Ronald Reagan: The General Electric Years and the Untold Story of His Conversion to Conservatism* (New York: Columbia University Press, 2006); Greg Grandin, *Empire's Workshop: Latin America, the United States, and the Rise of the New Imperialism* (New York: Metropolitan Books, 2006); Nigel Hey, *The Star Wars Enigma: Behind the Scenes of the Cold War Race for Missile Defense* (Washington, DC: Potomac Books, 2006); Preston, *War Council*, 245–246; Robert M. Collins, *Transforming America: Politics and Culture in the Reagan Years* (New York: Columbia University Press, 2007); John Patrick Diggins, *Ronald Reagan: Fate, Freedom, and the Making of History* (New York: W. W. Norton, 2007); Leffler, *Soul of Mankind*, 338–467; Richard Rhodes, *Arsenals of Folly: The Making of the Nuclear Arms Race* (New York: Alfred A. Knopf, 2007), 138–289; Weiner, *Legacy of Ashes*, 375–422; Vladislav M. Zubok, *A Failed Empire: The Soviet Union in the Cold War from Stalin to Gorbachev* (Chapel Hill: University of North Carolina Press, 2007); Sean Wilentz, *The Age of Reagan: A History, 1974–2000* (New York: HarperCollins, 2008); Steven F. Hayward, *The Age of Reagan: The Conservative Counterrevolution, 1980–1989* (New York: Crown Forum, 2009); James Mann, *The Rebellion of Ronald Reagan: A History of the End of the Cold War* (New York: Viking, 2009); *Los Angeles Times*, January 3, 2010, A27.

29. The following analysis of the Bush administration is based on these sources: Prados, *Keeper of the Keys*, 548–557; Michael J. Hogan, ed., *The End of the Cold War: Its Meaning and Implications* (New York: Cambridge University Press, 1992); Michael R. Beschloss and Strobe Talbott, *At the Highest Levels: The Inside Story of the End of the Cold War* (Boston: Little, Brown, 1993); Garthoff, *Great Transition*, 375–801; Millett and Maslowski, *For the Common Defense*, 655–656; McCormick, *America's Half-Century*, 237–258; William C. Wohlforth, ed., *Witnesses to the End of the Cold War* (Baltimore:

Johns Hopkins University Press, 1996); Berman, *America's Right Turn*, 143–163; Zegart, *Flawed by Design*; Herspring, *Pentagon and the Presidency*, 297–330; Patterson, *Restless Giant*, 218–253; Rothkopf, *Running the World*, 260–302; Westad, *Global Cold War*, 364–407; Carter et al., eds., *Historical Statistics*, 5:353–356, 367–268; Hey, *Star Wars Enigma*, 217–233; Preston, *War Council*, 245–246; Leffler, *Soul of Mankind*, 422–467; Rhodes, *Arsenals of Folly*, 271–309; Weiner, *Legacy of Ashes*, 423–435; Christopher Maynard, *Out of the Shadow: George H. W. Bush and the End of the Cold War* (College Station: Texas A&M University Press, 2008).

30. The following account of the Clinton administration is based on these sources: Millett and Maslowski, *For the Common Defense*, 655–656; William G. Hyland, *Clinton's World: Remaking American Foreign Policy* (Westport, CT: Praeger, 1999); Zegart, *Flawed by Design*; Chalmers Johnson, *Blowback: The Costs and Consequences of American Empire* (New York: Metropolitan Books, 2000); Robert S. Litwak, *Rogue States and U.S. Foreign Policy: Containment after the Cold War* (Washington, DC: Woodrow Wilson Center Press, 2000); Sidney Blumenthal, *The Clinton Wars* (New York: Farrar, Straus and Giroux, 2003); John F. Harris, *The Survivor: Bill Clinton in the White House* (New York: Random House, 2005); Herspring, *Pentagon and the Presidency*, 331–376; Patterson, *Restless Giant*, 254–425; Rothkopf, *Running the World*, 303–388; Carter et al., eds., *Historical Statistics*, 5:367–368; Preston, *War Council*, 245–246; Weiner, *Legacy of Ashes*, 439–476; Taylor Branch, *The Clinton Tapes: Wrestling History with the President* (New York: Simon and Schuster, 2009).

31. There is already practically a cottage industry devoted to the Bush administration, neoconservatism, evangelical Christianity, and other movements related to it. Some of the numerous volumes include the following: Helen Caldicott, *The New Nuclear Danger: George W. Bush's Military-Industrial Complex* (New York: New Press, 2002); Walter LaFeber, *America, Russia, and the Cold War, 1945–2002* (New York: McGraw-Hill, 2002); Bob Woodward, *Bush at War* (New York: Simon and Schuster, 2002); Bob Woodward, *State of Denial* (New York: Simon and Schuster, 2006); Michael Mann, *Incoherent Empire* (London: Verso, 2003); Clyde V. Prestowitz, *Rogue Nation: American Unilateralism and the Failure of Good Intentions* (New York: Basic Books, 2003); T. D. Allman, *Rogue State: America at War with the World* (New York: Nation Books, 2004); John Lewis Gaddis, *Surprise, Security, and the American Experience* (Cambridge, MA: Harvard University Press, 2004); Johnson, *Sorrows of Empire*; Chalmers Johnson, *Nemesis: The Last Days of the American Republic* (New York: Metropolitan Books, 2006); Chalmers Johnson, *Dismantling the Empire: America's Last Best Hope* (New York: Metropolitan Books, 2010); James Bamford, *A Pretext for War: 9/11, Iraq, and the Abuses of American Intelligence Agencies* (New York: Anchor Books, 2005); Andrew J. Bacevich, *The New American Militarism: How Americans Are Seduced by War* (New York: Oxford University Press, 2005); Larry Diamond, *Squandered Victory: The American Occupation and Bungled Efforts to Bring Democracy to Iraq* (New York: Times Books, 2005); Niall Ferguson, *The War of the World: Twentieth-Century Conflict and the Descent of the West* (New York: Penguin, 2006); Stephen Grey, *Ghost Plane: The True Story of the CIA Torture Program* (New York: St. Martin's Press, 2006); Damon Linker, *The Theocons: Secular America under Siege* (New York: Doubleday, 2006); Kevin Phillips, *American Theocracy: The Perils and Politics of Radical Religion, Oil, and Borrowed Money in the 21st Century* (New York: Viking, 2006); James Risen, *State of War: The Secret History of the*

CIA and the Bush Administration (New York: Free Press, 2006); Arnold A. Offner, "Liberation or Dominance: The Ideology of U.S. National Security Policy," in Bacevich, ed., *The Long War*, 1–17, 37–42; Perret, *Commander in Chief*, 299–392; Hal Brands, *From Berlin to Baghdad: America's Search for Purpose in the Post–Cold War World* (Lexington: University Press of Kentucky, 2008); Thomas Frank, *The Wrecking Crew: How Conservatives Rule* (New York: Metropolitan Books, 2008); Walter L. Hixson, *The Myth of American Diplomacy: National Identity and U.S. Foreign Policy* (New Haven, CT: Yale University Press, 2008); Godfrey Hodgson, *The Myth of American Exceptionalism* (New Haven, CT: Yale University Press, 2008); Joan Hoff, *A Faustian Foreign Policy from Woodrow Wilson to George W. Bush: Dreams of Perfectibility* (New York: Cambridge University Press, 2008), 156–203; Eugene Jarecki, *The American Way of War: Guided Missiles, Misguided Men, and a Republic in Peril* (New York: Free Press, 2008); Jonathan Mabler, *The Challenge: Hamdan v. Rumsfeld and the Fight over Presidential Power* (New York: Farrar, Straus and Giroux, 2008); Robert Scheer, *The Pornography of Power: How Defense Hawks Hijacked 9/11 and Weakened America* (New York: Twelve, 2008); Leslie H. Gelb, *Power Rules: How Common Sense Can Rescue American Foreign Policy* (New York: HarperCollins, 2009); Maria Hohn and Seungsook Moon, eds., *Over There: Living with the U.S. Military Empire from World War Two to the Present* (Durham, NC: Duke University Press, 2010); U.S. Bureau of the Census, *Statistical Abstract of the United States* (Washington, DC: Bureau of the Census, 2011), tables 501, 502; Amy Chun, "Which Way Do We Go," *New York Times Book Review*, October 25, 2009, 27; *Los Angeles Times*, December 30, 2009, A27. *Peace & Change* 34 (July 2009) devotes an entire issue to the Bush administration, including both articles and book reviews.

32. Many of the volumes cited above and below deal with civil-military relations to varying degrees and with differing levels of sophistication. For scholarship focusing principally on the subject, some recent titles include the following: Joseph G. Dawson III, ed., *Commanders in Chief: Presidential Leadership in Modern Wars* (Lawrence: University Press of Kansas, 1993), ix–xv, 1–47, 87–178; Robert K. Griffith Jr., *The U.S. Army's Transition to the All-Voluntary Force, 1968–1974* (Washington, DC: Center of Military History, 1997); Russell F. Weigley, "The Soldier, the Statesman, the Military Historian," *Journal of Military History* 63 (October 1999): 807–822; Peter Feaver and Richard H. Kohn, eds., *Soldiers and Civilians: The Civil-Military Gap and American National Security* (Cambridge, MA: MIT Press, 2001); Alex Roland, *The Military-Industrial Complex* (Washington, DC: American Historical Association, 2001); Eliot A. Cohen, *Supreme Command: Soldiers, Statesmen, and Leadership in Wartime* (New York: Free Press, 2002); Peter Feaver, *Armed Servants, Agency, Oversight, and Civil-Military Relations* (Cambridge, MA: Harvard University Press, 2003); Herspring, *Pentagon and the Presidency*; Andrew J. Bacevich, "Elusive Bargain: The Politics of U.S. Civil-Military Relations since World War II," in Bacevich, ed., *The Long War*, 207–264; James Burk, "The Changing Moral Contract for Military Service," ibid., 405–455; Alex Roland, "The Military-Industrial Complex: Lobby and Trope," ibid., 335–370; Adrian R. Lewis, *The American Culture of War: The History of U.S. Military Force from World War II to Operation Iraqi Freedom* (New York: Routledge, 2007); Beth Bailey, *America's Army: Making the All-Volunteer Force* (Cambridge, MA: Belknap Press, 2009); Rebecca L. Schiff, *The Military and Domestic Politics: A Concordance Theory of Civil-Military Relations* (New York: Routledge, 2009); Jason K. Dempsey, *Our Army: Soldiers, Politics, and American*

Civil-Military Relations (Princeton, NJ: Princeton University Press, 2010); Diane H. Mazur, *A More Perfect Military: How the Constitution Can Make Our Military Stronger* (New York: Oxford University Press, 2010).

Armed Forces & Society 24 (Spring 1998 and Summer 1998) includes a useful series of articles, critiques, and exchanges on civil-military relations and numerous bibliographic references. For a brief discussion and citation of sources for earlier analyses of civil-military relations, see Paul A. C. Koistinen, *Mobilizing for Modern War: The Political Economy of American Warfare, 1865–1919* (Lawrence: University Press of Kansas, 1997), 74–75, n. 5.

33. Bacevich, "Elusive Bargain," 209–210.

34. On the use of private contractors for carrying out military, intelligence, and related roles, see Johnson, *Sorrows of Empire*, 131–216; Johnson, *Nemesis*, 1–11, 137–207; Johnson, *Dismantling the Empire*, 96–106, 109–132, 183–184, 191–195; Deborah Avant, "Privatizing Military Training: A Challenge to U.S. Army Professionalism?" in *The Future of the Army Profession*, eds. Don M. Snider and Gable L. Watkins (Boston: McGraw–Hill, 2002), 179–196; Deborah D. Avant, *The Market Force: The Consequences of Privatizing Security* (New York: Cambridge University Press, 2005); P. W. Singer, *Corporate Warriors: The Rise of the Privatized Military Industry* (Ithaca, NY: Cornell University Press, 2003); Sarah Percy, *Mercenaries: The History of a Norm in International Relations* (New York: Oxford University Press 2007); Jeremy Scahill, *Blackwater: The Rise of the World's Most Powerful Mercenary Army* (New York: Nation Books, 2007); Andrew Alexandra, Deane-Peter Baker, and Marina Caparini, eds., *Private Military and Security Companies: Ethics, Policies and Civil-Military Relations* (New York: Routledge, 2008); "Forum on Military Privatization," *Armed Forces & Society* 36 (July 2010): 647–749 (addressing the issue from an international perspective, with excellent bibliographic references); Hohn and Moon, *Over There*, 397–408; Molly Dunigan, *Victory for Hire: Private Security Companies' Impact on Military Effectiveness* (Stanford, CA: Stanford University Press, 2011); and *Los Angeles Times*, September 30, 2007, M2; August 28, 2008, A26; July 22, 2009, A25; August 13, 2009, A1; August 20, 2009, A18; August 27, 2009, A15; December 11, 2009, A28; December 16, 2009, A13; January 1, 2010, A1; January 2, 2010, A21; January 8, 2010, A16; January 11, 2010, A16; April 17, 2010, A1; June 7, 2010, A7. See also chapter 6, dealing with think tanks and related institutions.

35. For an extended analysis of military professionalism and civil-military relations, see Paul A. C. Koistinen, *The Military-Industrial Complex: A Historical Perspective* (New York: Praeger, 1980), 5–22.

36. This topic is explicated in Paul A. C. Koistinen, *Beating Plowshares into Swords: The Political Economy of American Warfare, 1606–1865* (Lawrence: University Press of Kansas, 1996); Koistinen, *Mobilizing for Modern War*; and Paul A. C. Koistinen, *Planning War, Pursuing Peace: The Political Economy of American Warfare, 1920–1939* (Lawrence: University Press of Kansas, 1998).

CHAPTER TWO. CONGRESS

1. Executive-legislative relations during the interwar and war years are reasonably well covered and documented in Paul A. C. Koistinen, *Planning War, Pursuing Peace:*

The Political Economy of American Warfare, 1920–1939 (Lawrence: University Press of Kansas, 1998), chaps. 14 and 15; and Paul A. C. Koistinen, *Arsenal of World War II: The Political-Economy of American Warfare, 1940–1945* (Lawrence: University Press of Kansas, 2004), 439–444. Sources cited in chapter 1 on the presidents also include a great deal of information on executive-legislative relations during and after the Cold War years. For a convenient guide to congressional hearings on defense policy, see Richard Burt and Geoffrey Kemp, eds., *Congressional Hearings on American Defense Policy, 1947–1971: An Annotated Bibliography* (Lawrence: University Press of Kansas, 1974; published for the National Security Education Program).

2. James M. Lindsay, *Congress and the Politics of U.S. Foreign Policy* (Baltimore: Johns Hopkins University Press, 1994), covers the subject quite well, particularly chap. 3. David M. Barrett, *The CIA and Congress: The Untold Story from Truman to Kennedy* (Lawrence: University Press of Kansas, 2005), is the most recent study of Congress and intelligence agencies. Barrett is more positive than most on the quality of congressional oversight. See also chapter 1, notes 11 and 22.

3. Figures on spending for national defense are available in many sources. Standard sources include U.S. Bureau of the Census, *Historical Statistics of the United States, Colonial Times to 1970*, 2 pts. (Washington, DC: U.S. Bureau of the Census, 1975), 224–230, 1114–1116, 1123–1124; and Susan B. Carter et al., eds., *Historical Statistics of the United States: Earliest Times to the Present*, 5 vols. (New York: Cambridge University Press, 2006), 5:367–371. Alex Roland, *The Military-Industrial Complex* (Washington, DC: American Historical Association, 2001), 10–13, provides excellent charts on military spending from 1945 to 1995.

4. Robert D. Johnson, *Congress and the Cold War* (New York: Cambridge University Press, 2006), 1–104; Julian E. Zelizer, *On Capitol Hill: The Struggle to Reform Congress and Its Consequences, 1948–2000* (New York: Cambridge University Press, 2004), 1–91; Anne H. Cahn, *Congress, Military Affairs and (a Bit of) Information* (Beverly Hills, CA: Sage Publications, 1974), 5–60; Gary W. Reichard, "The President Triumphant: Congressional-Executive Relations, 1945–1960," in *Reshaping America: Society and Institutions, 1945–1960*, eds. Robert H. Bremner and Reichard (Columbus: Ohio State University Press, 1982), 343–368; Robert M. Collins, *More: The Politics of Economic Growth in Postwar America* (New York: Oxford University Press, 2000), 17–97. Julian E. Zelizer, *Arsenal of Democracy: The Politics of National Security—From World War II to the War on Terrorism* (New York: Basic Books, 2010), also traces post–World War II executive-legislative relations.

5. Stephen I. Schwartz, ed., *Atomic Audit: The Costs and Consequences of U.S. Nuclear Weapons since 1940* (Washington, DC: Brookings Institution Press, 1998), 105–123, 485–518. Schwartz's volume is an invaluable contribution. It examines and analyzes most aspects of nuclear policy and provides an excellent guide to the sources. See also James M. Lindsay, *Congress and Nuclear Weapons* (Baltimore: Johns Hopkins University Press, 1991).

6. The following analysis of the congressional resurgence in foreign and defense policies is based on these sources: Johnson, *Congress and the Cold War*, 69–189; Zelizer, *On Capitol Hill*, 5–155; Melvin Small, *Democracy and Diplomacy: The Impact of Domestic Politics on U.S. Foreign Policy, 1789–1994* (Baltimore: Johns Hopkins University Press, 1996), 80–109; Lindsay, *Congress and Politics of U.S. Foreign Policy*, 11–75; Michael Foley, *The New Senate: Liberal Influence on a Conservative Institution, 1959–1972* (New

˙Haven, CT: Yale University Press, 1980); James Clotfelter, *The Military in American Politics* (New York: Harper and Row, 1973), 148–182.

7. The discussion of the triumph of congressional reformers and their accomplishments is based on the following sources: Johnson, *Congress and the Cold War*, 144–225; Zelizer, *On Capitol Hill*, 92–205; Small, *Democracy and Diplomacy*, 110–140; Lindsay, *Congress and Nuclear Weapons*; William C. Banks and Peter Raven-Hansen, *National Security Law and the Power of the Purse* (New York: Oxford University Press, 1994); Barry M. Blechman, *The Politics of National Security: Congress and U.S. Defense Policy* (New York: Oxford University Press, 1990); Lindsay, *Congress and Politics of U.S. Foreign Policy*, 53–184; Loch K. Johnson, *The Making of International Agreements: Congress Confronts the Executive* (New York: New York University Press, 1984), 3–82, 116–175; Michael Barnhart, ed., *Congress and United States Foreign Policy: Controlling the Use of Force in the Nuclear Age* (Albany: State University of New York Press, 1987); Michael W. Kirst, *Government without Passing Laws: Congress' Nonstatutory Techniques for Appropriations Control* (Chapel Hill: University of North Carolina Press, 1969); James L. Holt, "View from the Hill: Why the U.S. Congress Established, Then Abolished the Office of Technology Assessment" (Ph.D. diss., University of Texas at Dallas, 2005); Robert L. Pfaltzgraff Jr. and Uri Ra'anan, eds., *National Security Policy: The Decisionmaking Process* (Hamden, CT: Archon Books, 1984), pt. 4; Alan Platt, *The U.S. Senate and Strategic Arms Policy, 1969–1977* (Boulder, CO: Westview Press, 1978); Alton Frye, *A Responsible Congress: The Politics of National Security* (New York: McGraw-Hill, 1975); Marc E. Smyrl, *Conflict or Codetermination? Congress, the President, and the Power to Make War* (Cambridge, MA: Ballinger, 1988), 3–59; Thomas M. Franck and Edward Weisband, *Foreign Policy by Congress* (New York: Oxford University Press, 1979); John Lehman, *The Executive, Congress, and Foreign Policy: Studies of the Nixon Administration* (New York: Praeger, 1974); Alan Platt and Lawrence D. Weiler, eds., *Congress and Arms Control* (Boulder, CO: Westview Press, 1978); Cahn, *Congress, Military Affairs, and Information*, 5–64; Barrett, *CIA and Congress*; Russell A. Miller, ed., *US National Security, Intelligence and Democracy: From the Church Committee to the War on Terror* (New York: Routledge, 2008).

8. The nation's swing to the right beginning in 1976 is covered in these sources: Johnson, *Congress and the Cold War*, 225–286; Zelizer, *On Capitol Hill*, 187–270; Blechman, *Politics of National Security*; Small, *Democracy and Diplomacy*, 137–170; Smyrl, *Conflict or Codetermination*; Lindsay, *Congress and Politics of U.S. Foreign Policy*; Johnson, *Making of International Agreements*; Douglas C. Waller, *Congress and the Nuclear Freeze: An Inside Look at the Politics of a Mass Movement* (Amherst: University of Massachusetts Press, 1987); Lawrence C. Dodd and Bruce I. Oppenheimer, eds., *Congress Reconsidered*, 8th ed. (Washington, DC: CQ Press, 2005); Daniel Wirls, *Buildup: The Politics of Defense in the Reagan Era* (Ithaca, NY: Cornell University Press, 1992); James R. Locher III, *Victory on the Potomac: The Goldwater-Nichols Act Unifies the Pentagon* (College Station: Texas A&M University Press, 2002); Richard D. Burns and Lester H. Brune, *The Quest for Missile Defenses, 1944–2003* (Claremont, CA: Regina Books, 2003); Nigel Hay, *The Star Wars Enigma* (Washington, DC: Potomac Books, 2006). See also William C. Berman, *America's Right Turn: From Nixon to Clinton*, 2nd ed. (Baltimore: Johns Hopkins University Press, 1998); Michael E. Tanner, *Leviathan on the Right: How Big-Government Conservatism Brought Down the Republican Revolution* (Washington, DC: Cato Institute, 2007); Bruce J. Schulman and Julian E. Zelizer, eds., *Rightward Bound: Mak-*

ing America Conservative in the 1970s (Cambridge, MA: Harvard University Press, 2008).

9. Paul M. Kennedy, *The Rise and Fall of the Great Powers: Economic Change and Military Conflict from 1500 to 2000* (New York: Random House, 1987).

10. A number of the sources cited above deal with Congress's ability to deal more effectively with foreign and defense policies.

11. Many of the volumes cited above analyze the effects of congressional reforms on foreign and defense policies. The most thorough and systematic presentation is offered by Blechman, *Politics of National Security*, 23–218.

12. For forthright examples of such an interpretation, see Franck and Weisband, *Foreign Policy by Congress*; and Lehman, *Executive, Congress, and Foreign Policy*.

13. Natalie H. Kaufman, *Human Rights Treaties and the Senate: A History of Opposition* (Chapel Hill: University of North Carolina Press, 1990), analyzes in detail the Bricker amendment. See also Johnson, *Making of International Agreements*, 85–115.

14. For a thorough analysis of the War Powers Resolution, see Smyrl, *Conflict or Codetermination*. See also various essays in Barnhart, *Congress and United State Foreign Policy*; and Blechman, *Politics of National Security*, 167–200.

15. These themes are pursued in Zelizer, *On Capitol Hill*, 194–262.

16. Many of the numerous studies on the subject are discussed or cited in Kenneth R. Mayer, *The Political Economy of Defense Contracting* (New Haven, CT: Yale University Press, 1991), chap. 5; see also chap. 6. For representative examples, see Bruce M. Russett, *What Price Vigilance? The Burdens of National Defense* (New Haven, CT: Yale University Press, 1970), chap. 3; and Stephen Cobb, "The United States Senate and the Impact of Defense Spending Concentrations," in *Testing the Theory of the Military-Industrial Complex*, ed. Steven Rosen (Lexington, MA: Lexington Books, 1973), chap. 8. See also William J. Weida and Frank L. Gertcher, *The Political Economy of National Defense* (Boulder, CO: Westview Press, 1987), 16–38; and James M. Lindsay, "Congress and the Defense Budget: Parochialism or Policy?" Kenneth R. Mayer, "Patterns of Congressional Influence in Defense Contracting," and Charlotte Twight, "Department of Defense Attempts to Close Military Bases: The Political Economy of Congressional Resistance," in *Arms, Politics and the Economy: Historical and Contemporary Perspectives*, ed. Robert Higgs (New York: Holmes and Meier, 1990), 174–280. Ann Markusen et al., *The Rise of the Gunbelt: The Military Remapping of Industrial America* (New York: Oxford University Press, 1991), analyzes at length how military production centers come into being and are sustained. See also Ann Markusen and Joel Yudken, *Dismantling the Cold War Economy* (New York: Basic Books, 1992).

17. The Base Realignment and Closure (BRAC) website provides full information on the Defense Base Closure and Realignment Commissions.

18. These legislative tactics are analyzed at length in the following sources: Lindsay, *Congress and Politics of U.S. Foreign Policy*; Lindsay, *Congress and Nuclear Weapons*; Kirst, *Government without Passing Laws*.

CHAPTER THREE. A BIG MILITARY

1. The following analysis of unifying the armed services is based on these sources: Lawrence J. Legere Jr., "Unification of the Armed Forces" (Ph.D. diss., Harvard Uni-

versity, 1950); James V. Forrestal, *The Forrestal Diaries*, ed. Walter Millis (New York: Viking, 1951), 59–65, 115, 117–121, 145–153, 159–170, 200–206, 221–236, 271–274, 291–297, 298–555 (intermittent); Paul Y. Hammond, *Organizing for Defense: The American Military Establishment in the Twentieth Century* (Princeton, NJ: Princeton University Press, 1961), 85–391; Robert G. Albion and Robert H. Connery, *Forrestal and the Navy* (New York: Columbia University Press, 1962), 250–286; Vincent Davis, *Postwar Defense Policy and the U.S. Navy, 1943–1946* (Chapel Hill: University of North Carolina Press, 1962); Vincent Davis, *The Admirals Lobby* (Chapel Hill: University of North Carolina Press, 1967), 157–321; Demetrios Caraley, *The Politics of Military Unification: A Study of the Conflict and the Policy Process* (New York: Columbia University Press, 1966); Perry M. Smith, *The Air Force Plans for Peace, 1943–1945* (Baltimore: Johns Hopkins University Press, 1970); James E. Hewes Jr., *From Root to McNamara: Army Organization and Administration, 1900–1963* (Washington, DC: Center of Military History, 1975), 163–374; Michael S. Sherry, *Preparing for the Next War: American Plans for Postwar Defense, 1941–45* (New Haven, CT: Yale University Press, 1977); Michael S. Sherry, *The Rise of American Air Power: The Creation of Armageddon* (New Haven, CT: Yale University Press, 1987); Alice C. Cole et al., eds., *The Department of Defense: Documents on Establishment and Organization, 1944–1978* (Washington, DC: Historical Office, Office of the Secretary of Defense, 1978); John C. Binkley, "The Role of the Joint Chiefs of Staff in National Security Policy Making: Professionalism and Self-Perceptions, 1942–1961" (Ph.D. diss., Loyola University of Chicago, 1985), 118–197; Jeffrey M. Dorwart, *Eberstadt and Forrestal: A National Security Partnership, 1909–1949* (College Station: Texas A&M University Press, 1991), 69–180; Townsend Hoopes and Douglas Brinkley, *Driven Patriot: The Life and Times of James Forrestal* (New York: Alfred A. Knopf, 1992), 319–350, 351–481 (intermittent); Michael J. Hogan, *A Cross of Iron: Harry S. Truman and the Origins of the National Security State, 1945–1954* (New York: Cambridge University Press, 1998), 23–68.

2. There is a vast and rich literature on UMT. For an introduction, see the following volumes and consult their indexes, citations, and bibliographies: Robert D. Ward, "The Movement for Universal Training in the United States, 1942–1952" (Ph.D. diss., University of North Carolina–Chapel Hill, 1957); Sherry, *Preparing for the Next War*; Lynn Eden, "Capitalist Conflict and the State: The Making of United States Military Policy in 1948," in *Statemaking and Social Movements: Essays in History and Theory*, eds. Charles Bright and Susan Harding (Ann Arbor: University of Michigan Press, 1984), 233–261; Hogan, *Cross of Iron*; Aaron L. Friedberg, *In the Shadow of the Garrison State: America's Anti-Statism and Its Cold War Grand Strategy* (Princeton, NJ: Princeton University Press, 2000).

3. For the step-by-step process of strengthening the DOD and Office of the Secretary of Defense, see John C. Ries, *The Management of Defense: Organization and Control of the U.S. Armed Services* (Baltimore: Johns Hopkins University Press, 1964), 125–212; Stanley L. Falk, *The National Security Structure* (Washington, DC: Industrial College of the Armed Forces, 1967); Harry B. Yoshpe and Theodore W. Bauer, *Defense Organization and Management* (Washington, DC: Industrial College of the Armed Forces, 1967), 23–224; Robert J. Art, *The TFX Decision: McNamara and the Military* (Boston: Little, Brown, 1968); Ralph Sanders, ed., *Defense Research and Development* (Washington, DC: Industrial College of the Armed Forces, 1968); James M. Roherty, *Decisions of Robert S. McNamara: A Study of the Role of the Secretary of Defense* (Coral

Gables, FL: University of Miami Press, 1970); Hewes, *From Root to McNamara*, 193–374; Randolph P. Kucera, *The Aerospace Industry and the Military: Structural and Political Relationships* (Beverly Hills, CA: Sage Publications, 1974), 34–59; Clark A. Murdock, *Defense Policy Formation: A Comparative Analysis of the McNamara Era* (Albany: State University of New York Press, 1974); Robert F. Coulam, *Illusions of Choice: The F-111 and the Policy of Weapons Acquisition Reform* (Princeton, NJ: Princeton University Press, 1977); Cole et al., eds., *Department of Defense*, 61–332; Douglas Kinnard, *The Secretary of Defense* (Lexington: University of Kentucky Press, 1980); Charles G. Carpenter and Stanley J. Collins, "Air Force Logistics: A Historical Perspective (1940–1983)" (M.A. thesis, Air Force Institute of Technology, 1983); Steven L. Rearden, *History of the Office of the Secretary of Defense*, vol. 1, *The Formative Years, 1947–1950* (Washington, DC: Historical Office, Office of the Secretary of Defense, 1984), 29–146; Doris M. Condit, *History of the Office of the Secretary of Defense*, vol. 2, *The Test of War, 1950–1953* (Washington, DC: Historical Office, Office of the Secretary of Defense, 1988), 513–531; Richard M. Leighton, *History of the Office of the Secretary of Defense*, vol. 3, *Strategy, Money, and the New Look, 1953–1956* (Washington, DC: Historical Office, Office of the Secretary of Defense, 2001), 21–43; Robert J. Watson, *History of the Office of the Secretary of Defense*, vol. 4, *Into the Missile Age, 1956–1960* (Washington, DC: Historical Office, Office of the Secretary of Defense, 1997), 243–291; Lawrence S. Kaplan, Ronald D. Landa, and Edward J. Drea, *History of the Office of the Secretary of Defense*, vol. 5, *The McNamara Ascendancy, 1961–1965* (Washington, DC: Historical Office, Office of the Secretary of Defense, 2006); Binkley, "Role of the Joint Chiefs of Staff"; Robert J. Art, Vincent Davis, and Samuel P. Huntington, eds., *Reorganizing America's Defense: Leadership in War and Peace* (Washington, DC: Pergamon-Brassey's, 1985); Marcel F. Coppola, *U.S. Army Materiel Command Organization, 1962–1987* (Alexandria, VA: Historical Office, U.S. Army Materiel Command, 1987); Thomas C. Hone, *Power and Change: The Administrative History of the Office of the Chief of Naval Operations, 1946–1986* (Washington, DC: Naval Historical Center, 1989), 53, 57–84, 88, 93, 96, 102–104, 110, 119–121; Frederick H. Hartmann, *Naval Renaissance: The U.S. Navy in the 1980s* (Annapolis, MD: Naval Institute Press, 1990), 57–59, 114–124; Harvey M. Sapolsky, *Science and the Navy: The History of the Office of Naval Research* (Princeton, NJ: Princeton University Press, 1990); George W. Baer, *One Hundred Years of Sea Power: The U.S. Navy, 1890–1990* (Stanford, CA: Stanford University Press, 1994), 367–393; Alex Roland, *The Military-Industrial Complex* (Washington, DC: American Historical Association, 2001), 19–24; Adrian R. Lewis, *The American Culture of War: The History of U.S. Military Force from World War II to Operation Iraqi Freedom* (New York: Routledge, 2007).

4. Quoted in Baer, *One Hundred Years of Sea Power*, 370.

5. These themes are pursued by Sherry, *Preparing for the Next War*; Sherry, *Rise of American Air Power*; and Smith, *Air Force Plans for Peace*. Other volumes cited in note 1 are also helpful.

6. Legere, "Unification of the Armed Forces," 420–436; Davis, *Postwar Defense Policy and the Navy*, 153–155.

7. For developments involving aircraft and the military during the interwar years, see Paul A. C. Koistinen, *Planning War, Pursuing Peace: The Political Economy of American Warfare, 1920–1939* (Lawrence: University Press of Kansas, 1998), 179–198.

8. H. L. Nieburg, *In the Name of Science* (Chicago: Quadrangle Books, 1966),

246–256; Gregg Herken, *Counsels of War* (New York: Alfred A. Knopf, 1985), 74–87.

9. William S. Hill Jr., "The Business Community and National Defense: Corporate Leaders and the Military, 1943–1950" (Ph.D. diss., Stanford University, 1980), 18–20, 69, 75–77, 84–111, 179–210, 259–275, 283–293, 350–381, 419–420, 426–437.

10. Sanders, *Defense Research and Development*, 19–26.

11. Ann Markusen et al., *The Rise of the Gunbelt: The Military Remapping of Industrial America* (New York: Oxford University Press, 1991), 3–25.

12. Friedberg, *In the Shadow of the Garrison State*, 245–320.

13. These themes are systemically traced and analyzed in Paul A. C. Koistinen, *Beating Plowshares into Swords: The Political Economy of American Warfare, 1606–1865* (Lawrence: University Press of Kansas, 1996); Paul A. C. Koistinen, *Mobilizing for Modern War: The Political Economy of American Warfare, 1865–1919* (Lawrence: University Press of Kansas, 1997); Koistinen, *Planning War, Pursuing Peace*; and Paul A. C. Koistinen, *Arsenal of World War II: The Political Economy of American Warfare, 1940–1945* (Lawrence: University Press of Kansas, 2004).

14. George V. Sweeting, "Building the Arsenal of Democracy: The Government's Role in Expansion of Industrial Capacity, 1940–1945" (Ph.D. diss., Columbia University, 1994); Friedberg, *In the Shadow of the Garrison State*, 250–264.

15. Friedberg, *In the Shadow of the Garrison State*, 264–272.

16. Michael H. Armacost, *The Politics of Weapons Innovation: The Thor-Jupiter Controversy* (New York: Columbia University Press, 1969); Nieburg, *In the Name of Science*, 47–49, 189–192, 202–203, 223, 230–236, 243; Robert L. Rosholt, *An Administrative History of NASA, 1958–1963* (Washington, DC: National Aeronautics and Space Administration, 1966), 44–48, 107–123; Leighton, *Strategy, Money, and the New Look*, 437–445; Watson, *Into the Missile Age*, 161–169, 174–183, 390–398; Friedberg, *In the Shadow of the Garrison State*, 272–277.

17. James Fallows, *National Defense* (New York: Vintage Books, 1982), 76–95; Edward C. Ezell, *The Great Rifle Controversy: Search for the Ultimate Infantry Weapon from World War II through Vietnam and Beyond* (Harrisburg, PA: Stackpole Books, 1984); Thomas L. McNaugher, *The M16 Controversy: Military Organization and Weapons Acquisitions* (New York: Praeger, 1984); William H. Hallahan, *Misfire: The History of How America's Small Arms Have Failed the Military* (New York: Charles Scribner's Sons, 1994), 405–535; Friedberg, *In the Shadow of the Garrison State*, 277–280.

18. Friedberg, *In the Shadow of the Garrison State*, 280–292. Detailed studies on private versus public plant and equipment in the 1960s are too few and too limited for definitive conclusions.

19. Thomas L. McNaugher, *New Weapons, Old Politics: America's Military Procurement Muddle* (Washington, DC: Brookings Institution, 1989), 17–51.

20. Gordon Adams, *The Politics of Defense Contracting: The Iron Triangle* (New Brunswick, NJ: Transaction Books, 1982), 95–102.

21. The following analysis of economic mobilization planning and mobilizing the economy for the Korean War is based on these sources: William Y. Elliott, *Mobilization Planning and the National Security (1950–1960): Problems and Issues*, S. Doc. 204, 81st Cong., 2nd sess., 1950; Harry P. Yoshpe, *The National Security Resources Board, 1947–1953: A Case Study in Peacetime Mobilization Planning* (Washington, DC: Executive Office of the President, 1953); Edward H. Hobbs, *Behind the President: A Study*

of Executive Office Agencies (Washington, DC: Public Affairs Press, 1954), 156–184, 192–203; Ries, *Management of Defense*, 93–95, 98–99, 129–130, 157–158; Theodore J. Panayotoff, *The Department of Defense Industrial Mobilization Production Planning Program in the United States* (Texarkana, TX: Army Materiel Command, 1972); U.S. Bureau of the Census, *Historical Statistics of the United States, Colonial Times to 1970* (Washington, DC: U.S. Bureau of the Census, 1975), 224–230, 1114–1116, 1123–1124; Susan B. Carter et al., eds., *Historical Statistics of the United States: Earliest Times to the Present*, 5 vols. (New York: Cambridge University Press, 2006), 5:353–362, 367–368; Cole et al., *Department of Defense*, 39–40, 46–47, 95–96, 157, 194–196, 241–244; Harry F. Ennis, *Peacetime Industrial Preparedness for Wartime Ammunition Production* (Washington, DC: National Defense University, 1980); Hill, "Business Community and National Defense," 298–303; Roderick A. Vawter, *Industrial Mobilization: The Relevant History*, rev. ed. (Washington, DC: National Defense University Press, 1983), 8–67; Rearden, *Formative Years*, 24, 32–33, 90–96, 129–132; Condit, *Test of War*, 501–506; Robert Cuff, "Ferdinand Eberstadt, the National Security Resources Board, and the Search for Integrated Mobilization Planning, 1947–1948," *Public Historian* 7 (Fall 1985): 37–52; Leon N. Karadbil and Roderick L. Vawter, "The Defense Production Act: Crucial Component of Mobilization Preparedness," in *Mobilization and the National Defense*, eds. Hardy L. Merritt and Luther F. Carter (Washington, DC: National Defense University Press, 1985), 37–43; Terrence J. Gough, *U.S. Army Mobilization and Logistics in the Korean War: A Research Approach* (Washington, DC: Center of Military History, 1987); Patrick M. Regan, "Organizing Societies for War: Domestic Pressures for and Foreign Policy Consequences of Mobilization in the United States and Great Britain, 1900–1985" (Ph.D. diss., University of Michigan, 1992); Hogan, *Cross of Iron*, 49–51, 65–66, 210–220, 341–335, 376–379; Paul G. Pierpaoli Jr., *Truman and Korea: The Political Culture of the Early Cold War* (Columbia: University of Missouri Press, 1999).

22. Information on economic mobilization planning after the Korean War is available in these sources: Charles J. Hitch and Roland N. McKean, *The Economics of Defense in the Nuclear Age* (Cambridge, MA: Harvard University Press, 1960), 7–19; Samuel P. Huntington, *The Common Defense: Strategic Programs in National Politics* (New York: Columbia University Press, 1961), 25–32; Hill, "Business Community and National Defense," 70–77; Mary Kaldor, *The Baroque Arsenal* (New York: Hill and Wang, 1981); U.S. Congress, House Committee on Armed Services, *The Ailing Defense Industrial Base: Unready for Crisis (Report of the Defense Industrial Base Panel)*, House Report no. 20, 96th Cong., 2nd sess., 1980; Vawter, *Industrial Mobilization*, 41, 49–91, 97–100; Luther F. Carter and Hardy L. Merritt, "Mobilization for National Defense: The Parameters of Research and Practice," Ralph Sanders and Joseph E. Muckerman II, "A Strategic Rationale for Mobilization," John W. Eley, "Management Structures for Industrial Mobilization in the 1980s: Lesson from World War II," Karadbil and Vawter, "The Defense Production Act," O. M. Collins, "The Impact of Corporate Resource Allocation Decisions on National Security Objectives: Dissynergism in Aerospace Resources Planning," and Robert C. Fabrie, "Structural Change in the U.S. Industrial Base: Its Impact on National Defense," in *Mobilization and the National Defense*, Merritt and Carter, eds., 2–3, 9–20, 35, 45–59, 63–83, 86, 90–92, 96–98, 100–104; Gerald Abbott, ed., *In Touch with Industry: ICAF Industry Studies, 1997* (Washington, DC: National Defense University, 1997); Carter et al., eds., *Historical Statistics of the United States*, 5:355–356, 367–368. The analysis of deindustrialization is confined here to its impact

on economic mobilization and planning for it. America's eroding industrial base and its declining international competitiveness are discussed and documented in chapter 8.

23. Carter et al., eds., *Historical Statistics of the United States*, 5:371; Center for Defense Information, *Military Almanac, 2007* (Washington, DC, 2007), 108–114. The *Almanac* provides figures from three different sources on U.S. and world military spending in 2005. I used the figures that appeared to be most sensible.

CHAPTER FOUR. THE DEFENSE INDUSTRY

1. The analysis of the aircraft and aerospace industries is based on the following sources: George V. Sweeting, "Building the Arsenal of Democracy: The Government's Role in Expansion of Industrial Capacity, 1940 to 1945" (Ph.D. diss., Columbia University, 1994), 250, 323–340; Herman O. Stekler, *The Structure and Performance of the Aerospace Industry* (Berkeley: University of California Press, 1965), 8–24, 47–49, 52–56, 96–153; H. L. Nieburg, *In the Name of Science* (Chicago: Quadrangle Press, 1966), 256–266; Robert L. Rosholt, *An Administrative History of NASA, 1958–1963* (Washington, DC: National Aeronautics and Space Administration, 1966), 274–276; Judith Reppy, "The United States," in *The Structure of the Defense Industry: An International Survey*, eds. Nichole Ball and Milton Leitenberg (New York: St. Martin's Press, 1983), 21–49; George V. D'Angelo, *Aerospace Agencies and Organizations: A Guide for Business and Government* (Westport, CT: Quorum Books, 1993); Donald M. Pattillo, *Pushing the Envelope: The American Aircraft Industry* (Ann Arbor: University of Michigan Press, 1998); Roger E. Bilstein, *The American Aerospace Industry: From Workshop to Global Enterprise* (New York: Twayne Publishers, 1996). See also *Los Angeles Times*, February 13, 2010, B-1. The websites of aircraft and aerospace firms are also helpful in tracing their origins, restructuring, mergers, acquisitions, and changing names.

2. Sweeting, "Building the Arsenal of Democracy," 338.

3. Roland explains that the air force concocted the term *aerospace* to stake out its claim to the space mission. See Alex Roland, "The Military-Industrial Complex: Lobby and Trope," in *The Long War: A New History of U.S. National Security Policy since World War II*, ed. Andrew J. Bacevich (New York: Columbia University Press, 2007), 343.

4. For a brief analysis of the aircraft industry in the interwar years and the citation of major publications on the subject, see Paul A. C. Koistinen, *Planning War, Pursuing Peace: The Political Economy of American Warfare, 1920–1939* (Lawrence: University Press of Kansas, 1998), 179–198, 371–374.

5. The analysis of the stability and concentration of the defense industry is based on these sources: Ann Markusen and Joel Yudken, *Dismantling the Cold War Economy* (New York: Basic Books, 1992), 74–82; Ann Markusen et al., *The Rise of the Gunbelt: The Military Remapping of Industrial America* (New York: Oxford University Press, 1991), 16–19, 33–34, 92–93; J. Ronald Fox, *Arming America: How the U.S. Buys Weapons* (Boston: Graduate School of Business Administration, Harvard University, 1974); John F. Gorgol, *The Military-Industrial Firm: A Practical Theory and Model* (New York: Praeger, 1972); Frederic M. Scherer, "The Aerospace Industry," in *The Structure of American Industry*, 4th ed., ed. Walter Adams (New York: Macmillan, 1971), 341–344, 347–352; William L. Baldwin, *The Structure of the Defense Market, 1955–1964* (Durham, NC: Duke University Press, 1967), 1–110, 147–179; Stekler, *Structure and Performance*

of the Aerospace Industry, 42–57, 96–118; Charles J. Hitch and Roland N. McKean, *The Economics of Defense in the Nuclear Age* (Cambridge, MA: Harvard University Press, 1960); Merton J. Peck and Frederic M. Scherer, *The Weapons Acquisition Process: An Economic Analysis* (Cambridge, MA: Harvard Business School Division of Research, 1962), 98–221, 581–595; Joan M. Cavanagh, "You Can't Kill the Golden Goose: A History of General Dynamics' Electric Boat Shipyard in Twentieth Century New London County, Connecticut" (Ph.D. diss., Yale University, 1996).

6. Jacques S. Gansler, *The Defense Industry* (Cambridge, MA: MIT Press, 1980), 128–161; Reppy, "United States," 21–49; M. Agapos, *Government-Industry and Defense: Economics and Administration* (Tuscaloosa: University of Alabama Press, 1975), 51–53; Peck and Scherer, *Weapons Acquisition Process*, 137–147, 386–404; Markusen and Yudken, *Dismantling the Cold War Economy*, 79–80, 216–219; Todd Sandler and Keith Hartley, *The Economics of Defense* (New York: Cambridge University Press, 1995); Pattillo, *Pushing the Envelope*.

7. Gansler, *Defense Industry*, 97–108; Franklin A. Long and Judith Reppy, eds., *The Genesis of New Weapons: Decision Making for Military R&D* (New York: Pergamon Press, 1980); Markusen and Yudken, *Dismantling the Cold War Economy*, 116–131; Reppy, "United States," 23–26, 30–31, 34–35; Scherer, "Aerospace Industry," 361–365.

8. Gansler, *Defense Industry*, 49, 73–77; Stekler, *Structure and Performance of the Aerospace Industry*, 78–95; Baldwin, *Structure of the Defense Market*, 122–134; Markusen and Yudken, *Dismantling the Cold War Economy*, 85–89.

9. The following discussion of defense industry profits is based on these sources: Richard F. Kaufman, "MIRVing the Boondoggle: Contracts, Subsidy, and Welfare in the Aerospace Industry," *Papers and Proceedings of the 84th Annual Meeting of the American Economic Association, American Economic Review* 62 (May 1972): 290–291; Reppy, "United States," 38–42; Baldwin, *Structure of the Defense Market*, 180–196, 227–229; Gansler, *Defense Industry*, 50, 82–96, 138–142, 205; Stekler, *Structure and Performance of the Aerospace Industry*, 58–71, 157–162; Scherer, "Aerospace Industry," 349–352; Peck and Scherer, *Weapons Acquisition Process*, 206–214, 405–418; Stuart D. Brandes, *Warhogs: A History of War Profits in America* (Lexington: University Press of Kentucky, 1997), 269–276.

The Senate Special Committee Investigating the Munitions Industry (the Nye Committee) concluded in the mid-1930s that establishing reliable figures on defense and war profits was nearly impossible, since legitimate controversies abounded and industry could manipulate and obscure vital information. See Koistinen, *Planning War, Pursuing Peace*, 266–271, 287–292.

10. Scherer, "Aerospace Industry," 335; Baldwin, *Structure of the Defense Market*, 122–124; Kaufman, "MIRVing the Boondoggle," 291–294.

11. Nieburg, *In the Name of Science*, 74–84, 93–94, 186–192, 198–199, 226–230, 288–303, 335–350; Richard F. Kaufman, *The War Profiteers* (Indianapolis: Bobbs-Merrill, 1970), 96–99, 105. See also sources cited in note 7, above.

12. Peck and Scherer, *Weapons Acquisition Process*, 19–54, 425–460; Scherer, "Aerospace Industry," 361–362; Walter Adams and William James Adams, "The Military-Industrial Complex: A Market Structure Analysis," *Papers and Proceedings of the 84th Annual Meeting of the American Economic Association, American Economic Review* 62 (May 1972): 279–287; Baldwin, *Structure of the Defense Market*, 125–128; Gansler, *Defense Industry*, 74–76, 90–92, 296n19; Kaufman, *War Profiteers*, 60–64, 69–74, 105–112.

13. Peck and Scherer, *Weapons Acquisitions Process*, 19–54, 425–460; Kaufman, *War Profiteers*, 64; Markusen and Yudken, *Dismantling the Cold War Economy*, 94–99. The best and most complete study of gold-plating within the context of larger MIC operations is Mary Kaldor, *The Baroque Arsenal* (New York: Hill and Wang, 1981).

14. Kaufman, *War Profiteers*, 63–64, 222–225. Numerous other volumes cited above and below discuss and analyze poor to failed weapons systems. See also the analysis and citations in chapter 8.

15. Ibid., 71, 116–118, 213, 225–227, 239. See also the analysis and citations in chapter 8.

16. James R. Kurth, "The Political Economy of Weapons Procurement: The Follow-on Imperative," *Papers and Proceedings of the 84th Annual Meeting of the American Economic Association, American Economic Review* 62 (May 1972): 304–311; James R. Kurth, "Aerospace Production Lines and American Defense Spending," in *Testing the Theory of the Military-Industrial Complex*, ed. Steven Rosen (Lexington, MA: D. C. Heath, 1973), 135–156; James R. Kurth, "The Follow-on Imperative in American Weapons Procurement, 1960–1990," paper presented at the Conference on the Economic Issues of Disarmament, University of Notre Dame, South Bend, IN, November 1990, cited in Markusen and Yudken, *Dismantling the Cold War Economy*, 264n53.

17. Berkeley Rice, *The C-5A Scandal: An Inside Story of the Military-Industrial Complex* (Boston: Houghton Mifflin, 1971); Gordon Adams, *The Politics of Defense Contracting: The Iron Triangle* (New Brunswick, NJ: Transaction Books, 1982), 309–313, 333–336; Alex Roland, *The Military-Industrial Complex* (Washington, DC: American Historical Association, 2001), 28–30; Kaufman, *War Profiteers*, 157–169, 225–227.

18. Walter A. McDougall, . . . *The Heavens and the Earth: A Political History of the Space Age* (New York: Basic Books, 1985); Roland, *Military-Industrial Complex*, 32–34. Many of the volumes cited above and below also deal with NASA. The Department of Homeland Security's contract with Boeing to install a "virtual fence" along the American-Mexican border has encountered many of the same difficulties characteristic of DOD and NASA contracting. See *Los Angeles Times*, October 22, 2010, A1.

19. Many of the sources cited above and below discuss the positive accomplishments of the defense industry. Roland, *Military-Industrial Complex*, 15–18, briefly summarizes the principal arguments.

20. Markusen et al., *Rise of the Gunbelt*; Markusen and Yudken, *Dismantling the Cold War Economy*, chap. 7. The following discussion of the Gunbelt is based principally on these volumes. See also Reppy, "United States," 35–38; Adam Yarmolinsky and Gregory D. Foster, *Paradoxes of Power: The Military Establishment in the Eighties* (Bloomington: Indiana University Press, 1983); Pattillo, *Pushing the Envelope*; and Edmund F. Wehrle, "Welfare and Warfare: American Organized Labor Approaches the Military-Industrial Complex, 1949–1964," *Armed Forces and Society* 29 (Summer 2003): 525–546.

21. The following analysis of aerospace and arms exports is based on these sources: Gansler, *Defense Industry*, 6–7, 49, 89, 204–218; Markusen and Yudken, *Dismantling the Cold War Economy*, 56, 60–64, 66–68, 78–79, 206, 211, 242–243; Adams, *Politics of Defense Contracting*, 223–444 (selected pages and tables on various corporations dealing with "Corporate Data," "Contracting History," and "Questionable Payments"); Koistinen, *Planning War, Pursuing Peace*, 191, 193–195, 257–266. See also the analysis and citations in chapter 7.

22. The following discussion of converting and diversifying the defense industry is based largely on Markusen and Yudken, *Dismantling the Cold War Economy*, 208–240. See also Barry Bluestone and Bennett Harrison, *The Deindustrialization of America: Plant Closings, Community Abandonment, and Dismantling of Basic Industry* (New York: Basic Books, 1982); Lloyd J. Dumas, ed., *The Political Economy of Arms Reduction: Reversing Economic Decay* (Boulder, CO: Westview Press, 1982); Suzanne Gordon and Dave McFadden, eds., *Economic Conversion: Revitalizing America's Economy* (Cambridge, MA: Ballinger Publishing, 1984); Gregory A. Bischak, ed., *Towards a Peace Economy in the United States: Essays on Military Industry, Disarmament and Economic Conversion* (London: Macmillan, 1991); and Lloyd J. Dumas, ed., *The Socio-Economics of Conversion from War to Peace* (Armonk, NY: M. E. Sharpe, 1995).

CHAPTER FIVE. "BIG SCIENCE"

1. Some representative and insightful volumes in this regard include Peter Galison and Bruce Hevly, eds., *Big Science: The Growth of Large-Scale Research* (Stanford, CA: Stanford University Press, 1992), 1–17 and various essays; Everett Mendelsohn, Merritt Roe Smith, and Peter Weingart, eds., *Science, Technology and the Military*, 2 vols. (Norwell, MA: Kluwer Academic Publishers, 1988), xi–xxix and various essays; Stuart W. Leslie, *The Cold War and American Science: The Military-Industrial-Academic Complex at MIT and Stanford* (New York: Columbia University Press, 1993), 1–13; and Roger L. Geiger, *Research and Relevant Knowledge: American Research Universities since World War II* (New York: Oxford University Press, 1993), 30–40. See also Don K. Price, *Government and Science: Their Dynamic Relation in American Democracy* (New York: Oxford University Press, 1962), and Don K. Price, *The Scientific Estate* (Cambridge, MA: Harvard University Press, 1965).

2. Daniel J. Kevles, *The Physicists: The History of a Scientific Community in Modern America*, rev. ed. (Cambridge, MA: Harvard University Press, 1995), 294–295; Irvin Stewart, *Organizing Scientific Research for War: The Administrative History of the Office of Scientific Research and Development* (Boston: Little, Brown, 1948), 71.

3. Kevles, *Physicists*, 296; Alex Roland, *Model Research: The National Advisory Committee for Aeronautics, 1915–1958*, vol. 1 (Washington, DC: National Aeronautics and Space Administration, 1985), 169–170.

4. Stewart, *Organizing Scientific Research for War*, 7.

5. A. Hunter Dupree, *Science in the Federal Government: A History of Policies and Activities to 1940* (Cambridge, MA: Harvard University Press, 1957), 302; Geiger, *Research and Relevant Knowledge*, 5–6.

6. Dupree, *Science in the Federal Government*, 302–325.

7. Ibid., 331–343.

8. Roland, *Model Research*, xi, 24; Kevles, *Physicists*, 296; Dupree, *Science in the Federal Government*, 370.

9. Alex Roland, "The National Advisory Committee for Aeronautics," *Prologue* 10 (Summer 1978): 68–81.

10. Dupree, *Science in the Federal Government*, 366–367; Geiger, *Research and Relevant Knowledge*, 3–4.

11. James L. Penick Jr. et al., eds., *The Politics of American Science, 1939 to the Present*

(Chicago: Rand McNally, 1965), 10–13; Dupree, *Science in the Federal Government*, 369–372; Kevles, *Physicists*, 296–301.

12. Carroll W. Pursell Jr., "Science and Government Agencies," in *Science and Society in the United States*, eds. David D. Van Tassell and Michael G. Hall (Homewood, IL: Dorsey Press, 1966), 223–249; Carroll Pursell, "Science Agencies in World War II: The OSRD and Its Challengers," in *The Sciences in the American Context: New Perspectives*, ed. Nathan Reingold (Washington, DC: Smithsonian Institution Press, 1979), 359–378; Carroll Pursell, *Technology in Postwar America: A History* (New York: Columbia University Press, 2007), 1–19; A. Hunter Dupree, "The Great Instauration of 1940: The Organization of Scientific Research for War," in *The Twentieth-Century Sciences: Studies in the Biography of Ideas*, ed. Gerald Horton (New York: W. W. Norton, 1972), 443–467; Stewart, *Organizing Scientific Research for War*, 35–49; G. Pascal Zachary, *Endless Frontier: Vannevar Bush, Engineer of the American Century* (New York: Free Press, 1997), 108–165.

13. Stewart, *Organizing Scientific Research for War*, 200–202.

14. Ibid., 18.

15. Geiger, *Research and Relevant Knowledge*, 9–13; Kevles, *Physicists*, 302–308; Stewart, *Organizing Scientific Research for War*, 20–25; Zachary, *Endless Frontier*, 166–183.

16. Stewart, *Organizing Scientific Research for War*, 49, 120–123; Vincent C. Jones, *MANHATTAN: The Army and the Atomic Bomb* (Washington, DC: Center of Military History, 1985), 21–28, 33–35, 44–46, 77–81; William Lawren, *The General and the Bomb: A Biography of General Leslie R. Groves, Director of the Manhattan Project* (New York: Dodd, Mead, 1988); Stephen I. Schwartz, ed., *Atomic Audit: The Costs and Consequences of U.S. Nuclear Weapons since 1940* (Washington, DC: Brookings Institution Press, 1998), 53–59; Zachary, *Endless Frontier*, 189–217; Pursell, *Technology in Postwar America*, 59–69.

17. Schwartz, *Atomic Audit*, 58–59; Geiger, *Research and Relevant Knowledge*, 7–9.

18. Most of the sources cited above comment on Bush's leadership style. The fullest analysis appears in Zachary, *Endless Frontier*; the shrewdest insights are in Pursell, "Science Agencies in World War II," 359–378.

19. Many of the sources cited above deal with this theme; the most detailed development is available in Pursell, "Science Agencies in World War II," 359–378.

20. Carroll W. Pursell Jr., ed., *The Military-Industrial Complex* (New York: Harper and Row, 1972), 338; James Phinney Baxter 3rd, *Scientists against Time* (Boston: Little, Brown, 1946), 125, 456–457, 460 (some citations and pagination are incomplete or garbled).

21. Stewart, *Organizing Scientific Research for War*, 19–20, 191–199, 204–205, 208–213, 221–231, 339–352.

22. The account of Bush, Kilgore, the OSRD, and the NSF is based on these sources: Vannevar Bush, *Science—The Endless Frontier: A Report to the President on a Program for Postwar Scientific Research* (1945; reprint, Washington, DC: National Science Foundation, 1960); Penick et al., eds., *Politics of American Science*, 13–21, 82–95, 120–137, 157–162, 172–180; Pursell, "Science and Government Agencies," 240–249; Pursell, "Science Agencies in World War II," 373–375; Daniel Lee Kleinman, *Politics on the Endless Frontier: Postwar Research Policy in the United States* (Durham, NC: Duke University Press, 1995); Kevles, *Physicists*, 341–348, 356–366; Daniel J. Kevles, "K1S2: Korea,

Science, and the State," in Galison and Hevly, eds., *Big Science*, 312–333; Zachary, *Endless Frontier*, 231–235, 246–260, 326–328, 331–332, 368–378; J. Merton England, *A Patron for Pure Science: The National Science Foundation's Formative Years, 1945–57* (Washington, DC: National Science Foundation, 1982), 3–110; Milton Lomask, *A Minor Miracle: An Informal History of the National Science Foundation* (Washington, DC: National Science Foundation, 1976), 39–57; Geiger, *Research and Relevant Knowledge*, 13–19; U.S. Bureau of the Census, *Historical Statistics of the United States, Colonial Times to 1970* (Washington, DC: Bureau of the Census, 1975), 966–967.

23. As quoted in Zachary, *Endless Frontier*, 326.

24. The following analysis of ONR is based on these sources: Harvey M. Sapolsky, *Science and the Navy: The History of the Office of Naval Research* (Princeton, NJ: Princeton University Press, 1990), 3–138; S. S. Schweber, "The Mutual Embrace of Science and the Military: ONR and the Growth of Physics in the United States after World War II," in Mendelsohn, Smith, and Weingart, eds., *Science, Technology and the Military*, 3–45; Penick et al., eds., *Politics of American Science*, 22–27, 180–188; Geiger, *Research and Relevant Knowledge*, 21–29, 32–33; David K. Allison, "U.S. Navy Research and Development since World War II," in *Military Enterprise and Technological Change: Perspectives on the American Experience*, ed. Merritt Roe Smith (Cambridge, MA: MIT Press, 1985), 289–328; Kevles, "K1S2," 312–333; Kevles, *Physicists*, 353–356; Roland, *Model Research*, 163; England, *Patron for Pure Science*, 198; Julius A. Furer, *Administration of Navy Department in World War II* (Washington, DC: Naval History Division, 1959), 737–808.

25. Sapolsky, *Science and the Navy*, 50, 132, table A-1. Accurate figures on ONR outlays are difficult to calculate from the statistics presented by Sapolsky.

26. Michael S. Sherry, *Preparing for the Next War: America Plans for Postwar Defense, 1941–45* (New Haven, CT: Yale University Press, 1977), 120–158.

27. Creation of the AEC is covered in most of the secondary sources cited above. The most detailed account is in the two-volume official history: Richard C. Hewlett and Oscar E. Anderson Jr., *New World, 1939–1946: A History of the United States Atomic Energy Commission* (University Park: Pennsylvania State University Press, 1962), and *Atomic Shield, 1947–1952: A History of the United States Atomic Energy Commission* (University Park: Pennsylvania State University Press, 1969). See also Gar Alperovitz, *Atomic Diplomacy: Hiroshima and Potsdam; the Use of the Atomic Bomb and the American Confrontation with Soviet Power*, rev. ed. (New York: Penguin, 1985); Martin J. Sherwin, *A World Destroyed: The Atomic Bomb and the Grand Alliance* (New York: Vintage Books, 1977); Gregg Herken, *The Winning Weapon: The Atomic Bomb in the Cold War, 1945–1950* (New York: Viking, 1982), 114–150; Kevles, *Physicists*, 349–353; and Sean L. Mallory, *Atomic Tragedy: Henry L. Stimson and the Decision to Use the Bomb against Japan* (Ithaca, NY: Cornell University Press, 2008).

28. England, *Patron for Pure Science*, 200. See also Kevles, "K1S2," 329.

29. Leslie, *Cold War and American Science*, 14–20, 44–75; Rebecca S. Lowen, *Creating the Cold War University: The Transformation of Stanford* (Berkeley: University of California Press, 1997); G. Stewart Gillmor, *Fred Terman at Stanford: Building a Discipline, a University, and Silicon Valley* (Stanford, CA: Stanford University Press, 2004); Peter Galison, Bruce Hevly, and Rebecca Lowen, "Controlling the Monster: Stanford and the Growth of Physics Research, 1935–1962," in Galison and Hevly, eds., *Big Sci-*

ence, 46–77; Robert Seidel, "The Origins of the Lawrence Berkeley Laboratory," ibid., 21–45; Henry Etzkowitz, "The Making of an Entrepreneurial University: The Traffic among MIT, Industry, and the Military, 1860–1940," in Mendelsohn, Smith, and Weingart, eds., *Science, Technology and the Military*, 515–540; Zachary, *Endless Frontier*, 40.

30. Schwartz, ed., *Atomic Audit*, 59–104; Geiger, *Research and Relevant Knowledge*, 173–197; H. L. Nieburg, *In the Name of Science* (Chicago: Quadrangle, 1966), 45–60, 211–217, 369; Robert L. Rosholt, *An Administrative History of NASA, 1958–1963* (Washington, DC: National Aeronautics and Space Administration, 1966), 66–67, 247–248, 251–325; Herken, *Winning Weapon*, 114–150; Leslie, *Cold War and American Science*, 133–159; Gordon Thompson, "The Genesis of Nuclear Power," in *The Militarization of High Technology*, ed. John Tirman (Cambridge, MA: Ballinger, 1984), 63–75. See also Walter A. McDougall, . . . *The Heavens and the Earth: A Political History of the Space Age* (New York: Basic Books, 1985); Paul A. Stares, *Space and National Security* (Washington, DC: Brookings Institution, 1987); and Roger E. Bilstein, *Orders of Magnitude: A History of NACA and NASA, 1915–1990* (Washington, DC: National Aeronautics and Space Administration, 1989).

31. Bureau of the Census, *Historical Statistics of the United States*, 966–967 (Veterans Administration expenditures are included with defense outlays, although the numbers are slight; however, R&D plant, with its substantial budgets, is not included); Susan B. Carter et al., eds., *Historical Statistics of the United States, Earliest Times to the Present*, 5 vols. (New York: Cambridge University Press, 2006), 3:446–456 (the headnotes and footnotes to the sections and tables explain the contents); Lloyd J. Dumas, "University Research, Industrial Innovation, and the Pentagon," in Tirman, ed., *Militarization of High Technology*, 125–132; Judith Reppy, "The United States," in *The Structure of the Defense Industry: An International Survey*, eds. Nicole Ball and Milton Leitenberg (New York: St. Martin's Press, 1983), 34–35; David C. Mowery and Nathan Rosenberg, *Technology and the Pursuit of Economic Growth* (New York: Cambridge University Press, 1989), 123–147; Kenneth M. Jones, "The Government-Science Complex," in *Reshaping America: Society and Institutions, 1945–60*, eds. Robert H. Bremner and Gary W. Reichard (Columbus: Ohio State University Press, 1982), 326–329; Geiger, *Research and Relevant Knowledge*, 166, 173–174, 178–179, 185–186, 193–195, 197. With so many variables involved, so much complexity, and limited official data in key areas, sources rarely agree on the amount of defense spending and its parts. Often, rough estimates are the best that can be offered.

32. Bruce L. R. Smith, *American Science Policy since World War II* (Washington, DC: Brookings Institution, 1990), 73–89; Jones, "Government-Science Complex," 315–342; U.S. Congress, House Committee on Science and Technology, Serial R, *Report Prepared for the Task Force on Science Policy*, 99th Cong., 2nd sess., September 1986; Geiger, *Research and Relevant Knowledge*, 157–197; Kevles, *Physicists*, 414–415.

33. Gregg Herken, *Cardinal Choices: Presidential Science Advising from the Atomic Bomb to SDI*, rev. ed. (Stanford, CA: Stanford University Press, 2000), 54–164; Geiger, *Research and Relevant Knowledge*, 166–168, 174.

34. James R. Killian Jr., *Sputnik, Scientists, and Eisenhower: A Memoir of the First Special Assistant to the President for Science and Technology* (Cambridge, MA: MIT Press, 1977); George B. Kistiakowsky, *A Scientist at the White House: The Private Diary of President Eisenhower's Special Assistant for Science and Technology* (Cambridge, MA: Harvard

University Press, 1976); Robert A. Devine, *The Sputnik Challenge* (New York: Oxford University Press, 1993); Benjamin P. Greene, *Eisenhower, Science Advice, and the Nuclear Test-Ban Debate, 1945–1963* (Stanford, CA: Stanford University Press, 2007); Zuoyue Wang, *In Sputnik's Shadow: The President's Science Advisory Committee and Cold War America* (New Brunswick, NJ: Rutgers University Press, 2008); Geiger, *Research and Relevant Knowledge*, 170.

35. Lomask, *Minor Miracle*, 261–278; Herken, *Cardinal Choices*, 146–225.

36. Leslie, *Cold War and American Science*, 251–252; Geiger, *Research and Relevant Knowledge*, 194–195.

37. This theme is taken up by many of the sources cited above and below. Some representative examples include Paul K. Hoch, "The Crystallization of a Strategic Alliance: The American Physics Elite and the Military in the 1940s," in Mendelsohn, Smith, and Weingart, eds., *Science, Technology and the Military*, 87–116; Jessica Wang, *American Science in an Age of Anxiety: Scientists, Anticommunism, and the Cold War* (Chapel Hill: University of North Carolina Press, 1999); Herbert N. Foerstel, *Secret Science: Federal Control of American Science and Technology* (Westport, CT: Praeger, 1993); Dumas, "University Research," 123–151; Warren F. Davis, "The Pentagon and the Scientist," in Tirman, ed., *Militarization of High Technology*, 153–179; Leslie, *Cold War and American Science*, 1–13, 256; Geiger, *Research and Relevant Knowledge*, 173; and Mark Walker, ed., *Science and Ideology: A Comparative History* (London: Routledge, 2003).

A number of substantial volumes on Oppenheimer have come out in the past few years. Among them are Gregg Herken, *Brotherhood of the Bomb: The Tangled Lives and Loyalties of Robert Oppenheimer, Ernest Lawrence, and Edward Teller* (New York: Henry Holt, 2002); Kai Bird and Martin J. Sherwin, *American Prometheus: The Triumph and Tragedy of J. Robert Oppenheimer* (New York: Alfred A. Knopf, 2005); Cathryn Carson and David A. Hollinger, eds., *Reappraising Oppenheimer: Centennial Studies and Reflections* (Berkeley, CA: Office for History of Science and Technology, 2005); Priscilla J. McMillan, *The Ruin of J. Robert Oppenheimer and the Birth of the Modern Arms Race* (New York: Viking, 2005); and Charles Thorpe, *Oppenheimer: The Tragic Intellect* (Chicago: University of Chicago Press, 2006).

38. Dumas, "University Research," 125.

39. Ibid., 129–132.

40. Leslie, *Cold War and American Science*, 25–32; Dumas, "University Research," 129–132.

41. The following discussion of Stanford is based on these sources: Leslie, *Cold War and American Science*, 44–75, 102–132, 160–187, 188–232; Lowen, *Creating the Cold War University*; Gillmor, *Terman at Stanford*; Galison, Hevly, and Lowen, "Controlling the Monster," 46–77; W. K. H. Panofsky, "SLAC and Big Science: Stanford University," in Galison and Hevly, eds., *Big Science*, 129–146. See also S. S. Schweber, "Big Science in Context: Cornell and MIT," in Galison and Hevly, eds., *Big Science*, 149–183; Geiger, *Research and Relevant Knowledge*, 58–61; and Dumas, "University Research," 125–132.

42. Geiger, *Research and Relevant Knowledge*, 230–242; Leslie, *Cold War and American Science*, 233–256. A vast literature is available on the tumult of the 1960s. The endnotes in Geiger's *Research and Relevant Knowledge*, 385–387, cite many of the important works; for additional citations, see James T. Patterson, *Grand Expectations: The United States, 1945–1974* (New York: Oxford University Press, 1996), 799–802.

CHAPTER SIX. OTHER ESTATES

1. Fred Kaplan, *The Wizards of Armageddon* (New York: Simon and Schuster, 1983), 52–58, 352–355; Stephen P. Waring, "Cold Calculus: The Cold War and Operations Research," *Radical History Review* 63 (Fall 1995): 29–51; Paul Dickson, *Think Tanks* (New York: Atheneum, 1971), 22–23, 64–65; Gene M. Lyons and Louis Morton, *Schools for Strategy: Education and Research in National Security Affairs* (New York: Frederick A. Praeger, 1965), 236–240; Bruce L. R. Smith, *The Rand Corporation: A Case Study of a Nonprofit Advisory Corporation* (Cambridge, MA: Harvard University Press, 1966), 2–3, 6–14; James A. Smith, *The Idea Brokers: Think Tanks and the Rise of the New Policy Elite* (New York: Free Press, 1991), 117–118, 164; Sharon Ghamari-Tabrizi, *The Worlds of Herman Kahn: The Intuitive Science of Thermonuclear War* (Cambridge, MA: Harvard University Press, 2005), 46–49, 297–298, 316; Alex Abella, *Soldiers of Reason: The RAND Corporation and the Rise of the American Empire* (Orlando, FL: Harcourt, 2008), 16–18, 23, 28, 58.

2. The following discussion of pre–Cold War research organizations is based on these sources: David W. Eakins, "The Development of Corporate Liberal Policy Research in the United States, 1885–1965" (Ph.D. diss., University of Wisconsin, 1966); David W. Eakins, "The Origins of Corporate Liberal Policy Research, 1916–1922: The Political-Economic Expert and the Decline of Public Debate," in *Building the Organizational Society: Essays on Associational Activities in Modern America*, ed. Jerry Israel (New York: Free Press, 1972), 163–179; Michael A. Lutzker, "The Formation of the Carnegie Endowment for International Peace: A Study of the Establishment-Centered Peace Movement, 1910–1914," ibid., 143–162; Donald T. Critchlow, *The Brookings Institution, 1916–1952: Expertise and the Public Interest in a Democratic Society* (De Kalb: Northern Illinois University Press, 1985); Donald T. Critchlow, "Think Tanks, Antistatism, and Democracy: The Nonpartisan Ideal and Policy Research in the United States, 1913–1987," in *The State and Social Investigation in Britain and the United States*, ed. Michael J. Lacey and Mary O. Furner (Washington, DC: Woodrow Wilson Center Press; New York: Cambridge University Press, 1993), 279–322; Ellen C. Lagemann, *The Politics of Knowledge: The Carnegie Corporation, Philanthropy, and Public Policy* (Middletown, CT: Wesleyan University Press, 1989); Paul A. C. Koistinen, *Mobilizing for Modern War: The Political Economy of American Warfare, 1865–1919* (Lawrence: University Press of Kansas, 1997); Paul A. C. Koistinen, *Planning War, Pursuing Peace: The Political Economy of American Warfare, 1920–1939* (Lawrence: University Press of Kansas, 1998); Paul A. C. Koistinen, *Arsenal of World War II: The Political Economy of American Warfare, 1940–1945* (Lawrence: University Press of Kansas, 2004).

3. Critchlow, "Think Tanks, Antistatism, and Democracy," 284.

4. The following discussion of think tanks and related institutions deals principally with a limited time period. Unless very recent secondary sources are available, as is the case with RAND, their later years can be traced on the Web. Moreover, the use of tense can be problematic. I have tried to use common sense in that regard. See also the discussion of private corporations carrying out a wide range of military responsibilities and activities in chapter 1.

5. The following analysis of the RAND Corporation is based on these sources: Smith, *Rand Corporation*; Dickson, *Think Tanks*, 23–25, 49–88, 110–111; Kaplan, *Wizards of Armageddon*, 10–11, 49–173, 201–231, 237–247, 249–257, 286–290, 356–391;

Gregg Herken, *Counsels of War* (New York: Alfred A. Knopf, 1985), 32–38, 74–101, 104–108, 140–162, 171–176, 204–207, 218–225, 259–260; Alex Roland, *Model Research: The National Advisory Committee for Aeronautics, 1915–1958*, vol. 1 (Washington, DC: National Aeronautics and Space Administration, 1985), 155–160; Michael H. Gorn, *Harnessing the Genie: Science and Technology Forecasting for the Air Force, 1944–1986* (Washington, DC: Office of Air Force History, U.S. Air Force, 1988); Smith, *Idea Brokers*, 113–121, 134–140, 302–303 (the volume also includes a very useful appendix, "Think Tank Directory," 270–310); David Hounshell, *The Cold War, RAND, and the Generation of Knowledge, 1946–1962* (Santa Monica, CA: RAND Reprints, 1998); S. M. Amadae, *Rationalizing Capitalist Democracy: The Cold War Origins of Rational Choice Liberalism* (Chicago: University of Chicago Press, 2003); Ghamari-Tabrizi, *Worlds of Herman Kahn* (the volume deals almost entirely with Kahn's years at RAND); Andrew Bacevich, "Tailors to the Emperor," *New Left Review* 69 (May–June 2011): 101–124; Abella, *Soldiers of Reason*. The last author has this to say about systems analysis: "While OR [operations research] referred to studies of existing systems to uncover more effective ways to perform specific missions, systems analysis addressed the far more complex problem of choice among alternate systems that had yet to be designed, where the degrees of freedom and uncertainty are large, and where the difficulty is deciding both what to do and how to do it" (58).

6. Herman Kahn, *On Thermonuclear War* (Princeton, NJ: Princeton University Press, 1960); Kaplan, *Wizards of Armageddon*, 109–110.

7. Ibid., 231.

8. Smith, *Rand Corporation*, 114–119; Dickson, *Think Tanks*, 88, 117–132.

9. Smith, *Rand Corporation*, 3–4, 119–125; Dickson, *Think Tanks*, 88, 155–157.

10. For the Hudson Institute, see Dickson, *Think Tanks*, 89–117, 137–140; Herken, *Counsels of War*, 189–192, 204–207, 221–222, 271, 309–312, 342–343; Kaplan, *Wizards of Armageddon*, 129–130, 220–231; Smith, *Idea Brokers*, 154–159, 288–289; Ghamari-Tabrizi, *Worlds of Herman Kahn*; Abella, *Soldiers of Reason*, 103–104; and Lyons and Morton, *Schools for Strategy*, 261–264.

11. For RAC, see the following: Lyons and Morton, *Schools for Strategy*, 9, 42–43, 238–240, 243–245; Dickson, *Think Tanks*, 149–150; Michael T. Klare, *War without End: American Planning for the Next Vietnams* (New York: Vintage Books, 1972), 77, 80–81, 105, 110–111, 227–229.

12. The analysis of IDA is based on these sources: Dickson, *Think Tanks*, 87, 140–147, 216, 247; Lyons and Morton, *Schools for Strategy*, 9, 43, 252–257, 306–307; Klare, *War without End*, 74–77, 79, 84–85, 91–93, 179–291, 367–371; Herken, *Counsels of War*, 60–63, 210–212, 217–220, 253–255, 292–293; James R. Killian Jr., *Sputnik, Scientists, and Eisenhower: A Memoir of the First Special Assistant to the President for Science and Technology* (Cambridge, MA: MIT Press, 1977), 102–204; Smith, *Idea Brokers*, 291–292; Ann Finkbeiner, *The Jasons: The Secret History of Science's Postwar Elite* (New York: Viking, 2006).

13. For Aerospace, see the following sources: H. L. Nieburg, *In the Name of Science* (Chicago: Quadrangle Books, 1966), 48–49, 189, 192, 200–217, 249–256, 266–269, 283, 341; Dickson, *Think Tanks*, 151–153, 157–160; Alex Roland, *The Military-Industrial Complex* (Washington, DC: American Historical Association, 2001), 26–27.

14. Dickson, *Think Tanks*, 151, 153–155, 220; Nieburg, *In the Name of Science*, 226, 245–246.

15. Dickson, *Think Tanks*, 147–149; Klare, *War without End*, 77–79; Irene L. Gendzier, "Play It Again Sam: The Practice and Apology of Development," in *Universities and Empire: Money and Politics in the Social Sciences during the Cold War*, ed. Christopher Simpson (New York: New Press, 1998), 83–85.

16. Dickson, *Think Tanks*, 138–140.

17. Michael A. Bernstein, "American Economics and the National Security State, 1941–1953," *Radical History Review* 63 (Fall 1995): 16–17; Smith, *Rand Corporation*, 142–143.

18. For national defense studies at Yale, Princeton, the University of Chicago, Johns Hopkins, and Columbia, see the following sources: Lyons and Morton, *Schools for Strategy*, 36–47, 59, 66, 70–71, 89–90, 102, 107, 127–144, 181–185, 213–214, 304, 309–311 (this volume is the most complete and systematic survey of the topic); Bruce Kuklick, *Blind Oracles: Intellectuals and War from Kennan to Kissinger* (Princeton, NJ: Princeton University Press, 2006), 72–87; Kaplan, *Wizards of Armageddon*, 13–23, 27, 29–32, 49–50, 79–86, 186–190; David Callahan, *Dangerous Capabilities: Paul Nitze and the Cold War* (New York: HarperCollins, 1990), 154, 500; Christopher Simpson, *Science of Coercion: Communication Research and Psychological Warfare 1945–1960* (New York: Oxford University Press, 1994), 52–53.

19. Kuklick, *Blind Oracles*, 86–87.

20. Allan A. Needell, "Project Troy and the Cold War Annexation of the Social Sciences," in Simpson, ed., *Universities and Empire*, 3–38; Bruce Cumings, "Boundary Displacement: Area Studies and International Studies during and after the Cold War," ibid., 163–164; Kuklick, *Blind Oracles*, 80; Smith, *Rand Corporation*, 67–73, 184–185; Kaplan, *Wizards of Armageddon*, 60–61, 125–127.

21. Christopher Simpson, "Universities, Empire, and the Production of Knowledge: An Introduction," in Simpson, ed., *Universities and Empire*, xi–xxxiv; Needell, "Project Troy," 3–38; Ellen Herman, ed., "Project Camelot and the Career of Cold War Psychology," in Simpson, ed., *Universities and Empire*, 97–133; Cumings, "Boundary Displacement," 159–188; Ellen Herman, "The Career of Cold War Psychology," *Radical History Review* 63 (Fall 1995): 53–85.

22. For the Russian Research Institute and Mosely, see Cumings, "Boundary Displacement," 167–171; the endnotes are particularly important.

23. Ibid., 169.

24. On Harvard and the Russian Research Center, see Sigmund Diamond, *Compromised Campus: The Collaboration of Universities with the Intelligence Community, 1945–1955* (New York: Oxford University Press, 1992), 24–150; Simpson, *Science of Coercion*, 52–62, 82, 86–87, 131–132; and Cumings, "Boundary Displacement," 163–167, 173–181. See also Hugh Wilford, *The Mighty Wurlitzer: How the CIA Played America* (Cambridge, MA: Harvard University Press, 2008), 123–148 (this volume provides a wealth of information on the CIA's secret propaganda operations at home and abroad designed to encourage and shape anti-Soviet views and responses); Liping Bu, *Making the World Like Us: Education, Cultural Expansion, and the American Century* (Westport, CT: Praeger, 2003); and Lori Lyn Bogle, *The Pentagon's Battle for the American Mind: The Early Cold War* (College Station: Texas A&M University, 2004). A recent scholarly publication on post–World War II Soviet studies in the United States provides a full and thorough survey and analysis of the field: David C. Engerman, *Know Your*

Enemy: The Rise and Fall of America's Soviet Experts (New York: Oxford University Press, 2009).

25. Needell, "Project Troy," 3–38.

26. The following account of CENIS is based on these sources: Nils Gilman, *Mandarins of the Future: Modernization Theory in Cold War America* (Baltimore: Johns Hopkins University Press, 2003); David C. Engerman et al., eds., *Staging Growth: Modernization, Development, and the Global Cold War* (Amherst: University of Massachusetts Press, 2003); David Halberstam, *The Best and the Brightest* (New York: Random House, 1972), 150–152, 155–162, 630–631, 635–640, 654–655, 659–660; Simpson, *Science of Coercion*, 4, 52–55, 81–86, 89–93, 113–115, 131–132; Klare, *War without End*, 88–92, 106–116, 273–275, 288–295; Kuklick, *Blind Oracles*, 1–2, 50, 80, 82, 146–150, 168, 225–226; Christopher Simpson, "U.S. Mass Communication Research, Counterinsurgency, and Scientific 'Reality,'" in *Ruthless Criticism: New Perspectives in U.S. Communication History*, eds. William S. Solomon and Robert W. McChesney (Minneapolis: University of Minnesota Press, 1993), 313–315; Needell, "Project Troy," 12, 21–22; Gendzier, "Play It Again Sam," 57–95; Cumings, "Boundary Displacement," 171–173, 187n35, 276; David Milne, *America's Rasputin: Walt Rostow and the Vietnam War* (New York: Hill and Wang, 2008), 44–46, 58–68, 79–81.

27. The account of Camelot is based on the following: Irving Louis Horowitz, ed., *The Rise and Fall of Project Camelot: Studies in the Relationship between Social Science and Practical Politics*, rev. ed. (Cambridge, MA: MIT Press, 1974); Herman, "Project Camelot," 97–133; Herman, "Career of Cold War Psychology," 53–85; Simpson, *Science of Coercion*, 84–87; Abella, *Soldiers of Reason*, 183–184; Klare, *War without End*, 77–78, 86–87, 92–105, 111; Dickson, *Think Tanks*, 133–137; Chalmers Johnson, *Blowback: The Costs and Consequences of American Empire* (New York: Metropolitan Books, 2000), 18–19, 68. For a more comprehensive version of Herman's analysis of psychology and public policy from World War II to recent times, see Ellen Herman, *The Romance of American Psychology: Political Culture in the Age of Experts* (Berkeley: University of California Press, 1995), chaps. 2–6, 11. A recently published article on SORO—the organization carrying out Project Camelot—is rich in citations on academic involvement in and responses to think tanks devoted to national security; see Joy Rohde, "Gray Matters: Social Scientists, Military Patronage, and Democracy in the Cold War," *Journal of American History* 96 (June 2009): 99–122.

28. Noam Chomsky, *Towards a New Cold War: Essays on the Current Crisis and How We Got There* (New York: Pantheon Books, 1982), 65; Pool is quoted in Simpson, *Science of Coercion*, 8. For the full development of Chomsky's argument, see chap. 1 of the cited work. David H. Price, *Anthropological Intelligence: The Deployment and Neglect of American Anthropology in the Second World War* (Durham, NC: Duke University Press, 2008), presents a thorough and balanced analysis of anthropologists' participation in World War II and consequences for the discipline then and in the future. Giuseppe Caforin, ed., *Social Sciences and the Military: An Interdisciplinary Overview* (New York: Routledge, 2007), presents a broad and international approach to the subject. For a positive view of American "cultural diplomacy" before and during the Cold War years, despite the dark underside of clandestine and manipulative operations by the CIA and others, see Richard T. Arndt, *The First Resort of Kings: American Cultural Diplomacy in the Twentieth Century* (Washington, DC: Potomac Books, 2005).

29. Klare, *War without End*, 31–116; Kaplan, *Wizards of Armageddon*, 252, 328–329; Dickson, *Think Tanks*, 85–87.

30. For the University of Michigan, see Klare, *War without End*, 70, 79, 82–87, 173–181; Deborah W. Larson, "Deterrence Theory and the Cold War," *Radical History Review* 63 (Fall 1995): 93, 98; and Lyons and Morton, *Schools for Strategy*, 6–7, 46, 66, 70–71, 193–197, 272–273, 304, 309–310.

31. Klare, *War without End*, 86.

32. Michigan State is covered in Klare, *War without End*, 70, 110, 261–263, 313–315, 332–333, 333n.

33. Jean M. Converse, *Survey Research in the United States: Roots and Emergence, 1890–1960* (Berkeley: University of California Press, 1987), 239–304, 315–323, 330–352, 373–378, 385–391; Simpson, "U.S. Mass Communication Research," 316, 332–335, 347n42; Simpson, *Science of Coercion*, 4, 26–30, 51–57, 61–81, 86–90, 94–106, 111–117, 126–127, 131–132; Simpson, "Universities, Empire, and the Production of Knowledge," xii–xiii, xviii–xix, xxxiii–xxxivn14; Gendzier, "Play It Again Sam," 75–76; Cumings, "Boundary Displacement," 170. See also Robert A. Jacobs, "Curing the Atomic Bomb within the Relationship of American Social Scientists to Nuclear Weapons in the Early Cold War," *Peace and Change* 35 (July 2010): 414–463. The book cosponsored by the Bureau of Applied Social Research and CENIS was Daniel Lerner with Lucille Pevsner, *The Passing of Traditional Society: Modernizing the Middle East* (Glencoe, IL: Free Press, 1958).

34. Simpson, "U.S. Mass Communication Research," 316.

35. Kuklick, *Blind Oracles*, 152–167; Lyons and Morton, *Schools for Strategy*, 146–154.

36. Steven L. Rearden, *History of the Office of the Secretary of Defense*, vol. 1, *The Formative Years, 1947–1950* (Washington, DC: Historical Office, Office of the Secretary of Defense, 1984), 313–316, 383–384, 402–405.

37. Killian, *Sputnik, Scientists, and Eisenhower*, 11–13, 67–93; Richard M. Leighton, *History of the Office of the Secretary of Defense*, vol. 3, *Strategy, Money, and the New Look, 1953–1956* (Washington, DC: Historical Office, Office of the Secretary of Defense, 2001), 287, 292–297, 301–302, 307, 396–398, 423–449, 454–455, 677–678; Kaplan, *Wizards of Armageddon*, 127, 130–131; Abella, *Soldiers of Reason*, 105–110.

38. Richard J. Watson, *History of the Office of the Secretary of Defense*, vol. 4, *Into the Missile Age, 1956–1960* (Washington, DC: Historical Office, Office of the Secretary of Defense, 1997), 136–141, 151, 155, 183–187, 191–196, 248–250, 300–304, 355–356, 388, 412–418, 475–477; Kaplan, *Wizards of Armageddon*, 125–154, 167–169, 213–215, 225–226; Herken, *Counsels of War*, 111–121, 124–127, 133; Killian, *Sputnik, Scientists, and Eisenhower*, 5–6, 27–28, 30, 88, 96–101; George B. Kistiakowsky, *A Scientist at the White House: The Private Diary of President Eisenhower's Special Assistant for Science and Technology* (Cambridge, MA: Harvard University Press, 1976), xxvi, xxviii, xxx–xxxi, xxxvi–xxxvii, lv–lvi, 336–337; Roger Hilsman, *To Move a Nation: The Politics of Foreign Policy in the Administration of John F. Kennedy* (Garden City, NY: Doubleday, 1967), 8–9; Callahan, *Dangerous Capabilities*, 166–177, 377; Abella, *Soldiers of Reason*, 110–115.

39. Kaplan, *Wizards of Armageddon*, 370–371; Herken, *Counsels of War*, 259–267.

40. Eisenhower quoted in Herken, *Counsels of War*, 116, 118.

41. Eisenhower's farewell address is reproduced in Gregg B. Walker, David A. Bella,

and Steven J. Sprecher, *The Military-Industrial Complex: Eisenhower's Warning Three Decades Later* (New York: Peter Lang, 1992), 361–367; quotations, 364.

42. Dickson, *Think Tanks*, 158–159.

43. Gregg Herken, *Cardinal Choices: Presidential Science Advising from the Atomic Bomb to SDI*, rev. ed. (Stanford, CA: Stanford University Press, 2000), 159–170; Herken, *Counsels of War*, 229–241; Killian, *Sputnik, Scientists, and Eisenhower*, 86–90.

44. Nieburg, *In the Name of Science*, 253. See also Dickson, *Think Tanks*, 86–87, and other citations on McNamara in note 3 of chapter 3.

45. U.S. Bureau of the Budget, *Report to the President of the United States on Government Contracting for Research and Development* (Washington, DC: Bureau of the Budget, 1962); Dickson, *Think Tanks*, 133–162; Nieburg, *In the Name of Science*, 218–243, 268–271, 279–287, 334–350, 371–378; Richard F. Kaufman, *The War Profiteers* (Indianapolis: Bobbs-Merrill, 1970), 96–99, 186–199 (scattered throughout this volume are numerous other references to the uses and abuses of think tanks).

46. For a formulation and elaboration of the analysis on think tanks, strategy centers, and defense intellectuals as they affected American Cold War policies toward the Soviet Union and the developing world, see the following works: Simpson, *Science of Coercion*; Kuklick, *Blind Oracles*; Needell, "Project Troy"; Gendzier, "Play It Again Sam"; Herman, "Project Camelot"; Cumings, "Boundary Displacement"; Waring, "Cold Calculus"; Herman, "Career of Cold War Psychology"; Larson, "Deterrence Theory"; and Kaplan, *Wizards of Armageddon*, 151, along with other publications cited earlier in the chapter.

CHAPTER SEVEN. WEAPONS

1. Barton C. Hacker, *American Military Technology: The Life Story of a Technology* (Westport, CT: Greenwood Press, 2006), 115–119; Stephen I. Schwartz, ed., *Atomic Audit: The Cost and Consequences of U.S. Nuclear Weapons since 1940* (Washington, DC: Brookings Institution Press, 1998), 113.

2. Gary E. Weir, *Forged in War: The Naval-Industrial Complex and American Submarine Construction, 1940–1961* (Washington, DC: Naval Historical Center, 1993); Hacker, *American Military Technology*, 125–130; Kenneth J. Hagan, *This People's Navy: The Making of American Power* (New York: Free Press, 1991), 346–355; George W. Baer, *One Hundred Years of Sea Power: The U.S. Navy, 1890–1990* (Stanford, CA: Stanford University Press, 1994), 352–359, 375–379, 434–645. See note 19 below for additional citations.

3. Donald M. Pattillo, *Pushing the Envelope: The American Aircraft Industry* (Ann Arbor: University of Michigan Press, 1998), 197–199.

4. Ibid., 206.

5. Ibid., 200–206. See also Roger E. Bilstein, *The American Aerospace Industry: From Workshop to Global Enterprise* (New York: Twayne Publishers, 1996), 79–159, and Bill Gunston, *World Encyclopaedia of Aircraft Manufacturers: From the Pioneers to the Present Day* (Annapolis, MD: Naval Institute Press, 1993).

6. James Fallows, *National Defense* (New York: Vantage Books, 1982), 35–49; Ray Wagner, *American Combat Planes*, 3rd ed. (Garden City, NY: Doubleday, 1982), 441–474, 522–548.

7. Fallows, *National Defense*, 26–34, 42–55, 95–106; Hacker, *American Military Technology*, 115–116, 159–160; Pattillo, *Pushing the Envelope*, 199, 259; Chester W. Richards, *A Swift, Elusive Sword: What If Sun Tzu and John Boyd Did a National Defense Review?* 2nd ed. (Washington, DC: Center for Defense Information, 2003).

8. William Greider, *Fortress America: The American Military and the Consequences of Peace* (New York: Public Affairs, 1998), 31–45, 57, 70, 79, 83, 90–91, 93–96, 105–106, 141–142; Center for Defense Information, *Defense Monitor* 37 (November/December 2008): 8–9. See also Fallows, *National Defense*, cited in notes 6 and 7 above. On a related subject, see Lee Gaillard, *V-22 Osprey: Wonder Weapon or Widow Maker? They Warned Us, But No One Is Listening* (Washington, DC: Center for Defense Information, 2006).

9. Greider, *Fortress America*, 13–14, 31–34.

10. Nick Kotz, *Wild Blue Yonder: Money, Politics, and the B-1 Bomber* (New York: Pantheon Books, 1988); David S. Sorenson, *The Politics of Strategic Aircraft Modernization* (Westport, CT: Praeger, 1995); Fallows, *National Defense*, 166–168; Pattillo, *Pushing the Envelope*, 272–273, 326–327, 339, 341, 348–349; Schwartz, ed., *Atomic Audit*, 113, 116–117, 119–123; Wagner, *American Combat Planes*, 417–440; Greider, *Fortress America*, 42–43, 111–118; Alex Roland, *The Military-Industrial Complex* (Washington, DC: American Historical Association, 2001), 14–15.

11. Greider, *Fortress America*, 3–17.

12. Ibid., 19–30; *Los Angeles Times*, January 11, 2009, A15. See also William W. Love Jr., ed., *The Chiefs of Naval Operations* (Annapolis, MD: Naval Institute Press, 1980), 137–379; Kenneth J. Hagan, ed., *In Peace and War: Interpretations of American Naval History, 1775–1984*, 2nd ed. (Westport, CT: Greenwood Press, 1984), 263–370; Hagan, *This People's Navy*, 333–387; Thomas C. Hone, *Power and Change: The Administrative History of the Office of the Chief of Naval Operations, 1946–1986* (Washington, DC: Naval Historical Center, 1989); Frederick H. Hartmann, *Naval Renaissance: The U.S. Navy in the 1980s* (Annapolis, MD: Naval Institute Press, 1990); Baer, *One Hundred Years of Sea Power*, 275–451; and Leslie A. Rose, *Power at Sea*, vol. 2, *The Breaking Storm, 1919–1945*, and vol. 3, *A Violent Peace, 1946–2006* (Columbia: University of Missouri Press, 2007), 2:167–189, 327–422; 3:43–63, 206–234, 267–306.

13. Hacker, *American Military Technology*, 133, 137–149, 157–159; Fallows, *National Defense*, 36, 51–55, 69, 110–119, 141; Greider, *Fortress America*, 137; Ward Just, *Military Men* (New York: Alfred A. Knopf, 1970), 151–184; A. J. Bacevich, *The Pentomic Era: The U.S. Army between Korea and Vietnam* (Washington, DC: National Defense University Press, 1986); Ingo Trauschweizer, *The Cold War U.S. Army: Building Deterrence for Limited War* (Lawrence: University Press of Kansas, 2008); George H. Quester, "The Politics of Conventional Warfare in an Unconventional Age," in *The Long War: A New History of U.S. National Security Policy since World War II*, ed. Andrew J. Bacevich (New York: Columbia University Press, 2007), 99–136.

14. Jacques S. Gansler, *Defense Conversion: Transforming the Arsenal of Democracy* (Cambridge, MA: MIT Press, 1995), 9.

15. Ibid., 9–11; Hacker, *American Military Technology*, 152–166; Greider, *Fortress America*, 121–138; Adrian R. Lewis, *The American Culture of War: The History of U.S. Military Force from World War II to Operation Iraqi Freedom* (New York: Routledge, 2007); Thomas G. Mahnken, *Technology and the American Way of War* (New York: Columbia University Press, 2008); P. W. Singer, *Wired for War: The Robotics Revolution*

and Conflict in the Twenty-first Century (New York: Penguin, 2009); Center for Defense Information, *Defense Monitor* 37 (November/December 2008): 10–11; Aaron Major, "Which Revolution in Military Affairs? Political Discourse and the Defense Industrial Base," *Armed Forces and Society* 35 (January 2009): 333–361. Search online for "Force XXI."

16. Jeremy Bernstein, *Nuclear Weapons: What You Need to Know* (New York: Cambridge University Press, 2008); David E. Hoffman, *The Dead Hand: The Untold Story of the Cold War Arms Race and Its Dangerous Legacy* (New York: Doubleday, 2009); Neil Sheehan, *A Fiery Place in a Cold War: Bernard Schriever and the Ultimate Weapon* (New York: Random House, 2009); Shane J. Maddock, *Nuclear Apartheid: The Quest for American Atomic Supremacy from World War II to the Present* (Chapel Hill: University of North Carolina Press, 2010). See also Paul Boyer, *By the Bomb's Early Light: American Thought and Culture at the Dawn of the Atomic Age* (New York: Pantheon, 1985); Michael S. Goodman, *Spying on the Nuclear Bear: Anglo-American Intelligence and the Soviet Bomb* (Stanford, CA: Stanford University Press, 2007); Robert A. Jacobs, "Curing the Atomic Bomb within the Relationship of American Social Scientists to Nuclear Weapons in the Early Cold War," *Peace and Change* 35 (July 2010): 414–463; and chapters 1, 3, and 4 of this volume.

17. Schwartz, ed., *Atomic Audit*, xxii, 1–3, 33, 102; Joseph Cirincione, *Bomb Scare: The History and Future of Nuclear Weapons* (New York: Columbia University Press, 2007), 77–78, 179n87; *Los Angeles Times*, January 12, 2009, A15, and May 4, 2010, A8; Center for Defense Information, *Military Almanac, 2007* (Washington, DC: Center for Defense Information, 2007), 26–31; Jeremy Bernstein, "Nukes for Sale," *New York Review of Books*, May 13, 2010, 44–46. Schwartz's edited volume is extremely valuable; researched and written by ten contributors, including the editor, it covers nearly all facets of nuclear armaments in detail, but from a broad perspective. Given that a great deal of documentation remains classified, the volume's accomplishments are even more impressive. Mahnken, *Technology and the American Way of War*, is also helpful in analyzing the impact and use of nuclear weapons among the various armed services.

The Center for Defense Information's *Defense Monitor* 39 (October/November/ December 2010) is devoted to an analysis of the New START between the United States and the Russian Federation. The treaty went into effect in February 2011, replacing the 2002 Moscow Treaty negotiated by the Bush administration. New START limits the number of deployed strategic warheads for each of the two powers to 1,550. This obligation must be met within seven years and constitutes a 30 percent reduction from the limitations set by the 2002 treaty.

18. Schwartz, ed., *Atomic Audit*, 111–123, 126–127, 130–132, 149–150, 160–161.

19. Ibid., 136–139, 141, 149–150, 158–160. Additional information on the SLBM-armed, nuclear-propelled submarines can be accessed by searching online for "submarines—Ohio class." See also Stephen Saunders, ed., *Jane's Fighting Ships 2010–2011* (Alexandria, VA: Jane's Information Group, 2010).

20. Bacevich, ed., *Pentomic Era*, 53–157; Trauschweizer, *Cold War U.S. Army*; Schwartz, *Atomic Audit*, 149–150, 153–158.

21. Schwartz, ed., *Atomic Audit*, 161–166.

22. Ibid., 22–27, 166–168, 184–189, 203–204; Fallows, *National Defense*, 139–170. See also Richard K. Betts, *Nuclear Blackmail and Nuclear Balance* (Washington, DC: Brookings Institution, 1987); Ronald E. Powaski, *March to Armageddon: The United*

States and the Nuclear Arms Race, 1939 to the Present (New York: Oxford University Press, 1987); Ronald E. Powaski, *Return to Armageddon: The United States and the Nuclear Arms Race, 1981–1999* (New York: Oxford University Press, 2000); Tami Davis Biddle, "Shield and Sword: U.S. Strategic Forces and Doctrine since 1945," in Bacevich, ed., *The Long War*, 137–206; and Paul F. Diehl, "Arms Races and the Outbreak of War, 1816–1980" (Ph.D. diss., University of Michigan, 1983).

23. Schwartz, ed., *Atomic Audit*, 7, 22–27, 184–195, 203–204, 519–541; Andrew J. Bacevich, "Elusive Bargain: The Pattern of U.S. Civil-Military Relations since World War II," in Bacevich, ed., *The Long War*, 227–228. For a candid view of air force attitudes about its unending requirements, see Jacob Neufeld, ed., *Reflections on Research and Development in the United States Air Force: An interview with General Bernard A. Schriever and Generals Samuel C. Phillips, Robert T. Marsh, and James H. Doolittle, and Dr. Ivan A. Getting—Conducted by Dr. Richard H. Kohn* (Washington, DC: Center for Air Force History, 1993).

24. Lynn Eden, *Whole World on Fire: Organizations, Knowledge, and Nuclear Weapons Devastation* (Ithaca, NY: Cornell University Press, 2004), 2, 7, 16, 271–277, 286–287, 291, 302–304; Janne E. Nolan, *Guardians of the Arsenal: The Politics of Nuclear Strategy* (New York: Basic Books, 1989), 29–33, 249–285; Schwartz, ed., *Atomic Audit*, 198–205, 463–468. See also the four-volume study of Richard Rhodes: *The Making of the Atomic Bomb* (New York: Simon and Schuster, 1986); *Dark Sun: The Making of the Hydrogen Bomb* (New York: Simon and Schuster, 1995); *Arsenals of Folly: The Making of the Nuclear Arms Race* (New York: Alfred A. Knopf, 2007); and *The Twilight of the Bombs: Recent Challenges, New Dangers, and the Prospects for a World without Nuclear Weapons* (New York: Alfred A. Knopf, 2010).

25. Schwartz, ed., *Atomic Audit*, 204–222, 261–263. See also the various essays on nuclear strategy in Ernest R. May, ed., *American Cold War Strategy: Interpreting NSC 68* (Boston: Bedford Books, 1993); William P. Bundy, ed., *The Nuclear Controversy: A Foreign Affairs Reader* (New York: Meridan, 1985); and Bacevich, *The Long War*. Additionally, see Ralph E. Lapp, *The Weapons Culture* (New York: W. W. Norton, 1968); Herbert York, *Race to Oblivion: A Participant's View of the Arms Race* (New York: Simon and Schuster, 1970); Lawrence Freedman, *The Evolution of Nuclear Strategy* (London: Macmillan, 1981); Lawrence Freedman, *Arms Control: Management or Reform?* (London: Routledge and Kegan Paul, 1986); John L. Gaddis, *Strategies of Containment: A Critical Appraisal of Postwar American National Security Policy* (New York: Oxford University Press, 1982); Robert Jervis, *The Illogic of American Nuclear Strategy* (Ithaca, NY: Cornell University Press, 1984); John Muller, *Retreat from Doomsday: The Obsolescence of Major War* (New York: Basic Books, 1989); David G. Coleman and Joseph M. Siracusa, *Real-World Nuclear Deterrence: The Making of International Strategy* (Westport, CT: Praeger, 2006); Sean L. Mallory, *Atomic Tragedy: Henry L. Stimson and the Decision to Use the Bomb against Japan* (Ithaca, NY: Cornell University Press, 2008); and David Tal, *The American Nuclear Disarmament Dilemma, 1945–1963* (Syracuse, NY: Syracuse University Press, 2008).

26. Schwartz, ed., *Atomic Audit*, 155–157, 177, 200–222, 261–268, 262n137; Fred Kaplan, *The Wizards of Armageddon* (New York: Simon and Schuster, 1983), 132–134; Gregg Herken, *Counsels of War* (New York: Alfred A. Knopf, 1985), 88–98; Center for Defense Information, *Defense Monitor* 33 (March/April 2004): 1–3, 7; Gabrielle Hecht and Paul N. Edwards, *The Technopolitics of Cold War: Toward a Transregional Perspective*

(Washington, DC: American Historical Association, 2007), 7–23. Paul Bracken, *The Command and Control of Nuclear Forces* (New Haven, CT: Yale University Press, 1983), reviews and analyzes the critical issues for the United States and, to a limited degree, the Soviet Union. Peter D. Feaver, *Guarding the Guardians: Civilian Control of Nuclear Weapons in the United States* (Ithaca, NY: Cornell University Press, 1992), carefully traces and analyzes operational policy concerning nuclear weapons and its effect on the critical issue of civilian versus military control.

27. Center for Defense Information, *Defense Monitor* 37 (November/December 2008): 1–7, *Defense Monitor* 39 (January/February/March 2010): 11, and *Defense Monitor* 40 (October/November/December 2011); Schwartz, *Atomic Audit*, 207. See also chapter 6.

28. William W. Keller, *Arm in Arm: The Political Economy of the Global Arms Trade* (New York: Basic Books, 1995), 10–12.

29. Ibid., 97–102, 125.

30. John Feffer, "Supporting Arms: U.S. Government Subsidies of the Arms Trade," Kevin Spears and Rear Admiral Stephen H. Baker (ret.), "Economic Arguments for Arms Export Reform," Jason Meyers, "Risky Business: The Security Implications of Arms Export Reforms," and Joseph P. Smaldone, "Foreign Policy Risks of Arms Export Reforms," in *Challenging Conventional Wisdom: Debunking the Myths and Exposing the Risks of Arms Export Reforms*, eds. Tamar Gabelnick and Rachel Stohl (Washington, DC: Federation of American Scientists and Center for Defense Information, 2003), 25–52, 53–64, 104–130, 131–152; Keller, *Arm in Arm*, ix–xii, 9, 11–15, 90, 100–104, 126; Greider, *Fortress America*, 97–110; Mary Kaldor, *The Baroque Arsenal* (New York: Hill and Wang, 1981), 132–168.

31. Keller, *Arm in Arm*, 65–92, 166–167, 177. See also chapter 6. A useful compendium on arms control is Jack Mendelsohn, ed., *Arms Control Chronology* (Washington, DC: Center for Defense Information, 2002).

32. Rachel Stohl and Tamar Gabelnick, eds., "Challenging Conventional Wisdom," in Gabelnick and Stohl, *Challenging Conventional Wisdom*, 9–17; quotation, Keller, *Arm in Arm*, 95.

33. Keller, *Arm in Arm*, 91–96, 152–158, 166–167, 177; Greider, *Fortress America*, 87, 89–90, 92–96. See also chapter 4.

34. Greider, *Fortress America*, 97–106; Keller, *Arm in Arm*, 90–91, 152–158. See also chapter 4.

35. Keller, *Arm in Arm*, 29–32, 52–59, 90–96, 102–104, 125–158, 166–173; Greider, *Fortress America*, 97–101; Wade Boese, "The Wassenaar Agreement," in Gabelnick and Stohl, eds., *Challenging Conventional Wisdom*, 173–181; Jullian Hayes and Theresa Hitchens, "The Missile Technology Control Regime," ibid., 182–194.

36. Keller, *Arm in Arm*, 11–12, 94–96, 170–173, 177; Ilan Peleg, "Models of Arms Transfer in American Foreign Policy: Carter's Restraint and Reagan's Promotion, 1977–1987," in *Arms, Politics, and the Economy: Historical and Contemporary Perspectives*, ed. Robert Higgs (New York: Holmes and Meier, 1990), 132–154. See also chapter 4.

37. David Albright, *Peddling Peril: How the Secret Nuclear Trade Arms America's Enemies* (New York: Free Press, 2010); Maddock, *Nuclear Apartheid*; Bernstein, "Nukes for Sale," 44–46; Keller, *Arm in Arm*, 27–29, 102–104, 125–135, 144–145; Greider, *Fortress America*, 108–109; Jonathan B. Tucker, *War of Nerves: Chemical Warfare from World War II to Al-Queda* (New York: Pantheon Books, 2006). For a reasonably posi-

tive view of progress on nuclear nonproliferation and weapons of mass destruction in general, see Cirincione, *Bomb Scare*, 125–157. See also Paul J. Magnarella, "Attempts to Reduce and Eliminate Nuclear Weapons through the Nuclear Non-Proliferation Treaty and the Creation of Nuclear Weapon–Free Zones," *Peace and Change* 33 (October 2008): 507–521, and chapter 4 of this volume. For an analysis of nuclear weapons, arms races, proliferation, and challenges within a global perspective, see Hecht and Edwards, *Technopolitics of Cold War*, 22–45.

38. Keller, *Arm in Arm*, 102–104, 146, 170–171; Greider, *Fortress America*, 108–111; "Form on Military Privatization," *Armed Forces and Society* 36 (July 2010): 647–749 (addressing the issue from an international perspective and including excellent bibliographic references); Michael Crowley and Greg Puley, "Toward Harmonized International Standards: The Framework Convention on International Arms Transfers," in Gabelnick and Stohl, eds., *Challenging Conventional Wisdom*, 195–201; Tamar Gabelnick and Rachel Stohl, "Conclusion: Developing Sound Export Control Reforms for Today's Security Environment," ibid., 202–223.

CHAPTER EIGHT. NATIONAL SECURITY AND THE ECONOMY

1. Lloyd J. Dumas, *The Overburdened Economy: Uncovering the Causes of Chronic Unemployment, Inflation, and National Decline* (Berkeley: University of California Press, 1986), 9–12; Lloyd J. Dumas, "Military Spending and Economic Decay," in *The Political Economy of Arms Reduction: Reversing Economic Decay*, ed. Lloyd J. Dumas (Boulder, CO: Westview Press, 1982), 17–24.

2. Seymour Melman, *Profits without Production* (New York: Alfred A. Knopf, 1983), 131–135. An extended analysis of the machine-tool industry is presented later in the chapter, along with a citation of sources.

3. Dumas, *Overburdened Economy*, 7–13; Dumas, "Military Spending and Economic Decay," 9–11.

4. The following discussion draws on these sources: Barry Bluestone and Bennett Harrison, *Deindustrialization of America: Plant Closings, Community Abandonment, and the Dismantling of Basic Industry* (New York: Basic Books, 1982), 112–115, 140–141; John E. Ullmann, ed., *The Improvement of Productivity: Myths and Realities* (New York: Praeger, 1980), 1–20; Dumas, *Overburdened Economy*, 3–16; Dumas, "Military Spending and Economic Decay," 17–24; U.S. Bureau of the Census, *Historical Statistics of the United States: Colonial Times to 1970*, pt. 2 (Washington, DC: U.S. Bureau of the Census, 1975), 1114–1116; Susan B. Carter et al., eds., *Historical Statistics of the United States: Earliest Times to the Present*, 5 vols. (New York: Cambridge University Press, 2006), 5:367–369. An extended discussion of the solid-state electronics industry is presented later in the chapter.

5. Joseph M. Jones Jr., "The Steel Industry," in Ullmann, ed., *Improvement of Productivity*, 228–244; John E. Ullmann, *The Prospects of American Industrial Recovery* (Westport, CT: Quorum Books, 1985), 143–158; John E. Ullmann, *The Anatomy of Industrial Decline: Productivity, Investment, and Location in U.S. Manufacturing* (New York: Quorum Books, 1988), 53–55, 104–106; Bluestone and Harrison, *Deindustrialization of America*, 4, 6, 36–37, 40–41, 127, 145–147, 156–158, 253–255; Melman,

Profits without Production, 188–199; Seymour Melman, *The Permanent War Economy: American Capitalism in Decline* (New York: Simon and Schuster, 1974), 86–87. See also Paul A. C. Koistinen, *Planning War, Pursuing Peace: The Political Economy of American Warfare, 1920–1939* (Lawrence: University Press of Kansas, 1998), chap. 5, for more information on the steel industry and additional bibliographic citations.

6. Bluestone and Harrison, *Deindustrialization of America*, 114.

7. The following analysis of the automobile industry is based on these sources: Charles W. Lott, "The Automobile Industry," in Ullmann, ed., *Improvement of Productivity*, 245–255; Ullmann, *Prospects of American Industrial Recovery*, 172–176; Ullmann, *Anatomy of Industrial Decline*, 68–71, 109–111, 171–173; Melman, *Profits without Production*, 28–37, 115–117, 120–124, 181–187, 200, 204–206, 295–297; Melman, *Permanent War Economy*, 75–76, 87, 101–102; Bluestone and Harrison, *Deindustrialization of America*, 4–6, 13–14, 36–37, 56–57, 71–72, 113–115, 138–141, 166–167, 175–178, 229n70; *Los Angeles Times*, May 3, 2009, A37, and October 24, 2010, B1.

8. The discussion of machine tools is based on these sources: John De Luca, "Machine Tools," in Ullmann, ed., *Improvement of Productivity*, 289–298; Ullmann, *Prospects of American Industrial Recovery*, 160–171; Ullmann, *Anatomy of Industrial Decline*, 57–61, 106–109; Melman, *Profits without Production*, 3–14, 103–107, 133–135; Melman, *Permanent War Economy*, 41, 81–84, 90–91, 329–331; David F. Noble, *Forces of Production: A Social History of Industrial Automation* (New York: Alfred A. Knopf, 1984); Tom Schlesinger, "Labor, Automation, and Regional Development," in *Militarization of High Technology*, ed. John Tirman (Cambridge, MA: Ballinger, 1984), 181–213; Koistinen, *Planning War, Pursuing Peace*, 150–155; Paul A. C. Koistinen, *Arsenal of World War II: The Political Economy of American Warfare, 1940–1945* (Lawrence: University Press of Kansas, 2004), 117–118.

9. The following analysis of the deindustrialization process that swept through the larger economy is based on these sources: Melman, *Profits without Production*, xi–xix, 1–81, 103–130, 181–206, 295–297; Bluestone and Harrison, *Deindustrialization of America*, 1–81, 111–190, 210–214, 252–255, 266–277; Richard J. Barnet and Ronald E. Muller, *Global Reach: The Power of the Multinational Corporations* (New York: Simon and Schuster, 1974); Ullmann, ed., *Improvement of Productivity*, 1–21 and various contributors' essays; Ullmann, *Prospects of American Industrial Recovery*, 3–26, 76–93, 181–204; Ullmann, *Anatomy of Industrial Decline*, ix–x, 1–24, 81–87, 119–128, 147–156, and essays on various industries; Seymour Melman, "Economic Conversion and Economic Renewal," in *Towards a Peace Economy in the United States: Essays on Military Industry, Disarmament and Economic Conversion*, ed. Gregory A. Bischak (London: Macmillan, 1991), xiii–xxii; Anthony DiFilippo, "Military Spending and Government High-Technology Policy: A Comparative Analysis of the U.S., West Germany, Japan, and Great Britain," ibid., 3–28; Lloyd J. Dumas, "National Security, Noncontributive Activity and Macroeconomic Analysis: Theoretical, Empirical and Methodological Issues," ibid., 57–77; Byung Yoo Hong, *Inflation under Cost Pass-Along Management* (New York: Praeger, 1979); Pat Choate and Susan Walter, *America in Ruins: The Decaying Infrastructure* (Durham, NC: Duke University Press, 1983); Suzanne Gordon and Dave McFadden, *Economic Conversion: Revitalizing America's Economy* (Cambridge, MA: Ballinger, 1984); Sar A. Levitan and Dianne Werneke, *Productivity, Prospects, and Policies* (Baltimore: Johns Hopkins University Press, 1984); Jeffrey A. Engel, *Local Consequences of the Global Cold War* (Stanford, CA: Stanford University Press, 2007).

10. Quoted in Barnet and Muller, *Global Reach*, 305.

11. The following analysis of the electronics industry is based on these sources: Robert B. Reich, "High Technology, Defense, and International Trade," in Tirman, ed., *Militarization of High Technology*, 33–43; Robert DeGrasse, "The Military and Semiconductors," ibid., 77–104; Lloyd L. Dumas, "University Research, Industrial Innovation, and the Pentagon," ibid., 123–151; Warren F. Davis, "The Pentagon and the Scientist," ibid., 153–179; Robert W. DeGrasse Jr., *Military Expansion, Economic Decline: The Impact of Military Spending on U.S. Economic Performance* (Armonk, NY: M. E. Sharpe, 1983), 77–108; DiFilippo, "Military Spending and Government High-Technology Policy," 3–28; Nance Goldstein, "Defense Spending as Industrial Policy: The Impact of Military R&D on the U.S. Software Industry," in Bischak, ed., *Towards a Peace Economy*, 29–53; David C. Mowery and Nathan Rosenberg, *Technology and the Pursuit of Economic Growth* (New York: Cambridge University Press, 1989), 123–296; Andrei Rozwadowski, "Semiconductors," in Ullmann, ed., *Improvement of Productivity*, 256–288; Ullmann, *Prospects of American Industrial Recovery*, 94–115; Ullmann, *Anatomy of Industrial Decline*, 63–68, 74–75, 106–109, 138–139, 170–171; Dumas, *Overburdened Economy*, 16–18, 214–217; Melman, *Profits without Production*, 199–200, 259–260, 264–269; Melman, *Permanent War Economy*, 23–25, 87–89, 101, 245–246, 340–353; Vernon W. Ruttan, *Is War Necessary for Economic Growth? Military Procurement and Technology Development* (New York: Oxford University Press, 2006), 91–190.

12. William Lazonick, *Sustainable Prosperity in the New Economy? Business Organization and High-Tech Employment in the United States* (Kalamazoo, MI: W. P. Upjohn Institute for Employment Research, 2009). Lazonick's seminal volume is based on years of research and many publications, a list of which is included in his book's bibliography. Lazonick summarizes the major lines of the book's analysis in a recent article: "Innovative Business Models and Varieties of Capitalism: Financialization of the U.S. Corporation," *Business History Review* 84 (Winter 2010): 675–702.

13. The term is used by J. Davidson Alexander, "Manufacturing Productivity and Military Depletion in the Postwar Industrial Economy," in Bischak, ed., *Towards a Peace Economy*, 78–117. An excellent bibliographic account of the evolving analysis and the effects of postwar defense spending is presented by John Tirman, "The Defense-Economy Debate," in Tirman, ed., *Militarization of High Technology*, 1–32. For a balanced and insightful analysis and extended bibliography of the subject, see Alex Roland, *The Military-Industrial Complex* (Washington, DC: American Historical Association, 2001).

14. See note 5 for a full citation of the volume. The book includes a citation of Melman's previous publications, which was updated in his 1983 volume *Profits without Production*. Inexplicably, his last book, *The Pentagon and the National Debt: The Consequences of the Global Military Mission of the United States* (Northampton, MA: Aletheia Press, 1991), could not be located through Interlibrary Loan services, various computer searches, and a number of personal inquiries to universities, scholars, and related persons.

15. See note 2 for a full citation of the volume. On business schools, see also Rakesh Khurana, *From Higher Aims to Hired Hands: The Social Transformation of American Business Schools and the Unfilled Promise of Management as a Profession* (Princeton, NJ: Princeton University Press, 2007).

16. Melman discusses the effects of the postwar economy on engineering at greater length in *Permanent War Economy* than in *Profits without Production*. See also Ullmann,

Prospects of American Industrial Recovery, 100, 167–168, 215–217; John E. Ullmann, "The Pentagon and the Firm," in Tirman, ed., *Militarization of High Technology*, 116–118; and Dumas, "University Research," 125–132.

17. See note 1 for a full citation of the volume. Dumas's other publications are listed in Lloyd C. Dumas, ed., *The Socio-Economics of Conversion from War to Peace* (Armonk, NY: M. E. Sharpe, 1995).

18. Ullmann has been prolific, publishing more than sixty books. His major works relevant to this subject have been cited in notes 4 and 5. See also John E. Ullmann, ed., *Social Costs in Modern Society: A Qualitative and Quantitative Assessment* (Westport, CT: Quorum Books, 1981), which includes his essay "The Military Sector."

19. Sources reflecting this outcome have been cited above, and others will be cited below. See also Tirman, "The Defense-Economy Debate," 1–32, and Joel S. Yudken and Michael Black, "Towards a New National Needs Agenda for Science and Technology Policy: The Prospects for Democratic Science and Technology Policymaking," in Bischak, ed., *Towards a Peace Economy*, 160–201.

20. Council on Competitiveness, *Picking up the Pace: The Commercial Challenge to American Innovation* (Washington, DC: Council on Competitiveness, 1988). See also Yudken and Black, "Towards a New National Needs Agenda," 161–173; Otis L. Graham Jr., *Toward a Planned Society: From Roosevelt to Nixon* (New York: Oxford University Press, 1976); and Otis L. Graham Jr., *Losing Time: The Industrial Policy Debate* (Cambridge, MA: Harvard University Press, 1992).

Recent reports by the Boston Consulting Group and Human Rights Watch state that current trends will result in the United States becoming one of the cheapest locations for manufacturing in the developed world by 2015. Based on its high productivity rate and low wages, such an outcome would make the nation, especially the South, the new China in terms of rapidly attracting the investment of foreign firms. This development has already been taking place at a gradual pace for several decades. Japan and European countries opened plants in the United States, which allowed them to take all the steps necessary to prohibit unions and deny their employees practically any rights. Such practices are prohibited throughout western and northern Europe, where labor unions are common, strong, and often represented on corporate boards. Ironies abound: for several decades after World War II, American corporations employed the same investment and production strategies abroad that are now followed by multinational and conglomerate corporations of Europe and Asia in this nation.

However, if the United States can muster the unity, leadership, energy, and will, the ignominious fate predicted might be averted. During the last fifteen years, in upstate New York and the Hudson River Valley, a promising project of manufacturing revitalization has been under way. The College of Nanoscale Science and Engineering (CNS&E) of the University of Albany has led the way. Nanotechnology involves working with materials at a microscopic level for purposes of producing computer microchips and other high-technology applications. CNS&E combines manufacturers, researchers, tool makers, and suppliers in a working partnership. It has been financed by more than 250 corporations, including giants such as IBM, donating over $6 billion. Additionally, and of critical importance, the State of New York (unlike skittish Washington) has contributed more than $1.4 billion in assistance, grants, and tax rebates to the effort, as well as fast-tracking construction permits and clearing other bureaucratic hurdles that slow down and increase the cost of building factories. The college has solicited the assistance and expertise of university professors and industrial leaders from the Silicon Valley and Japan. It has also been instrumental in luring high-tech firms to the area, including the 2012 opening of Advanced Micro Devices' $4.6 billion semiconductor plant located twenty miles from Albany.

CNS&E is attempting to duplicate the public-private partnership approach of Germany, Taiwan, South Korea, China, and others, which accounts in part for their domination of the global output of high-technology products. Some scholars believe that the New York effort, though highly commendable, is too late; others disagree. In the eyes of some, CNS&E is engaged in a form of state socialism, an approach that raises too many hackles in both the private and public sectors. Actually, the college is practicing a type of industrial policy typical of most developed nations. One possible result is that the CNS&E initiative will be taken up by an increasing number of blue states, while red states join Washington in saying no. Should that occur, the nation could become even more divided and troubled. For more information on these themes, see *Los Angeles Times*, May 15, 2011, A1, A11.

21. The following analysis of corporate-military relations prior to the Cold War years is based on material from the second, third, and fourth volumes of my political economy of warfare series, of which the current volume is the fifth and final one. See Paul A. C. Koistinen, *Mobilizing for Modern Warfare: The Political Economy of American Warfare, 1865–1919* (Lawrence: University Press of Kansas, 1997); *Planning War, Pursuing Peace*; and *Arsenal of World War II*. Although modified over time, brief accounts of the period 1914–1945 are available in Paul A. C. Koistinen, *The Military-Industrial Complex: A Historical Perspective* (New York: Praeger, 1980), chaps. 2–4, and Paul A. C. Koistinen, "Warfare and Power Relations in America: Mobilizing the World War II Economy," in *The Home Front and War in the Twentieth Century*, ed. James Titus (Colorado Springs: U.S. Air Force Academy, 1984), 91–110, 231–243. See also George V. Sweeting, "Building the Arsenal of Democracy: The Government's Role in Expansion of Industrial Capacity, 1940–1945" (Ph.D. diss., Columbia University, 1994).

22. The following economic analysis is based on these sources: Robert Pollin, *Contours of Descent: U.S. Economic Fractures and the Landscape of Global Austerity* (London: Verso, 2003); Jacob S. Hacker, *The Great Risk Shift: The New Economic Insecurity and the Decline of the American Dream*, rev. ed. (New York: Oxford University Press, 2008); Jacob S. Hacker and Paul Pierson, *Winner-Take-All Politics: How Washington Made the Rich Richer—And Turned Its Back on the Middle Class* (New York: Simon and Schuster, 2010); Naomi Klein, *The Shock Doctrine: The Rise of Disaster Capitalism* (New York: Picador, 2007); Lawrence E. Mitchell, *The Speculation Economy: How Finance Triumphed over Industry* (San Francisco: Berrett-Koehler, 2008); John Cassidy, *How Markets Fail: The Logic of Economic Calamities* (New York: Farrar, Straus and Giroux, 2009); Jeff Madrick, *The Case for Big Government* (Princeton, NJ: Princeton University Press, 2009); Charles R. Morris, *The Trillion Dollar Meltdown: Easy Money, High Rollers, and the Credit Crunch* (New York: Public Affairs, 2008); Justin Fox, *The Myth of the Rational Market: A History of Risk, Reward, and Delusion on Wall Street* (New York: HarperCollins, 2009); Iwan Morgan, *The Age of Deficits: Presidents and Unbalanced Budgets from Jimmy Carter to George W. Bush* (Lawrence: University Press of Kansas, 2009); Pablo Triana, *Lecturing Birds on Flying: Can Mathematical Theories Destroy the Financial Market?* (Hoboken, NJ: John Wiley and Sons, 2009); David Wessel, *In Fed We Trust: Ben Bernanke's War on the Great Panic* (New York: Crown Business, 2009); Tony Judt,

Ill Fares the Land (New York: Penguin, 2010); Nouriel Roubini and Stephen Mihm, *Crisis Economics: A Crash Course in the Future of Finance* (New York: Penguin, 2010); Judith Stein, *Pivotal Decade: How the United States Traded Factories for Finance in the Seventies* (New Haven, CT: Yale University Press, 2010); Louis Hyman, *Debtor Nation: The History of America in Red Ink* (Princeton, NJ: Princeton University Press, 2011); and citations in chapter 1 on Reagan, Bush Sr., Clinton, and Bush Jr.

The *New York Review of Books* (*NYRB*) from 2008 to 2010 has published an excellent collection of essays on the current economic situation. Some are reviews of relevant volumes; others are essays and symposium accounts. See George Soros, "The Crisis and What to Do about It," *NYRB*, December 4, 2008, 63–65; Robert Skidelsky, "Can You Spare a Dime?" *NYRB*, January 15, 2009, 28–30; Jeff Madrick, "How We Were Ruined and What We Can Do," *NYRB*, February 12, 2009, 15–18; Richard Parker, "Government beyond Obama," *NYRB*, March 12, 2009, 38–41; Amartya Sen, "Capitalism beyond the Crisis," *NYRB*, March 26, 2009, 27–30; Robert M. Solow, "How to Understand the Disaster," May 14, 2009, 4–8; "The Crisis and How to Deal with It" (a symposium on the economy including Bill Bradley, Niall Ferguson, Paul Krugman, Jeff Madrick, Nouriel Roubini, George Soros, and Robin Wells), *NYRB*, June 11, 2009, 73–76; Roger Alcaly, "How They Killed the Economy," *NYRB*, March 25, 2010, 43–45; Jeff Madrick, "Can They Stop the Great Recession?" *NYRB*, April 8, 2010, 54–58; Benjamin M. Friedman, "Two Roads to Our Financial Catastrophe," *NYRB*, April 29, 2010, 27–29; Paul Krugman and Robin Wells, "Our Great Banking Crisis—What to Expect," *NYRB*, May 13, 2010, 11–13; Jeff Madrick, "At the Heart of the Crash," *NYRB*, June 10, 2010, 37–39; Paul Volcker, "The Time We Have Is Growing Short," *NYRB*, June 24, 2010, 12–14; Paul Krugman and Robin Wells, "The Slump Goes On: Why?" and "The Way out of the Slump," *NYRB*, September 30, 2010, 57–60, and October 14, 2010, 14–16; George Soros, "The Real Danger to the Economy," *NYRB*, November 11, 2010, 16; John Cassidy, "The Economy: Why They Failed," *NYRB*, December 9, 2010, 27–29; and Jeff Madrick, "How Can the Economy Recover?" *NYRB*, December 23, 2010, 74–78. See also *Los Angeles Times*, January 2, 2011, A26; Harvey M. Schwartz, *States versus Markets: History, Geography, and the Development of the International Political Economy* (New York: St. Martin's Press, 1994); Robert M. Collins, *More: The Politics of Economic Growth in Postwar America* (New York: Oxford University Press, 2000); Jeffry A. Frieden, *Global Capitalism: Its Fall and Rise in the Twentieth Century* (New York: W. W. Norton, 2006), 253–476; "'Varieties of Capitalism' Roundtable," *Business History Review* 84 (Winter 2010): 637–674; and relevant volumes by Melman, Dumas, and Ullmann, cited earlier.

23. The following account of the DOD and armed services is based primarily on Winslow T. Wheeler, ed., *America's Defense Meltdown: Pentagon Reform for President Obama and the New Congress* (Washington, DC: Center for Defense Information, 2008). Thirteen authors contribute to this first-rate volume. Essays by Lt. Col. John Sayen, William S. Lind, Col. Robert Dilger, Pierre M. Sprey, Thomas Christie, and Wheeler, along with the latter's preface, all deal with the subject in a general way or provide a broad historical perspective. The major strength of the other contributors is more specific and detailed coverage that is still of great importance. A more recent volume edited by Wheeler enriches the analysis further: Winslow T. Wheeler, ed., *The Pentagon Labyrinth: 10 Short Essays to Help You Through It* (Washington, DC: Center for Defense Information–World Security Institute, 2011). Numerous issues of the Center for

Defense Information's newsletter, the *Defense Monitor* 30–39 (2000–2010), examine the subjects analyzed in Wheeler's volumes. The quality and coverage of this publication are not matched elsewhere. The Center for Defense Information's *Military Almanac, 2007* (Washington, DC: Center for Defense Information, 2007) and previous annual editions are also an enormously rich source of information on the American military and its comparative place in the world community. See also Jacques S. Gansler, *Affording Defense* (Cambridge, MA: MIT Press, 1991); Marion Anderson, *The Empty Pork Barrel: Unemployment and the Pentagon Budget* (Lansing, MI: Employment Research Associates, 1982); James R. Anderson, *Bankrupting America: The Tax Burden and Expenditures of the Pentagon by Congressional District* (Lansing, MI: Employment Research Associates, 1982); David Gold, *The Impact of Defense Spending on Investment, Productivity and Economic Growth* (Washington, DC: Center for Strategic and Budgetary Assessments, 1990); Samuel Bowles, David M. Gordon, and Thomas E. Weisskopf, *Beyond the Wasteland: A Democratic Alternative to Economic Decline* (London: Verso, 1984); Todd Sandler and Keith Hartley, *The Economics of Defense* (Cambridge: Cambridge University Press, 1995); Gabrielle Hecht and Paul N. Edwards, *The Technopolitics of Cold War: Toward a Transregional Perspective* (Washington, DC: American Historical Association, 2007); Andrew J. Bacevich, *The Limits of Power: The End of American Exceptionalism* (New York: Metropolitan Books, 2006); Andrew J. Bacevich, ed., *The Long War: A New History of U.S. National Security Policy since World War II* (New York: Columbia University Press, 2007); Andrew J. Bacevich, *Washington Rules: America's Path to Permanent War* (New York: Metropolitan Books, 2010); Thomas J. Mahnken, *Technology and the American Way of War* (New York: Columbia University Press, 2008); Melvyn P. Leffler and Jeffrey W. Legro, eds., *To Lead the World: American Strategy after the Bush Doctrine* (New York: Oxford University Press, 2008); Thomas C. Lassman, *Sources of Weapon Systems Innovation in the Department of Defense: The Role of In-House Research and Development, 1945–2000* (Washington, DC: Center of Military History, 2008); Ingo Trauschweizer, *The Cold War U.S. Army: Building Deterrence for Limited War* (Lawrence: University Press of Kansas, 2008); Chalmers Johnson, *Dismantling the Empire: America's Last Best Hope* (New York: Metropolitan Books, 2010), 163–180; and *Los Angeles Times*, December 20, 2011, A1. Chapters 1–7 also contain a multitude of sources directly or indirectly relevant to the subject matter.

In mid-May 2011 Senator Jon Tester (D-MT) called on Secretary of Defense Robert M. Gates to consider reducing or eliminating American military bases abroad as a means of cutting defense spending. With the Cold War over and American military technology far advanced, he argued, American military forces can be stationed at home and readily deployed abroad as necessary. In his letter to Gates, Tester in effect stated: "The U.S. currently operates more than 1,000 installations on foreign soil, including 268 in Germany, 124 in Japan and 87 in South Korea. Approximately 370,000 U.S. military forces are currently deployed in more than 150 countries around the world." See Tester's website (www.tester.senate.gov).

24. For the "Lightweight Fighter Mafia," see chapter 7. The air force's plans for a new bomber are outlined in *Los Angeles Times*, May 22, 2011, A1.

25. Winslow T. Wheeler, "Understand, Then Contain America's Out-of-Control Defense Budget," in Wheeler, ed., *America's Defense Meltdown*, 219. See also Linda J. Bilmes and Joseph E. Stiglitz, "A Costly War Machine: Fighting the War on Terror Com-

promises the Economy Now and Threatens It in the Future," *Los Angeles Times*, September 18, 2011, A31.

26. The Coburn letter of May 18, 2010, can be accessed through the senator's website (www.coburn.senate.gov). In *Defense Monitor* 39 (April/May/June 2010): 8–9 and (July/August/September 2010): 1–2, Winslow Wheeler cites Coburn's document and discusses its implications.

In documentation involving the DOD budget for fiscal year 2010, Congress directed the DOD to prepare a report on contract fraud during the past ten years. The department was able to cover only the years 2007 to 2009. Senator Bernie Sanders (I–VT) requested a copy of the DOD's preliminary report in January 2011 and put it on his office's website (www.sanders.senate.gov). In response to the report, a member of Senator Sanders's staff commented as follows:

> In this country, we have a $14 trillion national debt, and we are consistently running deficits of over $1 trillion. We cannot get this under control without looking at the Department of Defense. Since 1997, our defense budget, including the wars in Iraq and Afghanistan has tripled from $254 billion to over $700 billion. Much of this money is unfortunately contracted out to companies with a well-documented history of fraud. If we are to get our defense budget under control, the Department of Defense has got to start taking the problem of contractor fraud more seriously. . . .
>
> *Over a three-year period from 2007 to 2009, hundreds of contractors were found to have committed fraud in connection with a DOD contract. This apparently did not affect DOD's contracting behavior, however. During the same three-year period, DOD awarded $285 BILLION in contracts to the same companies!* [author's emphasis]

Along related lines, between March 2003 and May 2004, the Bush administration poured a total of $12 billion (in $100 bills) into Iraq to pay for reconstruction and other purposes. The money was handled casually, without proper control or accounting systems. After years of audits and investigations, the Pentagon cannot account for $6.6 billion, or nearly 50 percent of the total. The money appears to have been stolen, principally by Iraqis, it is presumed, or siphoned off by contractors. See *Los Angeles Times*, January 13, 2011, A1. In addition, Dina Rasor has recently published a well-researched and informative series of articles on the operations and abuses of DOD procurement. See dina@truthout.org.

27. Background about and articles by the so-called CDI group are available in Wheeler, ed., *America's Defense Meltdown,* and Wheeler, ed., *Pentagon Labyrinth*. The reforms are set forth in Wheeler, "Understand, Then Contain America's Out-of-Control Defense Budget," 236–241. However, Wheeler's proposals draw on the work of numerous other contributors to his edited volume.

28. For resistance to President Obama's modest efforts in behalf of national security reform, see *Los Angeles Times*, January 4, 2010, A1, May 8, 2010, A15, and May 9, 2010, A18; and Center for Defense Information, *Defense Monitor* 38 (April/May/June 2009): 1–11, (October/November/December 2009): 1–7, and 39 (April/May/June 2010): 8–9.

BIBLIOGRAPHICAL ESSAY

My approach to the military-industrial complex and the national security state, or warfare state, is broadly rather than narrowly conceived. That being the case, relevant sources are all but overwhelming. Consequently, this brief essay is a general guide to the available literature rather than an extensive enumeration and evaluation of articles, documents, and volumes.

Since the MIC is at the center of national power operations, any analysis of it should take that reality into account. Most historians, however, either bypass matters of power or deal with them only implicitly. A number of basic to sophisticated volumes provide an introduction to the subject: C. Wright Mills, *The Power Elite* (New York: Oxford University Press, 1956); G. William Domhoff, *Who Rules America?* (Englewood Cliffs, NJ: Prentice-Hall, 1967); Richard Gillam, ed., *Power in America: Interdisciplinary Perspectives on a Historical Problem* (Boston: Little, Brown, 1971); Kenneth Prewitt and Alan Stone, *The Ruling Elites: Elite Theory, Power, and American Democracy* (New York: Harper and Row, 1973); John C. Donovan, *The Cold Warriors: A Policy-Making Elite* (Lexington, MA: D. C. Heath, 1974); Gabriel Kolko, *Main Currents in Modern American History* (New York: Harper and Row, 1976); Philip H. Burch Jr., *Elites in American History*, 3 vols. (New York: Holmes and Meier, 1980); Michael Schwartz, ed., *The Structure of Power in America: The Corporate Elite as a Ruling Class* (New York: Holmes and Meier, 1987); Steve Fraser and Gary Gerstle, eds., *Ruling America: A History of Wealth and Power in a Democracy* (Cambridge, MA: Harvard University Press, 2005). A number of these authors have published other studies on or related to power operations.

William J. Novak, "The Myth of the 'Weak' American State," *American Historical Review* 113 (June 2008): 752–772, addresses somewhat indirectly American national power. His provocative article led to the journal's editors to organize a critique of Novak's work by John Fabian Witt, Gary Gerstle, and Julia Adams, which, collectively, is theoretical, analytical, and operational. See "*AHR* Exchange: On the 'Myth' of the 'Weak' American State," *American Historical Review* 115 (June 2010): 766–800.

Beginning in the early 1960s, a host of publications analyzed the MIC and the national security state. They include Fred J. Cook, *The Warfare State* (New York: Macmillan, 1962); Victor Perlo, *Militarism and Industry: Arms Profiteering in the Missile Age* (New York: International Publishers, 1963); John Kenneth Galbraith, *How to Control the Military* (Garden City, NY: Doubleday, 1969); John Stanley Baumgartner, *The Lonely Warriors: Case for the Military-Industrial Complex* (Los Angeles: Nash, 1970); Sidney Lens, *The Military-Industrial Complex* (Philadelphia: Pilgrim Press, 1970); Senator William Proxmire, *Report from Wasteland: America's Military-Industrial Complex* (New York: Praeger, 1970); Herbert L. Schiller and Joseph D. Phillips, eds., *Super State: Readings in the Military-Industrial Complex* (Urbana: University of Illinois Press, 1970); Berkeley Rice, *The C-5A Scandal: An Inside Story of the Military-Industrial Complex* (Boston: Houghton Mifflin, 1971); Walter Adams and William James Adams, "The Military-Industrial Complex: A Market Structure Analysis," *Papers and Proceedings of the 84th Annual Meeting of the American Economic Association, American Economic Review* 62 (May 1972): 279–287; Carroll W. Pursell, ed., *The Military-Industrial Complex* (New York: Harper and Row, 1972); J. A. Stockfish, *Plowshares into Swords: Managing the American Defense Establishment* (New York: Mason and Lipscomb, 1973); Steven Rosen, ed., *Testing the Theory of the Military-Industrial Complex* (Lexington, MA: Lexington Books, 1973); Stephen A. Van Dyke, "A Definition and Analysis of the Debate over the American Military-Industrial Complex to 1970" (Ph.D. diss., Bowling Green State University, 1976); Robert D. Cuff, "An Organizational Perspective on the Military-Industrial Complex," *Business History Review* 52 (Summer 1978): 250–267; Paul A. C. Koistinen, *The Military-Industrial Complex: A Historical Perspective* (New York: Praeger, 1980); Paul A. C. Koistinen, "Warfare and Power Relations in America: Mobilizing the World War II Economy," in *The Home Front and War in the Twentieth Century*, ed. James Titus (Colorado Springs: U.S. Air Force Academy, 1984), 91–110, 231–243; Aaron L. Friedberg, *In the Shadow of the Garrison State: America's Anti-Statism and Its Cold War Grand Strategy* (Princeton, NJ: Princeton University Press, 2000); Alex Roland, *The Military-Industrial Complex* (Washington, DC: American Historical Association, 2001); Helen Caldicott, *The New Nuclear Danger: George W. Bush's Military-Industrial Complex* (New York: New Press, 2002); Edmund F. Wehrle, "Welfare and Warfare: American Organized Labor Approaches the Military-Industrial Complex, 1949–1964," *Armed Forces and Society* 29 (Summer 2003): 525–546; and Alex Roland, "The Military-Industrial Complex: Lobby and Trope," in *The Long War: A New History of U.S. National Security Policy since World War II*, ed. Andrew J. Bacevich (New York: Columbia University Press, 2007), 335–370. Roland's *Military-Industrial Complex* is one of the most recent publications of substance on the subject, and it includes a complete and up-to-date bibliography.

The most comprehensive study of the effects of war and threatened war on American society is provided by Michael S. Sherry, *In the Shadow of War: The United States since the 1930s* (New Haven, CT: Yale University Press, 1995). Sherry also published two earlier studies involving national security. Between 1981 and 2002, Gregg Herken published or revised four important and informed volumes on nuclear weaponry and the key scientists involved with it, the war cohort, and scientists advising the president. All his works have been cited in the notes. See also the sources cited in note 34 of chapter 1 on the widespread and growing use of private contractors to perform nearly the full range of military functions. Studies on this crucial subject and its effects on the operations of the armed forces and civil-military relations are just getting under way.

As the works cited indicate, most publications on power operations and the MIC appeared in the 1960s and 1970s. Interest in these subjects was obviously stimulated by the tumult and agitation of the 1960s, particularly the growing protest against the Vietnam War. During the increasing conservatism of the late 1970s and 1980s, these subjects appeared to lose their appeal. At about the same time, American history professionals began to turn away from traditional and elite history to concentrate on social, cultural, and popular fields of study. In the last decade, scholarly publications on both the MIC and power structures have started to appear again.

By perusing the chapter endnotes or using the detailed and thorough index, readers can ascertain the sources I relied on to explicate a particular subject or analyze parts or the whole of the volume. Chapter 1 on the presidency and American foreign policy, national security, and civil-military relations cites numerous, though selected, studies. In general, these works, ranging from the first-rate to the serviceable, are more than adequate. Whenever possible, I have cited either bibliographic essays on the subject or sources that include good to excellent bibliographies. Literature for chapter 2 on Congress is much more limited in both quantity and quality than that on the executive. Nonetheless, a careful reading of the sources cited provides the necessary information and analysis to grasp the essential aspects of the legislative branch's trends, achievement, and failures.

A multitude of publications exist for chapter 3 on the armed services. However, as is typical with military history in general, sources that do not deal with specific operations tend to be limited in number and coverage. This is less true for the Cold War and post–Cold War periods than for previous times because of the military's size, reach, and budget; its role in policy making; and its interaction with the defense industry and other civilian institutions. Of particular importance in this regard are the publications of retired officers who are critical—often intensely so—of their former profession and institutions. Their critiques deal with flawed or failed operations, eroded professionalism, or improper and threatening behavior of the armed services as agents of the MIC. Some examples include James A. Donovan, *Militarism, U.S.A.* (New York: Charles Scribner's Sons, 1970); Richard A. Gabriel and Paul L. Savage, *Crisis in Command: Mismanagement in the Army* (New York: Hill and Wang, 1978); Richard A. Gabriel, *Military Incompetence: Why the American Military Doesn't Win* (New York: Hill and Wang, 1985); the numerous publications of Andrew J. Bacevich cited in the notes; various authors in Winslow T. Wheeler, ed., *America's Defense Meltdown: Pentagon Reforms for President Obama and the New Congress* (Washington, DC: Center for Defense Information, 2008), and in Winslow T. Wheeler, ed., *The Pentagon Labyrinth: 10 Short Essays to Help You Through It* (Washington, DC: Center for Defense Information, World Security Institute, 2011); and a number of publications of the World Security Institute's Center for Defense Information and its newsletter, the *Defense Monitor*. See also James Coates and Michael Killian, *Heavy Losses: The Dangerous Decline of American Defense* (New York: Penguin Books, 1985), and Richard Halloran, *To Arm a Nation: Rebuilding America's Endangered Defenses* (New York: Macmillan, 1986).

Publications on the defense industry, cited in chapter 4, are satisfactory at best. Most of the basic volumes were written quite early in the Cold War; others deal only with selected aspects of the subject. Company or corporate histories vary greatly in what they offer.

Chapter 5, on the physical sciences during World War II and the Cold War and their interaction with the armed services and the defense industry, is well documented. The quantity and range of publications are ample, and they offer differing and controversial points of view.

In chapter 6, some think tanks, such as the RAND Corporation, are the subject of numerous studies, while others have received only passing attention. The effects of the Cold War on universities and scholarly associations, research institutes, and like organizations are adequately dealt with in both general and specialized publications. Major national security review panels have been analyzed fully in both official and nongovernmental sources.

The literature on Cold War and post–Cold War weaponry, the subject of chapter 7, is extensive, particularly in the nuclear field. Available studies are both detailed and general and deal with aircraft, missiles, tanks, ships, and so forth, as well as categories of armaments.

The economics of national security during the Cold War and after is covered in chapter 8. A steady stream of books, articles, and other studies directly or indirectly addressing the subject continue to appear. They range from the detailed to the general, the scholarly to the polemical, the conservative to the radical, and the arcane to the accessible.

A number of departments, agencies, divisions, and subdivisions of the federal government have historical programs that publish or oversee the publication of studies relevant to national security. These include the Historical Office, Office of the Secretary of Defense; U.S. Army Center of Military History; Industrial College of the Armed Forces; National Defense University; Naval History and Heritage Command (created in 2008 to take over the Naval Historical Center); Air Force Historical Research Agency; National Science Foundation; and History Series, NASA. Other similar centers, agencies, and offices also exist.

The practice of government departments and agencies arranging for the publication of their official or semiofficial histories and other studies received a big boost during World War II at the urging of the Bureau of the Budget. See the bibliographic essay in Paul A. C. Koistinen, *Arsenal of World War II: The Political Economy of American Warfare, 1940–1945* (Lawrence: University Press of Kansas, 2004), for an explanation of why and how this took place.

INDEX

ABMs. *See* Antiballistic missiles
ABM Treaty (1972), 34, 49, 55
Abt, Charles, 153
Abt Associates, 153
Academic Advisory Committee on Thailand,
    154, 155
ACDA. *See* Arms Control and Disarmament
    Agency
Acheson, Dean, 13
Advanced Research Projects Agency (ARPA),
    143, 153
AEC. *See* Atomic Energy Commission
Aeronautical Laboratory (Cornell), 155
Aeronautics, 116, 129
Aerospace Corporation, 144–145
Aerospace industry, 83, 102, 103, 107, 110,
    170, 171, 231, 264n3
    airframe corporations and, 91
    analysis of, 264n1
    building, 90–96
    contractors and, 91, 92
    employment in, 105
    foreign sales and, 108
    high-tech, 88
    problems for, 93–94, 101
    profits for, 98
Afghanistan War, 59
    defense budget and, 236, 289n26
Agency for International Development (AID),
    154, 155, 156, 233
*Ailing Defense Industrial Base: Unready for
    Crisis* (Ichord Panel), 84
Airborne warning and control systems
    (AWACS), 57, 145
Aircraft, 169–170
    high-tech, 168
    nuclear-armed, 178
    production of, 78–79, 90–96
Aircraft industry, 67, 82, 88, 170, 264n4
    analysis of, 264n1
    future of, 90

    growth of, 96
    procurement and, 95
    relocation of, 104
Air force, 88, 102, 145, 164
    contracting by, 89
    Gunbelt and, 104
    missiles and, 169
    modernization projects by, 224
    plane production and, 78–79
    public relations campaigns by, 74
Air Policy (Finletter) Commission
    (1947–1948), 158
Allende, Salvador, 23, 51, 153
Alliance for Progress, 18
Allied-Signal, 93
Ambrose, Stephen E., 248n8
American Marietta, 94
American Political Science Association, 149
American Psychological Association, 153
American Telephone & Telegraph (AT&T),
    206, 211
American University, 152, 153, 156
Analytical Services Incorporated (ANSER),
    140
ANMB. *See* Army-Navy Munitions Board
Antiballistic missiles (ABMs), 22, 48, 49, 63,
    64, 141, 142, 164, 179
Apollo Program, 103
Applied Physics Laboratory (Johns Hopkins),
    117, 131
Arafat, Yassir, 33
Aristide, Jean-Bertrand, 32–33
Armaments centers, creation of, 104
Armed forces
    controlling/monitoring, 36–37, 42
    declining quality of, 223–227
    defense policy and, 243
    democracy and, 36
    growth of, 3, 75, 80
    influence of, 9, 37, 66–67, 220, 243
    leadership of, 38–39